Telling Migrant Stories

Reframing Media, Technology, and Culture in Latin/o America

TELLING MIGRANT STORIES

Latin American Diaspora in Documentary Film

EDITED BY

ESTEBAN E. LOUSTAUNAU AND LAUREN E. SHAW

University of Florida Press
Gainesville

Copyright 2018 by Esteban E. Loustaunau and Lauren E. Shaw
All rights reserved
Published in the United States of America

First cloth printing, 2018
First paperback printing, 2021

26 25 24 23 22 21   6 5 4 3 2 1

Library of Congress Cataloging-in-Publication Data
Names: Loustaunau, Esteban E., editor. | Shaw, Lauren E., editor.
Title: Telling migrant stories : Latin American diaspora in documentary film / edited by Esteban E. Loustaunau and Lauren E. Shaw.
Other titles: Reframing Media, Technology, and Culture in Latin/o America.
Description: Gainesville : University of Florida Press, 2018. | Series: Reframing Media, Technology, and Culture in Latin/o America | Includes bibliographical references and index.
Identifiers: LCCN 2017031784 | ISBN 9781683400233 (cloth : alk. paper) | ISBN 9781683403111 (pbk.)
Subjects: LCSH: Foreign workers, Latin American—United States. | Foreign workers, Latin American—Europe. | Latin America—Emigration and immigration. | United States—Emigration and immigration. | Europe—Emigration and immigration. | Illegal aliens—United States—History. | Documentary films—History.
Classification: LCC HD8081.A5 T45 2017 | DDC 791.43/6352968—dc23
LC record available at https://lccn.loc.gov/2017031784

UF PRESS

University of Florida Press
2046 NE Waldo Road
Suite 2100
Gainesville, FL 32609
http://upress.ufl.edu

Contents

List of Figures vii

Introduction: Documenting the Multiple Stories of Migration 1
   Esteban E. Loustaunau and Lauren E. Shaw

PART I. ENACTING POLITICS OF PLACE IN THE DIASPORA

1. *Harvest of Empire*: Affect and a Counternarrative of Latino/a Migration 19
   Lauren E. Shaw

2. Documenting Deportable Life: Knowledge, Performance, and Memory in *abUSed: The Postville Raid* and *Sin país* 39
   Jared List

3. Resisting Arizona's S.B. 1070 through Devotion to the Virgin of Guadalupe: Undocumented Immigrant Women's Contentious Repertoires in *The Vigil* 67
   Thomas Piñeros Shields

4. The Unending Journey of the Migrant Mother in *Los invisibles* and *De nadie* 88
   Esteban E. Loustaunau

PART II. (RE)MEMBERING PAST AND PRESENT LIVES

5. (Re)Membering the Pedro Pan Children's Exodus in Documentary Film 119
   Ada Ortúzar-Young

6. Migration, Exile, and Identities in *Abuelos*, by Carla Valencia Dávila 136
   Manuel F. Medina

7. *La Churona* and the Neobaroque Aesthetic: Mapping of a Transatlantic Ecuador 155
   Lizardo Herrera

PART III. MIGRANT IDENTITIES AND DISPLACED SUBJECTIVITIES

8. Testimonial Youth in Flux: Migration, Narrative, and Children in *Which Way Home* 175
   Ramón J. Guerra

9. Resistance in Motion: Small Cinemas by Cuban Women in the Diaspora 193
   Zaira Zarza

10. Who Documents the Migrant? Decolonial Aesthetics, Museo de América, and the Internet Documentary 217
    Juan G. Ramos

PART IV. CONVERSATIONS ON DOCUMENTARY FILM AND MIGRATION

11. Luis Argueta: Migrant Voices without Fear 241
    Interview by Esteban E. Loustaunau

12. Jenny Alexander: Breaking the Silence through Documentary Filmmaking 260
    Interview by Esteban E. Loustaunau

13. Tin Dirdamal: Intimate Gaze of Significant Concerns 275
    Interview by Lauren E. Shaw

14. Heidi Hassan: Love and Identity in the Cuban Diaspora 286
    Interview by Lauren E. Shaw

15. María Cristina Carrillo Espinosa: Filming Common Experiences of Migration 297
    Interview by Esteban E. Loustaunau

Appendix 319
List of Contributors 321
Index 325

Figures

1.1. The wall (*Harvest of Empire*, 2012) 21
1.2. Juan González (*Harvest of Empire*, 2012) 25
2.1. Gilda Ordoñez testifying before a congressional delegation in Postville, Iowa (*abUSed*, 2010) 49
2.2. Elida Mejía saying good-bye to her son at the San Francisco airport (*Sin país*, 2010) 54
3.1. Gina leading a march from the vigil to a Phoenix courthouse (*The Vigil*, 2014) 70
3.2. Vigil participants meeting for prayer and resistance (*The Vigil*, 2014) 74
4.1. Migrant mothers (*Los invisibles*, 2010) 98
4.2. Gael García Bernal and migrant mothers (*Los invisibles*, 2010) 98
4.3. María, at ease in front of the camera (*De nadie*, 2005) 106
4.4. María, as seen by two of her children in Honduras (*De nadie*, 2005) 107
6.1. Carla Valencia Dávila conducting research on the story of her Chilean grandfather (*Abuelos*, 2010) 141
6.2. Aunt Lily recalling her father's disappearance (*Abuelos*, 2010) 143
9.1. Lovers' intimate embrace (*Orages d'eté*, 2008) 201
9.2. Kaleidoscopic screen image (*Orages d'eté*, 2008) 202
9.3. Promotional film poster (*Extravío*, 2008) 204

Introduction

Documenting the Multiple Stories of Migration

ESTEBAN E. LOUSTAUNAU AND LAUREN E. SHAW

Since the fall of the Berlin Wall and the dissolution of the Soviet Union, the lines dividing the globe have changed from East/West to North/South, creating a new Other of political importance. While the global South suffers from climate change, neoliberal policies, and the effects of colonization, its people look toward the North for opportunity and in many cases for a safe haven. Governments of the North are stymied, and their citizens are also divided as to how to react: with a pathway to citizenship or harsher immigration laws, guest-worker programs or heightened border security, comprehensive immigration reform or tighter borders that include a 1,900-mile wall between the United States and Mexico? *Telling Migrant Stories: Latin American Diaspora in Documentary Film* works beyond these dichotomies and unsatisfactory binaries in its contributors' search for greater understanding of this migration pattern. Specifically, this volume addresses questions of social, political, and cultural concern around the issue of migration from Latin America to the North, be it the United States or Europe, as represented in contemporary documentary film. If the voices of today's migrants and refugees remain politically silent, documentary film in its many modes enables their voices to be heard.[1] Michael Chanan argues in *The Politics of Documentary*, "Documentary is one of the forms through which new attitudes enter wider circulation, through the form of its advocacy and the articulation of the social actors who participate as subjects" (7). The multifront political crisis in the United States barely a month into the Trump administration in 2017 produced unanticipated mass protests and clever use of documentary storytelling with persuasive results. On the eve of an executive order on mass immigrant deportations and just days after an executive ban on travel into the United States from seven Muslim-majority countries that sparked protests in the United States and around the world, the Pennsylvania-based building materials supply company 84 Lumber surprised millions of people watching the Super Bowl LI by introducing an ad featuring a migrant mother and daughter leaving their small village on their way to the United States. As Lauren Shaw further discusses the ad in chapter 1 of this volume, we are being reminded of the power of the discourse of affect in the media and the ways in which documentary film, in all its forms, can potentially introduce new attitudes and bring social change in the public sphere. *Telling Migrant Stories* is not a collection of essays on economic and political policies that attempt to meet the needs of either or both hemispheres. Rather, its chapters engage with a wide range of documentaries that reflect on this flow of people across borders, their journeys, their strategies of adaptation and cultural preservation, their agency in the face of policies and legal systems that attempt to render them powerless.

Documentary, because of its grounding in fact rather than fiction, can have a great impact on audiences. It has the power to educate, entertain, persuade, preserve culture, instill values, and share experiences. It differentiates itself from fiction by going beyond addressing "the viewer primarily as a private individual" and instead addressing "the viewer primarily as a citizen, a member of civil society, a putative participant in the public sphere" (Chanan vi). The mission of the International Documentary Association (IDA) points to the importance of this filmic form: "Documentary storytelling expands our understanding of shared human experience, fostering an informed, compassionate and connected world." Because of technological advances in digital photography and the editing process, documentary has become much easier to produce. Its approaches to storytelling have taken on a more personal shape, enabling the form to slip past the barriers of mainstream filmmaking. In their edited volume *New Documentaries in Latin America*, Vinicius Navarro and Juan Carlos Rodríguez stress the impact that some of these technological innovations have had on the production and distribution of nonfiction films in the region today (6). They explain how in Latin America, the coexistence of new technologies, mass media, and grassroots activism on the one hand provides new opportunities to critique and bypass mainstream forms of communication and on the other, makes the use of technology inseparable from everyday life. This convergence leads to alternative forms of film and video production and to creative partnerships and collaborations between filmmakers and social subjects (Navarro and Rodríguez 5).

In Latin America and beyond, the proliferation of documentaries has led to more opportunities for them to be screened at film festivals as well as online and even at local cinemas. For example, since 2005, Ambulante, a nonprofit organization in Mexico created by Gael García Bernal, Diego Luna, and other partners, promotes documentary film as a tool for social and cultural transformation. Each year, Ambulante brings documentary films and workshops to places where nonfiction film is rarely made available in order to generate social and cultural awareness and, echoing Chanan, turning viewers into active participants in the public sphere. International newspapers such as the *Guardian* produce lists of must-see documentary films. Netflix recommends 50 documentary films and refers to the genre as a form of mindful entertainment that often offers "braver and more compelling modes of storytelling" than fiction film (Scarano et al.). Additional online access to documentary films is now available on Amazon, Kanopy, Vimeo, and YouTube. Another indication of how popular culture has embraced documentary, the Independent Film Channel (IFC) has produced two seasons of *Documentary Now*, a series that parodies some of the classics of documentary filmmaking such as *The Thin Blue Line*, *Grey Gardens*, *Nanook of the North*, and *History of the Eagles*.

Access to viewing documentary is also evidenced by the creation of Op-Docs, an online section of the *New York Times* opinion pages. It was created in 2011 and features short documentaries by emerging or established filmmakers. Furthermore, in 2015 the Cannes Film Festival created a prize for documentary, L'Oeil d'or (Golden Eye), which interestingly enough has so far been awarded to films from Latin America.[2] Each year, more than 200 documentary film festivals take place around the globe. In addition, funding for documentary filmmaking has increased. Within the past two decades, the Ford Foundation and the MacArthur Foundation have added specific categories of grants to fund documentary projects. Other significant funding sources for documentary filmmakers are the Rockefeller Media Artists Fellowship, and grants from the AlterCine Foundation and the Sundance Institute; recipients of Rockefeller and Sundance funding include Tin Dirdamal, whose work is featured in this volume. Crowdfunding platforms like Slated, IndieGoGo, and Kickstarter connect aspiring documentarians of promising projects with real funders. Greater ease in production, more opportunities for screening, new chances for recognition, and a larger pool of funding have all contributed to the rise in documentary filmmaking and viewing. Combine that with a surge in migration stories and ongoing refugee crises and you have a plethora of documentaries on the subject.

Documentary is the merging of narrative storytelling with visual and audio media, and though migration in general shares some basic themes such as displacement, adjustment, and cross-cultural tensions, it is not a single story. This volume is a testament to that fact. Author Chimamanda Ngozi Adichie warns against the danger of a single story, which tends to misrepresent and stereotype complexities with its incompleteness. As human beings, it is our many stories that make us who we are, completely. It is in the telling of our own stories and hearing of these many stories that we realize we share more similarities than differences (Adichie). The essays in this volume offer multiple stories about migrants and migration from Latin America. Telling one's own story is empowering and can be an act of resistance against a dominant and false narrative. Because the documentaries of this volume publicly broaden the voices of the migrants they feature, they engage in empowerment through storytelling. And of equal importance, they fill in the gaps created by mainstream media, and they enable viewers to understand better the issue of migration. To this point it is important to be mindful of what Joanna Page calls "the sincerity of documentary," that is, that any documentary is always a social construct of reality, not objective reality itself (4). Rather than claiming objectivity in the production of documentary film, Stella Bruzzi treats documentary as a "negotiation between reality on the one hand and image, interpretation and bias on the other" (6).

In his book *The Figure of the Migrant*, Thomas Nail states,

> The migrant is the political figure of our time. Most people today increasingly fall somewhere, and at some point, on the spectrum of migration, from global tourist to undocumented laborer. As a result, they experience (among other things) a certain degree of deprivation or expulsion from their social status. In this sense, the figure of the migrant is not a "type of person" or fixed identity but a mobile social position or spectrum that people move into and out of under certain social conditions of mobility. (235)

Nail's affirmation that the twenty-first century will be known as the century of the migrant and that the migrant should be considered a fluid figure and not a type of person supports the focus and intention of this volume. By choosing the perspective of migration and movement we go beyond conventional static perspectives of people and place where movement is always considered to be "derivative" and "lacking" and, thus, adopt an alternative position in which movement becomes the primary and driving force of analysis (Nail 13). Even if the figure of the migrant falls somewhere between global tourist and undocumented laborer, all migrants experience a shift in economic, judicial, political, and social status. This shift, however, is drastically uneven across the spectrum of migration. The vast majority of migrants today face severe deprivation and various forms of expulsion even before being finally expelled from their native lands.[3] The collection of essays and interviews included in *Telling Migrant Stories* responds to the rise of Latin American migrations and how their histories tend to be decimated or forgotten and are often registered through alternative forms of artistic representation such as documentary film.

In the context of Latin American diasporas since the second half of the twentieth century, assumptions of community and identity as authentic, fixed, and unified are less relevant to people who are expelled, uprooted, and dispersed from their native lands. As displaced subjects, many migrants today struggle to reconfigure other meanings of personal and communal identity, place, and home. In many instances, they learn to articulate new meanings of recognition and belonging through cultural practices, religious rituals, and political and social activism rooted in individual and collective subjectivities (attitudes, feelings, devotions, and emotions). Salvadoran migrant artists in the United States belonging to the Central American diaspora that originated in the 1970s and 1980s metaphorically relocate Central America beyond the confinement of the isthmus located outside the United States. Reflecting on the work by the transregional and transnational poetry collective EpiCentroAmerica, Maritza Cárdenas observes that Central America "is now de-territorialized by its diaspora carrying the center in their hearts. Central America is not static—like its people, it is a migratory subject redefined by the metaphoric explosions from its diaspora" (112). Similar examples can be found in the multiple stories of other Latin American diasporas that emerged from Argentina and Chile since the years of dictatorship in the 1970s and 1980s, Colombia after the war in the 1980s, Cuba after Castro in the 1960s, the Dominican Republic after political turmoil and economic collapse since the 1960s, Ecuador most recently since the dollarization of the economy in 2000, Honduras after the devastation caused by Hurricane Mitch in 1998, El Salvador and Guatemala due to the rise in gang violence after the signing of the peace accords in the 1990s, and Mexico especially after NAFTA's implementation in the 1990s, to name a few.[4]

Beyond metaphorical resignification and social empowerment, documentaries have the capacity to merge activism with art, as happened with Errol Morris's famed 1988 film *The Thin Blue Line*; the film led to the dismissal of charges against Randall Adams, who was wrongfully convicted of murder in 1976. The search for truth can be an illusive subject, but in the case of *The Thin Blue Line*, it was lifesaving. Many of the films discussed in this volume uncover truths surrounding the issue of migration, and some have had a similar effect for migrants. Edited footage of films by Luis Argueta and Jenny Alexander (both featured in this book) has been used by immigration advocates and U.S. government officials to help reunite migrant families who have been detained in raids.

This volume is not meant to include all documentaries on the subject of migration, an insurmountable task for its authors. Nor is it an attempt to represent a certain group of migrants or the many different groups that come from a variety of backgrounds and geographies of Latin America. It bears no pretense of expertise on documentary and its different modes of filmmaking. It is not a how-to guide for filmmakers interested in the topic. It is an attempt to share the visual and spoken stories about migrants from Latin America with an English-speaking readership primarily from the United States.

Sheila Curran Bernard asserts in *Documentary Storytelling: Creative Nonfiction on Screen*, that documentaries can "contribute to our understanding of who we are, where we've been and what we might become" (11). She encourages documentarians to "take the viewer into a new world" (11). As editors and contributors to this volume, it is our hope that our readers be taken to the many worlds from which migrants depart, that readers become caught up in the migrants' struggles, ask questions about the single story, and begin to think about the multiple stories with compassion, solidarity, and a greater understanding.

The first section of this book, "Enacting Politics of Place in the Diaspora," begins with a historical perspective on Latino migration to the United States. In the chapter "*Harvest of Empire*: Affect and a Counternarrative of Latino Migration," Lauren Shaw examines how affect is woven into a rational discourse in the documentary *Harvest of Empire: The Untold Story of Latinos in America*

(2012) directed by Peter Getzels and Eduardo López. She underlines the way in which both the documentary and the book that inspired the film, *Harvest of Empire: A History of Latinos in America* (2000, revised 2011) by Juan González, are counternarratives to the Latino-threat narrative that pervades mainstream media and political discourse in the United States. Shaw distinguishes the film from the book by highlighting the documentary's persuasive power through the presentation of historical fact and archival footage as well as a diverse array of deeply emotional firsthand accounts of the migration experience. She also unveils some of the logistics of distribution that keep the counternarrative from mainstream audiences.

Jared List addresses the role of documentary film as a source of political advocacy on behalf of immigrant rights in the United States. List helps the reader understand how historically, the migrant has been relegated to exist outside of the realm of politics. That is, the migrant has been imagined as a social category that lacks the right to legal or political protection. As such, the notion of the migrant remains invisible to the law and as a consequence is perceived as being socially disposable, legally deportable, economically dispensable, and, thus, replaceable. List then turns to Luis Argueta's *abUSed: The Postville Raid* (2010) and Theo Rigby's *Sin país* (2010) as contemporary documentaries that expose and critique the public and official treatment of migrants as disposable and deportable life. List argues that one possible way of claiming the political rights of immigrants is by recognizing, remembering, and recording their histories. By performing memory through documentary film, migrants can make their voices be heard and their lives visible.

In his critique of Jenny Alexander's film *The Vigil* (2014), Thomas Piñeros Shields analyzes how a group of undocumented immigrant women in Phoenix resisted Arizona Senate Bill 1070 in 2010. *The Vigil*, Piñeros Shields contends, shows how public space can be rendered sacred through the act of devotion, which in this case also served as a political performance of protest. Piñeros Shields bases his chapter on Charles Tilly's concept of "repertoires of contention" to explain the meaning of the vigil enacted in front of the Arizona state capitol. He also analyzes the prefigurative act of these women evoking the justice they sought. The documentary contextualizes the Virgin of Guadalupe within Latin American and U.S. Latino cultures as a multifaceted symbol of protection of the poor and of unconditional motherly love.[5] Piñeros Shields builds on this symbolism to explain the diffusion of the Virgin of Guadalupe throughout Latin America as a symbol of indigenous resistance to colonial rule and more precisely in the film as a symbol of resistance to a contemporary form of injustice.

Completing part 1, Esteban Loustaunau's chapter examines variable degrees of critical agency of migrant mothers as represented in documentary film. He argues that migrant consciousness is often revealed in the human connections that filmmakers can establish with the migrant subjects. He then explains how in the short documentary *Los invisibles* (2010) the filmmaker Gael García Bernal stages a relation of accompaniment between himself and a group of Honduran migrant mothers traveling to the United States through Mexico, and in the film *De nadie* (2005) the director Tin Dirdamal forms a bond of trust with María Flores by becoming her confidant and messenger to her family in Honduras. Loustaunau argues that by establishing these human connections, the two films help viewers to better engage with the social conditions and, more importantly, the agency and self-awareness of the migrant mothers whose lives become unending journeys of both hope and despair.

The second section, "(Re)Membering Past and Present Lives," follows with Ada Ortúzar-Young's "(Re)Membering the Pedro Pan Children's Exodus in Documentary Film." She studies three related films on the subject of this mass exodus of children ages 2 to 16 from Cuba to the United States for nearly two years between 1960 and 1962. She compares *The Lost Apple* (1962); *Del otro lado del cristal* (1995); and *Operation Peter Pan: Flying Back to Cuba* (2011). Spanning a period of five decades, the three films as a whole show the experience over time and seem to complement each other. Interestingly, footage from *The Lost Apple* appears in the other two documentaries. Analyzing their styles and filmic techniques, Ortúzar-Young points to the different perspectives each film brings to that moment in Cuban-U.S. history. The central theme of loss of home and family pervades, however, regardless of the different (and opposing) political underpinnings the films possess. What is clear from the comparison of the three films is that Operation Pedro Pan is not fully represented in any one.

In his chapter Manuel F. Medina addresses questions of memory, identity, and migration in Carla Valencia Dávila's film *Abuelos* (2010). Medina analyzes Valencia Dávila's film about her personal family history of migration. Her migrant story begins with her Chilean father and Ecuadorian mother meeting as young students in Moscow. But soon Valencia Dávila turns her attention to the stories of her two grandfathers: *abuelo* Juan, a Chilean political activist who was murdered by the Chilean military dictatorship in 1973, and *abuelo*

Remo, an exceptional physician who shared with his granddaughter his secret for immortality. Medina's analysis of the film establishes connections between self-exile, exile, diaspora, and migration as perceived by a daughter and granddaughter turned filmmaker.

In the third chapter of part 2, Lizardo Herrera examines the cult of the Virgin of El Cisne by Ecuadorian immigrants in Spain in the documentary film *La Churona* (2010), by María Cristina Carrillo Espinosa. Herrera argues that the arrival of the Virgin of El Cisne in Madrid not only brings the migrant Ecuadorian community there closer together but also enables it to gain public visibility and with that, to increase its negotiating power for social inclusion in hostile settings. In the context of the wave of Ecuadorian emigration after the economic transition to dollarization in 2000, Herrera considers the emotional crisis that comes with territorial expulsion from Ecuador and the subsequent social discrimination against Ecuadorians in Spain. His criticism in *La Churona* of the devotion to the Virgin of El Cisne, from sixteenth-century colonial Baroque to twenty-first-century Neobaroque aesthetics, draws significant implications about that devotion and the ongoing Ecuadorian migration as a contested site of festive expression and sentimental hopelessness.

Part 3, "Migrant Identities and Displaced Subjectivities," addresses current patterns of migration as well as new forms of documentary film production. From the side of migration, it examines the latest wave of unaccompanied Central American migrant minors making their way to the United States atop the freight trains known as La Bestia (the Beast); from the side of documentary, this section explores recent forms of video production and dissemination as well as innovative approaches to first-person storytelling.

Ramón J. Guerra's chapter, "Testimonial Youth in Flux: Migration, Narrative, and Children in *Which Way Home*," relates the recent surge in child migrants from Mexico and Central America to the film *Which Way Home* (2009), directed by Rebecca Cammisa. More importantly, he expands upon John Beverley's definition of *testimonio* to apply it to the film in question. Steadily he builds the argument that this first-person documentary with an embedded cameraperson be understood as a *testimonio*, thereby capable of instigating change. His analysis of the film serves the purpose of supporting this theory as it describes key moments in the film's development: how it is structured, its narrative strategies, and above all how the documentary gives voice to the two main young adolescent boys it features—Fito, age 13, accompanying his friend Kevin, age 14, from Honduras to the United States. Along with other children and teenagers, Fito and Kevin travel motivated by the illusive American Dream as well as poor circumstances at home. Guerra distinguishes between representation (a sort of *costumbrismo*) and *testimonio*. With the latter's intent to effect change, its effectiveness also lies in the viewer's ability to hear the smaller voices of history in defiance of the larger voices that have created the plight of children like Fito and Kevin.

Zaira Zarza centers her chapter, "Resistance in Motion: Small Cinemas by Cuban Women in the Diaspora," on three young Cuban filmmakers, all graduates of the International Film and Television School in San Antonio de los Baños: Heidi Hassan, Susana Barriga, and Daniellis Hernández. Though their films are not usually studied in relation to each other, Zarza unites them through their intimate styles of storytelling, a cinema of affect in which the noncognitive and intuitive take precedence over the rational. Hassan's *Orages d'été* (2008) and *Tierra roja* (2007) and Barriga's *The Illusion* (2008) explore relationships in very personal terms. Zarza differentiates Hernández's *Extravío* (2008) from the other films, due to its less personal treatment and themes of blackness and difference, but ties it to *The Illusion* since both are steeped in disillusionment. She points to other commonalities among the three such as their childhoods set in the same collective past of the Cuban Revolution, their current residence in Europe, and the issues of Cubanness and displacement that surface in their work. Zarza briefly connects their sensibility and attention to stories of race, class, family, and self to the work of an earlier and distinguished Cuban filmmaker, Sara Gómez. She also raises the issue of feminism, something many Cuban women do not align with, even though their art may well indicate otherwise.

Today we are living in an era of broader access to image and video recording through the use of smartphones, tablets, and inexpensive digital cameras and an ample diffusion of images through social media and the Internet. Such an environment has significantly changed the ways we perceive the process of making films and videos. In his chapter, "Who Documents the Migrant? Decolonial Aesthetics, Museo de América, and the Internet Documentary," Juan G. Ramos discusses how contemporary documentary forms of production promote greater participation and encourage horizontal approaches to videomaking, including self-representation by migrants who tell their own stories and record their personal experiences of migration and movement. Ramos focuses on the portal Migrar Es Cultura (MigrarEsCultura.es) of the Museo de América in Madrid that invites migrants to post videos of their own personal stories of migration. Ramos considers the impact this new and democratizing form of documenting migrant voices has on authorship, production, and dissemination of documentary. He looks at various examples of videos posted to the museum's portal by Cuban, Guatemalan, Nicaraguan, and Salvadoran migrants living in Madrid.

A fourth section, "Conversations on Documentary Film and Migration," offers five interviews with prominent directors whose works are among the films analyzed in the chapter essays. This section assists the reader to better understand the production process of documentary films on Latin American migration, to listen to a filmmaker's account on the relation between film and politics, and to learn more about a director's personal experiences of working directly with migrant subjects. The directors consider the processes of filmmaking in various contexts of migration, from deportation, displacement, exile, and self-exile to undocumented migration particularly among women and children.

Esteban Loustaunau interviews award-winning Guatemalan director Luis Argueta, who describes his journey as a filmmaker beginning with making TV commercials to creating documentaries and becoming an advocate on behalf of Guatemalan immigrant families and children living in the United States. The many lessons he has learned from the migrants he has come to know in making films like *abUSed,* analyzed in chapter 2, *Abrazos,* and *The U-Turn* have led him to make a conscious decision to speak about things that people want to forget or have forgotten. Argueta is specially interested in challenging the viewer to face the injustice that dehumanizes migrants and to offer migrants a platform so they can denounce that same injustice freely and without fear.

Likewise, Jenny Alexander sees a clear connection between her role as documentary filmmaker and her commitment to social activism on behalf of immigrant women and youth. In her interview with Esteban Loustaunau, Alexander discusses filmmaking as a tool for social activism and the ways documentary can help migrants realize their social empowerment by listening to their own voices. In discussing two of her films, *Detained* (2007) and *The Vigil,* critiqued in chapter 3, Alexander describes how collaboration between filmmaker and migrant subject can lead to breaking the silence and fear that keep undocumented immigrants from demanding their rights. In a personal note, Alexander draws similarities between her family history of exile and Nazi persecution and the stories of discrimination and oppression of the migrant subjects in her films.

In his interview with Lauren Shaw, Tin Dirdamal reveals some of the processes and motives in his work. Documentary for Dirdamal is the medium through which he explores the world, investigates its perplexities, and arrives at a somewhat clearer view of its problems. Their conversation centers on his three documentaries *De nadie* (2005), *Ríos de hombres* (2011), and *Muerte en Arizona* (2014). Dirdamal also describes two interesting projects in the works: *Flesh* and *Ghosts of the Ship*. His film *De nadie* is considered in chapter 4, by Esteban Loustaunau. What appears as a stylistic convention in this film turns out to be the result of the filmmaker's ability to seemingly make the camera disappear while interviewing the migrants along their journey as well as of the limitations of sparse equipment during the filming process. His long view of events over time characterizes much of Dirdamal's explorations to date.

Filmmaker Heidi Hassan's interview with Lauren Shaw dovetails with chapter 9 by Zaira Zarza on first-person documentaries by Cuban women living in the diaspora. In addition to her two films discussed in that chapter, *Orages d'été* and *Tierra roja*, Hassan speaks of *Otra isla* (2014) and its impartial stance on the family that emigrated from Cuba but ended up camping out in a central square in Madrid. She also discusses her upcoming project in collaboration with her friend, compatriot, and collaborator Patricia Pérez Fernández. Hassan's connection to her first love, still photography, is woven through this conversation, as is her use of documentary for personal investigation of feelings. Her ambivalence about Cuba emerges, and though the subject matter of her films is ripe for political commentary, Hassan's eye turns to the more social and human aspects of her explorations.

In conversation with Esteban Loustaunau, the Ecuadorian anthropologist and filmmaker María Cristina Carrillo Espinosa draws a series of common experiences between her personal story of migration and the multiple stories of thousands of Ecuadorian immigrants who arrived in Spain in the early 2000s. Carrillo Espinosa says her film *La Churona* becomes a bridge between her own migration experience and those of so many Ecuadorian migrants living in Spain. One experience she shares with fellow Ecuadorians is finding herself living in Spain *sin papeles*, without papers, as a result of a change in migration policy by the Spanish government after the arrival of an Ecuadorian diaspora. In *La Churona*, studied in chapter 7, Carrillo Espinosa brings together the voices of Ecuadorian men and women trying to make sense of their new transnational identities and affiliations as characterized by a series of common migration circumstances that put them all in a horizontal plane. Carrillo Espinosa also discusses some of the differences of producing documentary films in Europe and in Latin America.

Acknowledgments

Bringing together a wide collection of ideas, images, and voices that help convey contemporary experiences of migration in documentary film could only have happened for us by working collaboratively. This is the product of years of friendship and professional collaboration on issues of Latin American migration and documentary film that started in 2010 at a NeMLA (Northeast Modern Language Association) convention in Montreal and that has continued to grow in panels and research collaborations at NeMLA, LASA (Latin American Studies Association), and other conferences in the Northeast, Chicago, Mérida, and Buenos Aires. Along the way, we gained new friendships and gathered ideas that have come together in this volume.

We thank our contributors, some of whom we met in panels we organized together and some we invited to be a part of this volume. We are also grateful to the filmmakers who generously accepted our invitations to be interviewed for this project. We value not only their friendship but, most of all, their passion and commitment to making films about the human existence of migrants, exiles, refugees, and the displaced.

The well-chosen readers for the manuscript provided us with invaluable feedback to sharpen our ideas. We thank Stephanye Hunter and Eleanor Deumens at University of Florida Press for being so efficient and responsive in the handling of the text. The series editors, Héctor Fernández L'Hoeste and Juan Carlos Rodríguez, were enthusiastically behind our project from the start. We thank the film journal *Archivos de la Filmoteca* for allowing us to publish a revised English version of Lizardo Herrera's article "*La Churona* y la réplica neobarroca: Cartografías de un Ecuador transatlántico."

Esteban Loustaunau is grateful to Assumption University, especially the provost, Louise Carroll Keeley, for supporting his sabbatical leave and research trips to Spain and Mexico. He thanks the members of the Faculty Development Committee for granting him summer research and course release grants to complete this volume. He is also thankful to his departmental colleagues in Modern and Classical Languages and Cultures for their ideas and support during the process of preparing this book. In the middle of working on this project,

Esteban lost his mother, Norma. He dedicates this volume to her memory and to his family—Kathy, Luci, and Diego—with endless love.

Lauren Shaw would like to express her gratitude to Elmira College for its support of her scholarship. Without the consistent funding of her research projects, her collaboration on this book would not have been possible. She thanks President Charles Lindsay; Provost Charles Mitchell; and Academic Vice President, Academic Dean, and Professor Emeritus Stephen Coleman, for their assistance throughout the years. She is grateful to Wendy Thompson-Márquez and Eduardo López for the valuable information they shared regarding the creation and distribution of the film *Harvest of Empire: The Untold Story of Latinos in America*. She also thanks Edward Dougherty for his act of generosity and the well-timed inspiration that it sparked. Lauren dedicates this volume to all migrants and to Wondwossen and Doug, with her heart and soul.

Finally, our gratefulness also extends to all the people who, in telling their stories of migration and displacement, in bringing aid to migrants in need, or in filming the migrant lives of others, enabled us to watch and learn from cinematic accounts of their courage and perseverance.

Notes

1. In *Latin American Documentary Filmmaking*, David William Foster raises an important point on the ways we have come to understand the various modes of documentary film over time. He states that despite the various ideological interpretations we give to the modes of documentary film, its production still reflects the same commitment to social issues as other forms of documentary such as testimonial, journalism, and autobiography (x).

2. The first prize for 2015 releases was awarded to the Chilean-Mexican film *Allende, mi abuelo Allende* (*Beyond My Grandfather Allende*) by Marcia Tambutti Allende. The prize for 2016 was given to the Brazilian film *Cinema novo* by Eryk Rocha.

3. Thomas Nail studies the conditions of migrants in four categories that are based on the particular types of expulsion and trajectories they face: the nomad, the barbarian, the vagabond, and the proletariat.

4. Today, the Latin American diaspora has dispersed across the world, with the majority living in the Americas and in Europe. More than 1 million Colombians live in the United States, and another 3 million live elsewhere in the Americas (Canada, Mexico, Costa Rica, Venezuela, and Ecuador) and in Europe (Spain, France, Italy, Germany, and the United Kingdom); 20 million people of Mexican ancestry live in the United States, and close to 2 million Puerto Ricans have found a home in New York City (*Cultural Diplomacy*).

5. Realizing that this is an imperfect solution, as editors of this volume we have agreed to use "Latino/a" as a noun referring to people and "Latino" as an adjective to describe concrete or abstract nouns.

Works Cited

About Us. International Documentary Association (documentary.org). N.d. Web. 10 June 2016.
Adichie, Chimamanda Ngozi. "The Danger of the Single Story." TEDTalk. 7 Oct. 2009. Web. 11 June 2016.
Bernard, Sheila Curran. *Documentary Storytelling: Creative Nonfiction on Screen*. 3rd ed. New York: Focal, 2010. Print.
Bruzzi, Stella. *New Documentary*. 2nd ed. New York: Routledge, 2006. Print.
Cárdenas, Maritza. "From Epicentros to Fault Lines: Rewriting Central America from the Diaspora." *Studies in 20th and 21st Century Literature* 37.2 (2013): 111–130. Print.
Chanan, Michael. *The Politics of Documentary*. London: British Film Institute, 2007. Print.
Cultural Diplomacy in Latin America. Institute for Cultural Diplomacy. N.d. Web. 8 June 2016.
Foster, David William. *Latin American Documentary Filmmaking: Major Works*. Tucson: U of Arizona P, 2013. Print.
Nail, Thomas. *The Figure of the Migrant*. Stanford, CA: Stanford UP, 2015. Print.
Navarro, Vinicius, and Juan Carlos Rodríguez. Introduction. *New Documentaries in Latin America*. Ed. Navarro and Rodríguez. New York: Palgrave Macmillan, 2014. Print.
Page, Joanna. "Introduction: Fiction, Documentary and Cultural Change in Latin America." *Visual Synergies in Fiction and Documentary Film from Latin America*. Ed. Miriam Haddu and Joanna Page. New York: Palgrave MacMillan, 2009. 3–13. Print.
Scarano, Ross, et al. "The 25 Best Documentaries on Netflix Right Now." *Pop Culture. Complex*. 16 March 2016. Web. 12 June 2016.

ENACTING POLITICS OF PLACE IN THE DIASPORA

1

Harvest of Empire

Affect and a Counternarrative of Latino/a Migration

LAUREN E. SHAW

In September 2012 the documentary *Harvest of Empire: The Untold Story of Latinos in America* was released in the United States. A year earlier, Penguin Books published a revised edition of the book *Harvest of Empire: A History of Latinos in America* by Juan González, originally published in 2000. These three versions of the same narrative on Latino/a migration produced during the beginning of the twenty-first century indicate the reading and viewing public's strong interest in what is mostly portrayed as a contentious issue: Latino/a immigration to the United States. Both the film and the book seek to illuminate the public's understanding of the intersection between U.S. and Latin American history and how that history relates to the numbers of Latinos who have migrated and continue to migrate north. Their message is clear and well supported by facts. The film is further substantiated visually with archival footage and emotionally charged with a range of interviews of Latinos living in the United States. It was codirector Eduardo López's desire to bring González's book to a wider audience with the hope of informing and improving the national debate on immigration.[1]

Narratives: False Threat, Factual Promise

While the film and book provide a consistently favorable account of Latinos as productive, hardworking, and contributing members of U.S. society, the narrative from mainstream U.S. media on the topic of Latino/a immigration stigmatizes Latinos as people who come to the United States only to take from the system, who refuse to learn English, and who resist assimilation to the majority culture. More precisely, this is a false narrative built on inaccuracies and a discourse of hate and fear effectively whipped up by public figures and newscasters to manipulate public opinion against Latino/a immigrants.[2] In his 2008 publication *The Latino Threat,* Leo Chavez refers to this false version as "the Latino threat narrative." He finds that it extends even to the belief that Mexican immigrants (the largest of Latino/a immigrant groups) migrate north as part of a grand conspiracy to reconquer the Southwest not only through migration but also through the "out of control fertility" ascribed to the reproductive capacities of Latinas (Chavez ix). Chavez explains the Latino threat narrative and then challenges its veracity, questioning the prevalence of its use in the media. My purpose in repeating this particular narrative is as a backdrop to the moment when González and later López were working on *Harvest of Empire,* the book and the film, respectively. López began working on the film in 2005 precisely because of this narrative, and it was through his reading of the book *Harvest of Empire* that he encountered a thorough foundation for the counternarrative that the film asserts (López interview). It is also noteworthy that while the Latino threat narrative is based on inaccuracies, fallacies, and emotions that divide the population, the counternarrative of *Harvest of Empire* is grounded on historical research from the period of Spain's conquest in the Americas to the early twenty-first century. It delivers hope, not fear, promise, not threat, and compassion rather than hate, despite the pain suffered by Latin Americans due to the U.S. involvement in Latin America since the mid-1800s. It seeks to unite rather than divide.

Shortly after the initial credits disappear from the screen the voice of the narrator, Juan González, connects the past and present to the future of the United States with the statistic that by 2050 more U.S. citizens will trace their heritage to Latin America than to Europe.[3] This reality is important to the argument because it provides the rationale for why other U.S. citizens need to see Latinos in the United States as something besides "aliens." They are and will be an even more important demographic within U.S. borders. And though for some this fact may play into the notion of a *reconquista* (reconquest), the film and the book substantiate the opposite, thoroughly explaining why Latinos are motivated to immigrate northward. As a counternarrative to the myth of the *reconquista,* the thesis of *Harvest of Empire* focuses on U.S. policies in Latin America and the Caribbean that have created the conditions causing immigrants to flee their countries. It is a thesis laid out and supported with deep

Figure 1.1. The wall (*Harvest of Empire*, 2012, Eduardo López).

factual, historical, statistical information, though not devoid of the anecdotal and personal stories of embodied experience. Without being alarmist, *Harvest of Empire* communicates an urgency for U.S. citizens to begin to understand why so many Latin Americans have left and continue to leave their homelands to come to the United States but also to begin to perceive them as something other than a threat.

The film *Harvest of Empire* establishes itself almost immediately as a counternarrative to that of the mainstream press. Its early visual and audio elements support a binary structure contrasting the aggressive and degrading portrayals of Latinos by the mainstream (white) press with positive images of them as individuals or groups. As the opening credits roll, the careful viewer notices black-and-white stills that alternate between anti-immigrant and sympathetic images of Latinos in the United States. Drawing the viewer into the world of the Latino/a immigrant, the photographs culminate into a color shot of the wall along the Mexican-U.S. border. The camera zooms through a rectangular hole in the wall to eventually pan out over footage of a massive demonstration in Los Angeles showing Latinos waving American flags. They carry banners affirming, "We're workers not criminals," as the voice of a demonstration speaker resounds with "We are America." Soft, uplifting music in the background is interrupted with the authoritative voice of Jack Cafferty, a former CNN talk-show host: "Once again the streets of our country were taken over by people who don't belong here." The scene of peaceful protest has cut to a contrasting excerpt of *The Cafferty File* with Cafferty referring to Latino/a immigrants as "illegal aliens" and people who do not and should not have rights in this country. The juxtaposition of narratives does not constitute a dialogue, but it does expose the inaccuracies of the mainstream narrative as well as its more negative affective appeal that so successfully plays into people's fears; "streets being taken over" does not describe a peaceful demonstration.

Much of the mainstream narrative about Latino/a immigrants revolves around the notion that they are different from earlier immigrants, Leo Chavez states:

> The Latino Threat Narrative posits that Latinos are not like previous immigrant groups, who ultimately became part of the nation. According to the assumptions and taken-for-granted "truths" inherent in this narrative, Latinos are unwilling or incapable of integrating, of becoming part of the national community. Rather, they are part of an invading force from south of the border that is bent on reconquering land that was formerly theirs (the U.S. Southwest) and destroying the American way of life. (3)

Juan González's premise is that Latino/a immigrants *are* different from other immigrants in the United States but not for reasons that support the Latino threat narrative. They are different only because of the reasons they leave their homelands for the United States. So much of the false narrative entertains the idea that Latinos come to the United States simply to take jobs from U.S. citizens, burden social systems with their needs, or worse, come as criminals. The counternarrative of *Harvest of Empire* is that Latinos come to the United States because they cannot live in their countries of origin due to decades and in some cases nearly two centuries of U.S. foreign policies enacted against Latin America and the Caribbean, rendering those regions uninhabitable due to economic conditions, political instability, and/or social collapse.

Book and Film

The subtitle of the documentary, *The Untold Story of Latinos in America*, signifies a slight change in connotation from that of the book, *A History of Latinos in America*. The different references, to *history* and to *story*, indicate a divergence in perspective and approach. Both works contain vast amounts of historical information and base their overall premise on the history of U.S.-Latino political relations, but the documentary also uses the device of storytelling through on-camera interviews.

The book is divided into "Part I: Roots," "Part II: Branches," and "Part III: Harvest," the last focusing on policy in the United States since the mid-1950s and the first dealing with the conquest and subsequent history up to 1950. It is part 2 that corresponds most neatly to the sections about countries explored in the documentary, with some discrepancies in which countries are discussed and in what order. The book includes Colombia and Panama and groups Nicaragua, El Salvador, and Guatemala into one chapter called "Central America," though it does not discuss Honduras or Costa Rica. With part 1, the book is able to include much more information to explain the deeper historical background of the Spanish conquest, the colonial period, and the U.S. role in continuing a form of colonial rule in Latin America. While important to the entire picture, this information is not vital to understanding the dynamic between the U.S. presence in Latin America and the Latin American presence in the United States. In the documentary and the book, discussion of each country builds the case for why Puerto Ricans, Cubans, Dominicans, Mexicans, Guatemalans, Salvadorans, and Nicaraguans leave their homelands and migrate to the United States. Part 3 in the book adds to the intricacies of how U.S. policy regarding migration affects Latino/a immigrants living in the United States.

In the epilogue of the book Juan González proposes six reforms dealing with U.S. domestic and foreign policy issues: Mexican labor, the colonial status of Puerto Rico, promotion of the Spanish language, improvement of inner-city schools, an end to militarism in the region, and discontinuation of the blockade against Cuba (309–311). They are essential to creating true Latino/a equality, and they represent a radical change in what González calls "the American empire" (309). Direct solutions are not proposed in the film, for its primary focus is to reach a public with little prior background in U.S. policies toward Latin America and to explain why Latino/a immigrants come to the United States. It seeks to inform and engage the viewer with its repetitive structure, compelling stories of Latinos and Anglos in the know, and the unifying presence of Juan González as narrator. The accumulation of what oftentimes are appalling facts serves to guide the viewer toward an empathic yet informed response about the insecure world of the Latino/a immigrant. While facts play a predominant role in the film, it is the stories of the interviewees on camera that affectively convey their experiences and evoke an empathic response.

The Film

Regardless of the importance of the epilogue and parts 1 and 3 of the book, the documentary is as compelling and persuasive for what it is able to offer. Its use of interviews is established from the early scenes in which González speaks of his personal history of coming with his parents to the U.S. mainland from Puerto Rico. He refers to their migration in the book as well, but in the documentary we hear his voice and can see him and pictures of his family as he shares the story. The highest-profile interviewee of the film is the Guatemalan activist and Nobel laureate Rigoberta Menchú, who speaks of the violent atrocities she, her family, and her people directly experienced. Each of the countries is represented through an interview of either a famous or not-so-famous individual who can speak directly about the social-political conditions from which he or she fled. The Pulitzer Prize–winning author Junot Díaz comments on Rafael Trujillo's U.S.-backed savage reign in the Dominican Republic and then testifies from his personal experience as an immigrant from the Dominican Republic that "here in the United States we make immigration a more horrific experience than it needs to be." Their faces and voices are credible, their stories compelling. The choice of González as narrator provides weight, legitimacy, and continuity to the narrative of *Harvest of Empire*, as do his on-camera interviews about each region and the shots of him co-anchoring *Democracy Now!* with the news program's host, Amy Goodman.

Viewers are introduced to González as the book's author and a journalist through close-up shots of him at work or long shots of him walking the streets of a Latino neighborhood in New York City; then the tone changes to convey a different side of González. About four minutes into the film, with his head bowed and arms crossed, a mid shot of him seated in a garden blurs and zooms out to include an American flag in the corner of the frame. It is a moment that marks the beginning of the film's affective mode delivered by eyewitness accounts of embodied experience. This particular scene, however, differs from the other interviews given by immigrants; here it is the narrator's voice that speaks of a past pain, as his body is rendered speechless and immobile. Bleak black-and-white archival footage and stills of what González calls "deep poverty" in Puerto Rico are interspersed with color footage of a seated González while in voice-over he speaks of the suffering passed down through generations. Roughly five minutes later, that same voice discloses having felt rage when exploring the history of Latinos, but a rage that was tempered by a

Figure 1.2. The author Juan González (*Harvest of Empire*, 2012, Eduardo López).

conviction that Americans are fair people and that if they have accurate information they are moved to combat injustice. In less than 15 minutes the narrator has been established as a rational figure of authority as well as a feeling being. The film begins to infuse the historical facts with personal lived experience, reason with affect, fact with feeling.

The on-camera interviews of Latinos directly affected by policies outlined in *Harvest of Empire* come to embody, to make tangible and visible, the film's ideas but also the feelings evoked from the interviewees. Their stories contest the voices of Cafferty and other media talking heads who portray Latinos disparagingly. In addition, their stories illustrate how U.S. policies in Latin America affected their childhood and continue to reach into their adulthood. Too short for the makings of a documentary of personal portraiture, these stories are invitations for the uninitiated Anglo audience to face the damage of U.S. policies in Latin America. *Harvest of Empire*, with its thesis and historical approach, is clearly of the expository mode of documentary filmmaking. However, it resembles, with its many interviews, the mode of personal portraiture because it touches on the "complex and revealing lives of specific individuals" as it draws "our attention to the social issues that unite and divide us as a people" (Nichols 248).

Several chapters in Sara Ahmed's *The Cultural Politics of Emotion* analyze, through a process of othering, how the British narrative regarding immigration and racial difference functions on what she calls economies of certain emotions: fear, hate, and even love. A subject's sense of belonging to the nation is inscribed in the narrative of love for the nation, which is threatened by the proximity of the other. She considers "the role of hate in shaping bodies and worlds through the way hate generates its object as a defense against injury" (42). Her examples coming from white-nationalist narratives resemble the Latino threat narrative, in that the object (in this case, the immigrant group) is seen as taking something away from the subject (the anti-immigrant group). According to Ahmed, hate explains the story of these opposing "bodies" (or groups, immigrant and anti-immigrant), but more importantly, she sees hate not as the root of the story but as what is affected by the story and also what renders the story affective (43).

The affective narrative of *Harvest of Empire* is not organized by hate but rather by pain, which serves to counteract the affective discourse of mainstream press regarding immigration. The interviews from a variety of Latino/a immigrants repeatedly replace the Latino threat narrative with a narrative around the issue of survival and the need to flee unlivable conditions in Latin America. The codirector Eduardo López has carefully chosen a wide range of interviewees, from Rigoberta Menchú, who works on behalf of the Maya Quiché, to the late Robert White, former U.S. ambassador to El Salvador.[4] Some of the other illustrious figures include the novelist Junot Díaz, the Pulitzer Prize–winning journalist Fabiola Santiago, musician Luis Enrique Mejía López, ACLU Executive Director Anthony Romero, and poet Martín Espada, to name a few. Each interview illustrates for the American population unfamiliar with Latinos the successes of the Latino/a population through the voices of Latinos who themselves or whose parents directly suffered the consequences of U.S. involvement in Latin America. Other interviews showcase prominent U.S. citizens like Robert White who can speak with pedigree and authority about U.S. involvement in Latin America: Melvin Goodman, former CIA division chief; Roy Bourgeois, priest and founder of the School of the Americas Watch;[5] and two Maryknoll nuns who survived the violence of the civil war in El Salvador that began in 1979. Each gives firsthand commentary on his or her experiences in Central America as well as on why and to what extent the United States was involved there. These voices counterbalance the anti-immigrant right-wing voices like Cafferty's; they support what Latinos testify to having experienced and substantiate the reality that Juan González narrates throughout the film.

In contrast to these public figures, Mariana Cabrera and her daughter Mariana Zamboni, from Guatemala, give heart-wrenching interviews that speak to the separation of family members so common in the immigrant experience. Zamboni details the failed first journey she made as a little girl to reunite with her mother in the United States and then mentions the second and successful attempt. She explains that it took 20 years for their undocumented status to change. Gratitude is the predominant emotion conveyed in this interview, especially when Zamboni expresses her appreciation that her own children will probably not have to migrate to survive and when her mother shows off her daughter's degree from Harvard University.

Undoubtedly the most emotional interview, however, is with María Guardado. Another noncelebrity, María embodies the extreme violence suffered by so many Salvadorans during the civil war that lasted more than twelve years between the military government and the FMLN (Frente Farabundo Martí de Liberación Nacional). The presentation of this interview resembles parts of Zamboni's story in which the most painful experiences are iterated while illustrated in black-and-white animated drawings. For Mariana Zamboni this stylistic turn presents itself at the moment she narrates her failure to cross the border. María's interview begins with a black-and-white illustration of eyes in darkness while a deep female voice begins to narrate. The camera cuts to a mid shot of a seated female speaker narrating her recollections of being blindfolded and of hearing people around her screaming in agony. She continues her horrific story while the camera cuts back to the black-and-white illustration. María is a torture survivor, left for dead by the soldiers who brutalized her. The documentary explains then that the United States, under the Carter and the Reagan administrations, gave massive amounts of military aid to the Salvadoran government whose death squads were responsible for the acts described by María. This is an untold story for the uninitiated in Latin American–U.S. relations, and it is unfathomable to most viewers who only hear sporadic references to these countries and are informed about immigration issues solely through mainstream media.

The accumulation of hard and ugly facts builds to a crescendo in the documentary. As the camera cuts from interviews to archival footage and eventually to statistics superimposed onto black-and-white images of violence, *Harvest of Empire* makes the point that U.S. aid, business interests, political policies, and trade agreements have devastated the countries investigated in the film. In the case of El Salvador, billions of dollars were sent in aid from the United States, most of which was spent on weapons and the military that brutalized its own people.

In contrast with María's account, a more affirming tone emerges as Dr. Alfredo Quiñones is interviewed, telling his story of having come from a small Mexican farming community and migrating north for a better life. Still shots of a young Alfredo on the family farm contrast with the adult Alfredo sitting in his office dressed in mint-green scrubs as director of the Brain Tumor Program at Johns Hopkins Medicine. He speaks of the hunger he experienced as a child, one of the effects on his family and his childhood, due to NAFTA and the subsequent devaluation of the Mexican peso. Seated in his office, he epitomizes Latino/a success, but only after suffering the consequences of U.S. policy in his native country. He also speaks out of a sense of gratitude and with a generosity of spirit, thus countering the Latino threat narrative. Taking into consideration all of the interviews in the documentary, *Harvest of Empire* has managed to tell many different stories representing the experiences of migrants from Latin America, stories that include a diversity of gender, age, origin, and even political persuasion.

Affect

Over the past few decades, affect has become a central focus in contemporary critical thought. Scholars from many divergent disciplines such as media studies, literary studies, history, political theory, neuroscience, psychology, sociology, and cultural studies have contributed to what has been coined the "affective turn" (Clough) or affect theory, "a recent interdisciplinary field devoted to the study of the role of affect and emotions and their various manifestations in human behavior, culture and society" (Blackwell). Some scholars distinguish between feeling, emotions, and affect (Shouse); some critique the separation of these closely related concepts (Leys), and some focus on economies of a specific feeling such as happiness or fear (Ahmed). Reception theory within film studies considers affect's impact on audiences' experiences and interpretations of films. Seigworth and Gregg, in their introduction to *The Affect Theory Reader*, define affect as "visceral forces beneath, alongside, or generally other than conscious knowing, vital forces insisting beyond emotion—that can serve to drive us toward movement" (1). I use "affective turn" here in recognizing the omnipresence of affect in American culture, media, and society as well as in understanding affect as a fundamental mode of exchange in public debate, influencing what gets debated and how issues get debated. Erika Doss notes, "Contrary to a Habermasian vision of a rational public sphere in which sensible citizens exchange ideas and come together in shared and progressive actions, contemporary American public life is marked by emotional appeals and affective conditions" (12).

Dierdra Reber's *Coming to Our Senses* speaks to the vibrancy and creative potential of this area of investigation. With close readings of films from the United States and Latin America, she demonstrates how a discourse of affect predominates throughout cultural expressions. It is my assertion that the effectiveness of the narrative structure of the film *Harvest of Empire* depends upon an interweaving of a rational and an affective discourse since the film's very premise is a call for understanding and compassion. Applicable to this study is Reber's analysis of *Diarios de motocicleta* (*The Motorcycle Diaries*, 2004) as a reshaping of the canonical figure Che Guevara into a "feeling soma" (161). Reber sees director Walter Salles's adaptation of the revolutionary's political awakenings documented in his diaries not through a presentation of discursive revolutionary speech (for which the historical figure is known) but rather as a feeling body "giving love to an oppressed Latin America" (Reber interview).[6] The film uses affect, "an emotion associated with an idea or set of ideas" (Oxford Dictionary), rather than a rational attack on capitalism, which is what the historical Guevara sought and expressed. While the film creates Che as an endearing figure, he is depoliticized, and so are the circumstances of his analysis and struggle. The discourse of affect in *Harvest of Empire* does not follow suit; rather, the film conveys the facts of Latin American history in relation to U.S. policies coupled with the pain and hardship its people have experienced because of them.[7] *Harvest of Empire* does not critique capitalism; it frames its thesis more softly in terms of U.S. policy generated by business interests. It proceeds from a historical perspective of U.S. history in relation to Latin America since the U.S.-Mexican War of 1846–1848.

Reber also notices that there is a generational divide between older audiences who still expect a more rational discourse and millennials who have come to expect a more affective discourse (Reber interview). Anne Rutherford in her *What Makes a Film Tick? Cinematic Affect, Materiality, and Mimetic Innervation* shares Reber's view that this affective pull is something even expected of certain audiences, such as many of today's college-age viewers who have become thoroughly conditioned to this mode of communication from the media. Rutherford also recognizes that older audiences still relate to a more rational discourse. Studying two documentaries dealing with the injustices committed against the aboriginals in Australia, she has found that undergraduate students were not moved by the documentary *Frontier* (1996, directed by Bruce Belsham) and that some even walked out. By contrast, the same audience viewing *Dhuway*, a documentary on identical subject matter, was much more interested and engaged. Like *Harvest of Empire*, the 1997 Australian documentary *Dhuway*, directed by Lew Griffiths, uses "archival footage and historical narrative, but weaves these components into a dynamic, living web in which history and historical evidence are actively inscribed in the lived experience of the people who are telling their stories" (Rutherford 230). Rutherford attributes the indifference of this group of viewers to the disembodied language of *Frontier* and the appeal of *Dhuway* to that film's mode of embodied affective expression. Furthermore, judging from the responses of a more general audience showing interest in *Frontier*, she claims a generational divide is responsible for a difference in expectations of viewers: "We have one audience requiring the mode of anonymous sources and legitimising structures of authority, and another, indifferent to these structures and unwilling to engage with material which does not address them in more direct and personal ways" (243).

Audience and Distribution

Harvest of Empire is screened at U.S. colleges primarily because of its distribution patterns that stem from the success of Juan González's book; it is a required text in at least 300 college courses in the country. The book and the film work well in concert as well as separately. In fact, it was the codirector Eduardo López's wish to do justice to the book with this film and to bring its central concept to a wider audience. In particular, he saw the film as a useful tool for journalists so that the national dialogue about immigration could take a different course. Unfortunately, this wish of his has not yet been realized. Moved by the book and with a desire to correct the misinformation in mainstream news, he and coproducer Wendy Thompson-Márquez began working on the documentary once they received rights from González in 2005. Not being able to find a TV partner made access to the film more difficult and with it, the goal of reaching a mass market. However, López has traveled to colleges to present the film and knows firsthand that "thousands have seen it, that it has opened minds and hearts, instigated dialogues, and raised important questions regarding immigration policy in this country" (López interview).

The documentary did meet most of the production team's aspirations, which were to create an award-winning film, obtain theatrical distribution in target cities, and receive strong and positive reviews. López has come to realize that the "subject matter is too strong and truthful for broadcast across the United States" (López interview). Wendy Thompson-Márquez speaks of *Harvest of Empire*'s inability to "break through to national newspapers or television programming" as their "greatest disappointment." During our interview she shared that the film was identified as "too fringe, too radical, and biased."[8] The disconnect between mass television access and the film's appeal is great. In contrast to the creative team's disappointment, for example, the documentary opened to sold-out audiences, extended runs, and favorable reviews. Thompson-Márquez recalls what occurred at the Regal Majestic Theater in Silver Spring, Maryland:[9]

> On opening night, the film had to be moved to the largest auditorium in the 20-screen multiplex in order to accommodate ticket sales. In fact, *Harvest of Empire* was the Washington region's highest grossing independent film of the weekend, besting the box office of any film showing at either one of the metropolitan area's two leading venues for independent film—the E Street Cinema and the Bethesda Row Cinemas. As a result of the public reaction the Regal Majestic extended the run for *Harvest of Empire* to a full three weeks. (Email)

The theatrical screenings, which opened at the Quad in New York and the Laemmle in Los Angeles, had extended runs from one week to one month due to the success in ticket sales and to reviews. Shortly after the opening of the film, *Harvest of Empire* received the ABC News Video Source Award from the International Documentary Association in Los Angeles. It even beat out an entry from Ken Burns for the honor, which is awarded to the film that best uses "news and archival footage as an integral component in a documentary" (Thompson-Márquez email). A year after the documentary opened, it won the Imagen Award as Best Documentary Feature for Film or Television. In the same year, June 2013, the organization representing commercial and documentary filmmakers throughout the East Coast, CINE, named *Harvest of Empire* Best Documentary and Best Independent Film of the Year. By early 2015 the film was chosen as one of the 15 Notable Videos for Adults by the prestigious

American Library Association. The ALA officially announced *Harvest of Empire* as a "comprehensive geopolitical picture of the economic and historical realities that have guided waves of Latin American migration to the United States" (Thompson-Márquez email). Despite these successes and after public relations experts were hired, the film was rejected by national television news programs that claimed immigration was not a "top priority, and when something breaks on the topic, they prefer to interview members of Congress" (Thompson-Márquez email).

Providing a counternarrative to the masses even on programming like *The Rachel Maddow Show*, *The Last Word with Lawrence O'Donnell*, *The Lead with Jake Tapper*, and *Anderson Cooper 360* has proven impossible since producers are not able to see the value in providing historical context to the issue and prefer to rely on their "large group of paid commentators who are brought in to discuss the issues of the day" (Thompson-Márquez email). Where the film has received attention, whether by interviewing López or showing short clips of the film, has been on MSNBC's *Joy Reid Show*, *Democracy Now!*, and *Moyers & Company*. Thompson-Márquez has been profiled in a major *Washington Post* article on her own personal immigration story as well as on her role as producer of *Harvest of Empire*.

Certainly not as splashy as being aired on national television but perhaps even more effective is López's input on the creation of a study guide to the documentary for all who are connected to the Common Core educational standard. Any teacher in the country has access to this guide, which was authored by curriculum writer and teacher Julia Hainer-Violand with the support of a grant from the Virginia Foundation for the Humanities (López interview). Such an act of service (rather than a commercial endeavor) seems an appropriate response to González's comment in the documentary that schools have not taught the history lessons explained in his book and in the film. As Michael Chanan states in *The Politics of Documentary*, "Where independent documentary remains outside the world of television, an alternative distribution constructs a parallel public sphere for its circulation, the documentarist has the advantage of a closer relationship with small but particular sectors of the public" (202).

Conclusion

Nichols asserts, "The task of documentaries is to move us towards a predisposition or perspective regarding some aspect of the world" (248). *Harvest of Empire* has the precarious task of appealing to an uninitiated audience without offending it for its lack of knowledge. It has to start by helping viewers realize they are not well informed, and from there it has the daunting task of assembling more than a hundred years of Latin American history into a cohesive and comprehensible 90-minute format. González's statement about the demographic changes in the United States can be compared with statements from Cafferty and Patrick Buchanan, for example, both of whom characterize Latino/a migration to this country as a threat.[10] The difference rests in how the information is communicated and in the contrasting emotions conveyed about a simple statistic: fear and resistance versus compassion and acceptance. Societies throughout the world, not just in the Americas, are moving toward the multicultural, multiethnic, and multireligious, as then UN High Commissioner for Refugees António Guterres (later UN secretary-general) stated during a conversation with TED's Bruno Giussani about the refugee crisis in Europe (Guterres). *Harvest of Empire* clarifies that many Latino/a immigrants are indeed refugees fleeing unlivable conditions in their homelands, conditions caused by U.S. intervention in the region. Historical fact in *Harvest of Empire* brought to life with a diverse array of interviews has uncovered a reality unfortunately deemed too true for U.S. mass media.

In the writing of this chapter, an unusual media event related to Latino/a immigration in the United States took place during the halftime ads at the 2016 Super Bowl. A 90-second commercial appeared for 84 Lumber, a Pennsylvania-based building supply company, featuring a young Mexican mother and her daughter traveling day and night to reach the U.S. border. Beautifully produced with barely any dialogue (the few words spoken were in Spanish), no voice-over, touching scenes between the two characters, and a tender and sensitive soundtrack, the ad itself might be grounds for encouragement or further discouragement about the treatment of immigration in this country, depending on one's interpretation of the short narrative, heavy on affect (the soundtrack, mother-daughter journey, hardship, even patriotism) as well as ambiguity. Its appearance, nonetheless, as one of the high-profile ads at the Super Bowl, gives cause for hope if only for the fact that it aired before millions of viewers without any reference to the Latino threat narrative. In fact, its empathic and favorable portrayal of migrants contradicts the Latino threat narrative without rhetoric of any kind. Also it is important that the issue of censorship was made obvious to the general public, with Fox claiming that the ad was too controversial for television.

Though the full commercial was banned by Fox, an agreement was made to cut the ending and reduce the 5:44-minute story to 1:31 minutes. The omitted portions consist of scenes of men constructing the wall, a long shot of the walled border, the mother-daughter pair confronted with the wall as an apparent obstacle, and their eventual discovery of the giant doors built into it. There are no guards, no border-control officials, no checkpoints, and the solitary pair passes through the sun-filled doorway of opportunity just before the ending. The tag line, "The will to succeed is always welcome here," appears over the last scene, showing lumber scraps from the wall construction lying in the bed of a pickup truck humming down an open road. Given what was cut, it appears the controversy existed in the portrayal of the wall itself, even as fantastical as it was, in the depiction of its construction by some men who quite possibly could be Latino and in the creation of a permissive opening at a site whose function is to refuse, reject, and separate. Associating those who embark on the journey north with the will to succeed and then welcoming those same people could even be seen as subversive to the official border politics of this era.

The success of Fox's censorship can also be debated. Because the end of the aired ad directed viewers to the uncut version with "See the conclusion at journey84.com," its site briefly crashed during the game as viewers rushed to take in the entire ad (Payne). Many complex issues surface with the appearance of this ad, both the cut and uncut versions and the divided response among viewers, but it confirms a major claim by Reber that we need to take heed of the power of affective discourse and comprehend it in rational terms (254). The ad exemplifies the effectiveness and pervasiveness of the discourse of affect in the media. Whether or not the ad brought more business to the previously little-known lumber company remains to be seen, but it did bring the entity out of obscurity. It also brought the debate on immigration into a bigger and more neutral arena.

Nielsen data show that more than 111 million people in the United States watched Super Bowl LI, estimating that 70 percent of homes with televisions were tuned into the game ("Super Bowl"), all of which indicates that at least one of the versions of 84 Lumber's ad was viewed by a massive audience. Applying to the issue of immigration reform Chenoweth's "3.5% rule" regarding social change and civil resistance, it will take 11 million Americans to participate fully and consistently in an effective movement to bring about a policy change. Aired at the initiation of the Trump administration's aggressive deportation agenda, which further criminalized unauthorized immigrants and subsequently labeled them "removable aliens," the ad humanizes the migrants' experience. Its depiction of a permeable wall is also counter to the reality of an immigration policy that only weeks after the ad aired was deemed a "military operation" (Hing).[11]

Responses to the ad were polarized, either with strong praise or equally strong criticism. The immigration scholar Yamil Velez attributes the divided reaction of viewers to the ambiguity of the ad:

> Ambiguity usually leads people to reinforce their prior beliefs. Whereas the expectation would be that when you give people mixed evidence they would maybe moderate their positions, we generally find that people reinforce their prior beliefs and attitudes . . . and interpret ambiguous evidence as supporting their preexisting notions of the world. (In Kauffman)[12]

Perhaps it is the portrayal of the door and beyond that can be construed as ambiguous, for what does that door really signify? What is being represented by that dreamy, sun-filled place into which the pair set foot? Heaven? An idealized United States? Success? Adding to the sense of ambiguity is the favorable portrayal of the migrants, which makes it compelling to be drawn into their drama and to root for them. How does any affective attachment sit for those whose stance on immigration might clash with feelings of empathy? Without the inclusion of a rational discourse, where does one turn for answers? *Harvest of Empire* is unambiguous in its almost relentless factual and empathic counternarrative to the singularly affective false mainstream narrative. The creative team of *Harvest of Empire* is a tiny part of the 3.5 percent needed for the seeds of change to be planted, but the power of the documentary to move its viewers emotionally and rationally to a deeply felt understanding of Latino/a immigration in the United States is massive, even if it doesn't reach the masses in one evening.

Notes

1. The documentary *Harvest of Empire* was codirected by Eduardo López and Peter Getzels. López also worked as coproducer with Wendy Thompson-Márquez. López and Thompson-Márquez first conceived of the project and were successful in obtaining rights from Juan González to make the film. During the last year and a half of the film's completion process the two producers hired Peter Getzels (Thompson-Márquez interview).

2. It is not my intention to highlight the Latino threat narrative or to give print space to those who espouse it. Suffice it to say that it can be heard on stations considered centrist such as CNN and MSNBC and accessed in mainstream print media such as the *Los Angeles Times*. Derogatory and dehumanizing terms referencing Latino/a immigrants as "illegal aliens" or just "illegals" and their children as "anchor babies" are still widely used in U.S. culture, which attests to the pervasiveness of this negative narrative.

3. The same statement is found on page xv of the introduction to González's book *Harvest of Empire*.

4. Robert White died at age 88 in 2015. For more information on his friction with the U.S. government due to his understanding and vocal criticism of U.S.-funded activities in El Salvador, see his obituary in the *New York Times* by Sam Roberts and another in the *Washington Post* by Pamela Constable.

5. On the School of the Americas Watch and Father Roy's founding role in it, see "SOA Watch."

6. Laura Podalsky also writes on *Diarios de motocicleta* in *The Politics of Affect and Emotion in Contemporary Latin American Cinema*, 60–61.

7. It was shortly after Guevara's famous trip through South America, made more famous with the film, that he traveled to Central America and witnessed U.S. policy acted out in Guatemala in the form of a U.S.-backed military takeover of a democratic and reformist government. The Arbenz government attempted to stand up against United Fruit, leading to an open confrontation with the United States. This was the defining moment that captivated Guevara and solidified his political vision for Latin America (Rowlands).

8. Having screened this film to college students and faculty, it is not my experience that viewers find it biased. Perhaps this label coming from mainstream television is an example of an ideological gap between the mainstream and the academy. Or perhaps this simply points to an acceptance of the false narrative as absolute and true.

9. In the spring of 2013 the film opened for one-week theatrical runs in Chicago, Philadelphia, Denver, San Francisco, Berkeley, Washington, DC, Phoenix, Santa Fe, Albuquerque, and Houston.

10. Patrick Buchanan's *State of Emergency: The Third World Invasion and Conquest of America* was published in 2008.

11. Hing describes Department of Homeland Security secretary's memos early in Trump's administration regarding the president's executive orders on immigration. They include raids; deportation of all removable aliens, not just criminal offenders; expansion of the U.S. deportation machinery; and harsher policies for asylum seekers, all of which amount to a mass-deportation agenda.

12. See Kauffman's article on how people of different views on immigration interpreted the ad.

Works Cited

Ahmed, Sara. *The Cultural Politics of Emotion*. 2nd ed. New York: Routledge, 2015. Print.
Blackwell Reference Online. Web. 10 Dec. 2016.
Buchanan, Patrick J. *State of Emergency: The Third World Invasion and Conquest of America*. New York: Thomas Dunne Books St. Martin's Press, 2008. Print.
Chanan, Michael. *The Politics of Documentary*. London: British Film Institute, 2007. Print.
Chavez, Leo R. *The Latino Threat: Constructing Immigrants, Citizens, and the Nation*, Stanford, CA: Stanford University Press, 2013. eBook Collection (EBSCOhost). Web. 3 Feb. 2017.
Chenoweth, Eria. "The Success of Nonviolent Civil Resistance." TEDxBoulder. Sept. 2013. Web. 18 Feb. 2017.
Clough, Patricia Ticineto. Introduction. *The Affective Turn: Theorizing the Social*. Ed. Patricia Ticineto Clough. Durham, NC: Duke UP, 2007. 1–33. Print.
Constable, Pamela. "Robert E. White, Who Criticized U.S. Policy in El Salvador, Dies." *Washington Post*, 15 Jan. 2015. Web. 10 July 2015.
Doss, Erika. *The Emotional Life of Contemporary Public Memorials: Towards a Theory of Temporary Memorials*. Amsterdam: Amsterdam UP, 2008. Print.
González, Juan. *Harvest of Empire: A History of Latinos in America*. New York: Penguin. 2011. Print.
Guterres, António. "Refugees Have the Right to Be Protected." TED, December 2015. Web. 17 Feb. 2017.
Harvest of Empire: The Untold Story of Latinos in America. Dir. Peter Getzels and Eduardo López. Onyx Films, 2012. DVD.
Hing, Julianne. "Trump Admits That His Deportation Agenda Is a Military Operation." *The Nation*. 24 Feb. 2017. Web. 26 Feb. 2017.
Kauffman, Gretel. "Does That 84 Lumber Ad Really Mean What You Think It Means?" *Christian Science Monitor*, 7 Feb. 2017. Web. 20 Feb. 2017.
Leys, Ruth. "The Turn to Affect: A Critique." *Critical Inquiry* 37 (Spring 2011): 434–472. Print.
López, Eduardo. Phone interview by the author. 29 Jan. 2017.

Nichols, Bill. *Introduction to Documentary*. 2nd ed. Bloomington: Indiana UP. 2010. Print.

oxforddictionaries.com. Web. 15 Dec. 2016.

Payne, Marissa. "84 Lumber CEO: Super Bowl Ad Showing Trump's Wall Wasn't Intended to Be Political." *Washington Post*, 7 Feb. 2017. Web. 15 Feb. 2017.

Podalsky, Laura. *The Politics of Affect and Emotion in Contemporary Latin American Cinema*. New York: Palgrave Macmillan, 2011. Print.

Reber, Dierdra. *Coming to Our Senses: Affect and an Order of Things for Global Culture*. New York: Columbia UP, 2016. Print.

———. Interview by Chuck Mertz. *This Is Hell!* 27 Feb. 2016. Web. 30 Nov. 2016.

Roberts, Sam. "Robert E. White, Ex-Ambassador to Latin America, Dies at 88." *New York Times*, 16 Jan. 2015. Web. 10 July 2015.

Rowlands. David T. "Guatemala: The Coup That Radicalised Che Guevara." *Greenleft Weekly*, 30 May 2014. Web. 15 Feb. 2017.

Rutherford, Anne. *What Makes a Film Tick? Cinematic Affect, Materiality, and Mimetic Innervation*. Bern: Peter Lang, 2011. eBook Collection (EBSCOhost). Web. 2 Feb. 2017.

Seigworth, Gregory J., and Melissa Gregg, eds. *The Affect Theory Reader*. Durham, NC: Duke UP 2010. Print.

Shouse, Eric. "Feeling, Emotion, Affect." *M/C Journal* 8.6 (2005). Web. 10 Dec. 2016.

"SOA Watch Staff—Fr. Roy Bourgeois." School of the Americas Watch, 25 April 2017. Web. 23 June 2017.

"Super Bowl LI Draws 111.3 Million TV Viewers, 190.8 Million Social Media Interactions." Nielsen, 6 Feb. 2017. Web. 12 Feb. 2017.

Thompson-Márquez, Wendy. Interview by Lauren Shaw, via email and phone. 17 Feb. 2017.

⟩ 2 ⟨

Documenting Deportable Life

Knowledge, Performance, and Memory in *abUSed: The Postville Raid* and *Sin país*

JARED LIST

Since 9/11, U.S. immigration policy has occupied a greater space in the national imaginary. Nightly and online news sources cover the contentious immigration banter between political parties; yet, a solution is always avoided. In these programs and articles we rarely hear from the immigrants themselves; their voices are not included. Millions of undocumented individuals living in the United States remain in limbo, hoping for a fair and just outcome that takes into account more than simply their legal status. While we could detain ourselves here to discuss the recent political efforts to address immigration and its potential reform, such a task might unnecessarily detract from my overall aim to examine the role of documentary in humanizing the lives of those caught in the middle, that is, documentary as means through which immigrants and their families can share their experiences, ideas, and opinions and, furthermore, be included in the discussions and debates. In this sense, documentary is a strategy to overcome exclusionary media practices.

Let me briefly highlight the problematic system upon which U.S. immigration policy is founded. In the introduction of her *Impossible Subjects: Illegal Aliens and the Making of Modern America*, Mae M. Ngai argues that a regime of restriction is what has governed U.S. immigration policy since 1776. She mentions the quota system as evidence of this paradigm, and I would add that by reading a short introduction to U.S. immigration policy, the reader comes to find out that U.S. immigration policy truly revolved around the framework of inclusion/exclusion (Ngai 2). Nonetheless, the paradigms of restriction and inclusion/exclusion are not as clear-cut as they may seem.

For example, let us examine the relationship between the U.S. economy and immigration policy. Ngai argues that "undocumented immigrants are at once welcome and unwelcome: they are woven into the economic fabric of the nation but as labor that is cheap and disposable" (2). From a juridical-national framework, they are excluded and their migration to the United States restricted, but from an economic one, they are included, marked as disposable life. The restriction and the exclusion proposed by the former engenders the latter, as Ngai describes: "Marginalized by their position in the lower strata in the workforce and even more so by their exclusion from the polity, illegal aliens might be understood as a caste, unambiguously situated outside the boundary of formal membership and social legitimacy" (2). Ngai calls individuals trapped in this situation "impossible subjects," whereas here I use the term "deportable life." The two terms convey nuance of the same subject: "the illegal alien as a *new legal and political subject*, whose inclusion with the nation was simultaneously a social reality and a legal impossibility—a subject barred from citizenship and without rights" (Ngai 4). So, the question I want to examine here is How do impossible or deportable subjects who have been excluded, marginalized, and dehumanized emerge from such a precarious position? And how can documentary challenge such marginalization and dehumanization? In this chapter, I demonstrate how documentary as a rhetorical form and strategy can play a fundamental role in a politics of inclusion and humanization. To do so, I will use Luis Argueta's 2010 documentary *abUSed: The Postville Raid* and Theo Rigby's 2010 short documentary *Sin país*.

I look at how these documentaries, as performances of memory, produce knowledge about recent U.S. immigration policy. Both films are interventions in a greater discourse on U.S. immigration reform. They not only inform the public of the emotional, psychological, and economic tolls related to current immigration enforcement practices, but they also reveal and humanize the very lives deemed deportable. In this way, the documentaries are performative acts that record and (re)present the trauma associated with deportation. They serve a tripartite purpose: to articulate an empathetic understanding between the self and the other through the presence and humanization of documentary's subjects—a group of individuals who are often left voiceless and faceless in dominant discourses—to use performance to unearth and remember marginalized, silenced histories (that is, putting the pieces of the past back together), and to construct knowledge that affirms life.[1] While each documentary uses different techniques to convey the injustices and consequences associated with current policy, both present deportable life, that is, lives whose geojuridical status teeters between bare life and disposable (or dispensable) life.

Here I use several terms that originate from the works of Giorgio Agamben and Walter Mignolo. "Bare life," a term originally used by Hannah Arendt and developed by Agamben, refers to life outside of politics. In other words, "bare life" refers to those lives that lack any legal or political protection. Bare life's counterpart would be politicized life, as Agamben argues, being that the law protects and confers rights to this conception of life. He tells us that bare life can be killed, and there is no juridical consequence given the lack of legal protection. His case study is the Holocaust. In Nazi Germany, Jews were stripped of their rights and protection and sent to concentration camps (Agamben 128–132). There they encountered a state of exception, where once politicized life is made bare (Agamben 169). In other words, the law is suspended, hence, the term "state of exception."

"Disposable life" refers to life that is economically dispensable; it can be replaced. In his essay "Dispensable and Bare Lives: Coloniality and the Hidden Political/Economic Agenda of Modernity," Mignolo gives us the example of slavery and the slave trade. Slaves were deemed property and thus dispensable (Mignolo 74–75). When discussing deportable life, the concepts of bare life, disposable (dispensable) life, and state of exception all enter into the equation—something Nicholas De Genova discusses in his essay "The Deportation Regime: Sovereignty, Space, and the Freedom of Movement." Briefly, for him, it is the possibility of deportation (read: bare life) that gives way to disposable life.

Deportable Lives: Exploitation, Dispensability, and Injustice in abUSed

I begin not with an example from Argueta's documentary but rather an anecdote I found in a newspaper article while researching this project. The story goes something like this. One January day, just south of Fresno, California, a plane streaked through the air. The year was 1948, and for those in the area, when they looked to the sky, they knew something was not right. An engine failed; a wing broke off; the unfortunate souls aboard were doomed (Marcum). The onlookers from the ground could only watch in horror, witnessing a modern-day marvel turn modern-day disaster. Who might be on that plane? What were they thinking as the plane disintegrated midair? Who would miss them? What were their names? The news outlets and investigators would surely give the public this information, so they could be properly mourned.

But for many of those passengers, no names were shared with the public. It turned out the January 28 flight was chartered by the U.S. Immigration Service to return immigrants to Mexico. Many had come to work through the Bracero program, while others had entered without documents. As expected, newspapers covered the crash, informing readers of the event. They published the names of the pilots, the flight attendant, and the immigration officers on board. The public could remember them; their names were recorded in the official record. As for the 28 others on the plane, they were not afforded the same right to be remembered; their names were not important, rather their legal situation was. They were to be remembered as "deportees," as the newspapers had named them (Marcum). Incensed by the poor treatment of the Mexican immigrants and their anonymity in national media coverage, Woody Guthrie wrote lyrics about the incident. A decade later Martin Hoffman set them to melody, and it was Pete Seeger who popularized the song known as "Deportee (Plane Wreck at Los Gatos)."

The deportees would never make it back to Mexico, their bodies interred in a mass grave at Holy Cross cemetery in Fresno with a single tombstone marking the men's final resting place. The inscription on the tombstone read, "28 Mexican Citizens Who Died In An Airplane Accident Near Coalinga California On Jan. 28, 1948 R.I.P" (Marcum). At a cursory glance, the inscription does not tell us much; 28 Mexican citizens died in a plane crash in California. For these men, any form of remembrance was reduced to their nationality and citizenship. Gender, birth date, socioeconomic status, personality traits, photos, religious orientation, and marital and familial status are all absent from the stone—all the information that you may find on gravestones if you were to wander through a cemetery in the United States.

Thus, the question becomes Why were these individuals not afforded the same dignity in death as the flight crew? Were not all their lives equal in value? Or did their treatment after death reveal something about their lives and status in life? Why, if they were identified as Mexican citizens, were their bodies not returned to Mexico? All these questions begin to address the consequences of deportable life.

However, I think it is important to make a distinction before moving on to the analysis of the Postville, Iowa, raid itself. The story of the plane crash in California first appeared in a newspaper article. It is narrativized through the written word on the page. In contrast, abUSed uses film as its medium to convey its message. While we could compare the effectiveness at transmitting the message to their respective audiences, what we can do here is briefly mention how abUSed effectively shares its message, primarily through a retelling of the events surrounding the raid. When we as viewers hear these testimonies, images accompany their words. We see the faces and their expressions—the sadness, the fear, the relief, the uncertainty, the joy—as they recount their experiences.

All of these expressions humanize and individualize a group of people who have been subject to depersonalization in the larger debate on U.S. immigration. As Luis Argueta states later on in this book in his interview with Esteban Loustaunau, one of his purposes in making the film "is to humanize the immigrants and to make them individuals, not numbers" (258). In this sense, abUSed (and Sin país) include the excluded and marginalized, interpolating the question of humanity into dominant discourses on U.S. immigration policy. What results is a polyphonic, diverse representation of voices that give testimony to injustice, exploitation, and their consequences. Such an interpretation offers a reality strategically rooted in the value and importance of human life. One of the documentary's narratives especially highlights and calls attention to the dehumanization, exploitation, and precarity of the undocumented workers and the ways in which justice was miscarried. While examining the event itself, we must keep in mind that the following examples give shape to the documentary's argument and its aim to effect change among its viewers.

In 2008, 60 years after the plane crash in California, members of the small Iowa town of Postville would find themselves looking up to the sky as well. This time, rather than a plane plummeting through the sky, helicopters cut through the air. It was at this moment that "everything started to go weird," eighth-grader Pedro Arturo Vega-López later comments in Argueta's abUSed. The boy had been sitting in his classroom at Postville Elementary on May 12, 2008, when the typical morning turned into a memorable one. At first, he, like the rest of his classmates, wondered why the helicopters were circling above. "And all of a sudden it struck him what it might be, and he just collapsed on his desk in sobs," his eighth-grade teacher Mrs. Olafsen recounts in the documentary (abUSed). It turned out that Pedro's hunch was correct. The helicopters were there for a specific reason; they were conducting an unannounced raid of the town's main employer, Agriprocessors. Not even the Postville Police Department knew of the raid (*abUSed*).

The kosher slaughterhouse and meatpacking plant had been in the small town since 1987 and employed 900 workers—an extremely large number, considering the town's population of 2,273. After the U.S. Immigration and Custom Enforcement officers raided the plant, nearly 400 employees had been detained.[2] The detained were taken just outside the plant and lined up to await transportation to the nearby city of Waterloo, Iowa. In the film, Kerry Dillon, a Postville high school teacher and volunteer emergency medical technician, describes the sight when she first pulled up in an ambulance outside of the slaughterhouse: "All the sudden I see lines and rows of Hispanic workers on their knees like dogs, and they were just chained. And I couldn't even . . . I had never seen anything like that before" (*abUSed*). Eventually the workers were loaded onto buses and transported to the National Cattle Congress in Waterloo. The complex was normally used for livestock shows and competitions along with fairs and rodeos; however, on this day it became the detention center for the arrested workers. Jen Krogstad, a staff writer for the *Waterloo Courier*, comments in *abUSed*, "I don't know who picked the cattle congress, but from the federal government's perspective, that is terrible PR [public relations]." It is precisely Krogstad's nuance here that I want to analyze, for he highlights a problematic relation between territory, rights, and life.

The makeshift prison at the National Cattle Congress did not meet federal requirements, certified federal interpreter Erik Camayd-Freixas states in the documentary. Present at the legal proceedings after the raid, he explains that the cubicles constructed within the gymnasium for defense attorney-client meetings did not ensure a minimum level of privacy. The cubicles were constructed of chain-link fencing inside the building, and in many cases, immigration and customs enforcement agents were present in the cubicles during these meetings. Camayd-Freixas says the makeshift detention center "did not fulfill the minimum requirements of a detention center, and in fact, it was never certified by the Department of Justice or the Bureau of Prisons because, in fact, it was not certifiable" (*abUSed*). Furthermore, the arrested workers often met with their attorneys in groups rather than individually. Given the large number of clients and the few attorneys, the meetings were often between the defense attorney and 10 clients. One of the attorneys, Sonia Parras-Konrad, even says that on the first day of her arrival to the detention center, she was not allowed to see any of her clients (*abUSed*).

The detainees were being tried in criminal cases as opposed to immigration proceedings. The prosecution had 72 hours to bring charges against the detainees, and if the charges were not filed, the right of habeas corpus would prevent them from being filed. Camayd-Freixas explains that charges were filed within the 72-hour limit; however, to do so, the employees of the court worked double shifts, himself included (*abUSed*). He along with others felt pressure from the prosecution to make sure charges were filed: "It was odd because . . . the court appeared to be working at the pleasure of the prosecution, bending over backwards in order to accommodate the prosecution. I've never seen that. I've never seen that" (*abUSed*). Once the charges were filed, the fate of the detainees was all but sealed.

In the documentary, U.S. District Court Judge Mark W. Bennett explains how he was unsettled to be sentencing 57 arrested workers on the same day, in groups of seven to ten at a time. For him, sentencing individuals in a group may keep them from speaking up or asking the court to clarify something they do not completely understand. Not only was the sentencing arrangement problematic for Bennett, he was also uncomfortable with those he was sentencing. None of the 57 individuals had ever been charged with a crime, Bennett remembers.

> Of the 57 people I sentenced, not one of them, not one of them had a criminal conviction in the United States, not so much as a misdemeanor conviction. To have 57 people in a row that don't even have a single misdemeanor among them is unheard of in federal court. So if anyone deserved mercy, and compassion, and fairness and justice, these 57 did, and I don't believe they received it, even though I'm the one who imposed the sentence because my hands were tied by the Department of Justice in the case. (*abUSed*)

When the sentencing was done, nearly all the arrested male workers were sent to prison for five to twelve months and then deported (Camayd-Freixas 3). In the cases of arrested female workers, many of those with children avoided deportation. Instead, they were fitted with GPS monitoring devices and restricted to a small radius in Postville so they could take care of their children (*abUSed*; Camayd-Freixas 16).

Argueta's documentary raises many concerns, as we have just seen, particularly in relation to life, rights, and territory; through this relation viewers can better understand the workers' precarious situations. An arrested worker, Laura Castillo, recounts in the documentary what happened to her. When she told an ICE officer that she was not going to say anything until she spoke with a lawyer—a right she believed she had—the officers "se comenzaron a reír y decir, 'ayyy sí, como si tuvieras muchos derechos aquí, éste no es tu país'" (began to laugh and said, "Oh yes, as if you had many rights here. This isn't your country") (*abUSed*). The argument in the documentary is articulated in such a way that it becomes apparent that in Postville the detainees are reduced to bare and disposable life. The National Cattle Congress becomes the site of exception. The sovereign power ignores or skirts laws that protect individuals' rights. Compounded with the suspension of the law in the case of Postville, the relation between life, territoriality, and citizenship permits the sovereign power to affirm, negate, or displace life—a relation that Saskia Sassen contends began during the Medieval period.[3] Nathalie Peutz and Nicholas De Genova state in their introduction to *The Deportation Regime: Sovereignty, Space, and the Freedom of Movement,* "The sovereign power to regulate and restrict human movement through space is thus never simply a matter of 'administration' or 'belonging.' It is the imposition of a power over life itself" (12–13).

De Genova claims in his essay "Migrant 'Illegality' and Deportability in Everyday Life" that "it is *deportability*, and not deportation per se, that has historically rendered undocumented migrant labor a distinctly disposable commodity" (438). It is here we arrive at deportable life, where the condition of deportability enables the use of life for economic ends.[4] It is where bare and disposable life meet, the former preceding and giving way to the latter.[5] Peutz and De Genova find,

> It is *deportability*, then, or the protracted possibility of being deported—along with the multiple vulnerabilities that this susceptibility for deportation engenders—that is the real effect of these policies and practices. *Deportation regimes are profoundly effective,* and quite efficiently so, exactly insofar as the grim spectacle of the deportation of even just a few, coupled with the enduring everyday deportability of countless others (millions, in the case of the United States), produces and maintains migrant "illegality" as not merely an anomalous juridical status but also a

practical, materially consequential, and deeply interiorized mode of being—and of being put in place. (14)

Thus, the question becomes Does the Medieval relation between territoriality, birthplace, and rights become a means to extract and exploit labor in the colonial/modern global capitalist system? I would argue, as do Peutz and De Genova, that deportability (that is, bare life) engenders disposable life. In other words, whereas social classification vis-à-vis race becomes the means to produce and justify disposable life, today the relation between birthplace and rights (citizenship)—in conjunction with race—determines what life is deemed disposable.

Peutz and De Genova highlight another condition that the state of deportability comes to bear—the fear of deportation, of dislocation, of displacement, and ultimately, of social death (14). Fearful of the ever-present possibility of deportation, undocumented individuals may be victims of workplace exploitation and crimes, and despite their victimization, they may not seek justice, fearful that their legal status may come to light. Thus, they remain voiceless in the face of exploitation. The documentary clearly articulates this fear and subsequent silence among the workers and community members in Postville.

The viewer learns in the documentary about the labor practices at Agriprocessors. On July 26, 2008, Congressman Luis Gutiérrez of Illinois led a congressional delegation that met at St. Bridget's Catholic Church in Postville to hear the testimonies of some of the workers in the meatpacking plant. There, the former workers' testimonies exposed the plant's exploitative and illegal labor practices. Gilda Ordoñez, who at the time of the meeting was 16 years old, is one of those who shared their experiences. She tells the delegation, "I worked there in the plant. I would work beginning at 7 p.m. and would leave at 6:30 or 7 a.m. I worked almost 12 hours. There I suffered a lot because I couldn't handle much in that job because I used scissors a lot and my hand would swell up. And in that, they treated us poorly. They yelled at us and always gave us hard work" (*abUSed*, my translation).[6] She goes on to say that the workers would be subjected to having water mixed with kill-waste (animal by-products from the slaughtering and meatpacking process) thrown on them (*abUSed*).

Following her testimony, Gutiérrez asked the audience if there were others under the age of 18 who had worked in the plant. Argueta's documentary includes three other young workers' testimonies that day, all of them having started work at the plant between the ages of 14 and 17. However, employing minors was not the only law the owners broke. Hired at the age of 17, Isaías López-Marroquín describes his daily routine in an interview in the documentary:

> At 6 on the dot I had to be wrapping tongues, that was the rhythm. Then I had to wash some carts. At 8 a.m. they would bring me more tongues, and I had to do more tongues. At 9:45 a.m. I had a 15-minute break. Then I would return to resume and at 12:15 p.m. we had a 30-minute lunch. And then from 12 to 12, I didn't have any more.... I had to hold it; I had to take advantage during lunchtime. I had to take the opportunity because they didn't give permission to use the bathroom, much less to eat. They didn't let us stop, not even to drink water.... If I worked more than 80 hours in a week, they only paid me 75 or 76. They didn't pay me the full hours.[7] (*abUSed*)

These accounts of exploitative and unjust labor practices remained hidden; initially, none of the minors wanted to speak to government officials. The attorney Parras-Konrad explains that Iowa Workforce Development (IWD) had been trying for two months before the raid to meet with the minors working in the plant to hear their experiences. Out of fear, none of the workers initially wanted to meet with them. "The only thing they knew was that they [IWD] were asking questions and that they were the government," states Parras-Konrad (*abUSed*). "It wasn't until I explained to them that what has happened to you is a crime in this country. If you help the investigators with their investigation, they can protect you. And all of a sudden they had rooms full of kids wanting to talk to them" (*abUSed*). The film reinforces Parras-Konrad's statement through a series of medium close-up shots of the minors who spoke out against the abuse. Immediately after those, the film cuts to the town meeting where politicians, including Gutiérrez, hear firsthand accounts of the exploitation and abuse, the first shots being close-ups of the faces of Gutiérrez and one of the minors. The emphasis on the face reinforces the weight of the moment and its immediacy. The workers are finally able to break their silence in a public manner (figure 2.1). The owners depended on the fear of deportability and the resulting silence to exploit their employees. Nevertheless, for the workers, breaking their silence came too late. They were double victims, victims of

Figure 2.1. The 16-year-old worker Gilda Ordoñez testifying before a congressional delegation in Postville, Iowa (*abUSed,* 2010, Luis Argueta).

exploitative, unfair labor practices and victims of the law's suspension in the court proceedings shortly after the raid.

Despite the injustice and hopelessness surrounding the Postville raid, we might find some consolation in the production of Argueta's documentary. What we note in the examples above is that, in many cases, the testimonies come from minors. Children are the ones telling their stories, and this strategy is effective in transmitting the film's message. As Argueta states in his interview with Loustaunau in this volume, including children's voices provides a less adulterated point of view. In this sense, their voices contribute, perhaps in an honest, more direct manner, to the overall message.

Furthermore, the manner in which the documentary and the children's experiences are framed makes their testimonies even more poignant and compelling. The documentary opens with images of Postville—classrooms full of children with their teachers, golden fields of corn, and community members enjoying their town. Accompanying these images are Woody Guthrie's "This Land Is Your Land" as the soundtrack and text over the images that gives background information on the town, one of the bits of information being Postville's slogan "Hometown to the World." In other words, the film portrays Postville as a diverse, friendly, Midwestern town where families can raise their children in a safe and welcoming environment. Many times this comes through in the documentary, whether it be the church's role in providing safe haven for the town's children or the teachers and school administrators who, in interviews, share their empathy and solidarity with the children and their families. It is the raid, symbolized through the sounds of helicopters at the beginning of the film, that disrupts the tranquility and safety that Postville afforded to many.

The film's strategy to juxtapose the peaceful, safe, and close-knit community with the injustices on the part of Agriprocessors and the U.S. government is to create an empathetic relation between the viewer and subject. Through the many voices, viewers come to empathize with the difficult, unjust situations in which the undocumented workers find themselves. Calling attention to deportable life and the aporia of the impossible subject—the excluded and, at the same time, included subject—becomes one of the film's strategies to highlight the inherent contradictions within U.S. immigration policy. Argueta's is not the only film to record and re-present the detrimental consequences and trauma associated with deportation and deportability; *Sin país* does so as well.

Traumatic Expressions: Displacement, History, and Memory in *Sin país*

In this section I demonstrate how documentary can play a fundamental role in a politics of inclusion and humanization, and to do so, I will use Theo Rigby's *Sin país*. Let's begin with a brief summary of the film. In 1992, Sam and Elida Mejía-Pérez decide to leave Guatemala and migrate north to the United States. Leaving behind a country torn by civil war, they settle in the San Francisco Bay area with their firstborn, Gilbert, in tow. Through a series of home videos that show a young Gilbert with his dad, the viewer captures a glimpse of the family's early years in the bay area. The videos portray a loving, doting father who holds his son's hand as they enjoy what appears to be a hilly or mountainous area near the bay. Off camera, Elida asks her husband and son if they are cold. "¿Sienten frío?" (Are you cold?), to which Gilbert replies, "Sí, tengo mucho frío" (Yes, I am very cold) (*Sin país*). But the cold does not hamper the outdoor excursion, as the reply to Elida's next question reveals. "¿Pero, están contentos?" (But are you happy?), she asks, and both respond, "Sí" (*Sin país*). More home footage follows of the family throughout the early years in California, with intermittent interruptions by Elida's voice, again off screen. "Cuando uno viene de su país, usualmente nos traemos sueño. Uno sueña a venirse para acá, a hacer un poquito de dinero. Pero luego todo cambia. Si cambia el tiempo, también la mentalidad cambia y hay cambios en la familia porque para ellos, no hay otro país que el de allá" (When one comes from his or her country, we usually bring with us a dream. One dreams of coming here to make a little bit of money. But then everything changes. If time changes, then the mentality as well and there are changes in the family because for them, there is no other country than the one over there) (*Sin país*).

The documentary then cuts to a long shot of a home decorated for Christmas. Text overlays the image, letting the viewer know that for the previous two years Elida and Sam had been fighting to stay in the United States after a botched 2007 immigration raid on their house—a case of mistaken identity. The officials were looking for someone else; despite the error, ICE moved ahead with the deportation process ("*Sin país*: In Context"). *Sin país* then jumps to one week before their deportation. What I would like to underscore regarding the documentary's introduction is the film's intent to humanize the subjects in question. Drawing on the narrative of the American Dream, the film juxtaposes the calm, happy years with the present—an uncertain future with perhaps insurmountable obstacles as a family is torn apart. For the Mejía-Pérez family the American Dream has become what appears to be the American nightmare, a reality that the family's lawyer notes (*Sin país*).

Rigby's documentary has two functions: to tell a story—the story of the Mejía-Pérez family—and to intervene in the immigration debate by exposing the faces of those in a state of precarity or deportability. My claim here may seem straightforward and simple: *Sin país*, or in more general terms, documentary, can humanize those who are dehumanized and include those who are excluded. Such claim draws from the work of subaltern studies and presupposes the political nature of literature and film. Documentary as a form of political and social expression is something Bill Nichols examines in his work *Introduction to Documentary*. For him, there is a subset of documentaries whose objective is to address social and political issues. For example, the documentaries of the 1960s and 1970s are concerned with what Nichols calls "history from below"—films that give voice and representation to the dispossessed and marginalized (152). *Sin país* follows such a tradition.

However, in the case of Rigby's film, the humanizing aspect cannot be overlooked or discounted for its supposed simplicity because it is through the documentary's humanizing attempts that the film seeks justice. What type of justice, we may ask. One may argue that justice, for the most part, has been absent in the history of the United States' immigration policy. Proponents of deportation might argue that undocumented immigrants have broken the law, but what happens when the law is not just? How might we understand immigration when looking at its history in the United States? Reading the United States' record on immigration policy will reveal its exclusionary, discriminatory nature that began with the passage of the Naturalization Law of 1795—a law decreeing that only "free-born white persons" could become naturalized citizens (Gerber 19). Later examples are the federal government's passage of the Chinese Exclusion Act in 1882, prohibiting the immigration of Chinese laborers, and the passage of the Immigration Act of 1917, which barred entrance of Asian immigrants into the country (Henderson 17, 30).

I include these examples to historicize the laws that have governed immigration in the United States since its birth as a nation. Given these examples, can we say for certain that U.S. immigration laws have been just? I came to this question after having read Shoshana Felman's chapter "The Storyteller's Silence: Walter Benjamin's Dilemma of Justice" in her book *The Juridical Unconscious: Trials and Traumas in the Twentieth Century*. In her chapter on Benjamin, Felman recapitulates his concern over the relation between history, law, and justice. While Benjamin's context is quite different from the scope of this chapter, Felman's analysis can be useful to dialogue with the one I present. Felman contends that Benjamin examines history as a struggle between injustice and justice within the context of the Nuremberg trials. Using various landmark trials of the twentieth century, her aim is to call into question the relation between justice and history. She notes that up until the middle of the twentieth century, history and justice had maintained a radical division (Felman 11).

Although *Sin país* does not capture in detail the legal proceedings for Sam, Elida, and Gilbert Mejía-Pérez, it does have a similar function to the trial, given that the court "provides a stage for the expression of the persecuted. The court allows (what Benjamin called) 'the tradition of the oppressed' to articulate its claim to justice in the name of a judgment—of an explicit or implicit prosecution—of history itself" (Felman 12). Taking Felman's argument into account, *Sin país* has the same function. It moves beyond the private/public divide and publicizes the private. It expresses the expressionless. The documentary is a trial of sorts; rather than an appeal to a judge in a court case, the documentary makes its case to the viewers who now occupy the jurors' bench, requiring them to make a judgment over the Mejías' situation.

By "expressionless" Felman means those who have been "deprived of expression; those who, on the one hand, have been historically reduced to silence, and who, on the other hand, have been historically made faceless, deprived of their *human* face—deprived, that is, not only of a language and a voice but even of the mute *expression* always present in a *living* human face" (13). For Felman, the court is the space that gives the expressionless the ability to share their stories and show their face (14). Here, the parallels between documentary and the trial need little explaining, for one of documentary's objectives is storytelling.[8] Thus, I would like to continue with the documentary as storytelling and as a platform for the expressionless.

One week before their deportation, Sam and Elida begin to say their goodbyes and pack up their belongings. After their arrival in the United States in 1992, they had two more children, Helen, now thirteen years of age, and Dulce, four years old. Both are U.S. citizens, but the deportation affects them in different ways. Helen is to stay behind with her brother, aunt, and uncle in the United States while Dulce accompanies her mom and dad back to Guatemala. Despite the imminent separation, the camera captures an attempt for normalcy. It is Sam's birthday, and the family is there to celebrate. However, Sam wants neither a celebration nor a cake. Nevertheless, a birthday celebration prevails, as the viewer sees Sam's frosting-covered face in the next shot.

The face is the focal point in the documentary's many close-up shots. Each family member's face, at some point, occupies the framing. The most notable example is the filming at the San Francisco airport. The camera is there to document the family's separation, and at this moment, the cinematography includes a series of close-up shots of the family members bidding farewell to each other. This moment in the documentary is the most emotionally charged one. The expressions on their faces transmit the pain and sadness that the forced separation has caused. Their expressions tell the story. Amid the tears, Elida says to her son, Gilbert, "No llores. Estamos vivos" (Don't cry. We are alive) (*Sin país*) (figure 2.2). Looking to comfort her crying son, she reminds him that they are, at least, still alive. In other words, she is able to tell her own story. Such a statement reminds the viewers of the precarity of the family's situation. Nonetheless, she must leave her son behind, the same son she carried 15 years before to the United States.

It is this leaving—this displacement—that warrants further examination. The title, *Sin país*, translates to "Without a country." The etymology of *país* finds its origins in the Latin word *pāgus*, also meaning *provincia* (province), *aldea* (town), and *pueblo* (town or people) (Roberts 293; Segura Munguía 472). For purposes of my argument, I use the semantic and etymological relation

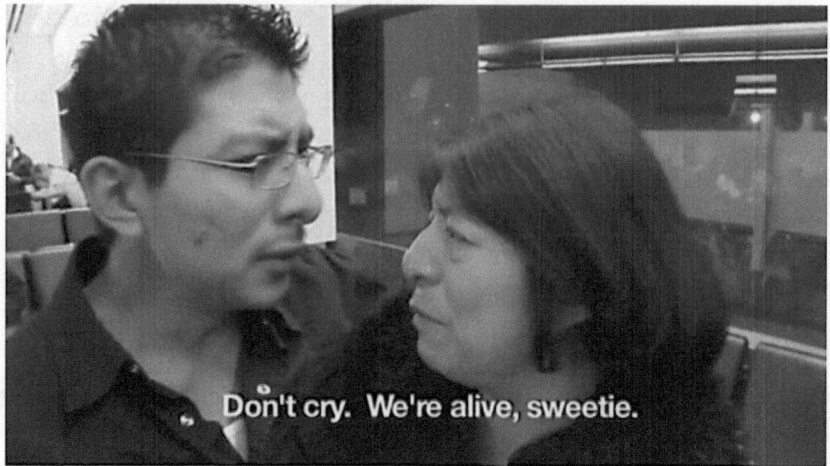

Figure 2.2. Elida Mejía saying good-bye to her son, Gilbert, at the San Francisco airport (*Sin país*, 2010, Theo Rigby).

between *país* and *pueblo*. *Pueblo* has two meanings; in English, the word can be translated as either "people" or "town." The semantic duplicity can offer various interpretations, and in this way, I use the term *país* to tease out the double meaning. On one hand, *Sin país* alludes to a sense of homelessness, that is, the removal from one's home and placement into a new environment that does not necessarily provide the familiarity, comfort, and safety that the former home once did. It conjures up a sense of belonging and membership in a community. Such an interpretation speaks to the affective and psychological relations that individuals hold with their countries or communities.

On the other hand, the term *pueblo* implicates the notion of a town or people related to the Greek term *polis*. Put differently, we can understand *pueblo* in the political sense, that is, the organization and administration of a group of people into a political unit, or city-state. This brings us to the other understanding of the title, the country as a state that confers rights to its citizens through a centralized body of power (government). In other words, when I discuss the two understandings of "country," what I am alluding to here is the notion of the nation-state. I argue that the title *Sin país* and the film's content implicate both.

When the removal process begins, individuals scheduled for deportation find themselves in a precarious situation, particularly those who have called the United States home for many years and do not really know their homelands. Such is the case for Sam, Elida, and their children. The difficult situation is compounded by the fact that the family members all have different legal statuses and levels of agency in the United States. Sam, Elida, and Gilbert are undocumented, while Helen and Dulce are U.S. citizens. Sam and Elida are removed from the country, and Gilbert remains in limbo as he waits for a judge to decide his fate. Dulce is too young to be without her parents, while Helen is old enough to have some autonomy; yet, the documentary notes the challenges that Helen faces in having her parents thousands of miles away. Three go to Guatemala; two remain in California. Beyond the three being physically displaced, the family members all experience displacements, emotionally and psychologically.

Their sense of home has been uprooted. The deportation disrupts any comfort, safety, and support that the physical immediacy of the parents provided. Ritualized practices like holidays and birthdays now have a new meaning, and this is something the film documents. In one scene we see Helen celebrating her birthday with Gilbert and extended-family members in California. Her parents are on the computer screen, virtually present to celebrate. What should be a happy moment is bittersweet. Through a close-up, we see a tear fall on Helen's cheek shortly after her parents appear on the computer screen.

Later, the family attempts to share a moment together on Christmas Eve, again, virtually. This time Helen—free to travel between Guatemala and the United States—is in Guatemala with her parents and sister. The film cuts between shots from both locations: Gilbert on the screen in Guatemala and the rest of the family on the screen in California. At one particular moment, Gilbert is the one on the screen as the camera captures the exchange. The holiday turns somber as Elida begins crying while talking to her son. She shares her Christmas wish: "Pero primero Dios, hijo, el otro año estamos juntos" (I hope to God that next year we are together) (*Sin país*). The scene captures the emotional toll of the forced displacement, and we might say that they are without country, without their community and home intact.

Deportation as displacement also leaves deportees without a country in the legal sense. In her essay "Exiled by Law: Deportation and the Inviability of Life," Susan Bibler Coutin discusses the consequences for some deportees who find themselves in politically and legally precarious situations. Using El Salvador as her case study, Coutin explains that individuals deported to El Salvador, where they were born and have legal citizenship, may find themselves in an undocumented situation as well: "Another NGO member characterized deportees as *doblemente mojados*, doubly 'illegal,' given their undocumented status in the United States and their difficulties obtaining identity documents in El Salvador" (Coutin 363). She explains that in their interviews, her subjects would share that it was a difficult, cumbersome process to obtain a national ID card. In some cases, the deportees would be subject to identity trials in which witnesses had to testify that the individuals were born in El Salvador (Coutin 362–363). Even more troublesome, Coutin states, is that "deportation can remove people not only from national territory but also from any legal means of supporting themselves and finally life itself" (368).

Such stories speak to a sense of statelessness that comes of deportable life. Hannah Arendt in her book *The Origins of Totalitarianism* develops what it means to be without a state. She examines the disintegration of rights for particular minority populations in Europe after World War I up until the end of World War II. In the chapter "The Decline of the Nation-State and the End of the Rights of Man," she problematizes the role of the nation-state and adherence to it as an organizing political unit when the state effectively makes its once citizens stateless by stripping them of their rights. Due to the rise of hatred toward specific populations and the emergence of totalitarianism, states stripped these individuals of their citizenship (Arendt 268). They effectively did not belong to a state. It is important to highlight a distinction between the stateless and deportable life. For Arendt, statelessness means undeportability "because there was no country on earth in which they enjoyed the right to residence" (276). This creates the state of exception and dovetails with the concept of bare life.

While in the case of *Sin país* one might argue that the direct correlation between statelessness and the Mejía-Pérez family does not exist, we can use Arendt's text to examine how the family is without a country, specifically through the terms "stateless" and "displaced persons." She argues that the term "displaced person" replaced "stateless" because the latter "at least acknowledged the fact that these persons had lost the protection of their government and required international agreements for safeguarding their legal status" (Arendt 279). The term "displaced person" ignores the statelessness that describes the individual's situation. In other words, the term avoids the implications of being stateless: "Nonrecognition of statelessness always means repatriation, i.e., deportation to a country of origin, which either refuses to recognize the prospective repatriate as a citizen, or, on the contrary, urgently wants him back for punishment" (Arendt 279).

I would argue that the dominant conceptual framework through which undocumented immigration is understood is more akin to that of displacement than of statelessness, in the sense that "displaced persons" (undocumented immigrants) can be deported to their country of birth even though they would not identify the country as their homeland. Yet, if we use statelessness as the analytical framework, it proves useful in further understanding deportable life.

The case of Gilbert serves as an example. Arriving in the United States as a young boy, around the age of six years old, he has spent most of his life in the United States, not Guatemala. He was educated in the U.S. school system, surrounded by American culture and traditions. Viewers even witness this in the documentary through the inclusion of an earlier video recording destined for his grandparents in Guatemala. He tells them, "Aquí estoy yo aquí en los Estados Unidos y ya estoy yendo a la escuela y estoy aprendiendo mis letras todo" (I'm in the United States. I'm going to school and I'm learning the alphabet) (*Sin país*). His undocumented status leaves him displaced in the sense of statelessness. His home has effectively been the United States even though he does not have the rights and privileges that a permanent resident or citizen has, thus rendering him stateless.

A return to Guatemala, his birthplace, does not remedy the statelessness either. For Gilbert, he has grown up in the United States, and as Coutin argues in her essay, a return to the home country does not necessarily mean immediate recognition of full citizenship—both in the legal and psychological sense. Deportation can leave individuals without a home in the affective and psychological understanding (nation) and the legal and political sense (state). Thus, Rigby aptly captures the precarious situation of the Mejía-Pérez family through his title *Sin país*.

It bears saying that forced displacement like theirs is traumatic, and one of the documentary's goals is to convey this trauma. Again, the close-up is the director's preferred shot to allow the viewer to observe the private moments of silence and inability to express oneself. After the deportation, Elida shares that the change has been difficult, particularly regarding the separation from her two elder children. She is especially troubled by her elder daughter's situation. As a U.S. citizen, Helen could leave the United States and live with her mother and father in Guatemala, but her mother recognizes the benefits of staying in the country. As she is weighing the pros and cons, silence consumes Elida. She stops speaking; the camera zooms in on her face as she is looking down. Slowly, she raises her head and looks at the camera. Tears fill her eyes. We might understand Elida's silence as a result of the trauma associated with the deportation. Elizabeth Jelin, in her work *State Repression and the Labors of Memory*, finds that trauma and its effects often involve gaps or voids in remembering the event as well as disruptions in narrating it (17). The silence the camera captures privileges documentary over other forms of storytelling, say, writing, for example. The viewer is able to see the subject's expression as silence falls over her.

For Helen, her parents' absence seems to be equally difficult. Her mother says her daughter has changed: "Todos los traumas que ella ha sufrido han hecho cambiar mucho su actitud y su carácter" (All the traumas she has suffered has made her attitude and character change) (*Sin país*). One of the most formidable struggles for Helen is the decision of whether to stay in California. Her home is California; yet, her family is in Guatemala. The documentary highlights the hardship of the forced displacement vis-à-vis the difficult and uncertain situation in which Helen finds herself—a teenager who looks to her parents for emotional, psychological, and economic dependence but loses all of that as a result of the deportation. Documentary, as the vehicle of expression, can capture that which evades translation into a linguistic code. Thus, to argue that *Sin país* humanizes the dehumanized, gives expression to the expressionless, and gives voice to the voiceless is to recognize the trauma that has been silenced, either because of its inexpressibility through language or its absence in the archive. It places the subject of the trauma in the public space, and it demands a response. Such a response came for the Mejía-Pérez family. Sam and Elida were granted humanitarian parole in 2010 and allowed to return to California as a result of "the extreme hardship that the Mejías . . . were suffering" ("*Sin país*: In Context").

Sin país puts a face to deportable lives, those individuals who suffer forced displacement based on a complex web of restriction and inclusion/exclusion. It attaches meaning to the cold, expressionless statistic of 3,782,000 individuals deported between 2000 and 2012 and does so by connecting with the audience through storytelling (Gonzalez-Barrera). Let's remember that storytelling is a dialogical event. The storyteller conveys a message to her or his reader or audience. The story as an event is important, for as Jelin notes, it separates habit from memory. For Jelin, the habit is an automated, iterative, mundane, and unmemorable action, whereas the memorable event is imbued with feelings and emotions that trigger a search for the event's meaning. The retelling or the memory of the event find expression in narrative form, and in this sense, the past and its meaning are narrativized (Jelin 16).

In other words, the remembered event necessitates an emotional or sensorial response, and *Sin país* attempts to elicit such reaction. It aims for its viewers to sympathize with the documentary's subjects. The storytelling evokes emotions and feelings, and accordingly, the viewing becomes a remembered event. This is significant because, at a moment in history when large-scale, habitual deportation is occurring, the documentary intervenes with another narrative, one that challenges juridical and national narratives of (il)legality and reveals the human face behind the statistic. Put differently, the alternative narrative challenges deportable or impossible life. Documentaries like *Sin país* propose an alternative collective memory to that of the faceless, voiceless, and dehumanized deportations that continue in the present. We might say that documentary serves a "vehicle for memory," to reference Jelin's use of Ernst van Alphen's term (in Jelin 25). Jelin writes,

> Memory, then, is produced whenever and wherever there are subjects who share a culture, social agents who try to "materialize" the meanings of the past in different cultural products that are conceived as, or can be converted into, "vehicles for memory," such as books, museums, monuments, films, and history books. Memory shows up also in actions and expressions that, rather than re-presenting the past, incorporate it performatively (van Alphen 1997). (Jelin 25)

Sin país and *abUSed*, thus, call into question the past and recent history of U.S. immigration policy by reframing the discussion from a juridical-national framework to a humanistic one, expressing the once expressionless and at the same time asking viewers to (re)consider their stance on current immigration policy.

Re-Membering the Past: Performances of Memory in *abUSed* and *Sin país*

Documentary can serve as a conduit of memory. Museums, films, books, and monuments are all vehicles, artifacts, and/or expressions of memory. Jelin finds that they re-present the past (25). While she does not include performances (theater, rituals, song) in her examples, we might add this mode of remembering to the list. In examining performance in relation to documentary and memory, I believe it is worthwhile to explain in what ways I use the term "performance"; I use performance theorist Richard Schechner's understandings of the term. For him, performance involves "being," "doing," "showing doing," or "explaining showing doing" (Schechner 22). Each element describes a particular aspect of performance. "Being" refers to existence, "doing" to an activity, "showing doing" to the act of performing, and "explaining showing doing" to performance studies. In the performance of memory, the first three understandings are of particular interest.

However, there is another definition of performance that must be addressed, that of performance as a "twice-behaved behavior" or a "restored behavior" (Schechner 28–29). By restored behavior, Schechner draws attention to the cultural, historical, social, religious, ideological, and biological frameworks and practices that constitute individual behavior. For him, an individual's behavior does not exist in a vacuum. Rather, the individual's actions, thoughts, and behavior draw upon previous, external models and influences: "Restored behavior includes a vast range of actions. In fact, all behavior is restored behavior—all behavior consists of recombining bits of previously behaved behaviors" (Schechner 28). Recognizing the dialogical nature of behavior allows us to understand the performativity of daily life. In other words, behaving, acting, thinking, and knowing are all performances, for "performance in the restored behavior sense means never for the first time, always for the second to *n*th time: twice-behaved behavior" (Schechner 29). So, how might we understand memory in relation to performance?

Like performance, memory is constructed. Jelin tells us that memory is socially, collectively, and culturally framed (11, 16, 22, 68). Despite the perceived individual, perhaps private nature of memory, it is indeed contingent upon exterior discourses and frameworks. By this Jelin means that memory is socially and dialogically continent, as it finds meaning through cultural practices, knowledge, behavior, emotions, and feelings whose meaning and conventions are derived from social interactions and socialization (9). Thus, memory is discursively produced and constructed in a particular time and place.

We have yet to define what memory is, though. Central to memory are the acts of remembering and forgetting. Let's not forget that to make an event or information memorable, emotions and/or meaning must be tied to it. Memory, consequently, is reactivated in the present. In other words, the past event or idea is restored in the present. In this way, performance is akin to memory. Memory is a restored idea or event from the distant or immediate past, just as performance is a restored behavior. We might say, then, that performance implicates memory—even when the performer is not conscious of it, as in habitual memory—as a reiteration or restoration of it. As Diana Taylor states in her essay "DNA of Performance: Political Hauntology," "Performance works in the transmission of social memory, drawing from and transforming a shared archive and repertoire of cultural images" (56).

The documentaries *abUSed* and *Sin país* have this function in transmitting social memory, and such transmission has as its objective to seek immigration reform and justice. In *abUSed,* performance exists on two levels. The most obvious, straightforward example is the camera's capture of the theatrical performance *La Historia de Nuestras Vidas: The Story of Our Lives.* The dramatization took place on May 12, 2009, in Postville's John R. Mott High School auditorium. The performers were seven men arrested in the raid. They were released after serving their five-month sentences and remained in the United States as material witnesses (*abUSed*). With few props on the set, among them cinder blocks and chains, the men recount their experiences through word and action. They tell their stories; they bear witness to their experiences. For Taylor, bearing witness is performative: "Bearing witness is a live process, a *doing*, an event that takes place in real time, in the presence of a listener" (53). Taylor's claim dovetails with Schechner's definitions of performance. The men's performance has two functions: to speak out against the injustices and to serve as a means to cope with the trauma. Taylor contends, "The telling and retelling offer victims a way of coping. That carrying through—the telling and bearing witness—is accomplished through the physical, live encounter of the victim and listener. The telling and retelling constitute a performance, understood as a reiterative, twice-behaved behavior" (54). At the same time, the men remember their experiences in the National Cattle Congress in Waterloo, which leads us to the second level of performance.

The documentary itself is a performance of memory, in other words, performed, publicized memories that attempt to halt or at least question the deportation machine. Both *Sin país* and *abUSed* protest U.S. immigration policy and wrongdoing; in the case of Postville the film employs reliving (living the past in the present as the memory is recalled) and re-membering two specific events in history. I use the dash to separate the word "remember" because documentary is particularly apt for telling the individual stories in a diverse, polyphonic manner. Like collages, both documentaries draw from many media, sources, and voices to construct the stories. They restore the past through a multiplicity of voices, or members. In this sense, they not only remember the past but also participate actively by re-membering the past. The result of such re-membering is an embodied collective memory ready to be logged into the archive and ready to challenge immigration policy by laying bare deportable life.

The documentaries' aim is to publicize individual experiences and subjugated narratives, allowing the viewer to empathize with the subjects' situations. For the viewer, watching the documentaries may give way to a memorable event in which individual memory becomes collective. Taylor recognizes the importance of such transmission in overcoming injustice and dealing with crisis. She analyzes photos as a form of resistance in the context of the Dirty War in Argentina: "Targeted by the armed forces, the arts played a central role in the articulation and transmission of collective memory during and after the Dirty War.... [Photography] has long brought the seemingly separate worlds of arts and politics together in mutually defining ways" (Taylor 76). Accordingly, the documentaries are political commentaries that emerge from the experiences and events of the voiceless and expressionless, that is, from deportable life. The memories perform through documentary's ability to transmit a message beyond the restrictions of textual testimonies and re-member events in recent history.

Ultimately, the memories perform through storytelling that partially evades textocentrism.[9] The documentaries establish a space for these memories in the archive, that is, their existence or "being" in the archive, and the films do so through their "doing," by way of their reflexive effort to publicize the private, collectivize the individual, and give expression to the expressionless. From this light, it is hard to separate documentary from memory, for documentary often relies on memory as a source of its content, and the finished product itself becomes part of the archive, available for viewing in the future. In this sense, documentary becomes an artifact of the past as it records and re-members a particular event or situation.

Conclusion

I want to return now to the air disaster in 1948 and the subsequent interment of the 28 lost souls in California. The victims were left nameless in the cemetery plot in Fresno; there was no marker to remember them, save their nationality and citizenship. Some 65 years later, in 2013, the names are finally in place, thanks to the actions of a few individuals. A new grave marker replaced the old one, giving the passengers' names on that ill-fated flight (Marcum). The action to change the grave markers with the passengers' names is significant, taking into account what Juan Carlos Mazariegos says in his essay "La guerra de los nombres" (The war of the names). Using the testimony of Gilberto Ramírez, a Kaq'chikel Maya who recounts his experience in Guatemala during the civil war, Mazariegos says that Gilberto is "una narración, un texto, una enunciación que se disemina en los vericuetos del relato; en muchos sentidos, Gilberto es una historia, una vida narrada" (a narration, a text, an enunciation that disseminates in the winding paths of the story; in many senses, Gilberto is a story, a narrated life) (15).

Elida Mejía-Pérez, Sam Mejía-Pérez, Gilbert Mejía-Pérez, Helen Mejía-Pérez, Dulce Mejía-Pérez, Isaías López-Marroquín, Gilda Ordoñez, Laura Castillo—each name is a story. The names listed here are those of individuals who all have been affected in some way by the precarious condition of deportability. The documentaries *abUSed* and *Sin país* capture their names, their voices, and their expressions and transmit their stories. The two documentaries combat the dehumanization, marginalization, and injustice that result from deportability by disseminating, performing, and archiving the individual experiences and memories, respectively, of the Mejía-Pérez family and the individuals affected by the Postville raid. To quote Argueta from his interview in this book, "For people who do not know immigrants, I think it is very important to show that immigrants are not that different from them, from us and our ancestors and our own families. I think documentaries can educate and transform people" (259). Sometimes sharing a story can be one of the most effective ways to enact change, and documentary facilitates such transmission.

Notes

1. In fact, *abUSed* registers performance on two levels, given that it captures a theatrical performance titled *La Historia de Nuestras Vidas*, which recounts the meatpacking-plant raid in Postville and the detention of seven of the hundreds of workers who were snared in it.

2. Roughly 75 percent of the detainees were Kaq'chikel Maya originally from Guatemala (Camayd-Freixas 2).

3. See Sassen's *Territory, Authority, Rights: From Medieval to Global Assemblages* for analysis of the relation between territoriality, citizenship, and birth beginning in the Middle Ages (18).

4. De Genova uses the term "deportable alien" as opposed to "deportable life" in his

essay "The Deportation Regime: Sovereignty, Space, and the Freedom of Movement" (46–47).

5. See De Genova's essay "The Deportation Regime: Sovereignty, Space, and the Freedom of Movement" for a further explanation of deportability and its relation to bare and disposable life.

6. The original quote in Spanish: "Trabajé allí en la fábrica. Trabajaba a las 7 de la noche y salía a las 6:30 de la mañana o las 7. Trabajaba casi 12 horas. Allí sufrí bastante porque no aguantaba mucho en ese trabajo porque agarré mucho la tijera y se me hinchaba mucho la mano. Y en eso, nos trataban mal. Nos regañaban y siempre nos daban trabajo duro." This and all other translations in the chapter from Spanish to English are mine.

7. The original quote in Spanish: "A las 6 en punto tenía que estar envolviendo las lenguas, así el ritmo. Luego tenía que lavar unos carros. A las ocho me llevaban las lenguas, y así tenía que hacer la lengua. A las 9:45 tenía un break de 15 minutos. Luego volvía a resumir y las 12:15, tenía el lunch de media hora. Y de 12 a 12, ya no tenía nada. Me tenía que aguantar; nada más tenía que aprovechar en el tiempo de lunch. Tenía que aprovechar porque no daban permiso para ir al baño, mucho menos comer. No nos dejaba bajar ni siquiera tomar agua. . . . Si yo trabajaba más de 80 horas en la semana, me pagaban sólo 75 o 76 así. No me pagaban las horas completas" (*abUSed*).

8. While storytelling in a documentary typically would imply an expository mode of documentary, as Nichols develops in his *Introduction to Documentary*, I would argue that *Sin país* combines both expository and observational modes, constructing a story while observing the Mejía-Pérez family before and after deportation.

9. In his essay "Performative Studies: Interventions and Radical Research," Dwight Conquergood argues that performance breaks from textocentrism. He is clear to express that text themselves are not a problem but rather the privilege of text over other forms of communication and expression (Conquergood 151). Documentary is a departure from textocentrism, given documentary's use of other forms such as music, photos, images, and bodily expressions.

Works Cited

abUSed: The Postville Raid. Dir. Luis Argueta. Maya Media, 2010. Film.
Agamben, Giorgio. *Homo Sacer: Sovereign Power and Bare Life*. Trans. Daniel Heller-Roazen. Stanford, CA: Stanford UP, 1998. Print.
Arendt, Hannah. *The Origins of Totalitarianism*. New York: Harvest Book, 1976. Print.
Camayd-Freixas, Erik. "Raids, Rights, and Reform: The Postville Case and the Immigration Crisis." *DePaul Journal for Social Justice* 2.1 (Fall 2008): 1–24. Print.
Conquergood, Dwight. "Performance Studies: Interventions and Radical Research." *Drama Review* 46.2 (Summer 2002): 145–156. Print.

Coutin, Susan Bibler. "Exiled by Law: Deportation and the Inviability of Life." *The Deportation Regime: Sovereignty, Space, and the Freedom of Movement*. Ed. Nicholas De Genova and Nathalie Peutz. Durham, NC: Duke UP, 2010. 351–370. Print.

De Genova, Nicholas. "The Deportation Regime: Sovereignty, Space, and the Freedom of Movement." *The Deportation Regime: Sovereignty, Space, and the Freedom of Movement*. Ed. Nicholas De Genova and Nathalie Peutz. Durham, NC: Duke UP, 2010. 33–65. Print.

———. "Migrant 'Illegality' and Deportability in Everyday Life." *Annual Review of Anthropology* 31 (2002): 419–447. Print.

Felman, Shoshana. *The Juridical Unconscious: Trials and Traumas in the Twentieth Century*. Cambridge, MA: Harvard UP, 2002. Print.

Gerber, David A. *American Immigration: A Very Short Introduction*. Oxford, England: Oxford UP, 2011. Print.

Gonzalez-Barrera, Ana. "Record Number of Deportations in 2012." *Fact Tank: News in Numbers*, 24 Jan. 2014. Pew Research Center. Web. 18 May 2014.

Henderson, Timothy J. *Beyond Borders: A History of Mexican Migration to the United States*. Malden, MA: Wiley-Blackwell, 2011. Print.

Jelin, Elizabeth. *State Repression and the Labors of Memory*. Translated by Judy Rein and Marcial Godoy-Anativia, Minneapolis: U of Minnesota P, 2003. Print.

Marcum, Diana. "Names Emerge from Shadows of 1948 Crash." *Los Angeles Times*, 9 July 2013. Web. 10 Oct. 2013.

Mazariegos, Juan Carlos. "La guerra de los nombres: Una historia de la rebelión, el genocidio y el ojo del poder soberano en Guatemala." *Glosas nuevas sobre la misma guerra: Rebelión campesina, poder pastoral y genocidio en Guatemala*. Guatemala City: Asociación para el Avance de las Ciencias Sociales en Guatemala (AVANCSO), 2009. 1–68. Print.

Mignolo, Walter. "Dispensable and Bare Lives: Coloniality and the Hidden Political/Economic Agenda of Modernity." *Human Architecture: Journal of the Sociology of Self-Knowledge* 7.2 (Spring 2009): 69–88. Print.

Ngai, Mae M. *Impossible Subjects: Illegal Aliens and the Making of Modern America*. Princeton, NJ: Princeton UP, 2005. Print.

Nichols, Bill. *Introduction to Documentary*. Bloomington: U of Indiana P, 2001. Print.

Peutz, Nathalie, and Nicholas De Genova. Introduction. *The Deportation Regime: Sovereignty, Space, and the Freedom of Movement*. Ed. Nicholas De Genova and Nathalie Peutz. Durham, NC: Duke UP, 2010. 1–29. Print.

Roberts, Edward A. *A Comprehensive Etymological Dictionary of the Spanish Language with Families of Words Based on Indo-European Roots*. Vol. 2. Bloomington, IN: Xlibris, 2014. Print.

Sassen, Saskia. *Territory, Authority, Rights: From Medieval to Global Assemblages*. Princeton, NJ: Princeton UP, 2008. Print.

Schechner, Richard. *Performance Studies*. London: Routledge, 2002. Print.

Segura Munguía, Santiago. *Lexicón etimológico y semántico del Latín y de las voces actuales que proceden de raíces latinas o griegas*. Bilbao: Universidad de Deusto, 2014. Print.

Sin país. Dir. Theo Rigby. New Day Films, 2010. Film.

"*Sin país*: In Context." POV. 2012. PBS. pbs.org/pov/sinpais/. Web. 18 May 2014.

Taylor, Diana. "DNA of Performance: Political Hauntology." *Cultural Agency in the Americas*. Ed. Doris Summer. Durham, NC: Duke UP, 2006: 51–81. Print.

❱ 3 ❰

Resisting Arizona's S.B. 1070 through Devotion to the Virgin of Guadalupe

Undocumented Immigrant Women's Contentious Repertoires in *The Vigil*

THOMAS PIÑEROS SHIELDS

On a morning in 2010 at the Arizona state capitol, two women arrive and transfer a statue of the Virgin of Guadalupe from a parked car to a park bench. They set up an altar with candles and flowers before securing the Virgin to the altar. In this opening scene from *The Vigil* (2014), a film by Jenny Alexander, the Virgin of Guadalupe stands silently on a park bench while in the background Rosa and Gina walk past with blue plastic containers and protest materials as the film's title appears on the screen. This title scene suggests that the Virgin is herself a character of the film, becoming a focal point for the women's activism during a contentious political event. The film shows undocumented immigrant women like Gina and Rosa and others maintaining this public vigil day after day from April 23 to July 28, 2010, despite their fears of being arrested and deported. The filmmaker recalls, "This became a transformative space of refuge and liberation" (Alexander, correspondence).

The Vigil is situated at the epicenter of one of the most contentious political episodes in the United States over the past decade. In 2010, the state legislature of Arizona passed the Support Our Law Enforcement and Safe Neighborhoods Act (Arizona S.B. 1070), which Republican Governor Jan Brewer signed into law on April 23, 2010. The new law gave unprecedented powers to local police to stop and search persons suspected of being in the United States illegally. As this bill passed, Arizona became a focal point of controversy while challengers within the immigrant rights community criticized the law for racial profiling and Maricopa County Sheriff Joseph Arpaio became a national symbol of the immigration enforcement debate. The political response against the law included a proposal by national immigrant rights activists for a boycott of the state of Arizona by sports figures, musicians, celebrities, local governments, and businesses from across the country. Immigrant rights activists organized protests nationally as well as a boycott and online petitions. The Arizona immigration controversy shaped a national discourse around immigration, and polls indicated that a majority of people in other states supported tough laws like Arizona's (Archibold and Thee-Brenan). In part, this encouraged lawmakers in five other states (Alabama, Georgia, Indiana, South Carolina, and Utah) to propose and pass similar laws to expand state and local enforcement of immigration laws. In the center of this whirlwind of public controversy, a group of Latino/a immigrants, many of them women and undocumented, maintained a sacred space through which devotional prayer to the Virgin of Guadalupe became a political act of resistance.[1]

The Vigil tells a story of resistance by Gina and Rosa and other immigrant women and men during the three months leading up to the planned implementation of Arizona S.B. 1070. The film provides insight into why, despite risks to their personal safety and given so many other possible forms of protest they could adopt, the women chose to resist the implementation of S.B. 1070 through a public vigil around the image of the Virgin of Guadalupe. I build upon these insights in analyzing the film's representation of contentious political resistance to the law by undocumented immigrant women through the deployment of a devotional vigil to the Virgin of Guadalupe. Charles Tilly's concept of "repertoires of contention" is relevant to the vigil as "limited, familiar, historically created arrays of claims-making performances" (*Regimes* vii). Certainly the multiple and changing meanings of the Virgin of Guadalupe in Mexico, Latin America, and the United States can be seen as such. Four themes emerge from an analysis of *The Vigil*: the transformation of public spaces into sacred spaces through devotion to the Virgin of Guadalupe, prefiguration as a contentious performance, gendered repertoires of contention, and motherhood and the DREAM movement. Following the work of other social movement scholars, with regard to the motherhood theme the film can be seen as a "cultural product" that has the potential to take advantage of discursive opportunities to advance the movement's goals of generating public interest, shaping discourse, or influencing policy making (Koopmans and Stratham; Vasi et al.). Finally, implications may be drawn for rethinking the sometimes traditional cultural practices of devotions to the Virgin of Guadalupe as political acts of resistance.

Contentious Repertoires in *The Vigil*

Much scholarship about community organizing emphasizes tactics and strategies as rational individual decisions by political actors (Alinsky; Ganz; Warren). Tilly challenges the use of rational and deliberative tactics and strategies as a theoretical framework for explaining social movement methods in high-risk political and public struggles around a collective claim. Instead, he offers the concept of a "repertoire of contention," which represents an array of possible public actions that are learned and acted out in concert with others (Tilly, "Contentious Repertoires"). In this way, a repertoire of contention represents a cultural tool for social change. As such, scholars have noted the modular quality of repertoires of contention, meaning that a given practice used in one context may be adopted or appropriated by actors to be applied to another event or contentious setting (Tarrow). Implicit in this concept of contentious repertoire adoption is the notion that a particular means for social change will, in part, be limited by the cultural experiences available to the social movement participants.

Furthermore, the theory of repertoires of contention applies the metaphor of a cultural "claims-making" performance to the public actions of activists, thereby linking one or more claimants with a target or object of claims (McAdam et al.; Tilly, *Contentious Performances*, *Regimes*). Scholars have applied the concept of contentious repertoires to explain social movement claims-making to a broad range of social movements including U.S. civil rights activism (McAdam); college shantytown protests in the late 1980s (Soule); post-communist national protest events in Slovenia, Slovakia, and Hungary in the early 1990s (Szabó); and online direct action (Rolfe).

In *The Vigil*, undocumented immigrant women assume the position of claimants as part of a dynamic interaction targeting the state of Arizona as well as national political leaders and the broader public. The film suggests the performativity of these undocumented immigrant women as they set the stage to construct the space for the vigil in the opening scene of the documentary. Likewise, Gina and Rosa and others in *The Vigil* draw from an established stock of available scripts to "perform" political acts. These scripts emerge from the sociocultural and structural position of the activists, in this case undocumented

Figure 3.1. Gina leading a march from the vigil to a Phoenix courthouse, with Jan Brewer campaign posters in the background (*The Vigil*, 2014, Jenny Alexander).

Latina immigrant women, whose stock of available scripts can be found in their cultural traditions, religious faith, and experiences of motherhood.

It is important to note that by depicting the activism of these undocumented immigrant women as performance the filmmaker does not suggest they are devoid of agency in making decisions or any less courageous. Instead, the film depicts how contentious repertoires change over time as social movement leaders readjust strategies, learn, and adapt to their changing environment of opportunities and threats (Tilly, *Contentious Performances, Regimes*). The film's focus on these strategic contentious repertoires emphasizes the relational and culturally situated nature of Gina and Rosa's activism that drew upon a familiar practice of devotion to the Virgin of Guadalupe (figure 3.1).

Background and Meaning of the Virgin of Guadalupe

In response to the threats to their everyday way of life, the women in *The Vigil* seek an approach to social change that is drawn from a familiar and established reservoir of beliefs, values, and practices. In so doing, they turn to the practices of devotion to the Virgin of Guadalupe, a cultural resource that, for Rosa and Gina as well as Latinos/as worldwide, provides a sense of collective protection and strength. In the film, Rosa introduces background about the Virgin of Guadalupe by describing how she feels protected by her presence at the vigil.

She goes on to explain the Mexican cultural origins of the Virgin: "The Virgin of Guadalupe is the virgin that we worship in Mexico. The Virgin appeared on the Hill of Tepeyac. Indigenous people were suffering the conquest by Spain. What you ask of her is like asking something of God." In this short explanation Rosa reveals how the Virgin of Guadalupe is a cultural symbol drawn from Rosa's Mexican heritage, but she also indicates the Virgin's religious and political symbolism. To Rosa, the Virgin at once represents a direct relationship with God but also a statement of political resistance originating in indigenous campaigns against Spanish colonization in Mexico. Gina continues to expand upon the meanings evoked from the origin narrative of the Virgin of Guadalupe.

> Juan Diego was an Indian. He was very isolated. While he was walking, he suddenly heard a beautiful voice, "Juan Diego, the smallest of my children." The loving way she spoke to him. Her message when she says "the smallest of my children," for me it means the most humble, in the eyes of society, he has no worth, but in the eyes of our Mother, he is the only one she entrusts her message to.

Gina emphasizes the indigenous roots of Juan Diego, demonstrating a sense of connection to the Virgin as part of her cultural identity. Also, Gina's repeated reference to the Virgin as mother as well as her recognition of the Virgin's words to Juan Diego as a mother's love for the smallest of her children suggests that she sees the Virgin as a maternal protector of those considered by society to be meek, humble, and weak. This scene provides insight into how the women in *The Vigil* drew inspiration for their activism from the Virgin of Guadalupe. According to the filmmaker, Jenny Alexander,

> The Virgin of Guadalupe, as a *mestiza* who appeared to an *indio* (this was very important to Gina, see the scene where she tells the story of Juan Diego), is a mother herself, and is a symbol of motherhood and unconditional love. As a brown virgin, she is accessible to the women both in the politics in Arizona, as well as the politics from where they come (mestizo/Mexican heritage). For me that is where the women of *The Vigil* (mothers) derived the power to lead their act of resistance and transformation. (Correspondence)[2]

The cultural accessibility of the Virgin of Guadalupe as an indigenous *mestiza* can be seen in the origins of the Virgin of Guadalupe that began in the middle of the sixteenth century on a hill near Mexico City. The Tepeyac Hill where the Indian Juan Diego had a vision of the Virgin was previously the site of the Aztec earth goddess Tonantzin (Kirk). Contemporary scholars recognize the Virgin of Guadalupe as a composite of Christian and Aztec symbolism that helped indigenous people in a region of Mexico to accept Christianity as a less foreign system of faith (Conover; Kennet; Kirk 53).

The Vigil depicts the devotion to the Virgin of Guadalupe as both a model of self-improvement and a symbol of political resistance. The meaning of the Virgin of Guadalupe has been a fluid one within Mexico—from its use as a tool for colonization and religious conversion, to its use as a collective symbol of national identity of Mexicans, and more recently as a source of divine intervention and protection for Mexico's people. So, too, the Virgin has been adopted by Latino/a diaspora communities in Latin America and the United States (Castañeda-Liles; Peña, "Beyond Mexico"). The Virgin gained followers and devotees especially across Latin America but also around the world including Mexican and other Latin American migrant communities in the United States (Gálvez; Peña, "Beyond Mexico").

In a three-year ethnography, Gálvez describes the collective mobilization of Mexican migrant communities in two New York City parishes dedicated to the Virgin of Guadalupe, as well as the citywide organization that links 40 committees together. She observes two alternative applications of devotion to the Virgin of Guadalupe in relation to collective political engagement, especially campaigns for immigrant rights (Gálvez). The first mode emphasizes more individual acts of devotion to the Virgin of Guadalupe based on an individualistic "self-improvement" model; the second mode of mobilization builds a collective identity among participants that extends to involving the parish in collective action (Gálvez). Both are present among the women in *The Vigil*.

In the film, Gina's and Rosa's use of physical objects such as statues of the Virgin of Guadalupe as instruments for performing sacred religious devotions and requests for intervention are part of the cultural landscape for many Mexicans (Norget). The statements by Rosa, Gina, and other participants of the vigil reflect expressions of religious devotion and belief in the Virgin's protective power that they derive from their sociocultural heritage. Across the Latino/a diaspora, people seek the intervention of the Virgin into their daily lives (Cuadrado and Lieberman; Norget).

In the film, Gina and Rosa articulate how the Virgin represents a source of personal faith and devotion through which they seek divine intervention to prevent the enactment of S.B. 1070 and to protect immigrant families from being separated and those attending the vigil from being apprehended and detained by police or attacked by anti-immigrant groups. Such an appropriation of the Virgin of Guadalupe by political resistance groups is also part of a long history among Latino/a activists in the United States (Peña, "Beyond Mexico"). For example, in 1966 the United Farm Workers (UFW) adopted the Virgin of Guadalupe during a march the organizers called "Pilgrimage, Penitence, and Revolution" to build ethnic solidarity in the face of criticism for being considered communist (Saganera 65). Later, Chicano/a nationalists adopted the Virgin of Guadalupe as an ethnic symbol around which they might coalesce and valorize claims of continuity with indigenous Mexican cultures (Saganera 66). In *The Vigil* we see Gina and Rosa physically transport the Virgin of Guadalupe from a space of individualized, sacred devotion to be used in public, contentious performances. In so doing, the historical symbolic meanings of the Virgin of Guadalupe from previous movements were leveraged to create and solidify a collective identity of political resistance among the women in the vigil. This resistance identity is described during a scene in which Gina repairs the broken statue of the Virgin while an off-camera voice of another woman in the room explains: "And she fought. She fought from her heart, and gave us her death so people would see that she fought." The example of the women in the vigil reinforces previous scholarship that such Guadalupan devotion can contribute to the emergence of collective resistance identities in response to increased immigration enforcement and an expansion of xenophobic discourse (Gálvez; Peña, "Beyond Mexico").

Transforming Space from Public to the Sacred

Early in *The Vigil*, the audience sees Maria Hinojosa, CNN, NPR, and PBS reporter and host of the NPR program *Latino USA*, saying,

> In the days since Arizona Governor Janet Brewer signed Senate Bill 1070 into law, this area here around the state capitol building has been transformed. It's a grassy lawn, but now it has become a place of vigils 24/7. There are toddlers here. There are activists here. There are high schoolers. There are police officers. There are musicians. This area of government activity in the capitol of Phoenix has been transformed.

The transformation of this space reflects the creation of a "sacred space" with people sitting in folding chairs, sometimes praying, in front of an altar to the

Figure 3.2. Vigil participants meeting for prayer and resistance at the altar of the Virgin of Guadalupe (*The Vigil*, 2014, Jenny Alexander).

Virgin of Guadalupe (Peña, "Beyond Mexico") (figure 3.2). In an in-depth ethnography with a Guadalupan community in a Chicago suburb ("Beyond Mexico"), Peña analyzes how devotional practices to the Virgin of Guadalupe could transform a place into a sacred space and in so doing, alter the contours of relations between migrants and the nation (723). She provides three primary insights into the construction of a sacred space. First, the sacred space is a physical space, with a replica of the original Virgin of Guadalupe shrine on the Tepeyac Hill near Mexico City constructed by a Guadalupan community in a Chicago suburb (731). A second insight about creating the sacred space is that the space becomes sacred through the embodied performances of devotees who hold daily reenactments of the apparition of the *mestiza* Virgin for tens of thousands of visitors per year; they pray and dance and care for the shrine through physical acts of labor (737). Third, the space serves as a site of political mobilization that deconstructs the binary between secular and sacred spaces when devotees hold immigration and citizenship clinics as well as speaking events about pending immigration legislation (740). It is not difficult to extend Peña's insights in "Beyond Mexico" into how Guadalupan devotions led to the construction of a public sacred space in *The Vigil*. Throughout the film we can see examples of attention to the physical construction of the shrine each day, the embodied labor including devotional prayer, songs, and care of the space by the women in Arizona, and how the space became a site of collective resistance and political consciousness raising.

In both the Chicago suburb (Peña, "Beyond Mexico") and the Arizona site depicted in *The Vigil*, devotional practice to the Virgin of Guadalupe led to the creation of sacred space. Such similarities between these different contexts exemplify the modular nature of repertoires of contention from one location, group, and time to another setting, collection of actors, and practice (Tarrow). The use of devotions to the Virgin of Guadalupe as a cultural practice also represents a performance drawn from a contentious repertoire that holds a great deal of resonance within the Latino/a diaspora and especially migrant communities.

However, there are several important differences between Peña's ethnography "Beyond Mexico" in the Chicago suburbs and the women depicted in *The Vigil*. The first obvious difference can be found in the nature of the perceived threat undocumented immigrants faced in the weeks after Jan Brewer signed S.B. 1070 into law. Social movement scholars have long debated the role of threat in mobilization. State actions that disrupt the daily life of a community or the quotidian have been more likely to predict collective action (Snow et al.). The film depicts how, for Latino/a immigrants in Arizona at the time, the threat to everyday routines was very real. Second, it is striking to consider the time frame through which the women in Arizona constructed their vigil. *The Vigil* portrays how sacred devotion to the Virgin so quickly transformed a public space into a site of political resistance. Within a few hours or days, the space was described as "transformed." Finally and perhaps most notably, the construction of a sacred space in the Chicago suburb stops just short of appropriating the sacred symbolism of the Virgin of Guadalupe for political resistance. In the Chicago suburb, the political work occurs off to the side of the sacred space of the Virgin (Peña, "Beyond Mexico" 738). In contrast, *The Vigil* portrays a public scene created with clear intention of sending a public political message to Arizona policy makers, the media, and the public at large.

Prefiguration as Contentious Performance

In one scene, the participants in the vigil conduct a special ceremony on the night that Gina, Rosa, and others board a van to travel to Washington, DC, to deliver letters asking the federal government to prevent the scheduled enactment of S.B. 1070 in the coming weeks. As the sun sets, about 40 to 50 members of the vigil lead a solemn procession toward the large glass-door entrance of the state house building. The group marches somberly, led by a man carrying an American flag, while those behind him are carrying images of the Virgin of Guadalupe, candles, crucifixes, and flowers. One man blows several long, slow notes on a trumpet. The procession stops, facing the glass entrance. One of the women from the vigil speaks: "In the Bible it says that on the seventh day, the walls of Jericho fell and the city was taken by Israel. It was God's promise to Josué. What we want to do is take down the walls of hate." The procession then turns abruptly and continues back to the site of the vigil from there. As they reenter the lawn of the state house, members of the procession begin to shout in celebration, "S.B. 1070 is already defeated! It doesn't exist! These walls crumbled!" This scene provides a dramatic example of prefiguration in *The Vigil*. "Prefigurative space" refers to an alternative vision for how the world might be, or should be, organized (Maeckelbergh; Polletta, *Freedom*). The practices associated with creating such a projection to an imagined future can be called "prefiguration" (Maeckelbergh).

In this scene the activists testify to their faith by prefiguring, with a sense of celebration that since God's promise is absolute, that by securing this promise they have already created the world they imagine. It is a performance with elements of magical realism that may even seem foolish or silly to more rational outsiders, since at that time the law remained scheduled to go into effect within a few weeks. After this celebration, Michael Nowakowski, a Latino city councilor in Phoenix, tells the group of travelers about to embark, "It is important that you take the word from Phoenix to DC, to the Capitol of the United States; prayer without action is nothing."

The city councilor's statement seems to suggest that prayer, processions, and devotions to the Virgin of Guadalupe are not in themselves actions that are likely to lead to concrete policy changes. His comment parallels a debate among activists and some social movement scholars about whether prefiguration can be a type of strategic action (Maeckelbergh 4; Polletta, *Freedom* 6). On the one hand, this debate suggests that within social movements, especially traditional movements of the Left, "action" refers to the inclusion of strategic instrumentality and institutional political targets, whereas prefiguration is "inward looking" by dealing only with personhood, identity, and culture but not practical social change (Maeckelbergh 4). In a study of alterglobalization social movement groups,[3] Maeckelbergh reinterprets prefiguration as a practice that has consequences for the movement that seeks to redesign relations of power (8). She theorizes a prefigurative strategy to fundamentally realign power relations in society by merging means and ends.

The Vigil presents an approach to political activism that is consistent with Maeckelburgh's argument of prefiguration as strategy. The women of the vigil seek to transform relations between migrants and the larger society by creating a space that imagines a world that is consistent with a more just and humane society. For the women of *The Vigil*, the choice is not prayer or action; rather, prayer *is* an embodied form of action that projects a redefinition of their identity to the larger world. Their prayers and devotions to the Virgin of Guadalupe prefigure the type of world the activists would like to see manifest; they create a space that is a powerful site for political mobilization in a time of a state-level overt repressive threat. I would argue that the statement by the city councilor, by focusing on a narrow political agenda, misses a key aspect of the vigil by these women not as an apolitical distraction but as a transformative strategy that prefigures a better society (Maeckelbergh).

Gendered Repertoires of Contention

The women in *The Vigil* invoke an approach to social activism that speaks to the intersection of a feminist theology and a gender politics that emerge from Latin American diaspora by depicting the ways that the women's tactical repertoires stand in contrast to other, more aggressive, traditionally male forms of resistance to state action.

In one scene a male attendee at the vigil reads a news story with the headline "Open Season" about Sheriff Arpaio's intent to sweep and arrest the immigrant participants at the vigil. He points out that "open season" means "to hunt," as if the women attending the vigil are animals. He tells Gina this, and she replies with a smile, "The people of the vigil will be here." The man does not seem satisfied with this response and calls on her to "respond to this, that is the way people need to be, to express ourselves; express ourselves." He is clearly angry and punches his fist into his hand as he speaks. Gina answers, "But at our vigil . . . that is not our message!" At this point a woman enters the conversation and asks, "You are going to let them step all over you?" This exchange in the film portrays the nature of the vigil as a peaceful, receptive listening space that stands in contrast with angry or aggressive responses by other activists. This portrayal in the film of the Latino male vigil participant reinforces a gendered contrast in an approach to social change and action. The film reinforces such gendered contrasts by switching between scenes of the women at the vigil and of the violent actions of the state of Arizona and especially Sheriff Arpaio. The portrayal of a gendered performance of public, contentious action is reminiscent of Las Madres de la Plaza de Mayo in Argentina, a group of mothers who took public action in the main square of Buenos Aires to push for public attention to their children who were "disappeared" during a period of state terrorism and dictatorship between 1976 and 1983 (Taylor). Taylor writes about the public performance of *las madres* who overcame traditional obstacles to women as active political agents by modeling themselves on the Virgin Mary (294). The Virgin allowed *las madres* to adopt traditionally acceptable "feminine" qualities of self-sacrifice and irrationality as innovative tactics that expose the violence of state oppression in contrast to deeply held and traditional notions of motherhood (Taylor 296).

An example of a similar nonviolent strategic approach to expose state violence through the deployment of traditionally accepted feminine roles can be seen in *The Vigil* when Gina and an older woman, *doña* Dora, sit at a kitchen table. Dora asks for a permanent marker and draws a large heart on a piece of 18"-by-24" red poster board. The two of them start cutting hearts out of tissue paper and pinning them to the board. Dora begins her dedication with the first heart she cuts: "This is the heart of whoever you want . . . of Joe Arpaio. And this heart is for you. There you stay in love, wrapped in love."

Gina repeats the words as Dora speaks, seeming to suppress a smile of surprise that they are praying for Sheriff Joe Arpaio. Dora goes on to explain, "He had something very traumatic in his life and he can't forgive and he got bitter." As Dora cuts another heart out of tissue paper, we see that there are several sheets of paper that she cut into many hearts. Dora explains:

> Look now how the love gets bigger and bigger. They keep growing and growing. Faith doesn't change even when things go wrong. I believe in God and it doesn't matter how things are going for me. I keep believing that God is light, that God is power, no matter how things are going for me. That is my faith.

Unable to suppress her laughter, Gina says, "I didn't know we had a teacher here!" In this scene Gina and Dora pray for the man who threatens to hunt down, detain, and deport them and their family members.

The film contrasts the gendered repertoires of contention with the state actors as well as other social change agents. As a respected elder in her community, Dora provides instruction and wisdom to Gina in a space that has been set aside for women's sharing through prayer as they affix small hearts onto a poster. In so doing, they create a shared understanding of social change that is distinct from many aggressive or angry responses to mistreatment by activists. Instead, the making of hearts (again) demonstrates the deployment of prefiguration as a contentious practice. The alternative vision here is of Sheriff Arpaio not as a threatening or racist authority figure but as a wounded and hurt soul in need of love. Furthermore, the scene shows an intergenerational transfer of this repertoire from an elder, *doña* Dora, to a younger woman, Gina. Such mentoring is consistent with the more nurturing and nonviolent social change repertoire at the vigil.

In contrast to the scene with these women, Sheriff Arpaio's system of state repression is depicted as an extension of patriarchal power through high-tech weapons, a brigade of deputies and officers, public spectacle, and rhetorical devices that shape discourses around an "immigrant threat" to sovereignty and security. The call for "firepower" in the form of militarized armored tanks and surveillance helicopters stands in stark contrast to the women and children of *The Vigil*. The women in the film respond with prayers of courage, forgiveness, peace, and unity in a manner that parallels the silent and consistent gaze of mercy and compassion from the Virgin of Guadalupe statue despite the chaos swirling around her.[4]

In *The Vigil* the audience's gaze is directed toward images of armored off-road police vehicles and small helicopters, as rows of men and women in various uniforms hold up their hands to be deputized by Sheriff Arpaio. The audience hears a recorded message from the Maricopa sheriff's phone service:

> Thank you for calling the Maricopa County Sheriff's Office. Someone will be with you shortly. No matter which way you look at it, entering the United States illegally is a crime. In Maricopa County, Sheriff Joe Arpaio takes a hard stance against illegal immigration. Arpaio's anti–illegal immigration unit of 160 deputies and officers is doing an excellent job of finding and arresting these violators.

In the next scene we see a montage of news stories about an immigration raid at a Burlington Coat Factory store in the weeks leading up to the passage of S.B. 1070. We see a young Latino man in plastic handcuffs being put into the back of a van, saying in perfect English, "We are American and they arrested me. I don't know why. I gave them my ID." The news reporter seemingly shrugs off the young Latino man's words, announcing, "Well, that's right, Sheriff Joe Arpaio conducting his seventeenth crime-suppression sweep." The news report then cuts to a press conference with Arpaio, who says, "Once again, I want to warn everybody, especially in Mexico, if you want to come through Maricopa County, we are going to have enough firepower to react!" News reporters amplify Arpaio's threat by referring to the repression of immigrants ordered by the governor as a "crime-suppression sweep."

The film then cuts to a male police officer standing on an armored SWAT vehicle pulling an assault rifle through a door on the roof of the vehicle. As the barrel of the rifle emerges, it is twice as tall as the white, male officer holding the weapon. The reporter comments, "Now for this one, the sheriff literally brought out the big guns!" Such media stories, of course, go beyond just reporting the news but frame and shape perceptions of the audience by telling stories that present heroes and villains (Polletta, "It Was Like"). In this case, media constructed narratives that fetishize weapons and power. These narratives are unquestionably male, representing both phallic and aggressive images that do not reveal the impact of their actions. This hypermilitarized posturing by the police develops an always implied and sometimes stated discourse in mainstream media of the "Latino threat narrative" (Chavez).

Unlike mainstream news media, the documentary filmmaker reveals the very human impact of this militarism on families and children. The scene shifts from the armored truck in the daylight raid to a nighttime scene in a parking lot. The audience can see a man and a women speaking through the windows of two parked cars. A male voice asks in Spanish, "Why was she taken away?" A female voice answers in Spanish, "For a parking ticket, the police tell me she is going back to Mexico." Immediately, the filmmaker cuts to an interview with two small children who look tired and upset. We hear the male voice ask, "What did the sheriff say to you?" The child replies, "To be quiet. But I couldn't because I wanted to go with my mommy."

In this scene the filmmaker demonstrates the power of documentary film in the production of a counternarrative to the dominant discourse. The counternarrative takes place in shadows of poorly lit parking lots that are less often seen and tells the stories of mothers and children being separated in the middle of the night. In that dark place a child cries. She cannot be quiet because she wants to go with her mommy.

Motherhood and DREAMers

When she traveled to Arizona, Jenny Alexander did not intend to make a film about Gina and Rosa or the other participants at the vigil. She had been active in the movement for immigrant rights for more than a decade and had made three short films that focused on immigration reform.[5] She arrived on the scene at the Arizona state house with the intention of following DREAMers, people who came to the United States by age 16 and aspire to stay. The name "DREAMers" is a reference to their status under the Development, Relief, and Education for Alien Minors (DREAM) Act that was first proposed as federal legislation in 2001.

A common media narrative about DREAMers is that they entered as children through no fault of their own, worked hard, and played by the rules, so now they deserve a chance to become legal residents in the United States. Since DREAMers entered the United States as children, they are seen as not responsible for their undocumented status and therefore should not be punished by being deported from the country where they have grown up. Implicitly this narrative suggests that the responsibility or fault for their undocumented legal status rests somewhere else, with an uncomfortable and usually unspoken blame laid on their parents.

While Alexander pondered these thoughts, she was informed of a group of women quietly holding vigil in front of the Arizona state house. Several of these women were the mothers of DREAMers themselves. Alexander wondered, "Who is telling their story?" So, she began to interview them. Alexander's intentions then are to tell a story that presents a narrative shaped by facts, but constructed nonetheless.

Motherhood emerges throughout the film and sheds light on the relationship between the contentious repertoires of the mothers and the next generation of immigrant activists, the DREAMers. The film especially focuses on the relationship between Rosa and her daughter Dulce. Dulce is a cofounder of the Arizona DREAM Act Coalition (ADAC) and a DREAMer herself, meaning that she is one of the approximately two million undocumented immigrants currently in the U.S. who had entered the United States as children. During

2010 several DREAMers began to escalate their political activity by engaging in civil disobedience to gain support for the DREAM Act. *The Vigil* presents the civil disobedience of Dulce through a television news report:

> Two ASU [Arizona State University] graduates won't give up their fight to stay in this country even after officers arrested them. They are here illegally, but that's not why officers locked them up. [Man:] Dulce Matuz is part of the group that refused to leave several senators' officers including John McCain's. They went to Washington to bring attention to the DREAM Act.

The film then cuts to Rosa driving her car, saying, "Then at five they told me Dulce had been arrested. I feel shaky. I can't be calm in my house while things are happening outside, so I came to the vigil. Now I'm the one looking for refuge here." Here the film depicts Rosa's nervousness about her daughter as an illustration of motherhood that parallels the Virgin of Guadalupe's role as protector. Rosa herself seeks such protection when she returns to the vigil to seek safety in the community that she helped establish.

This narrative finds closure when Dulce is released and Rosa goes to the airport to meet her. On the way, Rosa is clearly nervous. Dulce smiles as she approaches Rosa in the airport terminal, where they hug and kiss. Rosa asks, "How was the experience?" Dulce responds, "Good." Rosa then looks her directly in the eyes. "Let me see your face. . . . Well, in the face you can see if something bad happened." Dulce answers, "They treated us well." In this exchange, Rosa assumes an almost mystical power of motherhood in claiming to be able to assess her daughter's well-being by looking in her face. This subplot in the film about the mother and daughter activists is reminiscent of the work of Bloemraad and Trost, who identify the bidirectional nature of parent and child models of political socialization through an analysis of immigrant rights protests in spring 2006. They describe parent-to-child political socialization complemented by risk-taking and political attitudes whereby new forms of youth engagement influenced parental attitudes and behaviors towards activism. The depiction of Rosa and Dulce in *The Vigil* sheds light on this dynamic by depicting the ambivalent feelings of Rosa, who on the one hand is proud of her daughter's work and accomplishments in their shared struggle for immigrant rights and on the other hand worries about Dulce and wants to protect her from harm.

Gina also represents the theme of intergenerational activism in describing her hopes for her son to Blanca just days before the expected implementation of S.B. 1070. The two women discuss what they might lose. Gina is tearful as she says,

> If the law goes into effect, I don't know what I am going to do. What I do know is that I fought and I showed my son that he should fight and be a good citizen, to fight for the rights of the many people who don't have the opportunity. I think that is a beautiful thing that he will have, even if we lose. He will always have his head held high because it will be an important lesson for him.

As with Rosa's hopes for Dulce, Gina describes her own activism as a lesson and model for her son.

It is unlikely that the women in *The Vigil* would see motherhood as a contentious performance rather than a core identity and practice. At the same time, the film, as a cultural product, deploys motherhood as a contentious performance. Certainly the camera's focus on the Virgin of Guadalupe as the mother of God helps to leverage motherhood as a cultural performance within the contentious discourse about immigration in the United States today.

Conclusion

The Vigil depicts devotion to the Virgin of Guadalupe as a political repertoire of contention deployed primarily by immigrant women in Arizona during a period leading up to the intended enactment of the harsh anti-immigrant legislation S.B. 1070, a law that would have granted unprecedented authority for local law enforcement to arrest and detain undocumented immigrants. The film portrays how the three months leading up to the planned implementation of the law were fraught with anxiety for undocumented immigrants in Arizona, but at the proverbial 11th hour, on July 28, 2010, the law was blocked by an injunction issued by a federal judge in light of a lawsuit brought about by the U.S. Department of Justice.

A later scene in the film takes place in Washington, DC, as Gina, Rosa and Dulce gather to hear the U.S. Supreme Court decision about the future of the S.B. 1070 legislation. The U.S. Supreme Court delivered a split decision that found three of the major provisions of S.B. 1070 to be unconstitutional, although it kept in place the most notorious provision of the law (*Arizona v. United States*). By declaring three parts of S.B. 1070 unconstitutional, immigrants in Arizona would not be criminalized for being in the United States without papers or for working without papers, and people in the country legally could not be arrested for noncriminal deportable offenses. The fourth provision of S.B. 1070, sometimes referred to as the "Papers, please" provision, was upheld (*Arizona v. United States*). As a result, Arizona police may stop, detain, and check the immigration status of anyone suspected of being an undocumented immigrant (*Arizona v. United States*). This provision has been widely criticized as encouraging racial profiling by police; it was the subject of a six-year lawsuit that ended in September 2016 when the Arizona attorney general determined that officers should be instructed to not "prolong a stop, detention or arrest solely for the purpose of verifying immigration status" (Ware). Despite the eventual policy defeat of S.B. 1070, the moral panic in the public discourse about undocumented immigrants continues to grow, and new anti-immigrant policy threats continue to present themselves. *The Vigil* provides a lens into how a group of undocumented women responded to an impending draconian social order for the Latino/a community in Arizona. *The Vigil* tells the story of how Gina, Rosa, and the other participants in the vigil resisted this threat by adopting familiar cultural practices to build unity, establishing their dignity in the public eye, constructing safe spaces that prefigure a more humane and just society, and modeling courage for their children.

Notes

1. *The Vigil* focuses on the story of two undocumented immigrant women during a period of contentious action. Participants in the events that took place at this vigil included men and women, some of whom held legal status in the United States and some who did not. Since I focus on the film, discussions about these events reflect those as represented in the film.

2. Jenny Alexander shared this with me in an email.

3. "Alterglobalization social movement" refers to proponents of global cooperation and interaction in the civic and social sphere under the belief that another world is possible but who stand opposed to the harmful effects of neoliberal economic globalization.

4. Such responses to violence situate the response of these women within a long history of faith-based nonviolent action including the Fellowship of Reconciliation (FOR) formed after World War I and the Southern Christian Leadership Conference (SCLC) created during the U.S. civil rights movement as well as national networks

such as the Industrial Areas Foundation (IAF) and the PICO (Pacific Institute for Community Organizations) National Network that incorporate prayer into Alinsky-style community organizing (Polletta, *Freedom*; Warren).

5. Alexander's earlier short films are *DREAM Deferred* (2004), *Mario* (2006), and *Detained* (2007). All are available at ActiveVistaFilms.com.

Works Cited

Alexander, Jenny. Personal correspondence with Thomas Piñeros Shields. 6 Aug. 2015.
———. *The Vigil: Curriculum Guide*. Malden, MA: ActiveVista Media. 2014. Print.
Alinsky, Saul. *Rules for Radicals: A Practical Primer for Realistic Radicals*. New York: Random House, 1971. Print.
Archibold, Randal, and Megan Thee-Brenan. "Poll Shows Most in U.S. Want Overhaul of Immigration Laws." *New York Times*, 3 May 2010. Web. 8 June 2017.
Arizona v. United States. Supreme Court of the United States, Docket 11–182, 25 June 2012. SCOTUSblog. Web.
Bloemraad, Irene, and C. Trost. "It's a Family Affair: Intergenerational Mobilization in the Spring 2006 Protests." *American Behavioral Scientist* 52 (2008): 507–532. Print.
Castañeda-Liles, Maria del Socorro. "Guadalupe Unbound: Our Lady of Guadalupe in the Lived Religion of Mexican-Origin Women." Diss. U of California, Santa Barbara. 2011. Unpublished.
Chavez, Leo R. *The Latino Threat: Constructing Immigrants, Citizens, and the Nation*. Stanford, CA: Stanford U P, 2008. Print.
Conover, Cornelius. "Reassessing the Rise of Mexico's Virgin of Guadalupe 1650s-1780s." *Mexican Studies* 27.2 (2011): 251–279. Print.
Cuadrado, Mary, and Lieberman, Louis. "The Virgin of Guadalupe as an Ancillary Modality for Treating Hispanic Substance Abusers." *Journal of Religious Health* 50 (2011): 922–930. Print.
Cunningham, David, Colleen Nugent, and Caitlin Slodden. "The Durability of Collective Memory: Reconciling the 'Greensboro Massacre.'" *Social Forces* 88.4 (2010): 1517–1542. Print.
Gálvez, Alyshia. "'I Too was an Immigrant': An Analysis of Different Modes of Mobilization in Two Bronx Mexican Migrant Organizations." *International Migration* 45.1 (2007): 87–119. Print.
Ganz, Marshall. "Worksheet: Telling Your Public Story; Self, Us, Now." Cambridge, MA: Kennedy School of Government, Harvard University, 2009. Print.
Kennet, Frances. "Sor Juana and the Guadalupe." *Feminist Theology* 11.3 (2003): 307–324. Print.
Kirk, Pamela. *Sor Juana Inés de la Cruz: Religion, Art, and Feminism*. New York: Continuum, 1998. Print.
Koopmans, Ruud, and Paul Stratham. "Challenging the Liberal Nation-State? Postna-

tionalism, Multiculturalism, and the Collective Claims Making of Migrants and Ethnic Minorities in Britain and Germany." *American Journal of Sociology* 105.3 (1999): 652–696. Print.

Liptak, Adam. "Blocking Parts of Arizona Law, Justices Allow Its Centerpiece." *New York Times*, 25 June 2012. Web. 20 Feb. 2016.

Maeckelbergh, Marianne. "Doing Is Believing: Prefiguration as Strategic Practice in the Alterglobalization Movement." *Social Movement Studies* 10.1 (2011): 1–20. Print.

Matovina, Timothy. "The Origins of the Guadalupe Tradition in Mexico." *Catholic Historical Review* 100.2 (2014): 243–270. Print.

McAdam, Doug. "Tactical Innovation and the Pace of Insurgency." *American Sociological Review* 48.6 (1983): 735–754. Print.

McAdam, Doug, Sydney Tarrow, and Charles Tilly. *Dynamics of Contention*. Cambridge, England: Cambridge UP, 2001. Print.

Norget, Kristen. "Progressive Theology and Popular Religiosity in Oaxaca, Mexico." *Progressive Theology* 36.1 (1997): 67–83. Print.

Peña, Elaine. "Beyond Mexico: Guadalupan Sacred Space Production and Mobilization in a Chicago Suburb." *American Quarterly* 60.3 (2008): 721–747. Print.

———. *Performing Piety: Making Space Sacred with the Virgin of Guadalupe*. Berkeley: U of California P, 2011. Print.

Polletta, Francesca. *Freedom Is an Endless Meeting*. Chicago: U of Chicago P, 2002. Print.

———. *It Was Like a Fever: Storytelling in Protest and Politics*. Chicago: U of Chicago P, 2006. Print.

Rolfe, Brett. "Building an Online Repertoire of Contention." *Social Movement Studies* 4.1 May (2005): 65–74. Print.

Saganera, Roberto Lint. "Migration and Mexican American Religious Life, 1848–2000." *Immigration and Religion in America: Comparative and Historical Perspectives*. Ed. Richard Alba, Albert J. Raboteau, and Josh DeWind. New York: New York UP, 2009. 56–70. Print.

Snow, David, Daniel M. Cress, Liam Downey, and Andrew W. Jones. "Disrupting the 'Quotidian': Reconceptualizing the Relationship between Breakdown and Emergence of Collective Action." *Mobilization: An International Journal* 1 (1998): 1–22. Print.

Soule, Sarah. "The Student Divestment Movement in the United States and Tactical Diffusion: The Shantytown Protest." *Social Forces* 75.3 (1997): 855–882. Print.

Szabó, Máté. "Repertoires of Contention in Post-Communist Protest Cultures: An East Central European Comparative Survey." *Social Research* 63.4 (1996): 1155–1182. Print.

Tarrow, Sydney. *Power in Movement: Social Movements and Contentious Politics*. 2nd ed. New York: Cambridge UP. 1998. Print.

Taylor, Diana. "Performing Gender: Las Madres de la Plaza de Mayo." *Negotiating Performance: Gender, Sexuality, and Theatricality in Latin/o America*. Ed. Diana Taylor and Juan Villegas. Durham, NC: Duke UP, 1994. 275–305. Print.

Tilly, Charles. *Contentious Performances*. New York: Cambridge UP, 2008. Print.
———. "Contentious Repertoires in Great Britain, 1758–1834." *Social Science History* 17.2 (1993): 253–280. Print.
———. *Regimes and Repertoires*. Chicago: U of Chicago P. 2006. Print.
———. *Stories, Identities, and Political Change*. Oxford, England: Rowan and Littlefield. 2002. Print.
Vasi, Ion Bogdan, Edward T. Walker, John S. Johnson, and Hui Fen Tan. "'No Fracking Way!' Documentary Film, Discursive Opportunity, and Local Opposition against Hydraulic Fracturing in the United States 2010 to 2013." *American Sociological Review* 80.55 (2015): 934–959. Print.
The Vigil. Dir. Jenny Alexander. ActiveVista Media. 2014. Film.
Ware, Doug C. "Once-Feared Arizona Immigration Law Defeated as Part of a Civil Settlement." UPI, 16 Sept. 2016. Web. 11 Nov. 2016.
Warren, Mark R. *Dry Bones Rattling: Community Building to Revitalize American Democracy*. Princeton, NJ: Princeton UP, 2001. Print.

] 4 [

The Unending Journey of the Migrant Mother in *Los invisibles* and *De nadie*

ESTEBAN E. LOUSTAUNAU

A year after the 9/11 attacks, Elvira Arellano, a single mother and Mexican immigrant living in Chicago, sparked a nationwide sanctuary movement on behalf of millions of undocumented workers facing the risk of deportation. Arellano worked for a service company cleaning airplanes at O'Hare International Airport to support her American-born son, Saúl. However, she was arrested in 2002 in a raid known as Operation Chicagoland Skies, one of many federal sting operations that emerged across the United States following 9/11 (Zamudio 1–2). After her arrest, Arellano legally contested her deportation in a double attempt to remain together with her son and to advocate for a comprehensive immigration law. A few years later, Arellano made international news by taking refuge in the Adalberto United Methodist Church in Chicago's Humboldt Park neighborhood and thus opening a space for undocumented immigrants and human rights activist to enter the national immigration debate. Facing a controversial media feeding frenzy, Arellano soon became a symbol of the immigration reform movement by undergoing a transformation from invisible immigrant worker to immigration reform activist.[1]

In an interview for *Time* after being chosen the magazine's Person of the Year in 2006, Arellano states, "It's wrong to split up families. I'm fighting for my son, not for myself. It's a matter of principle. I don't want him treated like garbage. I am a mom and a worker. I am not a terrorist" (in Cole). Arellano's succinct words open up a space for a previously inaudible voice in the immigration political debate, where so often undocumented immigrants, especially women, are denied access. Her message reveals the critical consciousness of a multifaceted woman speaking as a mother and a worker who is aware of her labor rights and ready to participate in the immigration debate. In the climate of disbelief, fear, and uncertainty that emerged after the 9/11 attacks, many immigrants like Arellano were wrongly targeted as criminals or as potential terrorists with anti-American sentiments.[2] However, speaking as a migrant mother and as a worker, Arellano challenges immigration law and defies global economic policies that depend on immigrant labor but exhibit little regard for the human condition of migrant workers and their families. In asserting who she is (a caregiver and a protective mother) and who she is not (a terrorist, a criminal), Arellano enacts a consciousness that is rooted in a dual experience of migration and motherhood that does not conform to the designs of an unjust and broken immigration system enforced by the modern state.[3]

Arellano is not alone in articulating a defiant position against laws and global economic practices that continue to discriminate against the poor and socially disenfranchised. Just as she manages to expose the perils of an unjust immigration system that splits families apart, other Latin American migrant mothers are voicing their critical consciousness, as represented in contemporary documentary film. Recent documentary films on Latin American immigration to the United States represent the critical agency of migrant mothers. In many cases, migrant mothers choose to emigrate alone from their home countries, often leaving their children behind in the care of a close relative or friend. Migrant mothers face an unresolved paradox: to remain together with their children as caregivers or to migrate to the United States with the hope of providing the basic material things the children need to survive. Even though every migrant mother experiences motherhood in complex and different ways, this paradox becomes a common predicament for many mothers at some point in their migrant journeys. Many migrant mothers today confront the ambiguity by rethinking the meanings of motherhood in ways that better correspond with their present lives. At times, their decisions as mothers go against modern values of motherhood, just as their contradicting actions may transgress traditional expectations of motherhood imposed on them by their families and communities in their home countries.

In an analysis of the tensions between normative notions of motherhood and the particular experiences of migrant mothers, Pierrete Hondagneu-Sotelo and Ernestine Avila uncover some of the ways in which migrant mothers negotiate new notions of motherhood. These two sociologists have coined the term "transnational motherhood" to describe the rearrangement of traditional meanings of motherhood in order to accommodate the spatial and temporal separations due to migration (388). Hondagneu-Sotelo and Avila argue that when mothers migrate and leave their children behind with their husbands or other family members, "they are embarking not only on an immigration journey but on a more radical gender-transformative odyssey" (393). This transformation often involves "forsaking deeply felt beliefs" such as "that biological mothers should raise their own children and replacing that belief with new definitions of motherhood" (398). In this way, migrant mothers face a series of obstacles related to gender, identity, and place. In their migrant journeys they must learn new ways to define themselves as women who travel alone, as mothers who are physically and sometimes emotionally detached from their children, and as part of an invisible people who not only experience displacement from their home communities but also face the violence that runs through the migrant trail.[4]

My focus in this chapter is to study ways in which Latin American migrant women articulate a critical consciousness of motherhood as seen through the lens of contemporary documentary film. In accordance with Janet Walker and Diane Waldman, I argue that this consciousness is revealed in dialogue between the migrant subject and the filmmaker in which the filmmaker does not see the migrant as the Other who is subjected to the desires of the self but *as* self and addresses both the difference and the necessity for migrant women's voices to be heard (16). As a result, the viewer is exposed to a different view of undocumented migration that transmits the migrant subject's agency as well as some of the socioeconomic dynamics that force her to migrate in the first place.[5] I discuss this topic in two contemporary documentaries where migrant mothers take center stage: Marc Silver and Gael García Bernal's *Los invisibles* (2010) and Tin Dirdamal's *De nadie* (2005). These documentaries portray the migration experiences of Central American subjects. In the two films, the young male directors engage differently with the women as subjects, as their relations depend on conditions set by the subjects themselves. The films show that for undocumented migrant mothers, their journeys of love for their children and of despair in the face of uncertainty, violence, and death never really end.

In my analysis of the ways in which documentarians and migrant subjects meet and come to collaborate in each film, I pay close attention to the stylistics and thematics of each documentary in order to draw closer to the filmmaker's vision of reality and to find connections between the filmmaker, the migrant subject, and the viewer. Some of these connections include nonverbal forms of communication between filmmakers and subjects that not only bring them closer together but can also help the viewer to better appreciate the consciousness of the migrant subjects. In *Los invisibles,* the relation between Gael García Bernal and migrant women is based on accompaniment and conviviality; in *De nadie,* director Tin Dirdamal takes the role of confidant and messenger for María, one of the protagonists. But before discussing the films, I will introduce the notion of migrant motherhood as a defiant form of human agency.

Otras Formas de Mi(g)rar: Migrant Motherhood as Decolonial Consciousness

In her book *New Documentary,* Stella Bruzzi writes against the grain of traditional documentary film theory to rethink the meaning of this nonfiction medium. Instead of contributing to past debates over the objectivity of documentary film and its ability to capture reality, Bruzzi prefers to look at documentary as a "negotiation between reality on the one hand and image, interpretation and bias on the other" (6). In other words, documentary film can be thought of as a meeting point in which a real event, the limitations of representation, and the act of viewing are confronted and often remain unresolved (Bruzzi 7). Following Bruzzi, I am interested in analyzing the relation between committed documentary filmmakers and undocumented migrant mothers whose lives remain unresolved, split between hope and despair. As Julianne Burton suggests, the purpose of committed documentary filmmakers is to "use the film medium to expose and combat the culture of invisibility and inaudibility" (376). Because of this purpose, I place my attention on documentary film representations of undocumented migrant mothers who are hardly seen or heard, given that their life stories do not fit in with the linear narrative plots that lead to happy endings so favored by the mainstream film industry. Instead, the migrant mothers who speak in *Los invisibles* and *De nadie* generate a counterdiscourse to inform viewers about the conditions many undocumented immigrants face. Through their criticism of government political inaction and lack of economic opportunities at home, many migrant mothers confront a hegemonic culture that keeps them being invisible and inaudible (Noriega 223, 210, in Walker and Waldman 18).

In each of the films that I analyze in this chapter, the solidarity that is formed between filmmaker and migrant subjects raises the viewer's awareness of a dividing line between the values and dreams that migrant mothers hold dear and the false promises of modernity—embodied in unjust laws and unfair global economic strategies—that turn those dreams into nightmares. The recognition of such difference, of the existence of other ways of knowing that come from positions that have been subalternized, is at the heart of the project of decolonial thinking. For Walter Mignolo and for Nelson Maldonado-Torres, decolonial thinking seeks to absorb and displace normative forms of knowledge—and their consequential geopolitical classification of people, cultures, and places—into the perspective of the marginalized subject (Mignolo *Local Histories* 12). As Maldonado-Torres explains,

> [The] Decolonial Turn is about making visible the invisible and about analyzing the mechanisms that produce such invisibility or distorted visibility in light of a larger stock of ideas that must necessarily include the critical reflections of the "invisible" people themselves. Indeed, one must recognize their intellectual production as thinking—not only as culture or ideology. (262)

In *Los invisibles* and *De nadie*, the interactions between filmmakers and subjects help make visible the dreams and struggles of undocumented migrants. They accomplish this collectively by representing the experiences and perspectives of migrant mothers as legitimate sources of knowledge.

The filmmakers and women subjects in these documentaries come together to reveal what I call "otras formas de mi(g)rar," the fusion of other ways of viewing (*mirar*) the migrant and of experiencing migration (*migrar*) within the purview of what Mignolo describes as "geography and biography" ("I Am" 168–169). From a decolonial place of enunciation, Mignolo explains how geography stands for the socioeconomic and gendered factors that lead women in impoverished Latin American countries—notably Guatemala, Honduras, and El Salvador—to emigrate from their hometowns, risking their lives to provide better conditions for their children. For instance, natural disasters such as hurricanes, earthquakes, and droughts but also a lack of labor opportunities for adults and educational options for children are all geographical factors that can lead to migration. Likewise, Mignolo's treatment of biography in "I Am Where I Think" corresponds with the personal life stories of single mothers who are heads of household, responsible for the well-being of their families, and attempt to immigrate to the United States while leaving their children behind in the care of close relatives or friends. By generating a critical consciousness based on geography and biography, migrant women articulate the notion of "Soy donde pienso" (I am where I think), which, according to Mignolo, challenges the Cartesian universalist assumption of "I think, therefore I am." For Mignolo, the consciousness that emerges after "Soy donde pienso" questions the idea that thinking comes before existence and experience ("I Am"). It also disputes the premise that European philosophical and scientific knowledge, spread globally since colonialism, must remain the universal referent without taking into account other forms of knowledge generated by people considered incapable of thinking and self-governing who come from places declared peripheral and unruly. In contrast, Mignolo and Maldonado-Torres both argue that the Cartesian formulation "I think, therefore I am" privileges the self (the one who *thinks*) from others who think differently. This creates a separation of the self who *is* from others who are not (people not considered full beings, who are invisible, dispensable) (Maldonado-Torres 252; Mignolo, "I Am" 161). Instead, the decolonial articulation creates spaces for the coexistence of difference, of different beings coming together in solidarity by being fully aware of the particular role each plays in building coalitions of affinity, respect, and recognition (Maldonado-Torres 252). In this way, the female subjects in *Los invisibles* and *De nadie* embody a decolonial consciousness that challenges their invisibility and dispensability, and García Bernal and Dirdamal demand the right of these subjects to be seen as human beings, co-inhabitants of this world.

Los invisibles: Performing Critical Distance

Los invisibles is a 30-minute documentary about the plight of thousands of Central American migrants who venture through Mexico each year on top of La Bestia (the Beast), a network of freight trains migrants utilize to reach the U.S.-Mexico border from as far south as the state of Chiapas on the Guatemalan border.[6] *Los invisibles* is organized into four short segments; each one can be viewed independently from the others, symbolizing the fragmented reality of this particular migration experience. The film introduces various points of view that expose the dehumanization, pain, and violence that migrants, especially women and children, suffer in Mexico.[7] The title of the film refers to the real social, political, and economic conditions that force thousands of Central Americans to migrate each year and how these conditions remain hidden due to political inaction and a lack of media attention, thus keeping undocumented human migration invisible to large social sectors in Mexico and the United States.[8] As a result, poor, undocumented migrants traveling on top of La Bestia have almost no power against theft, extortion, kidnapping, rape, or even death, a sign of their severe dehumanization. To confront the rampant violence often faced by people who need to flee their countries in search of work and better opportunities for their loved ones, filmmakers Marc Silver and Gael García Bernal bring to light the lives of several Central American migrants crossing through Mexico and the participation of many volunteers who provide services and bring hope to the migrants in their journeys.

In 2010, Silver and García Bernal were invited by Amnesty International to produce a documentary that would address the reasons behind undocumented migration. In an interview on National Public Radio, García Bernal explains how in conversations with Amnesty International, he and Silver "came up with a format for these films to have a life of their own." He states, "We didn't have the aid, the money, nor the practicalities to do a long feature film about this. We needed something that was documented—we could finish it quickly and put it out there quickly" (in "Crossing"). One reason for their expeditious approach to making *Los invisibles* was their desire to finish the film in time for the Global Forum on Migration and Development that took place in Puerto Vallarta, Mexico, in November 2010. In addition, the film articulates a response to the crisis by displaying the migrants' hopes, dreams, and ideas to improve their conditions along the journey. A third contribution of *Los invisibles* is to raise awareness among film viewers in Mexico and elsewhere about the dire conditions of undocumented Central American migration through Mexico.[9] Finally, the making of the film seemed to have had a genuine and profound impact on García Bernal himself. Toward the end of the last segment of *Los invisibles*, he tells Father Alejandro Solalinde the migrants he met "are people who have clear insight into their situation. They are people with a very clear goal. I feel that if we were in their place we would have given up ages ago. I'm inspired by their strength and their will to carry on."[10] Silver and García Bernal followed up *Los invisibles* with another award-winning documentary on migration, *Who Is Dayani Cristal?* (2013). Two years later García Bernal was the protagonist of Jonás Cuarón's thriller *Desierto* (2015). It appears that the mega movie star was the one left starstruck by the ordinary people he interviewed on the migrant road.

In *Los invisibles*, the close interaction between García Bernal and the film subjects aims to turn invisible migrants into visible moral and social agents. García Bernal blends in with the migrant subjects in his attempt to speak with instead of at them. In each segment, the film breaks down the barrier between invisible/visible, death/life, as the viewer witnesses the expressions, feelings, emotions, and ideas of the migrant subjects through the stylistic characteristics employed by the filmmakers. The characteristics include giving the central roles to the migrants while García Bernal takes a secondary position as observer and companion, the use of close-up and still shots to represent the humanity of the migrants and expose the dreadful conditions of the migrant journey, and strategic positioning of the subjects on screen to enact their agency through verbal narration and body placement in outdoor surroundings marked by death and desolation.

Ironically, García Bernal confers his star power—and visibility as an international film actor—to the migrant subjects themselves. In *Los invisibles*, García Bernal appears surrounded by migrants sharing the same close spaces, conversing with children at eye level, and dressed informally like the migrants he encounters. By not having a clear distance between interviewer and interviewees, the migrants with whom García Bernal interacts become the protagonists who share their stories, experiences, and dreams as they reclaim their humanity through their voices and emotions. For example, the film opens with a series of still shots of male migrants of various ages, each with his torso exposed, looking straight into the camera. The images of half-naked men make the viewer recognize the existence of real people in extreme conditions. The transformation from invisible migrants into human beings becomes possible through the actual faces of the people, for the face, argues Emmanuel Levinas, is meaningful all by itself, beyond any contexts. Normally, we are defined by our character in a given context. Undocumented migrants are turned invisible in the eye of the law. But, Levinas explains, one becomes who he or she is by the face itself. The face "is what cannot become a content, which your thought would embrace; it is uncontainable, it leads you beyond" (Levinas 86–87). During the film the sound is an ongoing exchange of distorted noise and harmonious rhythms that reflect the slow tempo of the action and the characters' emotions. The exchange of chaotic noise and harmonious sound becomes the leitmotiv in each of the four segments of the film to address the chaos, isolation, and uncertainty of the journey but also to unfold the possibility of hope that is found in the shelters and in the communion of all migrants.[11] The clash of confusion and conciliation becomes what Sergei Eisenstein calls an "intellectual montage" (in Lesage 312), as the filmmakers use it to turn invisible migrants into human subjects who are visible and able to speak, be heard, and be seen by the viewer. The still shots also serve another purpose; they function as portraits of missing men, women, and children so that their loved ones and family members back home can feel hopeful after seeing them on screen. They may be able to identify a migrant husband, wife, son, or daughter and know that they are alive, still holding onto a promise and a dream.[12]

The film's second segment, "Seis de cada diez," looks at migration from the point of view of women, and therefore, it is the one on which I want to focus my analysis. The central subjects in this segment of the film are three young mothers from Honduras and a 17-year-old girl from El Salvador named Dalila, who along with her uncle and other men, is ambushed by a group of thieves near the train tracks days before her encounter with García Bernal at an unnamed migrant shelter in southern Mexico. The segment begins with the testimony of one of the three Honduran women who identifies herself and her two companions as single mothers and widows. She explains:

> All of us here are single mothers. My children's father left me. Her husband died [*pointing to a woman off-camera*] and hers as well [*motioning toward the woman beside her*]. Mine's as good as dead because he doesn't help us at all.[13]

Their reality of abandonment and despair is shared by many migrant mothers who face the dilemma of whether to stay by their children's side to care for them without the necessary financial means to live well or to migrate to the United States to provide for their children with enough money to survive but remaining physically absent. One interesting factor in this young mother's testimony is the way she contrasts her migration to her husband's irresponsible abandonment on the one hand and the state's lack of accountability on the other. Here we begin to see how the transforming action of migrant motherhood confronts the social and economic conditions in Honduras. In conversation with García Bernal, she shares her personal story of migration:

> Migrant mother (MM): I left my family behind. My children, my mom, my brothers...
> García Bernal (GB): Your children? How many children do you have?
> MM: I have two. My mom, my brothers. Well, everything I have I left behind. But I want to go to the United States to help them because

Honduras is in a bad situation, there is no work, everything's very expensive. It is bad, really bad.[14]

In her own words, the woman makes a connection between her personal experience and the need for change in private places (home) and public environments (Honduras). These are the spaces in which women systematically suffer patriarchal abandonment, exploitation, and oppression. The pressures of a single mother to support her children, mother, and brothers in a country with a high unemployment rate and cost of living lead to a new meaning of migrant motherhood that triggers this mother's social consciousness. In the film, the young mother articulates her own consciousness based on her geographical and biographical conditions. Her sense of self and her critical stand against patriarchy and state-mandated austerity policies empower her to move forward in the hope of improving her family's well-being.

In *Los invisibles*, the migrant subjects may lack the ability and resources to engage in systemic political change, but it is clear from their interactions with García Bernal and with the social workers and priests in the migrant shelters that they possess the experiential knowledge to stimulate their social awareness. While undocumented migration to the United States has become a byproduct of prolonged social inequality exacerbated by political and economic policies affecting the poor in Honduras, El Salvador, and other countries, *Los invisibles* represents particular ways in which migrant mothers articulate their collective interests and reveal their social agency.

The film represents migrant mothers as social subjects who, along with the filmmaker, imagine a space of resistance and protection against suffering, terror, and death in their journeys through Mexico. García Bernal conducts his interview with the three Honduran migrant mothers in an undisclosed location in southern Mexico.[15] The Honduran mothers whom García Bernal interviews speak out on behalf of their families, and the filmmaker represents their resistance by contrasting images of desolation with representations of trust. Speaking in voice-over while the viewer sees a series of sinister images from a nearby garbage dump—a venue of vultures resting on a dry tree, fumes coming out from the piles of garbage, broken dolls—one of the women tells García Bernal about the harsh conditions that led her and her two companions to emigrate from Honduras. The images correspond with the woman's disheartening story of poverty and loss. At the same time, while García Bernal and the women carry on their conversation, they do it in a manner that

Figure 4.1. Migrant mothers (*Los invisibles*, 2010, Marc Silver and Gael García Bernal).

goes completely against the images of death and destruction in the dump. In this scene, the migrant mothers and García Bernal appear seated on the inner edge of the train tracks facing each other (figures 4.1 and 4.2). The way their bodies are positioned transforms the rails into two short-legged benches, thus creating a sense of proximity and familiarity between the filmmaker and the women. At first, the use of close-up camera shots makes the viewer connect the words of despair with the images of demise in the dump. But then the camera angle shifts from a close-up to a medium shot, and the viewer becomes aware of the contrast between the textual testimony of sorrow and the visual

Figure 4.2. García Bernal conversing with migrant mothers on the railroad tracks (*Los invisibles,* 2010, Marc Silver and Gael García Bernal).

representation of companionship and trust. The shift happens when García Bernal asks the woman about her children. Doing that moves the viewer closer to understanding the migrant subjects' experiences as mothers, family members, and citizens. This proximity comes about in the interconnection of words, images, and action—particularly the staging of filmmaker and subjects on screen. Symbolically, the scene introduces a break from the environment of death and sorrow represented by the images of the garbage dump and the testimonies about the migrants' constant fear of being assaulted, kidnapped, and sexually abused on the road. Instead of reproducing a fixed image of migrant subjects as powerless victims in despair, the physical placement of the subjects on camera lets the viewer see a space of life and hope that is collectively constructed through dialogue between García Bernal and the migrant mothers.

In this alternative space symbolically separated by the train tracks, the viewer witnesses a transformation of the three women and García Bernal and their immediate environment. Forming a close circle of trust by facing each other as they sit on the inner edge of the rails, the three migrants and the filmmaker create a safe and comfortable place for dialogue, removed from all the desolation and violence that surround them. This other symbolic space is what Josefina Ludmer calls a "territory of the present," that is, an "urban island" in which the women find themselves simultaneously outside of what surrounds them—in their own makeshift living quarters—and inside the social space as they face the oppression and violence of undocumented migration (Ludmer 105). I would like to argue that being able to re-create their own migrant island enables these mothers to establish a critical distance from the forces that push against them and continue to overwhelm them in their journey.

Seated in this other social space, the female subjects reconfigure their sense of motherhood and migration. The migrant mother who serves as the spokesperson for the group describes the act of migration as a means to an end. She tells García Bernal,

> My mind was made up when my children began school. I didn't have enough money to buy them what they needed, school supplies and so on. And that made me feel really bad. So I decided to go to the United States so that I could give them everything they needed. That is what I desire the most in life. I want my children to have what I could never have, an education. That is what made me go to the States, and I know I will get there.[16]

This migrant mother articulates a profound love for her children and a strong determination by confronting a global systemic crisis that impedes her from raising her children by her side and poses unlimited obstacles for a guaranteed future. Her words register a collective will for hope and justice as she affirmatively envisions having a successful journey.

In *Los invisibles,* García Bernal meets the migrant subjects at the early stages of their journey through Mexico. Facing each other on the edge of the train rails, he asks the migrant mothers about their biggest fear on the journey. To that they answer "que nos secuestren, porque no tenemos cómo pagar un rescate, porque sí piden mucho dinero" (that someone will kidnap us because we don't have money to pay a ransom because they demand huge sums of money and we can't pay). The collective fear of kidnapping by armed gangs along the way is especially traumatizing to migrant women and children traveling alone in Mexico. This is a central issue in Tin Dirdamal's *De nadie,* where the filmmaker meets the migrant subjects halfway through their journey. By then, the hypothetical fear turns into a soul-breaking reality.

De nadie: Documenting by Obeying

Inspired by Eduardo Galeano's poem *"Los nadies"* (The nobodies), the documentary film *De nadie* portrays the migration experiences of a handful of undocumented Central American migrants whom filmmaker Tin Dirdamal interviewed in 2003 at the shelter Casa del Migrante (Home of the Migrant) in Orizaba, Veracruz. Located 600 miles northeast of the Mexico-Guatemala border, Orizaba marks a quarter of the distance of the migrant journey through Mexico, yet by then most migrants have already experienced some of the worst dangers of the journey through Mexico. The Guatemalan, Honduran, and Salvadoran migrant subjects in the film have been traveling in Mexico for several days or weeks, mostly by riding on La Bestia. The subjects in the film share similar reasons for leaving behind their countries: lack of jobs and educational opportunities, high cost of living, unaffordable health services, and devastating natural disasters. They also share similar sentiments of regret and affliction from being exposed to the harrowing violence of the journey.[17] Feeling physically and morally broken, many of the migrants who speak on camera do not regret their decision for leaving, but some recommend that potential migrants stay home rather than experience the horrors of the migrant trail. To introduce a comprehensive picture of this severe migration experience, Dirdamal weaves together various migrant voices and compares them with other points of view from public officials, railway supervisors, and pro-migrant volunteers.

Although Central American migration to the United States is not a new phenomenon, many immigration studies have focused on the socioeconomic conditions that push people away from their home countries and pull them into different regions across the United States (Sørensen 45). In recent years, however, a number of journalists in Mexico, for example, those belonging to the network Periodistas de a Pie (Grassroots Journalists Network), have put their lives on the line to report on the dehumanizing atrocities against Central American migrants making their way through Mexico. These journalists provide information on the systemic political and economic factors that have led to the tremendous violence against undocumented migrants.[18] In this regard, *De nadie* provides the viewer with similar information to better understand the persistence of violence and danger along the migrant trail.

In the film, a railway administrator explains how the neoliberal economic policies that the Mexican state began to establish in the late 1980s are at the root of the problem. Jaime Valdez, a representative of the private railway company Transportación Ferroviaria Mexicana (Mexican Railway Transportation), explains that shortly after taking office in 1994, Mexican President Ernesto Zedillo (1994–2000) led the privatization of the national train system, a 160-year-old state-owned company. This resulted in the concession of the entire network of railways to five private companies.[19] The yielding of more than 14,000 miles of railway to freight-based private companies suspended passenger rail services across Mexico and limited the resources and priorities of the state for safety surveillance in the train system. Following this account, a veteran employee of Ferrosur, the company that owns the railways that connect the state of Veracruz to Mexico City, candidly comments on camera, "El uso del ferrocarril es el transporte ideal por excelencia para llegar a la frontera, por una razón: porque no es vigilado" (Using the train is the ideal way to get to the U.S. border for one reason: nobody is watching). The observations by these two railway employees are critical because they show how the absence of the state in the railway system, premeditated by political action under free market capitalism, refers to a deeper disjunction between the state and society under neoliberal rule. It is as if the present system of political deregulation and economic free trade demands for individual citizens-turned-consumers to fend for themselves (Valencia 29). In countries with drastic social and economic inequalities, state deregulation has had a devastating impact on those with fewer economic resources. This includes more than half the population of Central America.[20] As a result, the abandonment and invisibility of the poor often has led to an increase in corruption and extreme violence.[21] The "nobodies" Dirdamal encounters have already been victims of assault, injury, or sexual abuse, and some have witnessed the death of a loved one. Meanwhile, all these crimes go unpunished. The environment of terror and death that Central American migrants face in Mexico is part of what Sayak Valencia calls "capitalismo gore." Valencia proposes this term as a category of discourse to help address the complex frameworks of crime, politics, and economics in contemporary Mexico that have given full range to indomitable violence to the point that it becomes a spectacle—carried out by "monstrous subjects"—and, therefore, a profitable commodity in a globalized world (26–27).[22] Coming face to face with this dehumanizing reality filled with death and despair turned Tin Dirdamal into a committed filmmaker.

In an interview shortly after receiving the 2006 Sundance Film Festival Audience Award, Dirdamal told the story of how his film career started by accident. It began as a reaction to hearing about the terrible injustices that many Central American migrants were suffering while making the journey through Mexico ("Park City"). At the age of 23, Dirdamal took a break from his studies in industrial engineering in the northern city of Monterrey to volunteer for the Jesuit Migrant Service Program in Orizaba. As migrants approached him with their stories of abuse, Dirdamal grabbed a handycam and started recording their testimonies. Unsure of what to do with the initial footage, in 2003 Dirdamal received funding from Catholic Bishop Raúl Vera to produce a documentary about Central American migration in Mexico. He also obtained a grant from his university to help cover the cost of production and to exhibit the film free of charge to wide audiences in the campus theater (Molina Ramírez).

Despite not having any prior formal training in filmmaking, Dirdamal created a multi-award–winning full-length documentary film by drawing on migrant daily life mostly captured through the lens of a hand-held camera.[23] Perhaps one of the reasons for the film's success is that its cinematographic simplicity leads the viewer to focus more closely on the migrants' social experience of daily life (Lesage 312). Although the viewer never sees Dirdamal on camera, his frequent off-camera interactions with the migrant subjects and the motion of the camera as he walks next to them give the viewer a sense of his proximity to the action (Molina Ramírez). Yet, this proximity should not be confused with intimacy. Whereas proximity brings different people to share a common space, intimacy—a sentiment of affinity, closeness, and trust—remains limited, depending on how far each migrant subject is willing to share information with Dirdamal. In the case of *Los invisibles,* García Bernal does not reveal the names of most of the migrant subjects with whom he interacts on film, including the three Honduran mothers with whom he shares a private moment chatting on the train tracks. This way, the viewer remains at arm's length from the migrant subjects. In the making of *De nadie,* even though Dirdamal spent long days traveling along with the migrant subjects in the film, he keeps his distance as a sign of respect. Furthermore, in the context of each film, it would be hardly plausible for the viewer to expect to reach an equal level of intimacy with the film's subjects, considering the shocking experiences of violence the migrants endured. Thus, as Doris Sommer wisely forewarns us, we must "proceed with caution" when viewing documentary films about undocumented migrant subjects so that we may be able to reach a better understanding of migrant consciousness by respecting their difference and acknowledging their particular histories (25).

Mindful of Sommer's caution, I find that the most interesting textual elements of the film appear in the interactions between filmmaker and subjects, especially when the migrants speak through their gestures, pensive pauses, contradictions, and commands. It is in reading these elements as "textual strategies" that we come closer to grasping the migrant subjects' consciousness (Sommer 126). One of the best examples of migrant consciousness in *De nadie* is the story of María Flores, a Honduran mother whom Dirdamal meets in Orizaba and continues to follow northward to the city of Monterrey, less than three hours' drive from the U.S.-Mexico border. In a film with limited cinematographic resources, the dialogue between Dirdamal and migrant subjects like María becomes primary. In the opening segment of the film, María first appears looking vulnerable, as if she has been crying. But as soon as she begins to interact with Dirdamal, her emotional vulnerability washes away and is replaced by a strong, defiant, and brave personality. María's voice remains stoic until Dirdamal asks if she has any children. At that moment, the viewer can sense María's voice beginning to tremble as she thinks about the children she has left behind in Honduras. But as I will demonstrate, her response is a signal of her defiant consciousness. After a brief pause, María mentions the ages of each of her four children without revealing their names, yet. As she does almost every time she talks about her past life in Honduras, she states that her children are the reason behind her migrant journey: "Me vine para trabajar para ponerles a estudiar, pero no sabía lo que me iban a hacer" (I left to earn money so that they can study, but I didn't know what was going to happen to me on the road). Her conscious decision to migrate corresponds with that of the migrant mothers in *Los invisibles*. However, if the migrant mothers in *Los invisibles* tell García Bernal that their greatest fear is being kidnapped on the road, María is not willing to share what has already happened to her from riding on La Bestia. Here is where the filmmaker *and* viewer must act responsibly by respecting María's difference (Sommer 126). Her choice of words to tell that some kind of unexpected and violent offense has happened to her without saying exactly what it is becomes a defiant counterdiscourse to the sensationalist tales of violence produced by the mass media industry.

Going one step further, María's refusal to spell out the details of her suffering is her way of resisting not just sensationalist mass media representations but gore reality itself (Valencia 86). That is, one can identify with María's consciousness as a decent woman and mother. As the film progresses, it becomes clear that in her interactions with Dirdamal, María creates an alternative space of control where she calls the shots. This is an intentional space in which María attempts to rebuild her self-respect and moral virtue as a woman, worker, mother, and wife. At the same time, the way she guards her difference and rebuilds self-respect informs the viewer of her own relationship with her family and community back in Honduras.

The night Dirdamal meets María in the streets of Orizaba is also the moment she begins to establish her difference as a woman, worker, migrant, and mother. Surrounded by mostly men in what appears to be the entrance to the shelter Casa del Migrante, María explains that one of the reasons she decided to leave Honduras was the destruction of her home caused by Hurricane Mitch.[24] Not only did Mitch take away María's home, it also wiped away the Honduran economy, based mostly on agriculture. At that point, Dirdamal asks María about her husband's employment. She states, "My husband doesn't work because he has a prostate illness. I am the one who works. I had a machine to grind corn, but that wasn't enough. Only 25 lempiras a day is not enough to eat. That's why I am here."

Once again, the viewer learns that contemporary Central American migration is a result of a weak economy where an ineffective state fails to support its citizens after a major natural disaster. Moments later, María enters a room where several migrants are watching television. At that point, she reveals another reason for her migration: "The time I waste watching television is time I waste not doing many other things. In my house I am man and woman. That is why I don't have time to watch television. Worst at night. Do you know when

I go to bed after sharpening the corn grinder? At eleven at night, because that's when there is running water. And that's why I am here."[25] If in her earlier remarks María outlines the economic and political conditions that pushed her away from Honduras, here she reflects on her daily routine and how her notion of motherhood has already shifted away from a more traditional sense as domestic labor by having to be "man and woman" at home. At the same time, in a room surrounded by migrant men, María's words represent a demand for respect of difference. She demands the recognition of her difference as a woman, mother, and worker as well as respect from male migrants and Dirdamal (and indirectly, the viewer) as she tries to disguise her vulnerability as a lonely female migrant on the road. Later in the film, the viewer learns that María is the only woman among a small group of Honduran migrants traveling together. As a lone woman on the migrant trail, she is fully aware of the need to protect herself from additional violent attacks and betrayal.

Dirdamal understands María's claim for respect. Never rushing to ask too much from María, he listens to her more than he asks. He is also aware of the difference that exists between him and María and the other migrant subjects with whom he comes into contact. Here, the decolonial notion "Soy donde pienso" (I am where I think) becomes relevant to understand both María's and Dirdamal's actions. Dirdamal treats María as a human being without idealizing or minimizing her existence and experience (figure 4.3). As the film advances, María appears to be more comfortable around Dirdamal. This becomes evident when they share a comical moment after she rejects a job offer to be a circus dancer and when they talk about her family back in Honduras. Dirdamal and María form a kind of "cautious complicity" based on mutual trust and recognition of difference, where the filmmaker does not intend to speak for the migrant subject or take her position but to fulfill the role that is his to play (Sommer 133). The relation that María and Dirdamal develop in the film resembles the Zapatista transformative political principle of "mandar obedeciendo" (leading by obeying), in which a true leader follows the will of the people, the desires and ideas of the larger community (Khasnabish 125). As if adapting this principle to the film, Dirdamal follows María's will and documents her story by obeying her in a double action of respect and affection. I would like to propose that as a committed filmmaker, Dirdamal takes a double role, as María's companion during a short period in her journey through Mexico and as her messenger, willing to take specific instructions from María. Toward the end of the film, the viewer sees how María insists that Dirdamal visit

Figure 4.3. María, at ease in front of the camera (*De nadie*, 2005, Tin Dirdamal).

her family in Honduras to let them know that she loves them, is doing well, and remains hopeful of reaching the United States.

Interpreting Dirdamal's role in the film as confidant and messenger allows the viewer to observe how he listens patiently to María's straightforward commands and detailed instructions. Once María is ready to continue on her northbound journey, she hands Dirdamal a written note with her home address and instructs him to ask for her husband, Antonio, or her sister Trina upon arrival. As she pictures this encounter in her mind, she is certain that her children will be there to welcome Dirdamal when he arrives. Nonetheless, when she begins to think of her children, the camera captures how María slowly turns quiet, focused again on her own thoughts. After a few seconds of a close-up shot of María thinking to herself, the image cuts to another moment in the film when she again has the same reflecting stance as in the previous scene. These and other times in the film when María is silent, looking away from the camera or her interlocutors, are not to be taken as signs of passivity or dead air but instead as moments to recognize María's consciousness. María's gestures enact her agency as a migrant mother concerned for her children whom she has not seen in several weeks. And as the viewer later finds out, these moments also represent María as a moral subject who feels unworthy to be reunited with her family after the horrendous experience she suffered while riding on La Bestia. As a form of respect for María's dignity, Dirdamal waits until the end of the film to reveal María's secret: a few days before arriving in Orizaba, she and a group of men from Honduras traveling together were attacked by nine armed men belonging to the Mara Salvatrucha.[26] According to María's testimony, she was gang-raped by two of the attackers. Feeling ashamed, unable to recover from the trauma caused by this horrific experience, she tells Dirdamal, "No voy a tener valor. Sólo de saber lo que me ha pasado, no voy a tener valor de hablar con mis hijos" (I won't be able to do it. After what happened to me I won't be able to talk to my kids). In the film, María never recovers the happiness she had prior to the sexual attack. Still, in her interactions with Dirdamal she finds someone she can trust and with whom she can begin to restore a lost sense of respect and control.

María's relationship with Dirdamal is meaningful to her at a point when she is unsure about the best way to continue moving north and is afraid to face her family again after what she has gone through on the journey. As an example of María's conflictive position as a migrant mother, she orders Dirdamal not to say a word about the attack when he visits her family. The evening before she leaves Orizaba, María tells Dirdamal, "Tell them that you saw me and that I was happy, do you hear? Don't you tell them that you saw me like this, dispirited. Don't you tell them that I am broken." These words show the strong bond between a committed filmmaker and a migrant subject to the point where María becomes Dirdamal's director who instructs him about what to say, what to include, and what to leave out from the story of her migrant life that he is to show to her family in Honduras (figure 4.4). In the film, the viewer is made

Figure 4.4. María as seen by two of her children in Honduras (*De nadie*, 2005, Tin Dirdamal).

aware of how Dirdamal's respect for María is part of a collective effort to restore hope in a migrant mother's endless journey of love and despair.

Conclusion

Contemporary documentary film about undocumented migration can be interpreted as a contested space open to dialogue and exchange between filmmakers, migrant subjects, and viewers. Central American mothers traveling alone on the migrant trail expose their lives to many dangers but at the same time carry with them the loving hope and promise for a better future for their children and families. Their documented testimonies of memory that link them with their children left behind enable these mothers to generate spaces of defiance in the midst of despair and death on the journey. The migrant mothers in *Los invisibles* and *De nadie* allow Gael García Bernal and Tin Dirdamal to enter into these spaces and learn to "co-move" with the migrants in reciprocity of their trust.[27]

The relationships developed in these films strike against the neoliberal policies of the past three decades. These political reforms and economic policies left a deep social void across a troubled region that includes the Central American Northern Triangle (Guatemala, Honduras, and El Salvador), Mexico, and the United States. Documentary film has the potential to remind viewers that this void is not a vacuum. Here I am thinking of Toni Morrison when she writes, "We can agree, I think, that invisible things are not necessarily 'not-there'; that a void may be empty, but not a vacuum" (11). Morrison's reference to the need to explore race relations in America as an ongoing interaction between dominant and marginalized racial groups is applicable to the demands made by migrant mothers like the activist Elvira Arellano, María Flores in *De nadie*, and the anonymous women in *Los invisibles*. These women's critical voices call for further analyses of the exchanges between nonmigrant nationals and migrant people, especially women and children who are otherwise considered invisible nobodies. *Los invisibles* and *De nadie* register the unspoken voices of the invisible and in the process, introduce alternative forms of knowledge that challenge the goring acts of extreme violence and impunity along the migrant trail. García Bernal learns his role from accompanying and listening to the migrants' stories of hope and deception; Dirdamal accomplishes this by becoming María's confidant and messenger. These filmmakers understand their social and political roles in making visible the invisible, in critiquing the systems that insist on making people invisible, and in creating spaces for dialogue and inclusion of migrant mothers' own decolonial consciousness. In the end, this critical interpretation leaves viewers with the responsibility to identify their own roles and put them into action to challenge the culture of invisibility and inaudibility against migrants today.

Notes

1. The 2006 pro-immigration reform movement will always be remembered by the millions of undocumented immigrants and their families across the country who came out of the shadows that spring to march on behalf of their rights for basic labor protection, mobility, education, and inclusion (Engler). Elvira Arellano and multitudes of others took to the streets across cities in the United States to publicly project their voices for social justice and equality while realizing their power for collective advocacy. In 2007 Arellano was deported to Mexico after leaving the church to participate in an immigration reform rally in California. Upon her return to Mexico, Arellano continued her struggle for immigration reform and migrant human rights by founding the organization La Familia Unida and helping to create the Movimiento Migrante Mesoamericano. Along with pro-immigration rights activists Martha Sánchez Soler and Rubén Figueroa, Arellano brought aid to Central American migrants at the shelter Albergue para Migrantes San José in Huhuetoca, Mexico. In 2014 Arellano returned to the United States along with other deportees to protest U.S. immigration laws and deportation practices (Hill).

2. Tanya Maria Golash-Boza explains that after 9/11 the U.S. federal government created the Department of Homeland Security with the purpose of protecting the country from the threat of further terrorist attacks. This translated to a dramatic increase in immigration law enforcement that included massive raids, detentions, and deportations, as many undocumented immigrants became de facto suspected terrorists even when there was no evidence against them. Golash-Boza argues that many of these official practices exemplified human rights violations that tore families apart and shattered many migrant communities.

3. Going one step further, Arellano's subjectivity as a migrant who is also a single mother and a worker challenges normative assumptions about identity. According to Thomas Nail, the modern nation-state defines the migrant "as a figure without its own history and social force" (3). Instead, Nail argues that movement and migration should not be treated as "derivative or lacking" but as "the constitutive force of social motion" (14). From this perspective, Arellano transforms her condition as a deportable migrant mother into her legitimate source of resistance, that socially constitutive power through which to bring social change.

4. Not every experience of migration is the same. In this chapter I focus on examples of undocumented migrant mothers in part because their combined history more

closely resembles the situation of most women migrants today. This shared history registers the economic, political, social, and territorial expulsion of women and the uncertainty, insecurity, and violence that come with it (Nail 2).

5. Recent documentary films that address the experiences of migrant motherhood with origins in Latin America include Sharon Genasci and Dorothy Velasco's *Troubled Harvest* (1990), Marta Bautis's *Home Is Struggle/Historias paralelas* (1991), Tin Dirdamal's *De nadie* (2005), Anayansi Prado's *Maid in America* (2005), Marc Silver and Gael García Bernal's *Los invisibles* (2010), Marcela Zamora's *María en tierra de nadie* (2010), Nicholas Bruckner's *La americana* (2011), U. Roberto Romero's *The Harvest/La cosecha* (2011), and Jenny Alexander's *The Vigil* (2014).

6. Since at least the mid-1990s, Central American migrants on their way to the United States have used La Bestia as their main mode of transportation through Mexico. However, after the surge in the number of unaccompanied minor migrants seeking refuge in the United States in the summer of 2014, the Mexican government, under pressure from the Obama administration, increased the number of checkpoints along the railways in what was called Operativo Frontera Sur (Operation Southern Border). The operation reduced the flow of migrants atop the trains by 90 percent, but now they face higher risks by taking on the dangerous journey through Mexico on foot without access to shelter, food, and medical attention (Isacson, Mayer, and Smith).

7. English translations are quoted from the film's subtitles. The segments of the film are "Seaworld," "Seis de cada diez" (Six out of ten), "Los que se quedan" (Those who remain), and "Gol" (Goal). Each segment informs the viewer about the inhumane conditions Central American migrants face in crossing through Mexico but also about the hope migrants find in each other and in the people who volunteer in shelters that offer aid to them along the way.

8. Jorge Bustamante contends that the sense of political inaction that exists when it comes to protecting the lives of migrants today has to do with the "contrast between what governments say and what they do about the problem of human rights of migrants, and why... this problem [is] widely perceived as growing" (338).

9. Since the release of *Los invisibles* in the documentary film festival Ambulante, cofounded by García Bernal and Diego Luna, Amnesty International has made the film readily available free of charge on its website, and it is available in YouTube.

10. "Son personas que tienen una lucidez para entender su situación. Es gente que tiene una meta muy clara pero siento que si nosotros estuviéramos en esa situación, siento que hubiéramos renunciado hace rato. Me contagio de su fuerza y de sus ganas de seguir adelante."

11. In "Seaworld," the first segment, García Bernal describes in voice-over the work done by volunteers in shelters located at various points along the rail line. He explains how in these shelters, migrants "rest, sleep, wash, and eat. But most importantly, here is where they find safety, something they will not find anywhere else on the journey. ... They meet other people like themselves from different countries who are also

making the same journey. They give each other support and share experiences that will help them on their way." The many Mexican volunteers who run these shelters give migrants "one of the best things possible in life: Hope."

12. For the past 10 years, dozens of Central American mothers have joined the Caravana de Madres de Migrantes Desaparecidos (Caravan of Mothers of Disappeared Migrants), a social movement founded by Emeteria Martínez, who searched for more than 21 years until she found her missing daughter. The mothers of La Caravana are women from Guatemala, Honduras, El Salvador, and Nicaragua who march along the migrant trail in Mexico holding photographs of their missing migrant children as they search for them in shelters, hospitals, brothels, and prisons and through other social networks. See the group's blog at caravanamadres.wordpress.com and Marcela Zamora's documentary *María en tierra de nadie*.

13. "Nosotras aquí todas somos madres solteras. Yo, pues, el papá de mis niños . . . me dejó. Ella, su esposo se murió. El de ella también. O sea, el mío como que también esté muerto porque no nos ayuda en nada."

14. "Madre migrante (MM): Yo dejé mi familia, mis hijos, mi mamá . . .
García Bernal (GB): ¿Tus hijos? ¿Cuántos hijos tienes?
MM: Dos. Mi mamá, mis hermanos. Bueno, todo lo que tengo lo dejé allá. Pero pienso llegar a Estados Unidos para ayudarles mucho. Porque Honduras está bien malo. No hay trabajo. Tenemos gastos, muchos gastos. Todo está malo, malo, malo."

15. From watching this and other segments in the film, the viewer can estimate that this interview was done near the shelter Hermanos en el Camino (Brothers and Sisters on the Road) in Ixtepec, Oaxaca.

16. "A mí me convenció mucho [la necesidad de migrar] porque mis hijos empezaron las clases y pues no tenía para comprarles todo lo que ellos necesitaban: sus útiles. Pues, eso me hizo sentirme muy mal. Dije, no. Yo tengo que viajar para Estados Unidos para poder darle a mis niños todo. Porque es lo que más deseo en la vida. Que ellos tengan lo que yo no pude tener, mis estudios. Eso fue lo que me motivó a viajar a Estados Unidos. Y sí sé que voy a llegar."

17. The main migrant subjects in the film include José Medina, a 16-year-old Honduran boy who lost both of his legs and his left arm after falling off the train; Adolfo, a young Central American teenager who witnessed a gang belonging to the Mara Salvatrucha rob and murder his parents near Orizaba; María Flores, a Honduran mother who survived a similar gang attack; and José María Salvador, a Salvadoran man hoping to reach the United States to seek work and much-needed medical assistance.

18. At the network's website, periodistasdeapie.org.mx, the journalists offer a series of articles and e-books on contemporary immigration in Central America and Mexico. Other leading works of journalism committed to bringing justice and visibility to the lives and memory of Central American migrants crossing through Mexico include Pulitzer Prize winner Sonia Nazario's book *Enrique's Journey*; Alma Guillermoprieto's

online altar in honor of 72 Central American migrants massacred in Mexico in summer 2010, 72migrantes.com; and Oscar Martínez's *Los migrantes que no importan* (translated as *The Beast: Riding the Rails and Dodging Narcos on the Migrant Trail*). Two academic works that explore the philosophical and political repercussions of liberalism's failure to control violence in Mexico are Ileana Rodríguez's *Liberalism at Its Limits: Crime and Terror in the Latin American Cultural Text* and Sayak Valencia's *Capitalismo gore*.

19. These companies are Ferromex, Ferrosur, Transportación Ferroviaria Mexicana, Transportación Marítima Mexicana, and Grupo México. In 2005, Transportación Ferroviaria Mexicana acquired Transportación Marítima Mexicana and was renamed Kansas City Southern de México. Coincidentally, after leaving office in 2000 President Zedillo became director of the board at Union Pacific Railroad, Grupo México's partner company.

20. In *De nadie*, Dirdamal includes statistical data that show how 56 percent of the population in Central America live under the poverty line.

21. Another statistic in the film is that 51 percent of reported abuses against migrants are inflicted by public officials.

22. After the elevated rates of unaccompanied Central American minor migrants made the news in the summer of 2014, the governments of the United States and Mexico agreed on creating the Plan Frontera Sur, a dual attempt to seal the Mexico-Guatemala border and eliminate the traffic of undocumented migrants on top of La Bestia. However, human rights and pro-immigrant activists such as Father Alejandro Solalinde reacted critically to this new plan, arguing that it did not begin to address the social, political, and economic factors that generate migration and that it would only increase the danger and violence against migrants, who would be forced to seek alternative routes to travel other than the trains (Gómez).

23. In 2005 *De nadie* won Best First Work at the Guadalajara Mexican Film Festival and an Ariel for Best Feature-Length Documentary from the Mexican Academy of Film. In 2006 the film was nominated for the Grand Jury Prize and won the Audience Award at the Sundance Film Festival.

24. In 1998, Hurricane Mitch caused catastrophic flood damage in vast regions of Honduras, Guatemala, and Nicaragua. Nearly 11,000 people died and more than 11,000 went missing by the end of 1998. In the countries affected by Hurricane Mitch, a total of 2.7 million were left homeless.

25. "Yo el rato que pierdo viendo televisión, pierdo en hacer muchas cosas. Yo en mi casa soy hombre y mujer. Por eso no me queda tiempo de ver televisión. Peor en la noche. ¿Sabe usted a qué hora me acuesto afilando los platos para el molino? A las once de la noche, como hay agua. Y por eso yo estoy aquí."

26. The Mara Salvatrucha (M-13) is a transnational criminal gang with origins in the Central American diaspora of children and young families to California at the height of the 1979–1992 civil war in El Salvador. Today, members of the M-13 are hired by the Mexican drug cartel of Los Zetas to extort and kidnap undocumented migrants riding on La Bestia. In *De nadie*, an estimated 5,000 M-13 gang members were said to

be in Mexico, with 25 to 50 new members crossing the Guatemala-Mexico border each day.

27. Gustavo Esteva and Madhu Prakash suggest that *"conmoverse* (co-move) does not mean merely moving onself with the other . . . it calls for joining heads as well as hearts and stomachs in the dance that brings cultural changes, interchanges, and exchanges" (142).

Works Cited

Bruzzi, Stella. *New Documentary*. 2nd ed. New York: Routledge, 2006. Print.
Burton, Julianne. "Democratizing Documentary: Modes of Address in Latin American Cinema, 1958–1972." *Show Us Life: Towards a History and Aesthetics of the Committed Documentary*. Ed. Thomas Waugh. Metuchen, NJ: Scarecrow, 1984. 344–383. Print.
Bustamante, Jorge A. "Immigrants' Vulnerability as Subjects of Human Rights." *International Migration Review* 36.2 (Summer 2002): 333–354. Print.
Cole, Wendy. "People Who Matter: Elvira Arellano." *Time,* 25 Dec. 2006. Web. 10 May 2014.
"Crossing: A Journey of Grave Perils." *NPR World News,* 11 Sept. 2011. Web. 10 Feb. 2015.
De nadie. Dir. Tin Dirdamal. Producciones Tranvía, 2006. Film.
Desierto. Dir. Jonás Cuarón. Esperanto Kino, Itaca Films, CG Cinema, 2015. Film.
Engler, Paul. "The US Immigrant Rights Movement (2004-ongoing)." International Center on Nonviolent Conflict, April 2009. Web. 17 May 2014.
Esteva, Gustavo, and Madhu S. Prakash. *Grassroots Postmodernism: Remaking the Soil of Cultures*. London: Zed Books, 1998. Print.
Golash-Boza, Tanya Maria. *Immigration Nation: Raids, Detentions, and Deportations in Post 9/11 America*. Boulder, CO: Paradigm, 2011. Print.
Gómez, Eirinet. "Plan Frontera Sur: Un nuevo flagelo para los migrantes." *e-veracruz.com*, 14 Feb. 2015. Web. 1 March 2015.
Guillermoprieto, Alma. *72migrantes.com*, Fall 2011. Web. 27 Feb. 2017.
Hill, Selena. "Immigration Reform News: Activist Elvira Arellano Returns to Chicago Church after Being Deported in 2007." *Latino Post,* 24 March 2014. Web. 28 April 2015.
Hondagneu-Sotelo, Pierrette, and Ernestine Avila. "'I'm Here, but I'm There': The Meanings of Latina Transnational Motherhood." *Women and Migration in the U.S.-Mexico Borderlands. A Reader*. Ed. Denise A. Segura and Patricia Zavella. Durham, NC: Duke UP, 2007. 388–412. Print.
Isacson, Adam, Maureen Meyer, and Hannah Smith. "El control aumentado en la frontera sur de México: Una actualización sobre la seguridad, la migración y el apoyo de EE.UU." WOLA, Nov. 2015. Web. 27 Feb. 2017.
Khasnabish, Alex. *Zapatismo beyond Borders. New Imaginations of Political Possibility*. Toronto: U of Toronto P, 2008. Print.

Lesage, Julia. "Women's Fragmented Consciousness in Feminist Experimental Autobiographical Video." *Feminism and Documentary.* Ed. Diane Waldman and Janet Walker. Minneapolis: U of Minnesota P, 1999. 309–337. Print.

Levinas, Emmanuel. *Ethics and Infinity: Conversations with Philippe Nemo.* Trans. Richard A Cohen. Pittsburgh, PA: Duquesne UP, 1985. Print.

Los invisibles. Dir. Marc Silver and Gael García Bernal. Amnesty International, 2010. Online film.

Ludmer, Josefina. "Territorios del presente. En la isla urbana." *Pensamiento de los confines* 15 (2003): 103–110. Print.

Maldonado-Torres, Nelson. "On the Coloniality of Being: Contributions to the Development of a Concept." *Cultural Studies* 21.2–3 (March/May 2007): 240–270. Web. 15 Jan. 2015.

María en tierra de nadie. Dir. Marcela Zamora. Women Make Movies, 2010. Film.

Martínez, Oscar. *The Beast: Riding the Rails and Dodging Narcos on the Migrant Trail.* London: Verso, 2014. Print.

———. *Los migrantes que no importan.* Barcelona: Icaria, 2010. Print.

Mignolo, Walter. "I Am Where I Think: Remapping the Order of Knowing." *The Creolization of Theory.* Ed. Françoise Lionnet and Shu-mei Shih. Durham, NC: Duke UP, 2011. 159–192. Print.

———. *Local Histories/Global Designs: Coloniality, Subaltern Knowledges, and Border Thinking.* Princeton, NJ: Princeton UP, 2000. Print.

Molina Ramírez, Tania. "*De nadie.* Documental del paso por México de los migrantes centroamericanos: Retrato de 'los invisibles.'" *La Jornada* 8 Jan. 2006. Web. 28 Feb. 2015.

Morrison, Toni. "Unspeakable Things Unspoken: The Afro-American Perspective in American Literature." *Michigan Quarterly Review* 28.1 (1989): 1–34. Print.

Nail, Thomas. *The Figure of the Migrant.* Stanford, CA: Stanford UP, 2015. Print.

Nazario, Sonia. *Enrique's Journey. The Story of a Boy's Dangerous Odyssey to Reunite with His Mother.* New York: Random House, 2006. Print.

Noriega, Chon. "Talking Heads, Body Politic: The Plural Self of Chicano Experimental Video." *Resolutions.* Ed. Michael Renov and Erika Suderburg. Minneapolis: U of Minnesota P, 1996. 207–228. Print.

"Park City '06. Tin Dirdamal: 'I Became a Filmmaker by Accident.'" *Indiwire,* 21 Jan. 2006. Web. 16 Feb. 2015.

Rodríguez, Ileana. *Liberalism at Its Limits: Crime and Terror in the Latin American Cultural Text.* Pittsburgh: U of Pittsburgh P, 2009. Print.

Sommer, Doris. *Proceed with Caution, When Engaged by Minority Writing in the Americas.* Cambridge, MA: Harvard UP, 1999. Print.

Sørensen, Ninna Nyberg. "Central American Migration, Remittances, and Transnational Development." *Handbook of Central American Governance.* Ed. Diego Sánchez-Ancochea and Salvador Martí i Puig. New York: Routledge, 2013. 45–58. Print.

Valencia, Sayak. *Capitalismo gore*. Barcelona: Melusina, 2010. Print.
Walker, Janet, and Diane Waldman. Introduction. *Feminism and Documentary*. Ed. Diane Waldman and Janet Walker. Minneapolis: U of Minnesota P, 1999. 1–35. Print.
Who Is Dayani Cristal? Dir. Marc Silver and Gael García Bernal. Pulse Films, 2013. Film.
Zamudio, María Inés. "Elvira Arellano: From Undocumented Immigrant to International Activist." *Chicago Reporter*, 16 Jan. 2014. Web. 17 May 2014.

(RE)MEMBERING PAST AND PRESENT LIVES

5

(Re)Membering the Pedro Pan Children's Exodus in Documentary Film

ADA ORTÚZAR-YOUNG

> The ones who go away are always the children,
> their fingers fastened to the huge suitcases
> where mothers hide dreams and horror.
> On the platforms and in the airports
> they take note of everything
> and it is as if they were saying, "Where do we go today?"
> It is the children who always go away.
> They leave behind bits of string, nervous, invisible.
> At night, insistent, they tug at our skin,
> but they always go away, somersaulting, singing
> to each other—some leave weeping—
> until not even a father is able to hear them.
> —Heberto Padilla, "The Ones Who Go Away
>   Are Always the Children"

> It lay in my memory
> —like, in a sealed coffer,
> a precious stone.
> It glittered within there, hidden,
> illuminating the opaque face of things.
>   —Josie Crespo, "A Land for One Who Returns"

Yo recuerdo muy poco . . . yo recuerdo que eran unos tiempos de mucho. . . .
          De que se hablaba mucho en voz bajita
   (I remember very little . . . I remember these were times of much. . . .
          When everyone spoke in a very low voice)
          Vivian Otero, in *Del otro lado del cristal*

In 1990 Yvonne M. Conde stood in disbelief as she read page 122 in Joan Didion's *Miami*; the words glared defiantly at her. "How could over 14,000 children be sent alone by parents or guardians still living in Cuba? How could there have been such a mammoth exodus of Cuban children, and I had never heard of it?" She knew that at age 10 her parents had sent her to the United States alone, and she asked, "Did that mean that I was part of that exodus?" (Conde xii). On March 9, 1962, an article that appeared in the *Miami Herald* spoke of an "underground railway in the sky," a semiclandestine program that was secretly transporting Cuban children alone from Havana to Miami (Torres 8). It is widely believed that still today there are many people who are unaware that they were part of this program. The exodus would later be known as Operation Pedro Pan, after the literary figure created by James M. Barrie, about a homeless boy who could fly and who never grew up. The operation lasted 22 months, from December 26, 1960, to October 23, 1962, when flights were abruptly and indefinitely stopped after the missile crisis. At least 14,048 Cuban children between the ages of 2 and 16 left the island under the auspices of this program. Approximately half of those children were received by family members or friends upon arriving in Miami. The others were cared for by the Miami Catholic Welfare Bureau (Catholic Charities) and housed in temporary refugee camps created for that purpose before being relocated to more than 100 cities in 30 states and placed in boarding schools, foster homes, or orphanages (Abreu 82).

Unlike the character of the British fairy tale, the Pedro Pan children did grow up. Since the 1990s there has been an effort by historians and scholars, but particularly by those who were sent, to "re-member"—in the sense of recalling but also putting together, making whole—their story. The three documentaries that are the focus of this chapter are a small yet significant part of the by-now extensive academic studies, works of fiction, exhibits of photographs and memorabilia, blogs, and presentations that have been made public on the subject. *The Lost Apple* was produced in 1962 by the U.S. Information Agency, directed by David Susskind, and narrated by Mexican actor Ricardo Montalbán. *Del otro lado del cristal* (From the other side of the glass), filmed in the United States and Puerto Rico, was directed by Guillermo Centeno, Marina Ochoa, Manuel Pérez, and Mercedes Arce and produced in 1995 by the Instituto Cubano de Arte e Industria Cinematográficos (ICAIC). And *Operation Peter Pan: Flying back to Cuba*—better known in Spanish as *Cerrando el círculo* (Closing the circle)—was directed by Estela Bravo and produced in 2011 by

Bravo Films. Although filmed at very different historical moments, the three documentaries share, above all, the experiences of the Pedro Pan children over time. Overall, they complement each other, presenting various aspects of the operation and documenting the events and changes in Cuba at the outset of the Cuban Revolution that gave impetus to the exodus. Each one adds new pieces to the puzzle and sheds light on the architects of the program, on who was sent, and on reasons for doing so. Footage and images from *The Lost Apple*, a foundational Pedro Pan documentary, reappear at key moments in the other two films, giving these images an iconic character and acknowledging the cumulative although independent efforts of a recovery project that has helped elucidate this part of the larger Cuban diaspora.

The Lost Apple documents daily life in the Florida City refugee camp, one of the facilities set up by the Miami Catholic Welfare Bureau under the leadership of a young Irish priest named Bryan O. Walsh, to house the children arriving alone and without family or friends in the United States. The camera follows closely the children's daily activities but focuses on an eight-year-old boy named Roberto from the time he is brought to the camp carrying all his possessions in a small suitcase. Upon arriving to the processing center of the children's camp, this disoriented child is processed by employees, also Cuban, who speak to him in Spanish in reassuring voices and take the role of temporary house parents in the camp until foster parents are found for the children. Roberto is of humble origins. His father is a bricklayer; his mother does the washing for other people. The camera follows him at times, finds him often alone and sometimes rubbing his eyes at night as he tries to fall asleep. Other children also come under the camera's eye: Gladys, a well-adjusted 12-year-old who wants to be placed in the state of Washington, where she has friends, and more poignant characters such as Serafina, almost five, always seen holding a big doll, who "almost never smiles." A small child tries to drink from a water fountain but cannot reach it, emphasizing his helplessness and tender age. The facilities are austere, but life goes on. There are numerous random images of camp life such as a large dining hall full to capacity with children. Some, too small to eat by themselves, are helped by older children. They are images of helplessness but also of adaptability and survival. They are all well dressed and well fed, with attentive Spanish-speaking personnel tending to their needs. The refugees (as they are often called) are taught about Halloween, learn English, and play ball. A talent night offers some relief as they sing Cuban prerevolutionary patriotic songs. Father Cistierna ("a refugee too"), director of the camp, addresses the children during this event: "You are a constant reminder that there is something very wrong in the world. I would like you to be boys and girls with a great sense of responsibility, because the new society, a new world, is waiting for you to rebuild your homeland. That new world can only be built with new men. Cuba is waiting for you." Their activities are occasionally interrupted by phone calls from their families. Every day someone arrives, others depart. It is a transitory place where children get ready to go somewhere else more permanent but always keep in mind that Cuba will soon be free and they will return to their homeland. Together, these images convey a powerful message of the plight of the children.

While *The Lost Apple* revolves around the children, they seldom speak. It relies on two effective filmic techniques to convey voice: an anonymous surrogate, a voice-of-God commentator, whom we hear but do not see, who also translates from Spanish and inserts his own commentaries; and the popular Hispanic nursery rhyme "Señora Santana," which is heard throughout the documentary, particularly at key moments to accentuate the film's message of the loss of home and to guide the viewer to the desired interpretation. The voice of Ricardo Montalbán dominates the film from beginning to end. According to Bill Nichols, this surrogate voice "arose in the 1930's as a convenient way to describe a situation or problem, present an argument, propose a solution, and sometimes evoke a poetic tone or mood" (59). Montalbán speaks English with a heavy Spanish accent that lends authenticity to his role. He becomes an intermediary and speaks on the children's behalf. His tone of voice is soft and paternalistic, almost soothing, as if he wanted a child to understand what he is saying, but he is not speaking to them. His function is larger than that. He advocates for the children and explains their situation to a larger audience who is not familiar with it. The children need temporary families until the political situation changes in Cuba, and they hope to be placed in good American homes or in boarding schools. Gladys comes to the office to find out if she has been placed. "Not at this time," she is told. Montalbán's words assume their messianic tone with biblical allusions: "I was hungry and you fed me. I was thirsty and you gave me a drink, I was a stranger, and you took me in" (Matthew 25:35–40). This message is clearly directed to a non-Cuban audience and prospective American foster parents.

The other, equally powerful voice is provided by the song "Señora Santana." This popular lullaby, widely known throughout Latin America, makes reference to a boy crying after losing an apple. The child is offered another one, or even two, but he wants his. Only the one he lost will satisfy him. The lyrics of the song are not placed randomly, but strategically, such as the time when Gladys finds a foster home and departs the camp. Montalbán's voice asserts, "Sometimes it takes a long time to find the lost apple." In the meantime Gladys will have to accept another one.

The loss of home and family, the central theme of *The Lost Apple*, continues to portray the Pedro Pan child even today. On the 50th anniversary of the children's exodus, in 2012, a sculpture titled *The Tower of Snow* was inaugurated in front of Freedom Tower in downtown Miami. For many years this building housed the Cuban Refugee Center, the first stop where the new arrivals received assistance. It is now a museum that includes an exhibit of Pedro Pan memorabilia. The 11-foot-tall bronze sculpture depicts a boy on crutches bending over and carrying a house on his back. The young, squalid figure seems overwhelmed by the weight as he tries to move forward. The sculpture reminds the museumgoer of Roberto's arrival to the Florida City camp, carrying his suitcase, his house. Significantly, the image of Roberto carrying his suitcase appears in numerous representations of the Pedro Pan children, among them the documentaries *Del otro lado del cristal* and *Operation Peter Pan: Flying back to Cuba*. The two films rely largely on interviews of a few adults who were Pedro Pan children. After their three or four decades of silence, they have become successful professionals and have families of their own. Often they speak to the camera sitting comfortably in well-appointed living areas or in gardens.

"The other side of the glass" in the documentary title *Del otro lado del cristal* refers to the enclosed room at Havana airport, nicknamed the *pecera* (fishbowl) at the time, where those who had been cleared waited to board their flights. The small room is a site of trauma where the separation from family becomes real for the first time. Those departing could see those staying, but they could not hear each other. Vivian recalls the confusing moment: "Yo me iba embullada" (I was excited about leaving), but everyone in her family was crying. Lourdes describes the other side of the *pecera* as being almost surreal, while Rosa remembers the gestures and the anguish it caused since they could not hear each other.

The *pecera* returns again as a site of rupture in the film *Flying back to Cuba* and in some diasporic Cuban fiction. At the beginning of the film a voice announces that separation is the topic of the documentary, narrated by eight Cuban women. The simple statement conceals the complexity of the situation and what the viewer will encounter in the film. Among the three documentaries in this study, *Del otro lado del cristal* presents the most comprehensive picture of this historical moment at the height of the Cold War and the transformations that were taking place in the country as a result of the Cuban Revolution. They are private stories resulting from public events in which humans became pawns of larger circumstances they could not control.

Del otro lado del cristal begins with a hesitant statement by Rosa Irigoyen, as if she were searching back in her memory: "Bueno . . . que mi mamá tenía un miedo, ella tenía un miedo" (Well . . . my mother was so afraid, she was so afraid). It sums up what families felt at the moment and ultimately what led them to send their children alone to the United States. The documentary does not follow a strict lineal storyline in the reconstruction of those events that families feared so much. Like memory itself, which is often triggered by random objects or thoughts, a gradual reconstruction of history and the story of separation takes place. In order to do so, the film relies extensively on found footage from public newsreels placed strategically to corroborate the connection between the private and the public. Immediately following Rosa's words that open the film, the viewer is presented with a series of snapshots—in newsreel fashion and with an unseen commentator—of events dating from December 1960 to the October 1962 missile crisis—the time coinciding with the exodus. The opening resembles a television newscast by an emotionless reporter, thus lending authority and objectivity to what is presented as news events. It states that parents have authorized the departure of their children with special visas granted by the U.S. government. The operation has been carried out by Catholic organizations in both countries with the support of counterrevolutionary groups in Cuba that have printed for clandestine distribution a false law stating that the Cuban government will take away the parental authority (*patria potestad*) from parents and give it to the state.

The opening presents video clips of major changes taking place as a result of the revolution affecting children, such as the 1961 literacy campaign in which the state sent 100,000 adolescents to live in the countryside to teach peasants to read and write. And it shows images of the 1962 October crisis that brought the world to the verge of nuclear war and abruptly stopped the operation. The series of events is immediately followed by the introduction of eight Cuban women who do not react to this introduction. At this point the story turns personal, and the eight women speak to the camera. Nichols reminds us that documentary film can speak to us through its composition of shots, use of images, edits, and cuts and how these are juxtaposed, all of which serve to support its message (Nichols 67, 72). As such, *Del otro lado del cristal* introduces different voices. The Pedro Pan story does not take place in a vacuum; the historical and the very personal and subjective face each other, as the sequence of events in the introduction makes evident.

The introductory newscast montage is followed by the recollections of the eight women, each presenting memory fragments consisting of brief comments about the rapidly evolving conditions on the island as motivating factors for their parents' decision. Their comments are accentuated by brief quotes on the screen that sum up a few key words by one of the speakers: "La nube que nos envolvió" (The cloud that surrounded us) are Rosa's words. Ileana Fuentes then explains, "What is coming is communism, the state control over young generations, depriving parents of authority at home, the control of schools by the state." Ileana comments that when the government declared itself Marxist-Leninist, everyone panicked. Others point to the implementation of a socialist state and abolition of private property, such as the exchange of money, when bank accounts were confiscated, leaving families with only 200 Cuban pesos each. These are events that intensified fear and eroded people's trust in the government. The women's statements throughout the film are interrupted by short video clips such as of Fidel Castro addressing crowds, the rapid militarization of Cuba with tanks and soldiers parading in the streets, air attacks during the failed Bay of Pigs invasion in 1961, and prisoners taken during that invasion. These events lead up to the actual moment of separation from the family at the *pecera* in Havana's airport and the beginning of a new life. Historical and personal memories are reconstructed with small pieces of information.

Titles, many hand-written, distinguish segments of the documentary; one says, "¡y vi dónde estaba Minnesota!" (and I saw where Minnesota was!). The segment titles signal the intervention of the filmmaker to sort out and organize the random recalling of events by the eight women and direct the viewer's attention to what the filmmaker considers important. Memories of the first experiences in the camps show the fear of the unknown and the unexpected and how the children's lives become unsettled. The women recall having been driven at night on a dark road leading to the camp, the conglomeration of girls they did not know, some experiencing drastic reactions at the surroundings and more so upon learning that they would be sent to orphanages in distant places such as Minnesota. The segment concludes with an image of the Statue of Liberty with the words "en la torre hay un fantasma" (in the tower there is a ghost). There are other stories of disappointment, accentuated by video clips of a fast-moving subway train or images of bridges as desired connections that do not take place or of water marking the separation of children, including brothers and sisters. Eventually the segment title "todo lo borró el agua" (the water wiped out everything)—again, taken from a phrase from one of the women—signals that as time goes by memories fade away. The eventual reunion of children and parents proved difficult. Over time, children changed, and the younger ones learned English and found it difficult to communicate with their parents when they were reunited years later. Some of the women expressed their desire to return to Cuba to visit, and a few had done so. For others, it would be unthinkable to return to the island with the Castro government still in power.

The film concludes with a display of photos and memorabilia of Pedro Pan children. Marianne Hirsch reminds us of their importance: "In lives shaped by exile, emigration and relocation, such as my family's, where relatives were dispersed and relationships shattered, photographs provide even more than usual some illusion of continuity over time and space" (xi). The photographs maintain a unique relation to the exiles since "the referent is both present (implied in the photographs) and absent (it has been there but is not there now" (5). They tell a story of family separation and are a tangible vestige of a bygone past.

Operation Peter Pan: Flying back to Cuba begins with very personal stories—the desire of six Pedro Pan adults to bring closure to their journeys by returning to Cuba as a group. Some of these Pedro Pans had already made the trip back on their own. This documentary is framed in much the same way as the other two. The first scene shows a clip from *The Lost Apple* of Roberto arriving at the Florida City camp carrying his small suitcase. As with *Del otro lado del cristal*, too, *Flying back to Cuba* presents photographs and memorabilia at various places. In these ways a connection and a continuity are established among the three films. The six Pedro Pan adults, in attractive homes or garden surroundings, introduce themselves to the camera. This is a sharp visual contrast to the austerity and temporality conveyed by the Florida City camp. One of the women, Flora, had also participated in *Del otro lado del cristal*, and another, Candi, sang a patriotic song in the talent show of *The Lost Apple*. Like *Del otro lado del cristal*, the film goes beyond the very personal stories of the six participants and expands into the operation as a historical event. It presents interviews with key figures who conceived and carried out the transport of the children as well as others who have opinions about it. They all provide their assessments, in retrospect, of the operation, often expressing starkly conflicting views. There is a noticeable difference between the Pedro Pans who seem to express themselves in short bits and at times very emotionally but freely and spontaneously and the other speakers who appear to be answering questions posed by a person whom, with few exceptions, the audience does not see or hear. These dissonant voices introduce two different discourses: on the one hand, their very personal experiences, and on the other, a series of debatable and ideological viewpoints. Nonetheless, slowly, the story is woven together. *Operation Peter Pan: Flying back to Cuba* can be broadly divided into three parts: the recollections of six Pedro Pan adults, narrated in either Spanish or English, and some recorded around 10 years prior to the releasing of the documentary; interviews with leaders who organized or participated in the exodus and others who claim to have known about it at the time; and the return of five Pedro Pans to Cuba, thus "closing the circle." The sixth one, Elly Chovel, had passed away by the time the film was made.

Elly Chovel, the first person to be presented and founder of the Operation Pedro Pan Group, Inc., spent many years searching for and establishing communication among its members. She sums up what they all experienced: "It is very unusual for Cuban children, or any child in the world, to leave their family and their land and grow up separated from everything that was familiar to them, and this is what happened not just to my sister and I, but to 14,000 Cuban children. It happened in a short period of time. It was 22 months." In fact, according to Ressler et al., "Unaccompanied children have existed in virtually every past war, famine, refugee situation, and natural disaster" (3). For example, at one point during the 1936 Spanish Civil War "the number of orphaned and abandoned children was reported to be 90,000," although the total number of children separated from their parents remained unknown (Ressler et al. 10). Conde reports that in 1937, parents hastily evacuated more than 20,000 Basque children in search of safe heavens in several European countries and Mexico (xi).

Another notable program, Kindertransport (German, for children's transport) was internationally organized during the nine months prior to World War II in an effort to help Jewish parents send their children to safety in fear of the increasing hostility and persecution in territories dominated by the Nazis. By the end of the war nearly 10,000 children had been sent to the United Kingdom. They were placed in British foster homes and schools, and in many cases they were the only members of their families who survived the Holocaust. As would happen with the Pedro Pan children, many of the surviving children from the Holocaust became prominent figures. In addition to the extensive historical and scholarly documentation of their exodus, several documentary films have been made on the subject. Among them is *My Knees Were Jumping: Remembering the Kindertransports*, released in 1996 and directed by Melissa Hacker, the daughter of a Kindertransport child. *Into the Arms of Strangers: Stories of the Kindertransport*, directed by Mark Jonathan Harris and released in 2001, was produced by Deborah Oppenheimer, also a daughter of a Kindertransport child. *The Children Who Cheated the Nazis* (2000) is a British documentary directed by Sue Read and produced by Jim Goulding. It is narrated by Richard Attenborough, whose parents had responded to the appeal of the Jewish families by taking two girls into their family. More recently, at the end of the Vietnam War, more than 10,000 orphaned children were hastily evacuated on April 3–26, 1975, as Saigon was falling under the communists. Under Operation Babylift, as it was known, the infants and children were received by the United States, Canada, Australia, and France. Their stories have been widely documented in websites, films, and scholarly writings as well as in works of fiction.

After Chovel's brief introduction, *Operation Peter Pan: Flying back to Cuba* presents the voices of other Pedro Pan children. Silvia Wilhem explains, "It was a program sponsored by the Catholic Church and the U.S. State Department to get children out of Cuba as soon as possible. It was all very secret. We couldn't tell anyone." Flora elaborates, "My parents felt that the Cuban Revolution was not going to last . . . that we would come to the United States and we would receive an English-speaking education, and we would return to Cuba." Their comments and those of the other Pedro Pans are punctuated with photos of visa waivers that allowed them to enter the United States, flight attendants carrying in their arms small children, and passports of some of the children. According to Chovel, the first to leave were the oldest children of wealthy families, then children of any age from the middle class, and finally the very small ones. The comments made by the six participants indicate that some had good experiences and some did not. They recall the distress caused by the separation of siblings. Silvia Wilhem expresses the dismay that she, a member of a distinguished Cuban family and very pampered, felt when she was sent alone to an orphanage in Buffalo, New York. Ed Canler, who was sent to a private boarding school, acknowledges that it was a very good educational environment. Two of them had bad experiences; Candi Sosa recalls being molested by her foster father, and Alex López reports abuses by priests who were trusted with his care. The operation was truncated by the Cuban missile crisis, making the separation indefinite, something that no one had anticipated. When parents were eventually reunited with their children, the time that passed had transformed some of them and eroded their familial bonds; among the smallest children, as they learned English their Spanish deteriorated and impeded communicating with their parents. Candi Sosa recalls the wonderful feeling of their reunion in a new house when her parents came to the United States and hoping that their relationship would pick up where they had left off. Not so. She soon realized that they had changed, and so had she. Alex, who had to wait five years to be reunited with his parents, had reached adulthood and felt a sense of independence.

Given the secrecy with which this underground transport was conceived and carried out, it has given way to a broad spectrum of myths and speculations, often tinted with ideological controversies, as the second part of the documentary makes evident. One important part of *Flying back to Cuba* is the voice accorded to the key architects of the operation: Father (later Monsignor) Bryan O. Walsh, James Baker, Penny Powers, "Mongo" and Polita Grau, and some of their closest associates. The embodiment of these figures in images and their own words complements the extensive research and documentation about their roles found in many studies on the Pedro Pan exodus. The filmmaker assumes the viewer already has this background knowledge, thus creating a vacuum of information for those unaware of the various people's roles that is crucial to judging the key issues debated. Walsh became aware of the plight of unaccompanied minors when in November 1960 a homeless 15-year-old boy named Pedro was brought to the Catholic Welfare Bureau because his destitute relatives could not provide for him. Realizing that there would be more youngsters like this one and anticipating the needs presented by the increasing flow of Cuban refugees in Miami (by that time around 60,000), Walsh brought the situation to the attention of a representative of President Eisenhower's administration, in search of funding. On December 12, 1960, Walsh and James Baker, headmaster of the prestigious Ruston Academy, an American school still functioning in Havana at the time, met at the request of students' parents to discuss how they could help secure papers and finances to assist Cuban children whose parents desired to send them to the United States. Upon returning to Havana, Baker created an underground network, and the operation was born. The first Pedro Pan children arrived on December 26, 1960 ("Cuban Children's Exodus").

One way to define documentaries, Nichols asserts, is that they "are what the organizations and institutions that produce them make" (16). Documentaries are not a reproduction of reality but a representation of the world they occupy, based on documents. Nichols finds that documentaries stand for a particular view and "the question of whose story is it leaves considerable room for ambiguity" (13). In *Flying back to Cuba,* Bravo attempts to shape how the viewer regards the children's exodus. An important component is the center portion of the documentary, which is devoted to putting forward the notion that it was a program of the CIA with the intention to destabilize the Cuban regime. Prominent pro-Castro individuals speak in the film in favor of the regime and against the children's exodus, among them Eusebio Leal, who at the time was the Havana city historian and who has held numerous important positions in the Communist Party. To him, this operation is a dark page of history. Francisco Aruca of the Radio Progreso station in Miami declares his pro-Castro affiliation and says there was a plan drawn to convince Cuban parents that the government was going to take away their parental rights and would have control over the children's education. Other interviewees report on rumors of such a law being circulated, and one testifies about seeing a draft signed on August 31, 1961. Given that the documentary relies on a series of interviews, the viewer cannot ascertain whether this is the only origin story explored by the documentary or whether the director, through scripting and structuring this information, selected them in order to shape the historical creation of the Pedro Pan exodus.

The issue of possible CIA involvement is presented to Walsh on several occasions. The viewer can hear how the interviewer—who is not seen or heard in other parts of the documentary but is heard at this time—insists on directing the conversation to this topic and determining the extent of CIA involvement. Walsh replies, "First of all, if the CIA didn't know what we were doing, they were negligent. It was their job to know. I have no evidence whatsoever, and never had, of a direct CIA involvement." The interviewer presses further as to whether false visas were used, and Walsh replies they were not false. He says a "visa waiver" meant that no visa was required. Visas had been waived for all children up to 16 years of age. They simply used a photocopy and filled it out with the names, birth dates, and other information about the children. Walsh reaffirms his commitment and support of the operation: "I feel a tremendous respect for parents who exercise their human right in giving them the opportunity to make that decision. It was their decision."

Once a documentary is released it becomes part of a wider dialogue. New voices join the discussion. One such debate took placed at the screening of *Flying back to Cuba* in San Pedro, California, on June, 27, 2011. Some Pedro Pans were in attendance and objected to the director, Estela Bravo, not presenting an accurate picture of the reasons for the Pedro Pan exodus. Others pointed to the CIA and the false claims of a *patria potestad* law—which the film dated as August 31, 1961, after the operation had been functioning for more than eight months—as what motivated the parents to send their children alone. The Pedro Pans in attendance tried to refute Bravo's interpretation and called the film a "pseudodocumentary" during the question and answer period that followed the screening. They were not allowed to do so. The brief exchange was recorded by the Pedro Pans, as Bravo responded, "You have your opinions. Everybody has different opinions. I have the right to make my film." As seen in the exchange, Bravo's reply corroborates Nichols's assertion that representations in documentaries reflect the people who make them. A longtime resident of Cuba, Bravo's sympathy for the Cuban Revolution is widely known. Her militant prorevolutionary ideology is reflected in documentary films on Cuba and Fidel Castro as well as on other leftist leaders and subjects and numerous similar causes. As Bravo affirms in response to the Pedro Pans, *Flying back to Cuba* reflects her opinions, and this is achieved through the selection of interviewees. Furthermore, in several scenes viewers may have the suspicion that the interviewer is manipulating the questions and the content of the documentary to guide them to her desired interpretation of the operation.

As a result of the discussion after the screening and to contest Bravo's personal opinions, the group created its own short documentary, *Pedro Pan of California Responds to Estela Bravo's Documentary*. Besides refuting Bravo's manipulation of history, what triggered the exodus, in the view of the group, was the creation of Committees for the Defense of the Revolution (block organizations), implementation of a *ficha escolar* (Ficha Escolar Acumulativa, Accumulative Student Index established in December 1960 to collect family data), closing of the schools, and the government's encouragement for children to spy on their parents. The early stages of the revolution as a battleground for the minds of children have been researched and documented by Anita Casavantes Bradford:

> Between 1960 and 1961, childhood emerged as one of the primary sites of struggle in which the forces of the Revolution and an emerging Counter-revolution battled to determine Cuba's destiny. As the Castro government implemented increasingly radical economic and social policies, officials and the state-sponsored media relied heavily on representations of children to explain the Revolution's sharp turn to the left.... At the same time, Fidel Castro sought to consolidate his position as supreme leader and father of the Cuban nation by operating new understandings and practices of childhood, establishing exclusive government control over the education and ideological formation of children. (92)

Other signs by the government of changes to come were the declaration of 1961 as the Year of Education and the government's decision after the failed Bay of Pigs invasion to exile priests and nuns, who had been heavily involved in the many private Catholic schools in the country (Torres 108, 118).

Operation Peter Pan: Flying back to Cuba allows other prominent witnesses to address this moment in history. According to Wayne Smith, a former U.S. diplomat in Cuba, "In 1960 you had a growing conflict between the Catholic Church and the Cuban government, and so, especially parents who were devoutly Catholic and close to the church, were very concerned and afraid that their children would be sent to atheist schools or the Soviet Union." The main actors of the operation discuss their involvement. Baker reports spending 12 to 15 hours a day at the Miami airport helping Walsh receive the children; they never knew exactly how many would arrive or when.

Key parts of the Havana operation also come to light as a result of these interviews. Liaison figures in Miami were Penny Powers, a British English teacher in Cuba, and anti-Castro leaders Mongo Grau and Polita Grau, brother and sister of former Cuban President Ramón Grau San Martín. Both spent years in prison for their role in the children's program and are considered martyrs by the exile community. Penny Powers, a former Baker employee, worked at the British embassy and had assisted during World War II in the Kindertransport evacuation of Jewish children from Germany (Torres 71). Albertina O'Farrill, who was also part of the underground group in Havana distributing visa waivers, discusses how the waivers were prepared at the Graus' home and taken to cooperating embassies before they were distributed to the children. After the failed Bay of Pigs invasion, the demand for children's visas skyrocketed. O'Farrill views the operation favorably: "I am happy I was part of Operation Peter Pan. It was one of the best operations in the world. All those children we saved have shown us that our sacrifices were worth it."

The second part shows a collection of photographs and found footage from the children's camp in *The Lost Apple*, often the same images that appear in *Del otro lado del cristal*. It concludes with Candi Sosa singing at the talent show in the camp, with her voice projecting over that of Montalbán's. The third and final part of *Flying back to Cuba* centers on the return of five Pedro Pans to Cuba. Reactions vary. Ed Canler comments on his feelings upon arriving in the Havana airport: "What is a refugee doing in Cuba? . . . So stupid. . . . I'll never get out again. . . . I am not getting off. . . . I am scared to death." Candi and Flora visit their childhood homes to relive their memories. These parts are spontaneous and recounted with nostalgia and heavy hearts. Others seem staged, as the Pedro Pans walk in the Plaza de la Revolución and are handed flowers by children from the theater group La Colmenita. Candi realizes her dream of singing at the Tropicana nightclub. A final event takes place at the Casa de las Américas. Silvia closes the farewell event: "We left Cuba in the early '60s, because of a decision our parents made, thinking this was best for us. Today, the decision to return is ours."

In *Del otro lado del cristal*, too, some of the Pedro Pans try to understand their parents' decisions. Ileana reflects, "At age 46 I understood, and felt compassion for the decision my parents had made." Flora, on the other hand, states, "I feel angry for my parents for having participated in this, but I understand their decision. I don't know what I would have done."

The three documentaries are part of a larger and continuing debate, a collective act of recalling, gathering, and rebuilding. It is widely accepted that 14,048 children participated in this program. Yet, fewer than a dozen of the adult Pedro Pans appear in *Del otro lado del cristal* and *Operation Peter Pan: Flying back to Cuba*. How representative are their voices of the whole group? How and why were they chosen? Conde made extensive efforts to collect names and data but only reached 3 percent of the participants in the program. Why don't other Pedro Pan adults come forward and make their stories public? Some have pointed to the fear of being used for political propaganda. Others have decided to look forward and not to the past, evidence perhaps that they were not adversely affected by the program. Those who speak add new dimensions to popular memory and social history and to rebuilding their stories. They reveal as much as they conceal. The nature of the filmic texts, with their optics supported by the spoken word, constitutes powerful and convincing evidence, even after some of the participants have passed away, as have Father Walsh and Elly Chovel. The participants authenticate their existence. They are engaging and persuasive. Hirsch asserts that in analyzing the family—and she was referring to the traumatic events of the Holocaust—photographs "offer a prism through which to study the postmodern space of cultural memory composed of leftovers, debris, items that are left to be collected and assembled in many ways, to tell a variety of stories, from a variety of often competing perspectives" (13). The *lieux de mémoire* such as the photographs of the Pedro Pan children are being used and reused to negotiate new and sometimes conflicting versions of their stories. Together, however, they are ultimately (perhaps unbeknown to each other) adding new dimensions to their stories, thus remembering—recalling, piecing together, recording—the voices of this story of migration and dispersion.

Works Cited

Abreu, Jean. ¡*No te dejes quitar a tu hijo! Operation Pedro Pan and the Cuban Children's Program*. Diss. Durham, NC: Duke University, 2008. Unpublished.

Bradford, Anita Casavantes. *The Revolution Is for the Children. The Politics of Childhood in Havana and Miami, 1959–1962*. Chapel Hill: U of North Carolina P, 2014. Print.

Conde, Yvonne M. *Operation Pedro Pan. The Untold Exodus of 14,080 Cuban Children*. New York: Routledge, 1999. Print.

Crespo, Josie. "A Land for One Who Returns." Trans. David Frye. Bridges to/from Cuba. 2016. Web. Originally published as "Tierra del que regresa."

"The Cuban Children's Exodus." *Pedro Pan History*. Operation Pedro Pan Group, n.d. Web. 1 June 2016.

Del otro lado del cristal. Dir. Mercedes Arce, Guillermo Centeno, Marina Ochoa, and Manuel Pérez. Instituto de Arte e Industria Cinematográficos, 1995. Film.

Didion, Joan. *Miami*. New York: Simon and Schuster, 1987. Print.

Hirsch, Marianne. *Family Frames: Photography Narrative and Memory*. Harvard UP. 1997. Print.

Into the Arms of Strangers: Stories of the Kindertransport. Dir. Mark Jonathan Harris. Warner Home Video, 2001. Film.

"Kindertransport." Internet Archive, 21 Oct. 2006. Web. 1 March 2017.

The Lost Apple. Dir. Cliff Solway. U.S. Information Agency, 1962. Film.

My Knees Were Jumping: Remembering the Kindertransports. Dir. Melissa Hacker. Docurama, 1996. Film.

Nichols, Bill. *Introduction to Documentary.* 2nd ed. Bloomington: Indiana UP, 2010. Print.

"Operation Babylift." Vietnam Babylift. Web. 1 March 2017.

Operation Peter Pan: Flying back to Cuba. Dir. Estela Bravo. Bravo Films. 2010. Film.

Padilla, Heberto. *The Fountain, A House of Stone.* Trans. Alexander Coleman and Alastair Reid. New York: Farrar, Straus & Giroux, 1991. Print.

Pedro Pan of California Responds to Estela Bravo's Documentary. YouTube. 29 June 2011. Web. 1 June 2016.

Ressler, Everet M., Neil Boothby, and Daniel J. Steinbock. *Unaccompanied Children: Care and Protection in Wars, Natural Disasters, and Refugee Movements.* New York: Oxford UP, 1988. Print.

The Children Who Cheated the Nazis. Dir. Sue Read. FilmRise, 2000. Film.

Torres, María de los Ángeles. The Lost Apple: *Operation Pedro Pan, Cuban Children in the U.S., and the Promise of a Better Future.* Boston: Beacon, 2003. Print.

Triay, Victor Andres. *Fleeing Castro. Operation Pedro Pan and the Cuban Children's Program.* Gainesville: UP of Florida, 1998. Print.

Migration, Exile, and Identities in *Abuelos*, by Carla Valencia Dávila

MANUEL F. MEDINA

Most documentaries on immigration and Latin American diasporas are split between migration to either the United States or Europe, mainly Italy and Spain. The former emigrate from Central America and Mexico, the latter from Peru and Ecuador. In Ecuador the list includes documentaries such as *Problemas personales* (Personal problems, 2002),[1] directed by Lisandra Rivera and Manolo Fernández; *Pasaje de ida* (One-way ticket, 2003), from the director Rogelio Gordon; *Bienvenido a tu familia* (Welcome to your family, 2009), by Diego Ortuño; *Abuelos* (Grandfathers, 2010), by director Carla Valencia Dávila; *La Churona* (*The Migrant Virgin*, 2010), by María Cristina Carrillo Espinosa; *Vengo volviendo* (*Here and There*, 2015), by Gabriel Paéz Hernández and Isabel Rodas León; and *Prometeo deportado* (Prometheus deported, 2011), directed by Fernando Mieles. I chose *Abuelos*, the 2010 documentary by Ecuadorian filmmaker Carla Valencia Dávila, because it differs from most of the other works that I studied in its approach to immigration. Rather than emphasizing the experience of traveling to another country and the subsequent cultural adaptation or assimilation process, *Abuelos* turns the camera onto the daughter of immigrants who searches for her heritage and identity by exploring her roots.

Carla Valencia Dávila fits the classic definition of a daughter of the diaspora because her father left his native land of Chile due to the unsafe and unstable political conditions there and decided to settle in Ecuador, his wife's homeland. In the context of *Abuelos*, immigration relates closely to exile and its consequences for the future of those forced to abandon their home countries and seek asylum elsewhere. In "Reflections on Exile," Edward Said elaborates on the horrors of this type of immigration, comparing it to the metaphorical death of the individual:

> Is it not true that the views of exile in literature and, moreover, in religion obscure what is truly horrendous: that exile is irremediably secular and unbearably historical; that it is produced by human beings for other human beings; and that, like death but without death's ultimate mercy, it has torn millions of people from the nourishment of tradition, family and geography? (140)

Exile occurs not only because of economic conditions for parents seeking a better life for the family but also because people fear for their lives and must leave their homelands. Exiles face the choice of staying and perishing or leaving and surviving but perishing emotionally. They always belong elsewhere, the place where they developed a sense of national identity: "Nationalism is an assertion of belonging in and to a place, a people, a heritage. It affirms the home created by a community of language, culture and customs; and, by so doing, it fends off exile, fights to prevent its ravages" (Said 139).

The promotional material for *Abuelos* bills it as one of the most highly acclaimed Ecuadorian documentaries because, to date, it has received the most awards and recognition in the history of that country's film production. The documentary is Valencia Dávila's first feature-length production; her short film *Emilia* premiered in 2007. Valencia Dávila has emerged as a key player in the prolific Ecuadorian film scene. She has worked as an editor, writer, production designer, and art director as well as film director. *Abuelos* has earned accolades and praise from reviewers and merited invitations to many prestigious festivals (Matamoros). By competing in several contests the director was able to raise the necessary funds to complete the film. This began with the prize for Best Pitch Trailer in the Haciendo Otro Cine contest in Ecuador in 2006. Her proposal won Best Documentary Project in Chile at the 2008 DocSantiago Taller de Presentación de Proyectos. Back in Ecuador, when she released the film she earned the 2008 Premio Nacional de Cine Augusto San Miguel to the best documentary by an Ecuadorian director.

The documentary centers on the story of the protagonist, director, and narrator, Valencia Dávila, who embarks on a search for her grandfathers' stories and her own identity. The film opens with shots ranging from zoom to full as the director experiments with the deep focal points in a very innovative way to display the natural beauty of the Cuenca region of southern Ecuador. She uses this background to narrate the story of her maternal grandfather. The audience, while seeing the skillfully photographed scene, hears about her immediate ancestors. In voice-over Valencia Dávila narrates how her parents met in Moscow, where both pursued their college degrees. Her mother, then 17 years old, had traveled there all the way from Ecuador, and her father, at 19, from Chile. Their romance began when they toured the southern Soviet Union as part of a folkloric dance ensemble. They married while living abroad and planned to return to Chile and start their life together there, but the overthrow of the Salvador Allende government in 1973 changed their plans, and they decided to move to Ecuador instead. The coup in Chile directly affected their lives, and the director set out to make the documentary to explore and come to terms with the fact that she grew up with immediate family living in two different places: one nearby and familiar and the other a distant, distinct, and for a while inaccessible one. Although she mentions it quickly at the beginning of *Abuelos*, Carla Valencia Dávila waits until halfway through the film to show pictures of her parents as they left their respective family nests, traveled to the Soviet Union, met, got married, and had their first child. Instead, she opens the film by concentrating on the characterization of her two grandfathers, Remo Dávila in Ecuador and Juan Valencia in Chile, who emerge as the main protagonists of her story. We learn the result of the experiences of self-exile, exile, diaspora, and migration as perceived by a daughter and granddaughter as she directs a film that explores all these issues.

Through the documentary Valencia Dávila attempts to fill the emotional void she felt about her grandparents, hence the documentary's title, *Abuelos*. The director takes advantage of natural scenarios to frame the mise-en-scène she uses to introduce her grandparents to the viewing audience. A river or brook and the Cuenca region's green landscapes stand out as the dominant focus of the shots as she details and restages the lives of her grandfathers. Long and medium shots of the river flowing are set against a background of plants and trees as the narrator reminisces about her maternal grandfather, Remo, whom she did meet. He lived in a village near Cuenca, a city in the southern Ecuadorian Andes, and later in Quito, the country's capital. She had grown up believing that Remo would one day discover a way for human beings to live forever, as he had promised her.

The film changes location and moves to Chile, and the director-narrator chooses to frame the first scene there against the backdrop of the northern Chilean desert. She pans the camera from left to right displaying extreme long shots of mountains and valleys where it never rains. The sequence accentuates the marked contrast between the two stages: water and lush vegetation contrasting stark desert. Accompanying the views of monochromatic elevations, Valencia Dávila shares the history of her paternal, Chilean grandfather, Juan, who lived in Iquique in the northernmost part of the country, west of the Atacama desert. At the beginning of the military dictatorship that ruled the country after overthrowing Salvador Allende, Juan was sent to a concentration camp and soon after was killed. Valencia Dávila did not have the opportunity to know him; she only learned of him as a teenager when she saw his picture and felt the impact of the resemblance between him and her own father. She says, "De eso no se habló" (We did not talk about that), and Juan's fate remained the family's well-kept secret. Her father chose to live in exile, severing contact with his motherland and in doing so, erased his memory of Chile.

Valencia Dávila continues looking for her grandfather Juan so she can understand him and get closer to that side of the family, whose existence and presence her father Héctor had denied her because he chose to forget his early life and Chile and start over in his adopted nation. But his exiled self had not been able to prevent his daughter from seeking her heritage and discovering the majestic, subversive figure of her *abuelo* Juan.

The viewer may get the sense that the director set out to make the documentary to recover or rescue the unvoiced story of Juan mediated through her own voice-over; as director and narrator she tells the story both visually and orally. She communicates what she discovers about her grandfathers as the film displays well-photographed and dramatically edited shots that place the story spatially on a stage where the audience can also feel the emotion behind her words. The film relies heavily on her narration of the story that belongs to her; she literally lends her voice to the stories. Through her narration her grandfathers acquire the means to express themselves. She even allows her grandfather Juan to speak with his own voice in one of the film's final scenes. The director rescues her grandfather's voice and converts the audio reel into a format that lets her play it in modern devices. She literally serves as a mediator who gives voice to Juan, her grandfather. She wants to discover her *abuelo* using the photograph in which her grandfather Juan resembles her father as a point of departure. We can easily trace the documentary's genesis to this moment in her life, as she hints at the beginning of the film:

I grew up believing in Remo's immortality, and I ran into Juan's death. It divided me in two. While a part of me moved forward and became stronger, the other remained buried in the desert. This grandfather whom I could not meet lived looking at the Pacific Ocean, where my Ecuadorian grandfather's river ends.[2]

The director's search for her identity in her missing grandfather evokes the Lacanian desire defined as the emptiness a child feels when looking in the mirror she realizes that she and her mother represent two separate entities and then spends the rest of her life attempting, in vain, to fill the void. A person never accomplishes that impossible task because the void cannot be filled. Her grandfather Juan's image showing a stark similarity between her father and grandfather could be metaphorically interpreted as the mirror that sets up the chain of events that led to Valencia Dávila's decision to research her genealogical roots and document her search in the film. We could extend the metaphor by commenting that according to Lacan, the presence of the father provokes the end of the mirror stage, the completion of the split between mother and child (Fink 89). Juan's picture (mirror) makes the director realize the link between her father and grandfather, and it awakens her desire to get to know the erased figure of her *abuelo* Juan.

Valencia Dávila's travels to research her grandfathers' identities resemble those of a pilgrim in the sense that the trip itself already represents achieving a goal: "the essence of the journey is movement" (Coleman and Elsner 14). She visually documents her roaming from place to place by opening the film with shots that leave no doubt that she has embarked on this search. They range from zoom, where she can get close to the analyzed subject, to extreme long shots, where she can study it from a reflective distance; varying the shots emphasizes her desire to learn and understand the spaces left behind by her parents. We can read her journey to Chile and to Cuenca, Ecuador, as migratory experiences because she goes back to her grandfathers' beginnings. The film documents the expeditions, and the director uses the chronological order of her discoveries as the linear narrative structure of her text. At the beginning, the director introduces her reasons for making *Abuelos*: to reconcile with the figures of her two grandfathers. She sets out on a pilgrimage to discover her *abuelo* Juan, whom she did not know. Tracking down where her maternal grandfather, Remo, came from stands out as her other, equally important reason for making the film. Valencia Dávila allows viewers to see how she writes

Figure 6.1. The director-narrator in a rare moment of letting the camera film her research the story of her Chilean grandfather (*Abuelos*, 2010, Carla Valencia Dávila).

the script in a way that they can witness her learning new information about her subjects. From her point of view the audience can watch as she conducts research, interviews relatives and friends, drives down the road, contemplates beautiful settings, and learns more. In fact, we only see Carla as a character of her own film when she allows the camera to capture her as she places a phone call early in the film, conducts Google searches to track down details about her grandfather Juan and his role in the election of Salvador Allende, and rides back from Pisagua in northern Chile after completing her work there (figure 6.1). Otherwise, the audience only perceives her presence because of the narration that controls the story, the storytelling, and the rhythm of the film.

The director structures the documentary to dedicate equal cinematographic space to both grandfathers, and the story travels back and forth between the village near Cuenca and Quito and northern Chile near Iquique, where grandfather Juan lived and died. The documentary uses stunning photography to complement the narrative line and the graphic delivery of the story, and it employs the geographical settings and water as pictorial guides to frame the presentation of each piece of the story. The opening shots show the beauty and stillness of the terrain and the persistent humidity to depict the region where her maternal grandfather lived, near Cuenca. The director utilizes the calming rhythm of the water as it rolls along a creek as a diegetic sound to emphasize the bucolic setting. The second scene employs a different scenario to display a starkly contrasting view: a barren desert in northern Chile, an equally beautiful shot to depict its majestic characteristics. Next, the narrator-protagonist carries the camera with her, focusing on the sandy and rocky path as she walks along it. She explains her mission: to learn more about her paternal grandfather, who died at the hands of the oppressive forces of Augusto Pinochet. As viewers walk with the protagonist, they may immediately notice that the rocky terrain does not retain her footprints. The image suggests that she has embarked on a search for a path that has been erased. This second scene foretells, or at least suggests, the difficulty of her mission.

The audience receives the story of *abuelo* Juan through the theatrical storytelling of Lily, Carla's aunt. She remembers in great detail and narrates with her mouth and hands to emphasize her story and perhaps to gain credibility. Aunt Lily seems vested in avoiding the stereotype assigned to relatives of the disappeared ones, of exaggerating to place blame on the innocent regime responsible for their loved ones' disappearance. As she talks, Aunt Lily corrects her discourse for the sake of accuracy. For instance, she recounts the words of a soldier who ordered her to stop during a visit with her father: "If you take one more step, I'll kill you." And then she quickly modifies the wording: "No, If you take another step, I'll shoot you." The director positions Lily in a carefully arranged space, an arch in the brick wall that separates the dining room from the kitchen. The setting frames the aunt as she remembers and reenacts the visit with her father when he was detained by the military (figure 6.2). She recounts the story, switching back and forth between the past and the present. She has relived and retold the story many times and her narration suggests that she has not forgotten any details. It seems as if it happened just yesterday. Lily uses the opportunity to denounce the murder of her father at the hands of the oppressive forces of Pinochet.

Curiously enough, in this particular instance of the storytelling, the camera captures her narrative and performance and immortalizes her plea and memory as she recounts the history of Juan's last days and their last encounter. To avoid the monotony of recording a static subject who narrates, the director presents a series of shots that choreograph the aunt's emotional soliloquy. The camera pans alternately between the desert mountains, a mound of junked cars piled on top of each other, the aunt speaking, and the military installation where *abuelo* Juan was incarcerated. The director invites the audience to imagine with her the atrocity of imprisonment and the destruction of lives shortened, as the camera focuses on the vestiges of the army quarters. Valencia

Figure 6.2. Aunt Lily recalling her father's disappearance by order of Pinochet (*Abuelos*, 2010, Carla Valencia Dávila).

Dávila's recovering of history from people's memories echoes Ana M. López's comments in her masterful reading of *The Battle of Chile* and its presentation of information: "[The film] simultaneously positions the spectator as reader/observer of the 'real' and as the observer of a preconstructed, intentional operation, directed as a fiction is directed" (280). The director of *Abuelos* also positions the audience as reader/observer by placing viewers in the military facility where her grandfather spent his last days.

One could argue that the shot of the pile of junked cars emerges as the film's most telling image. The former military installation now houses these vehicles that have exhausted their usefulness and have been discarded onto this empty lot. The recurring shot of the abandoned cars suggests the metaphorical relation between them and the men the dictatorship killed and buried in common graves, their bodies piled one on top of another. This type of burial suggests that the military arbitrarily decided that the men had exhausted their usefulness to the country, and it ended their existence.

As the storytelling moves along, the narrator-protagonist uses a similar technique to visually record and depict *abuelo* Juan's birthplace. She films the remains of a town where, as the camera shows, only rubble and debris now attest to its previous existence and the persistence of destruction. The audience cannot identify the objects that lie in ruins, but the narrator helps by describing what the camera captures: church, school, bank, plaza, and so forth. All the vestiges confirm that barren terrain has replaced the fertility of life. The audience learns how the military regime destroyed the town, its buildings, houses, and people because it labeled them as communists who had to be destroyed:

> In this chill of overwhelming heat and cold that cut through the skin, he lived the first years of his life.... People were expelled and this camp destroyed and ransacked during the dictatorship years for being, as the military said, a communist's nest.[3]

The camera pauses at a structure that contrasts with the pulverized buildings. It is a house that resisted the military assault and had not completely fallen; the walls and a doorframe still stand erect. The shot seems to suggest that the military could not completely conquer those whom they labeled subversive who, like the house, had resisted.

Using a cinematographic technique similar to the one utilized when filming Lily talking about the capturing of her father, the director focuses on objects enhancing the delivery of the story told by Alberto Newman, a doctor who witnessed the execution of her *abuelo* Juan by firing squad, as he narrates the gruesome details of the event. In a sequential rotation are shots of the doctor, especially when he becomes emotional on remembering the ruins of the military camp and the now remodeled place. The new pink and white façade of the old building helps the director set up the sharp contrast between 1973 and now. It portrays men whose lives the dictatorship so prematurely ended as they moved about in the yard, perhaps not fully aware of the fate that awaited them. The scene switches back to the ruins and then to the newer installation erected there perhaps as an attempt to erase or cover up the horrors of the military dictatorship's violent acts. Often, the shots freeze on the screen to allow the audience ample time to ponder the story at times emotionally relived and at times utterly devoid of emotion by this firsthand witness. The director decides to deliver in black and white the presentation of the makeshift memorials erected in the place where the bodies were discarded. This photographic technique emphasizes the persistence of the tragedy and the emotional pain carried by the victims' relatives 40 years later. For instance, the camera stops and remains still as it captures the view of an iron cross, adorned by the picture of a victim and faded artificial roses. Then the camera pans out to a view of similar crosses from which empty picture frames hang. Rather than implying that their relatives have not kept it up, the makeshift memorial suggests an even louder cry of resistance. The unadorned, rusted iron crosses stand as a voiceless yet expressive message that cannot be ignored. The ocean waves have not been able to wash away the pain and suffering caused by the horrors of the annihilation of precious human life. The tattered Chilean flag that seems to preside over the place suggests the status of the country after the dictatorship destroyed civil rights and liberties, and now one can only find remains of Allende's *suave patria* (sweet country).

As the film moves along, we observe how different protagonists try to recreate Chile circa 1972 and *abuelo* Juan Valencia from memory. When they interpret or explain the artifacts of *abuelo* Juan's life at different times, they seem to read items from a palimpsest that records the efforts of several individuals who, before Carla, undertook the hard task of piecing together Valencia's last days. The director lets the witnesses express their versions of the story as they reason or maybe speculate about motives behind the tragedy of his premature departure. At the end, the film concludes, just like the collective voices who try to reconstruct the figure of Juan so his granddaughter might get to know him, that his commitment to the leftist movement led by Salvador Allende precipitated his murder on the hands of forces loyal to Pinochet. The director in an effort to cut the distance between the audience and the subjects who reconstruct the figure of Juan invariably uses medium shots to bring them closer to each other.

Carla, as the narrator, explains that each story helps her finally reconstruct the missing pieces in the true story of her grandfather that had remained hidden, maybe even in plain sight, "de una época que no viví pero de la que oí hablar toda mi infancia. Un país al que nunca pude ir a pesar de haber viajado tantas veces a Chile. Mi abuelo Juan vivió todas estas épocas. Apoyó a Salvador Allende en cada una de las campañas, en el 52, 64, 1970" (from a time that I did not live but from which I heard about throughout my childhood. My grandpa Juan lived all these times. He supported Salvador Allende in each one of his campaigns, '52, '64, and 1970). She choreographs her words with pictures of revolutionary posters and slogans that flash on the screen. As we see a poster, the narrator once again ponders her recently gained knowledge about those who fought with her grandfather as she identifies the image's content as "el nombre del abuelo Juan y de otros de quienes he aprendido mientras hacia este documental" (the name of *abuelo* Juan and others about whom I have learned while making this documentary).

In a move that parallels or echoes her *abuelo* Remo seeking the cure for mortality, Carla Valencia Dávila brings her *abuelo* Juan back to life through the magic of recording. The audience had learned early in the film about the existence of this tape and the director's frustration as she procured a place that would convert it from an audio reel to a format that could be reproduced using current technology. The director allows Lily to once again address the camera as she remembers her father, but this time she seems to invent him rather than narrate him. Her description and memories seem to enhance her perception of her father, who departed so long ago. But the director jumps back to the unveiling of the tape as if to confirm her aunt Lily's words as she introduces it: "Esta cinta salió de Chile hace 50 años y nadie la ha vuelta escuchar desde entonces" (This tape left Chile 50 years ago, and no one has heard it since then). Grandpa Juan confirms his sister Lily's memories of him. He utters a moving speech in which he celebrates and rejoices in the party's triumph. He sounds as good as the earlier depiction of him by the characters. As Juan speaks, the director focuses on the mountains that become a suitable background for his speech. The permanence and indestructibility of the mountains appear to metaphorically suggest that *abuelo* Juan and his noble ideals of equality in Chile will also live as long as the Andean mountain range that appears grand and free on the screen.

As the family gathers around the portable computer to listen to Juan Valencia talk about the achievements of the political movement that he helped lead, his words bring his flock together. The director puts together shots of the Dávila family in Chile listening to the tape and of her father listening to it in Quito. The wonders of technology have helped Juan reach out and bring his family together one more time. The tape left Chile in 1973, and it still served his original purpose of reaching out to his son, who then studied in the Soviet Union. The film uses imagery to emphasize this message by displaying shots that depict rooms with closed glass doors or windows that impede the possibility of an exit. These pictures transition the story into the retelling of another main event in their lives: the day when the family received the news that Juan had been executed by Pinochet's forces after overthrowing Allende, who then killed himself. Using medium shots to get the subjects closer to the audience, the three siblings take turns sharing their news of how they found out about the tragic fate of their father: Lily came home and mistakenly assumed her father had been released from prison; her brother in Chile was threatened when he tried to claim the body; Carla's father was in Moscow and received the news from the dean of the university where he studied.

The director chooses to close with a visit to the site where in 1990, thanks to the witness Alberto Newman, they located the remains of Juan Valencia. On the way there, the camera captures the white lines that mark the lane boundaries on the highway. The image masterfully reemphasizes the topic of the search and the traveling as a pilgrim latent throughout the documentary. The scene resembles the one shown earlier in the film when Carla walks on a rocky or sandy path that swallows up her footprints. Likewise, this asphalted road cannot keep track of her presence there either. However, the film itself confirms her visits to these places where she has brought to light the larger-than-life figure of her grandfather Juan. The documentary ends with a narration of how Juan's body was unearthed from the makeshift common grave on a hillside near Pisagua, close to the Pacific Ocean. Metaphorically, *Abuelos* also digs out Juan Valencia, who cannot remain hidden any longer because his granddaughter, with the help of digital film technology, has brought him out from the virtual anonymity where he had remained for so long. The forbidden topic cannot remain so any more. Carla can return home and start her work of piecing together the task of sharing her findings with the world. The director, in another rare appearance, allows the camera to show her as she travels back, leaving Pisagua behind as she contemplates the Andean mountains and the calm sea where her grandfather Juan had been buried for so long. The film displays pictures of *abuelo* Juan Valencia Hinojosa alive.

The documentary divides the cinematographic space evenly between the two grandparents. However, the experience of searching for *abuelo* Remo differs greatly from her search for *abuelo* Juan because Carla had grown up close to her mother's father. Carla Valencia Dávila uses the focus and the narrative perspective of an acting and contemplating being. The first one narrates herself into the story from the point of view of her childhood and adolescence. The contemplative being provides a more mature perspective as a narrator who can look at the past with nostalgia, subjectivity, and at times, more objectivity. Her presentation of her maternal grandfather centers on his possible supernatural powers, attributed to him by a young granddaughter, an acting being. The film opens with Carla sharing the promise she received from her grandfather: "Cuando yo tenía 16 años mi abuelo Remo me dijo, 'tú no te vas a morir nunca. Yo estoy descubriendo la inmortalidad.' Me dejó flotando con esa idea. Yo le creí" (When I was 16, Grandpa Remo told me, "You are never going to die. I am discovering immortality." He left me floating with that idea. I believed him). Just as the director equally researched her *abuelo* Juan's story, she travels to Cuenca, Ecuador, to recover and unveil the true essence of her grandfather who so confidently assured her that he would find a cure for death. Her research includes a journey to *abuelo* Remo's spaces and interviews with his daughters and patients. Grandpa Remo had made a living as a self-taught physician who practiced alternative medicine. Her pilgrimage takes her from the city to a less urban or more rural area. The director uses shots that depict nature as the background to narrating Remo's story. She photographs leaves on trees and a river flowing through the mountains to compose a piece of highly aesthetic value. The documentary opens with images that reveal the director's superb craft.

Carla Valencia Dávila attempts with the help of her aunts on her mother's side to piece together a story of this greater-than-life figure to whom Carla as a child attributed supernatural powers: "Mi abuelo podía hacer llover" (My grandfather could make it rain). An aunt verifies the story, explaining that she also fell victim to his charm, as when he asked, "¿Quieres ver cómo se aclara el cielo?" (Do you want to see how the sky clears up?). And indeed it happened, therefore establishing Remo's credibility. Carla chooses to film her aunt in a natural setting, sitting on a rock on a riverbank, to establish the close connection between *abuelo* Remo and nature. His granddaughter summons the help of former patients and neighbors to attest to Remo's miraculous achievements. She employs medium shots to film patients who chose Remo to cure them as they tell their convincing stories. They all testify to Remo Vásquez's ingenuity as a physician. His success earned him the title of shaman because his craft, skill, and success resemble those of a healer from one of the autochthonous nations of Ecuador. He shied away from conventional medicine and used herbs and medicinal plants; one of his patients testifies that Remo cured him with a regime of seeds. They all reach a similar conclusion: his practice was a kind of miracle. One says, "The treatment I followed with Remo cured me." A woman who qualifies herself as Remo's greatest achievement prides herself on being a unique case: "No fui una paciente muy normal. Los demás tenían que pagar. Supongo que les cobraba" (I wasn't a very normal patient. Others had to pay. He charged them, I suppose).

But Remo eventually left the southern Andes and migrated to Quito, where he spent his final days in this world. The departure of the man who promised to conquer death and discover immortality hit Carla hard. Cinematographically, the director depicts the news of his death by showing blurred shots of nature, mostly greenery, leaves, and water. The images contrast with the shots that appear at the beginning of the film, when we learn of *abuelo* Remo, showing aesthetically pleasing pictures of nature in its splendor. The director sets the camera on the ground pointing toward the sky as if to give the audience the perspective of her *abuelo* Remo buried on the ground.

Valencia Dávila once again acts as both an acting being and a contemplating being as she narrates herself into the story and gives us her perspective of the event from a more recent time after she has had the opportunity to ponder and reach conclusions. She has grown from being a little girl to a young woman and then to an adult who has never stopped worshiping and idolizing her grandfather. But Carla Valencia Dávila, the documentary's director and narrator, attempts to reach a certain objectivity. When describing her *abuelo* Remo's passing, she proclaims, "El inmortal murió esa noche: tenía 70 años" (The inmortal one died that night. He was 70 years old). A touch of irony is evident in her employment of the term "immortal" that semantically works well in its metaphorical and literal meanings. How can an immortal being die? Or he can die but still lives among us, and we have not forgotten this amazing human being. Carla's speech continues to switch back and forth as she tries to remain objective while providing the somewhat more subjective view from a granddaughter who remembers the night of her grandfather's departure:

> It impressed me that people wept for his death with such great pain. I remember a sweet smell and my grandpa silent in the middle of the room. I don't know who began, but all of the grandchildren began one by one to abandon the living room. . . . On that occasion and for the first time, we confessed to each other that we were all Grandfather's favorite granddaughter or grandson.[4]

Carla's aunt makes a similar comment, suggesting that her father preferred her over her siblings: "Don't tell anyone: I am very, very special." The comments attest to Remo's true love for his family and his keen ability to make every one of them feel special and more important than the rest. The documentary closes with shots of *abuelo* Remo alive, even as the audience receives the news of his death.

Upon closing the presentation of *abuelo* Remo, the documentary shows letters from people thanking her grandfather for curing them and saving their lives. This scene stands as the best homage to her grandfather by the director-granddaughter because it supports the stories narrated by his daughters. In this carefully edited scene we read the words from these patients as the narrator reads them out loud; the letters are piled up to make the audience aware of its large quantity. They come from both remote and nearby places: France, Italy, Cuenca, Quito, and so forth. Then Carla reads Grandpa Remo's medical and research notes as if trying to decode his formula for the cure to mortality. The key seems to emanate from the intoxication of human beings: "Éramos un montón de dioses intoxicados y que a medida que nos curamos nos íbamos desintoxicando" (We were a bunch of intoxicated gods, and as we heal ourselves, we began to become detoxified). But no one can decipher *abuelo* Remo's secret to immortality, and the documentary serves as a tribute to his magnificent life. Now, thanks to the film, Remo will live forever.

As already demonstrated, the director carefully selects each aspect of the visual setup of every scene and its corresponding shots. Carla Valencia Dávila uses her voice-over narration to avoid duplicating information provided in the images themselves, as expected from a proper documentary. For instance, she insistently uses scenes of water as the visual backdrop or as a sound effect. The ocean, river, and brook serve as metaphors that aid in the characterization of both grandfathers. In shots of Pisagua the ocean looks and sounds turbulent and restless. The first obvious symbolism relates to *abuelo* Juan's personality, as a man who fought the establishment to bring about a leftist government that tried to even the odds regarding wealth distribution and opportunities for the underprivileged. But the ocean's troubled waters also allude to the concentration camp where *abuelo* Juan was imprisoned and to the mass grave where he was buried, both places near the Pacific Ocean. His body remained there until 1990, when it was exhumed and given a more proper burial and gravesite. Lastly, the ocean waves' constant ebb and flow serve as a soothing therapy for Lily and her family as they mourn her father's violent and unfair killing. Lily speaks as the camera holds a shot of the ocean:

> My grandmother, when my dad died, during those terrible times, gave us the strength we needed. "So they won't see us cry," she said. "Those bastards won't see us cry because they didn't murder any common criminal, so we won't cry any more." She got us to go to the beach every day, which really helped us. Every day we went down to the beach; the sea soothes and calms you down.[5]

In another scene Lily recounts how *abuelo* Juan showed great excitement when he learned that he had just became a grandfather. The director places Lily in front of the calming sea as she sits in the frame, off center, sharing the other two-thirds of the shot with the calming waters that effortlessly move across the sand.

In contrast, the scenes dedicated to the characterization of Grandpa Remo show a less turbulent body of water, usually a river flowing steadily along. Often the director sets the scenes in front of a brook, when she films her maternal aunts narrating their stories about her Ecuadorian *abuelo*. The framing often suggests calmness and stillness and includes water and its interactions with the natural surroundings. The documentary itself opens with shots of a very humid place as the narrator introduces the audience to *abuelo* Remo and explains that this peaceful space of moisture and clear water represents her grandfather's domain and the setting for his amazing discoveries: "En este lugar, él debe haber caminado y respirado este mismo aire que hoy respiro: un aire de humedad, agua dulce, de insecto escondido" (In this place, he must have walked and breathed this same air that I breathe today: humidity in the air, sweet water, and hidden insects). In another scene, as Carla's aunts share the story of their father, Remo, and his struggle with cancer, the director displays a shot of underground water taken from below the surface. She tries to illustrate the buzzing sound constantly present inside his head by duplicating the perspective of an insect or similar animal as it travels from the surface to the bottom of the riverbed or the ocean floor. These shots suggest Grandpa Remo's predisposition to look beyond the surface and discover what less observant people might have missed.

Water, as an image and a symbol, permeates the whole film. The title of the documentary appears 3 minutes and 15 seconds into the film totally submerged in water surrounded by fish and aquatic flora and fauna. The narrator proclaims that both grandfathers lived near bodies of water that literally connect them; the Ecuadorian river flows into the Pacific Ocean. The director often uses water to transition between scenes that change not only the subject matter but also the geographic location, going from talking about one grandfather to talking about the other one.

At the end, Valencia Dávila links the two stories, saying that the violence of the military dictatorship abruptly ended when it assassinated her *abuelo* Juan. The director comments that it had finally rained in the desert where Grandpa Juan had been buried in a mass grave: "*Abuelo* Remo ha hecho llover en el desierto del abuelo Juan" (*Abuelo* Remo has made rain in the desert of *abuelo* Juan). The scene displays shots of flowers growing in the desert. Carla proclaims both her grandfathers' successes in their own endeavors. Her two grandfathers achieved their goals: one to cure the ill and the other to give Chile three years of democracy. They both lived their lives to make others' lives better. Her final words attest to her findings and serve as a fitting conclusion:

> This journey has allowed me to get closer to my other family and to a country that I have been able to recover thanks to my grandfather. I have been able to unearth stories from the desert and to place flowers on his grave. It has allowed me to tell my dad things he did not know. After the death of Remo, life has moved on as if life could continue even without the most important people. All of my family continued to take immortality pills until they ran out. Some ingredients expired; others ran out. I suppose that none of us felt able to take his place; two faces of a same story have told me where I came from: death and immortality, immortality and death.[6]

And then, in the final shot, the sun sets over the Andes. The stories of both grandfathers has been uncovered for the benefit and redemption of everyone involved.

The director chooses to deliver one more message, even after the movie ends. Valencia Dávila sings the song that accompanies the closing credits: "Piedra y camino" (Rock and road) from composer Atahualpa Yupanqui. Carla chooses the musical arrangement of a Chilean folk song that once again emphasizes her mixed identity and place on the metaphorical border: half Ecuadorian, half Chilean, someone who grew up far from the land of her exiled father. The selection of a song by Atahualpa Yupanqui sounds even more appropriate when we realize that he, like a pilgrim because of political persecution, lived in numerous locations after being born in Buenos Aires: Uruguay, Entre Ríos, Santa Fe, Rosario, Córdoba, Santiago del Estero, Tucumán, Salta, Jujuy, La Puna, and La Rioja (Márquez). The lyrics tell the story of a traveler whose fate dictates that he must move from place to place, trekking on rocky roads. The song's theme and pathos capture the spirit of the documentary and allow the director to have the final word, even after the narrative portion of the film ends. Carla Valencia Dávila has carefully taken care of every single detail of *Abuelos*, even this very last one.

In closing, the director uses her own story as the basis for her examination of the effects of immigration provoked by political causes in the descendants of those who must leave their countries and establish themselves in a new land.

The immigrants live forever in exile and must pass through the traditional ritual of cultural adaptation and assimilation. However, we often disregard the emotional burden placed on the shoulders of their children who grow up without close contact with their relatives who stayed behind in places that they cannot reach for political, economic, or whatever reasons. They all suffer the consequences of this exile. Carla Valencia Dávila delivers a great story in which the narration and the photography complement each other. These techniques invite the audience to feel her sense of loss and her desire to fill the void left in her because she did not get to know her paternal grandfather, Juan, who lost his life at the hands of the repressive Chilean government. She accomplishes a similar feat with the search for the identity of her maternal grandfather, whom she met but now, through the documentary, she can understand from the perspective of an adult observer rather than that of a little girl fascinated by his charm.

Notes

1. In cases where the producer or director has not provided an official English language title, I have provided a literal translation for informational purposes.

2. "Yo crecí creyendo en la inmortalidad de Remo y me encontré con la muerte de Juan. Me fraccioné. Mientras una parte de mi avanzaba y se fortalecía, la otra estaba enterrada en el desierto. Este abuelo que no pude conocer vivió mirando el océano Pacífico que es en donde este río de mi abuelo ecuatoriano va a desembocar."

3. "En este frío de calores aplastantes y fríos que cortan la piel vivió los primeros años de su vida.... La gente fue desterrada y este campamento totalmente destruido y saqueado en la época de la dictadura por ser, como le decían, un nido de comunistas."

4. "Gente que lloraba su muerte con un dolor que me impresionó. Recuerdo que el olor era dulce y allí estaba mi abuelo en la mitad de la sala y en silencio. No sé quién empezó pero todos los nietos uno a uno fuimos abandonando la sala.... En esa ocasión nos confesamos por primera vez unos a otros que todos éramos el nieto favorito."

5. "[Mi abuela], cuando mi papá murió, ella en el momento más terrible que pasamos, nos dió las fuerzas. 'Para que no nos vean llorar,' decía. 'Estos desgraciados no nos van a tener que ver llorar por que no mataron a ningún delincuente. Así que no lloremos más.' Y nos hacía cruzar a la playa todos los días. Eso nos ayudó más. Todos los días bajábamos a la playa. Que el mar como que te apacigua, te calma."

6. "Este viaje me ha permitido acercarme a mi otra familia y a un país donde he podido recuperar a mi abuelo. Desenterrar historias del desierto y poner flores en su tumba. Me ha permitido contarle a mi papá cosas que él no sabía. Después de la muerte de Remo la vida ha seguido pasando como que si la vida pudiera continuar sin las personas más importantes. Toda mi familia siguió tomando las cápsulas de

la inmortalidad hasta que se acabaron. Algunos ingredientes caducaron; otros se acabaron. Supongo que ninguno de nosotros se sintió capaz de tomar su lugar: dos caras de una misma historia me han contado de donde vengo: de la inmortalidad y la muerte; de la muerte y la inmortalidad."

Works Cited

Abuelos. Dir. Carla Valencia Dávila. Cinesud, 2010. Film.
"'Abuelos': Uno de los documentales más premiados del cine ecuatoriano." Review. Cinesud. 16 April 2013. Web. 5 Aug. 2014.
Bienvenido a tu familia. Dir. Diego Ortuño. Domino, 2009. Film.
La Churona. Dir. María Cristina Carrillo Espinosa. Ecuador para Largo, 2010. Film.
Coleman, Simon, and John Elsner. *Pilgrimage: Past and Present in the World Religions*. Collingdale, PA: Diane, 1995. Print.
Fink, Bruce. *The Lacanian Subject: Between Language and Jouissance*. Princeton, NJ: Princeton UP, 1995. Print.
López, Ana M. "*The Battle of Chile*: Documentary, Political Process, and Representation." *The Social Documentary in Latin America*. Ed. Julianne Burton. Pittsburgh, PA: U of Pittsburgh P, 1990: 267–288. Print.
Márquez, Chucho. "Comentario." Folklore del Norte. N.d. Web. 6 Aug. 2014.
Matamoros, Ileana. "Vivir la muerte." *Revista Vistazo*. 16 Oct. 2013. Web. 5 Aug. 2013.
Pasaje de ida. Dir. Rogelio Gordon. De Fe y Esperanza, 2003. Film.
Problemas personales. Dir. Lisandra Rivera and Manolo Fernández. Pequeña Nube, 2002. Film.
Prometeo deportado. Dir. Fernando Mieles. Other Eye Films, 2011. Film.
Said, Edward. "Reflections on Exile." *Reflections on Exile and Other Essays*. Convergences: Inventories of the Present. Cambridge, MA: Harvard UP, 2002. 136–149. Print.
Vengo volviendo. Dir. Gabriel Páez Hernández and María Isabel Rodas León. Filmarte, 2015.

7

La Churona and the Neobaroque Aesthetic

Mapping of a Transatlantic Ecuador

LIZARDO HERRERA

The documentary *La Churona* (2010), directed by María Cristina Carrillo Espinosa, tells the story of a traveling Virgin, the Virgin of El Cisne, or La Churona, as Ecuadorians affectionately call her.[1] This image, a replica of the Virgin of Guadalupe of Spain, arrived in the late sixteenth century to El Cisne, the present province of Loja, in southern Ecuador. At the beginning of the new millennium, La Churona took a reverse journey: one of her copies reaches Spain, specifically the district of Lavapiés in Madrid. On the one hand, the replica of the Virgin of Extremadura (the Virgin of Guadalupe in Spain) was sculpted by Diego de Robles in 1596 in Quito, and at that time it changed Loja's religious geography. In La Churona's sanctuary, the indigenous pantheon merged with the Catholic devotion through the Baroque penchant for miracle-making. On the other hand, after her return to Europe, La Churona re-created a sense of Ecuadorian identity, implementing an imaginary Ecuador in the heart of Madrid while producing a revival of Catholicism in the secularized Spanish society of the twenty-first century.

In the first part of the documentary, as La Churona makes her way from El Cisne to Loja, pilgrims sing the following verses: "She has come to America, has come to America to bring peace. We Ecuadorians call her mother, true mother." These lines connect two historic moments in Ecuador: first, the arrival in Hispanic America of a Catholic Virgin with all its imagery and second, the emergence of nationalism. An image coming from Spain more than 400 years earlier has become the mother of contemporary Ecuadorians. What is the link between these two very different moments in history?

We begin our analysis with a historical tour. A good point of departure is *También la lluvia* (*Even the Rain*, 2010), directed by Icíar Bollaín, a contemporary of Carrillo Espinosa's *La Churona*. This transnational film production takes the opposite journey from the Ecuadorian documentary, going from Spain to today's Bolivia, to re-create, among other issues, the complicity between colonialism and Catholicism during the sixteenth century. Costa and Sebastián, two of the main characters, want to make a film about Bartolomé de las Casas, who together with Antonio de Montesinos will make history as one of the main advocates of indigenous people against the *conquistadores'* abuses.[2] Sebastián's film project requires transporting a giant cross by helicopter to a semijungle area in Cochabamba, and once it is in place, they put it up as if they were planting a tree.

The analogy between the cross and a tree condenses the undertaking of the Conquest in the sixteenth century. The cross constitutes a phallus penetrating the ground, which it feminizes, as Spain taking possession of the new territory by impregnating it. The process represents a militant Catholic justification for possession. In religious terms and from the point of view of the Spaniards, we are in a period of great optimism, with mass indigenous baptisms, since it was believed that the large number of new converts meant the triumph of faith. Here, religious images, in spite of lacking the phallic nature of the cross, work like seeds implanting a Catholic sentiment. When *conquistadores* arrived in America, they executed native priests, destroyed their temples, and wiped out the images that were considered idols; in their place, they built Catholic chapels and disseminated religious images, convinced that these actions would spawn devotion and end idolatry. The arrival of the cross in *También la lluvia*, therefore, represents the arrival of a policy where the Catholic faith had clear geopolitical and economic objectives tied to the Conquest. The takeover was not purely territorial and economic, but spiritual as well.[3]

A few years later, a second generation of missionaries arrived in America, opposing the *conquistadores* by redefining the Conquest as an eminently spiritual enterprise. These religious men were alarmed to discover that Indians were still worshiping their former divinities; the clerics did not understand that the indigenous polytheism easily accepted the Christian God without abandoning existing gods. This second generation, therefore, was more careful with evangelization and tried to better organize the use of Catholic images. According to Jacques Lafaye, their ideal was "of Erasmian inspiration, suspicious of images and devotions" (318; my translations unless otherwise indicated). Their project thus restricted religious images to a pedagogical setting, putting aside spirituality or anything that could relate to the supernatural. Although the policy of the missionaries was to choose persuasion, not violence, in spiritual terms it was more radical than that of the conquistadores. While rigorously studying pre-Columbian religions, the missionaries' goal was to make tabula rasa of them, that is, to efficiently eradicate the religions to ensure a genuine Catholic conversion. Missionaries sought to possess/fertilize the indigenous intellect, a pursuit that brought about the implementation of a paternalistic policy infantilizing indigenous people, disempowering them further not only in terms of economic, sexual, and territorial exploitation but also symbolic.

By the third quarter of the sixteenth century, the historical context underwent major transformations. We enter a period of colonial solidification, as the era of conquest, the conquering epic came to an end. The new colonial system did not see the Indians as a threat or a population in need of conversion; the goal now was to integrate them into a new society. The arrival of the Jesuits, moreover, put into crisis the Erasmist approach. In Europe, after the Council of Trent, the Counter-Reformation was consolidated, and its program gave more importance to "the sacraments, to frequent communion and service" (Lafaye 318).[4] In America, a hyperritualized religion replaced the rationalized missionary doctrine; unlike the latter, the new religious approach did not hesitate to appropriate pre-Columbian rituals or to be contaminated by them. While Erasmus missionaries sought doctrinal purity, the new Baroque religiosity resorted to "miracles, apparitions, dreams, and visions to shore up the supernatural system that sought to communicate to the faithful" (Gruzinski 112). Thus, as indicated by Serge Gruzinski, a mix of indigenous and Catholic imagery was favored, while neither dissociated images from the represented divinity.

Lafaye argues that Mexico's colonial religious beliefs—one can say the same for the Andes—were "the unstable product of heterogeneous religious contributions due to ethnic groups unequal in importance and influence" (67). According to this author, contact between two traditions resulted in modifications for both. Either through prohibitions, persecutions, clandestine hidings, or distance, indigenous religions, along with those of African and Jewish origin, maintained their residual character, but Catholicism retained its status as the official religion. Nevertheless, this residual nature, far from resulting in tabula rasa, gave way to substitutions and/or assimilations that resulted in a cultural syncretism. The colonial Baroque image, therefore, is a syncretic image in which on the one hand, the official doctrine appropriated indigenous rites and utopias incorporating them into the Catholic worship but on the other, remnants of other religions contaminated and therefore also modified official Catholic ritual.

Bolívar Echeverría understands Baroque ethos as a *codigofagia*, which means a code that eats (consumes) another code or appropriates it in order to force it to overcome a malaise or discontent impossible to satisfy (Echeverría 48–56). In the colonial context, for example, Catholic ceremonials ate native symbols or religious practices, making them a part of itself. However, given the syncretic nature of Baroque rituals, codigofagia referred to by Echeverría works in two directions. The first consists of the Church and the Creole elites appropriating indigenous practices or symbols to enhance the magnificence of their own rituality, thereby facilitating the imposition of colonial hegemony. The second direction, and more important, is that indigenous or other popular traditions also appropriated the Catholic rituals, thus modifying themselves. But codigofagia's use was to meet a demand that went far beyond what the official Catholic doctrine could give them—an attitude of cultural resistance that twists and writhes, modifying Catholic ritual to counteract the fragmentation or complete disappearance of the indigenous traditions.

Caroline Dean's contributions go even further to exemplify Baroque ethos's attitude of cultural resistance. The American historian studies the celebrations of the canonization of Ignatius of Loyola and Corpus Christi in the seventeenth century in Cuzco, where the Inca elites actively participated. This means, according to Dean, the emergence of a new political pact, one that does not simply accept imperial sovereignty. Inca elites recognized the Spanish king as their sovereign who engaged in their festivities, but in doing so, they resorted to a dialectic that served to remind him of the services provided during his fight against the *chunchos*, indigenous rebels—or "barbarians." It also showed the disruptive force of the indigenous population both for its majority in number and because of the excesses of the celebrations—*borracheras* (drunken exultations)—that besides reviving indigenous ways of remembrance like the Taqui-Onkoy dances, encouraged the fear of a possible rebellion (Dean 149). In this political performance, Inca elites ate the Baroque ceremonial, but paradoxically, while participating in the grandeur of the ritual, they also subverted it by proposing a new system of alliances. Their codigofagia, in this sense, is the result of a deep discontent that knows that to become visible it has no other choice but to join and twist the victor's ceremonials. Inca elites'

Baroque ethos is masked in the excesses of the performance; however, its mask is no praise of the winner, but a disguise that allows it to challenge its colonial condition.

I would like to bring your attention back to the verses of the song sung by the pilgrims in *La Churona*, that the Virgin has come to America to bring peace. We can say that the image of the Virgin did bring peace after the violence of the Conquest or the attempted tabula rasa of the missionaries, but we are not talking about the Catholic pax. It is clear that La Churona appears in 1594 in a context in which the natives' military defeat was undeniable and the struggle between the conquerors and the Crown decided in favor of the latter. The colonial system, meanwhile, sought to consolidate hegemony by integrating heterogeneous social groups. The use of religion was crucial to promote a mixture of different cultural registers in conditions of considerable inequality. But if we see it from the reverse point of view, considering that the Indians first promoted the cult of La Churona, the peace brought about by this image, more than the pax brought by the colonial project, it was a mechanism of resistance. The vanquished ate Catholic doctrine to counteract social fragmentation, but it was a failed venture from the start because that doctrine was the colonial system's basis. In other words, it is possible to argue that the resistance of the vanquished brought peace because it suppressed the conflict of war, but this process, far from showing spiritual harmony, is the reflection of an intense drama that reconfigures the political-religious ceremonial aiming to propose a new system of alliances.

If we jump to the present, we can see that what connects colonial history with the contemporary is the Baroque codigofagia as a form of cultural resistance. La Churona prevails into the twenty-first century accompanying some Ecuadorian immigrants to Spain in a time of deep crisis. The crisis we see in the film is not only economic but also emotional. After the implementation of dollarization in Ecuador in 2000, a large number of Ecuadorians left the country to Spain, but the migrants felt extremely discriminated against in Spain, as is shown in the film by what an Ecuadorian female migrant says: "It's okay if they humiliate us, but not the Virgin." In *La Churona*, discontent is also seen during public demonstrations by immigrants against Euskadi Ta Askatasuna (ETA), protesting that Ecuadorians who are killed in terrorist attacks are not second-class citizens but are human beings, just like Spaniards. In this sense, it was not religious elites or Ecuadorian authorities who brought the Virgin of El Cisne's cult to Spain, but rather some migrants seeking a better quality of life.

Thanks to this image, migrants re-create a sense of Ecuadorianness in a foreign context that they find unfavorable or even hostile.[5]

What the Ecuadorian immigrants experience in the twenty-first century is similar to what Indians in the late sixteenth did, since they likewise are aware that they cannot confront nor resolve their discomfort. The immigrants know that contact with Ecuador is too fragile, and they do not have the strength to confront Spanish authorities; the colonized indigenous people endured a cognitive or representational crisis because their previous beliefs were lost. Both groups have lived a drama in which La Churona not only serves the purposes of the Catholic Church or the Ecuadorian nation but also functions as an integrating element in a context of radical disintegration. From this perspective, the religious image does not mean spiritual peace; it is more a reflection of a discomfort impossible to alleviate, where the drama of many displaced people unfolds: they turn to a religious image to be able to cope with helplessness. La Churona, then, is the result of a codigofagia that is aware of its crisis and resorts to excessive ritualism that, although it guarantees a channel of expression or a festive moment of satisfaction, is, unfortunately, unable to help overcome its embedded emotional dissatisfaction.

Baroque Replica and Neobaroque Nationality

According to the legend, as narrated by Teresa Mora Valdivieso in the documentary, in the late sixteenth century La Churona appeared in El Cisne, an ancient indigenous sanctuary. Faced with a severe drought and food shortage due to an infestation of mice, it is said that the Virgin brought rain and saved people from starvation, making it possible for the indigenous people of the region to remain in their town. In exchange for her miracles, the Virgin demanded the construction of a chapel on the site.[6] In other words, when she arrived, La Churona revealed her miraculous powers, earning the favor of the indigenous people and, over time, of Ecuadorians in general, who worship her with processions, pilgrimages, and so forth and appeal to her in times of need. An annual three-day pilgrimage is organized and attended each year in Ecuador by about 200,000 devotees.[7]

Because the image of the Virgin of Guadalupe who came to El Cisne was not the original, but a copy that local people commissioned from Diego de Robles, what is the relation between the copy and the original, and how does a replica become an image to which the faithful attribute a higher miraculous power? Walter Benjamin studied the aesthetics of allegory to understand the culture of the Baroque. For him, this culture has Renaissance and Classical influences, and unlike the Medieval, it recognizes the natural world. This means that for the Baroque, the divine is not something external or remote from the world; on the contrary, it is constantly manifesting itself in the world; the sacred is within nature, although in a partial and transient form. For this reason, Baroque allegory, unlike romantic symbolism, does not represent a full reunion with the essential truth; its character is, rather, fleeting and fragmentary. If we use religious terms, while the divine truth is initially present, it then disappears from allegorical image, meaning the nature of truth in the allegory is temporary and unstable (Benjamin 151–183).

Because allegory contains fleetingly divine truth means that the image is also ephemeral. The Baroque allegorist sees countless traces of the divine in the natural world, but as soon as it is reunited with the essential truth, it loses contact because the sacred has abandoned the image. Such transience, according to Benjamin, forces the allegorist to produce a new image and then another and another, in a process that immerses itself in the vertigo of an image's infinite proliferation. Allegory, then, does not have nature as its referent but always refers to something else that abandons it while representing it. Or, if preferred, while the sacred is manifested in nature temporarily, any object or image can serve as a support for the divine. If we think of Baroque allegory as a language, it does not refer to what is natural, but it brings an unlimited semiosis in which any sign is a sign of another sign infinitely, that is, a *mise-en-abyme* of the significance.

La Churona is an allegory of the Virgin Mary, but at the same time it is a replica of another miraculous image, Our Lady of Guadalupe of Extremadura. As such, Baroque allegory is not trapped by the ideology of the original; instead, it brings with it a proliferation of images in which the copy may have the same or even more relevance than the one from which it originated. While, as Lafaye notes, the Virgin of Guadalupe became important in America because a significant number of the conquistadores came from Extremadura, and it was not the original image that produced miracles in Loja, but one of its replicas. The fleeting nature of allegory implies that the power of the image is not in its sole existence or unique character but rather in its ability to multiply. The sculpture in El Cisne, for example, is not unique in Ecuador. Diego de Robles carved other replicas to which the faithful also attribute miraculous powers, such as the Virgin of Guápulo, the Virgin of El Quinche, outside Quito, and the Virgin of Cicalpa in the province of Chimborazo (Moreno Yánez).

If the cross functioned as a phallic symbol fertilizing geography, as shown in *También la lluvia*, La Churona's image, though it does not have a phallic appearance, also redefines geography because it transforms territory into holy ground. The divinity that is manifested in La Churona does not penetrate the ground, nor does it feminize it; instead, God becomes feminine. It transvests as Mary, a traveling Virgin walking around freely interacting with people and protecting them.[8] Thus, Loja's geography as well as Quito's, through the sister replicas of La Churona, become the territory chosen by the transvestite divinity. La Churona will not only be known as the traveling Virgin, but as time goes by, and as the song says, she will be all Ecuadorians' true mother.

The documentary accompanies this mother during the three days of the 75-kilometer pilgrimage from El Cisne to Loja, passing through San Pedro de la Bendita and Catamayo. Since La Churona has become an allegory of Ecuadorianness, I would like to describe the role police play in the pilgrimage as they are in charge of looking after the image during the trip, and when it reaches the city of Loja, they make a formal transfer of custody of the Virgin to the bishop. This transfer of custody is accompanied by full-throated singing of the national anthem. In this sense, the religious imagery of the Baroque's protective mother fuses with the national discourse of Mother Nation that emerges in Ecuador after the nineteenth century. This relation between the police and La Churona has even deeper ties. In the sixteenth century the Virgin of Guadalupe had a military component and was the patroness of the Conquest; today, La Churona has the title of Generalísima and is recognized as the armed forces' patroness in contemporary Ecuador.

How can we analyze the relation between Baroque allegory, the proliferation of images, and national discourse? The answer takes us to the sixteenth century. According to Lafaye, from the beginning, the Conquest undertaking defined American geography as an exceptional territory that in turn highlighted the effort of the *conquistadores* as exceptional too. Also, the first missionaries in Mexico understood their evangelizing work as a titanic chore replicating that of the Twelve Apostles marking the birth of a new era. The "New World," as the name suggests, acquired a millenarian importance in the economy of salvation. In the seventeenth and eighteenth centuries, Creole elites fought for the continent's cultural possession over the colonial metropolis, and in order to differentiate or legitimate themselves from Spain or Europe, they constructed the image of America as a land chosen by God's mother. It was following the publication of Miguel Sánchez's *Imagen de la Virgen María* in 1648, that the myth of Guadalupe was consolidated in Mexico, a discourse that Lafaye identifies as the origin of Mexican national sentiment.

In El Cisne, although there is no apologetic text like Sánchez's, something similar occurred. At the end of the sixteenth century, Fray Luis López de Solís, who had an active role in the Third Council of Lima in 1583, became the bishop of the diocese of Quito. Unlike his predecessor, Fray Pedro de la Peña, who had an Erasmist approach, López de Solís was very close to the Jesuits and heavily promoted devotion to La Churona along with her sister replicas (Ramón Valarezo). La Churona thus became an integrating element, a mother who put everyone under her wing in a very heterogeneous society, redefining Loja's geography and subsequently Ecuadorian territory as holy land.[9]

Today, the faithful fill the sanctuary's walls with many images; some attest to La Churona's miraculous powers, and others—which we can call minor—are prayer cards or simple tokens of appreciation. With its ephemeral nature, allegory is required to saturate geography or space with new allegories in an endless procession. We are witnessing, therefore, a proliferation not only of replicas of La Churona produced in smaller statues or pictures but of countless images and colors that have been saturating the sanctuary walls throughout history.

The power of allegorical replica, however, leads the religious sphere toward the secular realm. Today, for example, a replica is tied to a mass reproduction process that regulates the economy of salvation while also generating its own economy. The director of the documentary, María Cristina Carrillo Espinosa, told me in a personal conversation that she left out images of nuns in El Cisne working as cashiers in a bank that manages migrants' money. Contemporary allegorical production is also affected by copyright. One of the most interesting scenes in the film shows the production workshop of La Churona replicas. Antonio Jaramillo acquired the reproduction rights and produces hundreds of copies for migrants to carry abroad. In his workshop, sculptures are separated from accessories like crowns and the baby Jesus and other items so they can be transported in planes. Such is their devotion, says Jaramillo, that some faithful migrants refuse to check the figures as baggage. Instead they buy them their own plane seats. Mass production in this workshop includes carved wooden accessories, but dresses and wigs are the devotees' responsibility, and they never cease to provide luxurious wardrobes, generating a proliferation of new clothing.

During the pilgrimage the documentary shows that religious devotion happens within a festive atmosphere. Prayer cards or videos (digital replicas) of the Virgin are sold, while a magnificent triumphal arch is prepared to receive La Churona in Loja. Additional fireworks and concerts are also organized in her honor. We are witnessing a huge cultural *champús*,[10] a mix in which images so heterogeneous intermingle as family photos, home videos produced by Diego Jiménez for migrants in Spain, beauty pageants, the Virgin's dresses, and provisional posts with food and meats and so forth. La Churona accepts and embraces that her altars, squares, and roads fill with images different from each other because thanks to them her ritual celebrations acquire power and splendor. Cultural *champús* around La Churona, then, consists of an inclusion matrix. The Virgin is a mother in a religious but also cultural sense, as she accepts devotees' prayers as well as young people's concerts, dresses given by her faithful, fireworks, the national anthem, military greetings, plates of food, and beverages, among many other offerings.[11]

Although this cultural *champús* is permeated by the official Ecuadorian national discourse, La Churona is not synonymous with national unification. Carrillo Espinosa's documentary is not a naive celebration of popular sectors' contribution to the Ecuadorian myth of exceptionalism. Although nationalist discourse eats the Virgin of El Cisne's ritualism, transforming it into a national holiday and creating celebrations to consolidate its hegemony, it does not account for heterogeneity of the process. The Virgin and her images' proliferation are the result of the codigofagia drama, not by official institutions but by the defeated or, in this case, the Ecuadorian emigrants. In the documentary, the image of the police singing the national anthem contrasts with that of Jonathan, a teenager whose mother migrated to Spain, leaving him under his grandparents' care at a very young age. This young man's devotion and that of his family's are not the result of a spiritual peace or national pax but the product of a painful dissatisfaction, the alleviation of which the nation has been unable to prevent family fragmentation.[12]

Jonathan makes his pilgrimage to ask the Virgin to help him reunite with his family. The national discourse, in Jonathan's particular case, is substantially responsible for the boy's crisis. He is suffering because Ecuador as a nation has been unable to guarantee a decent life for his family. Diego Jiménez's videos or the images that come out of Antonio Jaramillo's workshop do not reflect the triumph of Ecuador as a nation. The consumers of these images are people who left the country because they were unhappy with their living conditions in Ecuador. In other words, while the migrants in the documentary miss Ecuador, they also feel excluded in Spain and long to re-create their Ecuadorianness although at the same time, they resent the lack of opportunities in their home country. The codigofagia behind Carrillo's *La Churona* is a way to express a deep discontent. Through the Virgin, her devotees re-create a sense of belonging to a site where they feel they have no place. La Churona and her neobaroque proliferation, in this case, represent a protective space in a time of crisis, but it is an ephemeral consolation because migrants know that in Ecuador there is no place for them, either.

The Ecuadorian Female Migrants and Their Mother

The idealization of the mother has been a constant in Latin American culture, and since we are talking about movies, I want to examine a Mexican film from the golden age of cinema, a period highlighted by promotion of the Marian ideal. *Cuando los hijos se van* (When the kids leave, 1941), directed by Juan Bustillo de Oro, tells the story of a mother in the middle of a conflict between her children and their father. The father, hardworking and responsible, represents tradition, while his ambitious children represent modernity. The emergence of modernity, with its desire for money and individual success, disrupts the traditional family, putting the father's authority in crisis. The father, instead of solving problems, makes it all worse by punishing the only unambitious child. The mother, Lupe (Guadalupe's nickname) is caught between tradition's rigid authoritarianism and modernity's greed. Her role is that of a selfless woman who in her eagerness to prevent family fragmentation is capable of any sacrifice, even if it jeopardizes the family's heritage. The wife and mother wants to mediate between two irreconcilable forces—the protection of her children against their father's inflexibility and the absolute legitimacy of her husband's sovereignty.[13]

Lupe's drama has many similarities with that of the Virgin of El Cisne; both are allegories of the Virgin of Guadalupe, in women fulfilling the role of selfless mothers. Lupe will do anything for her children, whom she defends despite their reprehensible behavior; La Churona brings rain and saves people from starvation without discriminating whether one person is more of a sinner than another; the Virgin Mary answers and attends to those who seek her. In the images of the Virgin and of Lupe, the mother's ideal is part of a Catholic hegemony through which rigid gender identities hold women at home to care for children and serve husbands. However, if we maintain the view that La Churona is an allegory of a transvestite divinity, things get complicated. First, the father figure disappears or appears as a woman in the sculpture of the Virgin; that is, in the religious image, the father's authority is also in crisis and, furthermore, absent. Second, migrant women featured in the documentary do not behave like Lupe. Carmen Barragán, the person who first brought La Churona to Madrid, clashes with Spanish priests, questioning their authority. This is a woman who gets into the business world by creating the Fundación Virgen del Cisne (Virgin of El Cisne Foundation) to promote Ecuadorian identity in Madrid.

It would be wrong, however, to idealize the work of Barragán as the image par excellence of cultural resistance in the twenty-first century. The Fundación Virgen del Cisne itself condenses the contradictions of a project that is compatible with the colonial-national hegemony. This woman reified and idealized the image of Ecuadorianness, victimizing migrants to obtain economic returns for her foundation, thus imposing a commercial logic or even profit that has nothing to do with devotion. But at the same time, Barragán was the main promoter of La Churona's festivities in Madrid. Her celebrations, as the priest Juan José told the documentary's director during an off-camera conversation, break the Church's solemn or sober logic, transforming the party into something more pagan. A Baroque or neobaroque ethos, previously referred to as cultural resistance, therefore, is not within the idealization of Ecuadorian identity, nor is it within the victimization of migrants, but in what the priest rejects as a form of desecration. Barragán, in her celebrations, mixes beauty contests, "mad cow" fireworks,[14] music concerts featuring characters like Máximo Escaleras, and more. The mix creates a spectacular on-stage cultural *champús* that transcends and subverts the ecclesiastical prescriptive, redefining celebration from a number of viewpoints.[15]

Female migrants in *La Churona* thus share some traits with Amalia, the ambitious daughter of Lupe who sacrifices love for money and social prestige. The women do not submit to the father authority, the priests, who promote the Marian image of the sacrificing or suffering woman. The women leave home to carve their own destinies without necessarily carrying the stigma of being bad women. Jonathan's mother did not leave home for purely selfish reasons but to achieve a better quality of life for her children. She is not opportunistic, nor is her desire to thrive born of a capricious attitude. She is a working woman struggling to thrive. Unlike Amalia, Jonathan's mother is not content with coming home to mourn her sorrows on her mother's lap. Although she suffers from being separated from her children, she is not passively waiting for their return as is Lupe. It was she who left home, and she seeks a way to bring her children to live with her in Spain.

La Churona's daughters do not repent for their sins as do Lupe's children, who leave for Mexico City dazzled by progress and disgusted by the insignificance of their own small town. Actual female migrants often do not wish to break with their Ecuadorian identity but want to keep it despite the distance. That is why they restage the cult of the Virgin of El Cisne in Madrid. The girls are more like Raimundo, Lupe's son, who was unfairly punished by his father and will rescue the family's estate with his sacrifice. *La Churona*'s female migrants were unjustly punished by Ecuador, a country that did not give them opportunities and forced them to go abroad and, ironically, survives on remittances that migrants send. However, unlike Raimundo, who joyfully accepts his sacrifice, these women's dramas are not resolved within the family; they are always present. They do not carry the sins of the rest of Ecuador on their shoulders, nor are they the hope of the nation, but show the failure of Ecuador in its role as both father and mother; in the first case, it was arbitrary and exclusionary, in the second, it was unable to protect its offspring.

If we think from a codigofagia point of view, Lupe's drama eats symbols of Christian tradition in order to find answers to a crisis that threatens her family. At the end of *Cuando los hijos se van* after Raimundo's sacrifice, the drama is resolved; peace comes to Lupe, who never gave up her role as a mother and always sacrificed her personal satisfaction for the family's welfare. Spiritual harmony, in this case, is the triumph of a hegemonic project that requires women to fulfill their roles as mothers and wives. The codigofagia of Ecuadorian female migrants does not bring such calm. The drama of separation from Ecuador and their families continues. The female Ecuadorian migrants are not like Lupe, who is resigned to wait for a miracle to redeem her family; these women try to take control of their destinies through their hard work. They turn to La Churona; they eat Catholic rituality to resist and fight a painful separation. Some bring their children to Spain, others continue being separated from their families, but they know that reunion with the nation—the great Ecuadorian family—is impossible. La Churona guarantees them a meeting place to overcome the crisis, but separation continues, and the memory of Ecuador in Madrid remains painful, if not traumatic.

Geography of a Transatlantic Ecuador

The second part of Carrillo Espinosa's documentary takes place in Spain. The Virgin of El Cisne came to the parish of San Lorenzo in Lavapiés, Madrid, first as a painting, then as the sculpture brought by Carmen Barragán. Initially, Barragán put the statuette on one of the temple's altars, but because of economic and image control conflicts, she removed it and later displayed it at a bar. Then, this choice of location caused a scandal, and Barragán was forced to move the figure again, this time taking it home. After a dispute that the media made public, the priest Juan José decided to travel to Ecuador to become familiar with the cult of La Churona and to personally bring a new replica from San Antonio de Ibarra. According to San Lorenzo's parish priest, Father Emilio, who at first did not know who La Churona was, the Virgin's arrival brought about a miracle. A nearly empty temple began to be frequently visited by many migrants. Ironically, La Churona's integrative powers among Ecuadorians marked the rebirth of a dying church in Spain. In the film Father Emilio magnifies the miraculous narrative, indicating that despite all the controversy, La Churona wanted to be in San Lorenzo's parish, and she had to come, as she did.

Comparing La Churona's trip to Madrid with her appearances in the late sixteenth century, we see that the cult's origin is not born from religious elites' actions, nor is it brought to Spain by national authorities. In the first case, the image appeared to some Indians who were at risk of starvation—and they were the ones who built the chapel and commissioned the image from Diego de Robles. In the second case, La Churona reached Lavapiés in the hands of a female migrant who then got in trouble with the Church. One can reasonably object that in the first case, miraculous devotion obeyed colonial policy and that it was the Church that ate indigenous religiosity to incorporate it into its rituals. It is also noted that before the conflict arose in Madrid, the priests brought the image reasserting the symbolic authority of the father. Priest Juan José goes even further. While blessing a migrant family's house in Madrid, he cleverly replaces the image of the Virgin of El Cisne with a replica of his, redefined as the Virgin of Lavapiés, and also imposes another prayer card among the proliferation of stuffed animals in the younger daughter's room. Also, it can be argued that by re-creating a strong sense of identity, La Churona is a conservative idealization of the nation. It is true that there was and is a codigofagia practice from religious or national elites seeking to impose a Catholic pax or a national pax, but this explanation, though necessary and correct, does not reflect the phenomenon in its entirety.

When La Churona came to Madrid, to the amazement of the locals she presented immediate competition to the Virgin of Almudena, the city's patroness. For two consecutive years, a procession was organized that filled the Plaza Mayor, a site that until then was reserved exclusively for Madrid's sacred image. In these processions, there is one detail that I would like to highlight: La Churona's dress. Besides the luxurious clothes and wig, the Virgin of El Cisne wears over her chest a band with the Ecuadorian flag, a garment much like the presidential sash used in Ecuador. Here three elements stand out: first, Madrid's geography; then, a foreign Virgin's procession implanting an imaginary Ecuador in Madrid; and finally, one of the most important symbols of Ecuadorian politics.

La Churona's cultural *champús* mixes heterogeneous and, in many cases, even contradictory elements, such as the Ecuadorian presidential sash and the Plaza Mayor in Madrid. Let us return to the cross and the tree analogy. Although the presidential sash is not a phallic symbol, it is one of power. This band does not penetrate the streets but instead spreads a feeling of Ecuadorianness. It's like Ecuador, the previously feminized America, spreading its seed in the center of Spanish power. In the sixteenth century, the *conquistadores* destroyed the Indian symbols, replacing them with Christian images. Ecuadorian migrants, though they do not destroy Spanish symbols, do reinvent the city's geography thanks to an image that redefines a space of exclusion into an inclusive one; in addition, it offers them visibility in the Spanish mass media.

In the sixteenth century, imperial Spain took possession of America; in the twenty-first century, a large number of excluded migrants take possession of Madrid's Plaza Mayor. But there are important differences: Europeans' status in conquered America was always superior to the natives, while the migrants' status is not. The latter experience humiliation and social exclusion. Whereas Spanish occupation was violent and permanent, migrants' is momentary and highly symbolic. The Ecuador that goes through the streets of Madrid has nothing to do with Ecuadorian authorities, nor is it sponsored by them. It is an allegorical Ecuador that, like La Churona, as soon as it appears, it disappears but paradoxically never vanishes completely because the Ecuadorian migrants remain in Spain.

To conclude, the presidential sash worn by La Churona as an allegory does not show us how national discourse eats popular practices; it shows precisely the opposite. La Churona's procession carrying the presidential sash creates an Ecuadorian geography in contemporary Madrid, but it is an ephemeral Ecuador that foremost makes visible a feeling of exclusion. Migrants' codigofagia thus reflects a drama that suffers local hostility and is urged to re-create a sense of belonging. Paradoxically, they know that the doors back to their country are closed, and that is why they are forced to find ways to enable themselves to integrate into Spanish society. In other words, following Echeverría's categories, migrants appropriate the presidential sash worn by La Churona to force this symbol of power to solve the discomfort it has created. In the film *La Churona*, therefore, we do not see the symbolism of power itself, but a population that refuses to be excluded and ignored. Hence, the film makes clearly visible not only Madrid's contradictions and hypocrisy but Ecuador's fractures and inabilities as a nation.

Notes

The first version of this chapter was published in Spanish as "La Churona y la réplica barroca: Cartografías de un Ecuador transatlántico," *Archivos de la Filmoteca* 72 (2013): 63–77.

1. *La churona* means the curly-haired woman or girl.

2. Costas and especially Sebastián seek cheap labor and give more importance to their film than to the struggle of indigenous Daniel, who is protecting water. Thus, the two characters replicate colonialism in its roles as both conquistador exploitation and religious paternalism.

3. The *bulas* of Alexander VI granted possession of American lands to the crown of Castilla in exchange for evangelizing its inhabitants. Also, the *encomienda* shows the overlap between religion and politics. For an analysis of the Conquest's legal discussions, see Brading.

4. The Counter-Reformation also meant a centralization of ecclesiastical power. In the colonial context, the Church began transferring Indian doctrines from religious orders to the secular clergy that was directly under the bishops' command.

5. In Italy, Ecuadorian migrants also use popular religiosity, especially the religious festivals of the Virgin of El Cisne and El Quinche, as a negotiating mechanism to achieve greater social inclusion (Lara Reyes).

6. Galo Ramón Valarezo, in his article "La Virgen de El Cisne: De la acción a la devoción," provides an excellent and concise history of the origin of La Churona. María Cristina Carrillo Espinosa, in her doctoral dissertation, also provides a history of this devotion.

7. Simón Bolívar established the procession from El Cisne to Loja in 1829. Given her miraculous powers, Loja wanted to retain La Churona, harming El Cisne. The decree stated that the Virgin was to leave August 15 to Loja and remain there until November 1, and then she would return to her original sanctuary (Carrillo Espinosa).

8. The significance of transvestism is vital in the Baroque and neobaroque. For a discussion on transvestism in neobaroque literature see Herrera.

9. Gilles Deleuze, in *El pliegue*, defines the Baroque as a wrapping line and a line of inclusion.

10. *Champús* is a traditional Ecuadorian beverage in which various ingredients are mixed. I owe the idea of cultural *champús* to film director Miguel Alvear (see Herrera).

11. I am working on the importance of the party in Baroque and Neobaroque rituals in the 2006 Peruvian Andean film *Madeinusa*, directed by Claudia Llosa.

12. The movie *Vengo volviendo* (*Here and There*, 2015), directed by Gabriel Páez Hernández and Isabel Rodas León, tells the story of immigrants' children who stayed in Ecuador with their grandparents while their parents emigrated to the United States or Europe. In the future I plan to trace some parallelisms and differences between *La Churona* and *Vengo volviendo* in regard to popular religiosity, family, and the drama of immigration.

13. Ana M. López understands melodrama in the Mexican golden age of cinema as a contradiction between a declining traditional hegemony and a modern hegemony unable to impose its values. The female characters of the period, López finds, are victims of social imbalances caused by male authoritarian behaviors.

14. A "mad cow" is a puppet in the shape of a cow that is covered in fireworks, lifted by a person, and run through the crowd.

15. Giulio Carlo Argan and Gilles Deleuze understand multiperspectivism as one of Baroque's most important features.

Works Cited

Almeida Durán, Napoleón. "La churona lojana." *Revista de la Universidad del Azuay* 27 (2002): 233–252. Print.

Argan, Giulio Carlo. *Renacimiento y Barroco II: De Miguel Ángel a Tiépolo*. Madrid: Ediciones Akal, 1999. Print.

Benjamin, Walter. *El origen del drama barroco alemán*. Madrid: Taurus, 1991. Print.

Brading, David A. *Orbe Indiano, de la monarquía católica a la república criolla 1492–1867*. Mexico City: Fondo de Cultura Económica, 1991. Print.

La Churona, Dir. María Cristina Carrillo Espinosa. Ecuador para Largo, 2010. Film.

Cuando los hijos se van. Dir. Juan Bustillo Oro. Grovas-Oro Mexico Films, 1941. Film.

Dean, Caroline. "War Games: Indigenous Militaristic Theater in Colonial Peru." *Contested Visions in the Spanish Colonial World*. Ed. Ilona Katzew. Los Angeles: Los Angeles County Museum of Art, 2011: 132–149. Print.

Deleuze, Gilles. *El pliegue: Leibniz y el Barroco*. Buenos Aires: Ediciones Paidós, 1989. Print.

Echeverría, Bolívar. *La modernidad de lo barroco*. Mexico City: Ediciones Era, 1998. Print.

Espinosa Carrillo, María Cristina. *La Churona en Madrid: Familia, comunidad y nación en la migración ecuatoriana en España*. Diss. Universidad Autónoma de Madrid, 2016. Print.

Gruzinski, Serge. *La guerra de las imágenes, de Cristóbal Colón a "Blade Runner" (1492–2019)*. Mexico City: Fondo de Cultura Económica, 2010. Print.

Herrera, Lizardo. "El champús de *Blak Mama*: Reflexiones sobre el neobarroco en el Ecuador andino." *Argus-a: Artes y Humanidades* 1.5 (July 2012). Web. 15 June 2013.

———. "*Cobra* y el juego de la simulación." *Kipus: Revista Andina de Letras* 20 (2006): 139–154. Print.

Jiménez, Armando. "Proceso histórico de la advocación de Nuestra Señora de El Cisne e influencia en la vida cristiana de los devotos." Congreso Mariano UTPL (Universidad Técnica Particular de Loja). 2010. Web. 10 June 2013.

Lafaye, Jacques. *Quetzalcóatl y Guadalupe: La formación de la conciencia nacional*. Mexico City: Fondo de Cultura Económica, 2006. Print.

Lara Reyes, Ruth. "Prácticas religiosas en contextos de migración: El caso de los ecuatorianos en Milán." *Cultura y Religión: Revista de Sociedades en Transición* 6.2 (2012): 43–63. Web. 7 June 2013.

López, Ana M. "Tears and Desire: Women and Melodrama in the Old Mexican Cinema." *Mediating Two Worlds: Cinematic Encounters in the Americas*. Ed. John King, Ana M. López, and Manuel Alvarado. London: British Film Institute, 1993. Print.

Moreno Yánez, Segundo. "La magia de un escultor." *Hoy*, 7 Nov. 2012. Web. 20 Nov. 2012.

Ramón Valarezo, Galo. "La Virgen de El Cisne: De la acción a la devoción." *El Comercio*, 11 Sept. 2016. Web. 5 Oct. 2016.

También la lluvia, Dir. Icíar Bollaín. Image Entertainment, 2010. Film.

Vengo volviendo. Dir. Gabriel Páez Hernández and María Isabel Rodas León. Filmarte, 2015. Film.

PART III

MIGRANT IDENTITIES AND DISPLACED SUBJECTIVITIES

8

Testimonial Youth in Flux

Migration, Narrative, and Children in *Which Way Home*

RAMÓN J. GUERRA

In the 2010 Academy Award–nominated documentary film *Which Way Home*, cameras are embedded with several young Central American migrants, ages 12 to 14, as they board the train—La Bestia, the beast—northbound from Central America, through Mexico, and ultimately to the United States. The resulting film, directed by Rebecca Cammisa as a product of her Fulbright Fellowship for Filmmaking, is a harrowing, witnessed account of young people's unique dangers experienced while attempting to cross borders and seek a better life in the United States, where the imperceptible goal resembles something akin to the vaguely muttered statement by one young man, "Maybe I'll meet a nice rich lady and she'll adopt me." The significance of the routine nature of this journey—several other children, some as young as nine, are encountered, interviewed, and monitored along the way—is palpable in the brazen attitudes of the two main young men Cammisa's film follows. Their perspectives, from their homes in Honduras through the many stops along the route, provide unfiltered testimony to the life of many Latin American youths who have been inspired by stories of the United States' seemingly abundant opportunities. This testimony drives the powerful narrative of the documentary, carefully shedding light on the newly shifting global community and the voices of those affected by the fallout of globalization—in this particular case, the voices of the very young—who have often been neglected in favor of grander narratives of immigration, typically centered on top-level policy makers and generalized notions of national security.

Past scholars have researched the narrative of *testimonio* in the form of first-person written accounts as a means of seeing the world but also instigating change in the world. With this in mind, documentary films like *Which Way Home* provide a testimonio-style text that professes personal experiences in the form of first-person narrative; eyewitness accounts of the subject dominate in this case. The film helps articulate the homelessness overarching the children as they are by-products of the immigration process who are often only misled by grossly uninformed portraits of an American Dream. As they give their testimonies on-screen, there is a dominant emotion of feigned hope, almost as if they want to hope for a better future (making it to the United States, having a U.S. family adopt them, and so forth) but somehow realize the futility of even hoping for such impossibilities.

Which Way Home

The presentation of the documentary *Which Way Home* is beautifully tragic and poetic. It is constructed by virtue of what can be termed an "embedded journalist" framework, with the cameraperson living alongside and experiencing firsthand the same incidents that the subjects of the narrative endure. In this film, the central narrative component on which the events hinge entails riding dangerously atop the northbound border-to-border trains as a means of shuttling immigrant hopefuls from Central America through Mexico to the southern border of the United States. Riding on top of La Bestia is the primary narrative force behind the documentary and allows the story of the two boys from Honduras to emerge over the 83 minutes of the film in an episodic form interspersed with other firsthand experiences of migrant excursions. The film is largely reliant on images that are slowly developed, with a musical score, an absence of any controlling voice-over narration, and intermittently displayed captions explaining various bits of background information that help establish the history and larger narrative to which this perspective will speak. As an example of this method, the film's opening shots reveal the image from several angles of an unidentified body floating in the river at the U.S.-Mexican border and the various crowd reactions as authorities work to fish it out. A local law enforcement official mentions that several drowned bodies have been recovered recently in the region, some that were even children, underscoring that this occurrence is not uncommon. From this statement, the film then transitions to a collage of images of many young children riding the trains along with the caption "Mexican freight trains are used by migrants traveling to reach the United States. Among the thousands that ride the trains, roughly 5% are children traveling alone."

Most of the ongoing narrative of the film is presented by the boys themselves through their actions and their answers to questions with which the cameraperson prods them from time to time. After the opening scene, the film introduces the two major protagonists; both are from Honduras, and both come from very low-income families and homes that are disheveled and dilapidated. Kevin is 14 years old and lives with his mother and his stepfather. They work hard but have little money and food, and Kevin feels that he is a bother to them, an opinion that is shared by his stepfather in a later conversation that indicates the man's resentment toward Kevin's reluctance to work or help his mother in any way to provide for their family. Kevin seems largely driven to go north by his limited exposure and by his familiarity with a mythos of American Dream–like characterizations of the United States as a final destination. His friend Fito is 13 years old and lives with his grandmother because his parents are unable to take care of him due to both poverty and drug use. His grandmother is mostly absent, and Fito experiences a life that is aimless; he projects a desire to go north primarily as a means to follow Kevin, out of loyalty. Both boys are a paradox—young men and yet sustained childhood. They are depicted as still quite playful in their wrestling with each other and enjoyment of a playground at a stop along their way. Later in their journey, when the boys encounter the migrant helpers Grupo Beta,[1] they are starstruck, like young kids seeing a version of an athlete idol or a comic book hero. They are mostly ignorant and oblivious to the true nature of their journey, consciously choosing to reflect on the potential gains of America over the dangers that they at first consider mere inconveniences. At one point later in the film, Kevin is asked if he knows all of the potential risks as they get closer to Mexico City and eventually to the border; seeming almost annoyed by the question, he casually runs through the list of dangers as if he has heard them all before and has them rehearsed. The boys are desperate and resourceful as well, as illustrated by scenes of them begging and finding food to sustain themselves. While it appears that they have an incomplete knowledge of the perilous trek awaiting them, they do not readily shirk any of the hardship; instead, they are seemingly girded by a preternatural sense of determination that is well beyond their years. Perhaps this is an indication of the general premise that the multitudes of young children pursuing this route have both a youthful experience and a tragic, undeservedly experienced youth.

As they set forth on the journey, hopeful and optimistic about the vaguely determined goal of some rich woman who might adopt them, their plight appears to be both ominous and illusory. At one point Kevin points to the truly breathtaking landscape of mountains and green valleys in southern Mexico in astonishment and amazement, as if they were vacationing rather than seeking an escape along a route well-defined by its known dangers (kidnappers, sexual predators, abandonment, corrupt officials, and so forth). The backdrop is an ironic scene—immensely beautiful but juxtaposed against the train tops overloaded with the desperate, hungry, tired, dirty, and sometimes ill-intended migrants rushing over the tracks and past nature's grandeur. Kevin's and Fito's joy in seeing this part of the world that they have never before seen rings with notes of sadness; the sense of joy is genuine, but there is an undeniable suggestion that their joy is keeping them from other, hidden emotions such as fear, sadness, and regret. The juxtaposition is experienced in many other places as well, between the binaries of young and old, sadness and joy, safety and danger, and dreams and illusions, among others. The end result is a coming-of-age narrative account that relies on lessons learned through the antithetical relation of hope and hopelessness. While there exists the possibility that they will survive the journey north, cross successfully into the United States, find some manner of employment, residence, and opportunity, the perpetual sense of failure in all its forms is omnipresent and manifests in their persistent desires to either ignore it or distract themselves from it.

A number of interspersed stories of other young children's experiences are scattered among Kevin and Fito's narrative. The interspersed stories aim to create a commonality and the notion of a widespread epidemic. One of the themes that emerges is the variety of stories pertaining to child migrants and their parents. The narratives typically resemble one of three manifestations: young children leaving for the North in an effort to reconnect with both or one of their parents who left for the United States earlier; young children leaving or being sent to the United States to find work and help their parents who stay and wait in their home country; or a variation of the second scenario, with young children setting out for the United States intending to start their own new lives separate from their parents. The last category describes Kevin and Fito, who leave unbeknown to their parents and Fito's grandmother and only let them know once they are already on their way. For other children in interspersed scenes, the desire to rejoin a beloved parent whom they have not seen for months or even years is more prominently depicted.

This particular scenario as portrayed in the documentary format is both comparable and dissimilar to the depiction of such fictional presentations as the 2007 film *Under the Same Moon/La Misma Luna*, directed by Patricia Riggen. In that film, a nine-year-old boy sets out from central Mexico to find his mother in Los Angeles after his grandmother dies. He and his mother have been separated since he was five years old, and his journey is improbably aided by another migrant who reluctantly offers him help and protection from all of the well-researched dangers. In the end the young boy reaches his mother in Los Angeles, and the film closes on their two teary-eyed faces preparing for a better future that will come off-camera. While this fictional treatment addresses the emotional pull that severed parent-child relationships create as well as the corruption of *coyotes*, drug runners, prostitution rings, and other impossible obstacles, the overarching representation of the young boy's ostensible luck and capability suggests that the improbable outcome is available with steadfastness and hearty optimism. Even in its realistic presentation, *Under the Same Moon* wallows in fairy-tale style devices that effectively elicit pathos-based responses, and it seems to almost relish rather than attempt to hide its sense of fantasy.

When the outcome of *Under the Same Moon* is compared with the depictions of children in *Which Way Home*, the horrific file images from Border Patrol evidence displaying victimized young children smuggled into the United States stuffed inside glove compartments and behind seat cushions are enough to combat that heartstring-pulling effect of the fictional portrayal with the gut-wrenching, gruesome realities on full display. One story involves a rescued nine-year-old boy who had suffered a broken arm and been abandoned in the desert until a sympathetic woman returned for him out of compassion. His grandmother remarks that if he had not been returned, the *coyote* she hired to smuggle him into the country would never have told her about his abandonment; she would have had no word of his fate. The overwhelming sense from this account is the general expendability of young children as by-products and afterthoughts in the grand scheme of immigration.

As the film continues and the train with the boys and hundreds of other migrants keeps moving north, Kevin and Fito befriend two other boys looking for companionship, and together they make their way toward the border sharing dreams of their arrival and acknowledging the dangers awaiting them as they go. Before reaching one particularly notorious train station checkpoint, the boys and the cameraperson make plans to rendezvous on the other side of that station. The boys never make it, and the cameraperson is forced to track them down by asking other migrants who have been riding the train and by making phone calls back to their homes in Honduras. Eventually it is learned that Kevin and Fito split up over a fight, and Fito and another companion were deported. Meanwhile, Kevin had turned himself in at the border and was being held at a U.S. shelter where he was enrolled in some educational courses while awaiting his being sent home. When he returns home, he shows off the grades he earned while there, and it is evident that he gained a sense of pride from his work in that situation. It is at this point that, after an initial welcoming phase from his mother, she expresses dissatisfaction with his return to the same situation as before, of Kevin's burden on the family. His stepfather specifically explains to the camera that Kevin's mother was happier when he was gone, and together they wished that he had found another family in the United States to take him in. Soon Kevin regrets his return to Honduras. The closing captions of the film provide the information that feels imminent: nine months later, after meeting up with Fito again, the boys once more leave for the United States. While Fito eventually returns to Honduras, Kevin makes it to a more permanent shelter in the state of Washington, where he remains, having completed his journey for the time being.

Testimonio Visualized: Expressing One's Experience on Screen

To understand the concept of testimonio as it can be applied to a documentary film like *Which Way Home*, we must consider that the purpose of providing testimony through literature or other media—much like its courtroom context suggests—is to provide an eyewitness encounter of an experience. The writing or telling can act as a witness, giving voice to those who have seen, experienced, or taken in the actuality of a momentous period rather than those who simply seek to report it. It must also be asked how the structure and style of traditional testimonial writing are translated to other genres of contemporary personal narrative such as memoir, autobiography, semi-autobiographical fiction, and most significantly for this essay, documentary film. Furthermore, what are the ways that these smaller voices of history complement, contradict, or attempt to expand an ongoing historiography or understanding of a particular phenomenon or occurrence? These types of personal narratives allow different opportunities for the oppressed or the subaltern to raise their voices against a larger, continuous voice attempting to define existence.[2] In the 2001 anthology *Telling to Live: Latina Feminist Testimonios*,[3] the Latina Feminist Group outlines its approach to crafting testimonio in a way that addresses the emergence of their voices as well as the recognition that their stories can and should do purposeful work in reshaping existent models.[4] The members met many times prior to establishing the anthology to confirm their goals and shape the outcome of their work by instituting several guiding questions to telling their stories.

> Initially, we addressed the following key questions: How do we bear witness to our own becoming? How do we define who we are? How have we made testimonio the core of our work? What are some important turning points of consciousness? What is our relationship to political identities and intellectual work? What is our relationship to building new paradigms or models? What are we transgressing? (Latina Feminist Group 12)

This set of questions can be applied to other types of personal expression as well, including documentary films based on first-person voiced experiences. In this defined approach to testimonios, testifying or bearing witness to a particular set of experiences becomes the underlying theme of the expression. The group also dissects the purpose of testimonio as they view it: "Testimonio was critical for breaking down essentialist categories, since it was through telling life stories and reflecting upon them that we gained nuanced understandings of differences and connections among us" (11). The concepts of bearing witness and providing testimony reveal the incorporation of the subaltern or Other into history through the solidifying aspects of relating one's own story, recognizing that story as part of a larger story and moving beyond fixed constructions of a historiography.

Looking at testimonio in this way requires a reexamination of how it has been defined by scholars in the past. Among them, John Beverley provides a "provisional definition" in reference to written narratives only and specifics of length, genre, and other characteristics. Beverley's definition restricts testimonio a bit but ultimately suggests the same core traits that I have taken and extended into texts like documentary film that may not, in his provisional definition, constitute testimonio. In discussing specifically written texts, Beverley states in his *Testimonio: On the Politics of Truth*,

> By *testimonio* I mean a novel or novella-length narrative in book or pamphlet (that is, printed as opposed to acoustic) form, told in the first person by a narrator who is a real protagonist or witness of the events he or she recounts, and whose unit of narration is usually a "life" or a significant life experience. (31)

He goes on to mention several textual categories that may be subsumed under his definition, including oral history, memoir, and nonfiction novel, among others, and he finishes his characterization with the profession that "any attempt to specify a generic definition for it [testimonio], as I do here, is at best provisional, and at worst repressive" (31). This recognition for potential expansion is crucial to my approach to fully envelop documentary films into the specific characteristic traits of testimonio.

The expanded application of testimonio based on Beverley's provisional definition is also strengthened by developed categorizations of "diaristic" forms of filmmaking as mentioned by Christian Quendler. In "A Series of Dated Traces: Diaries and Film," Quendler writes that filmmaking has incorporated new language and that "diaristic forms and testimonial genres informed a number of film movements in the second half of the twentieth century" (339). Quendler goes on to indicate that the innovation of media formats and availability have had an increased effect on the advancement of this particular nature of filmmaking:

> Whether serving as a vehicle of personal reflections or formal innovations, diary formats are frequently exploited to probe new media technologies. Innovations in recording technologies (digital cameras, camcorders, cell phones, etc.) are often embraced for new diary effects. When camcorders became common objects in everyday tourist and entertainment life, for instance, new diary film types involving "lost-and-found" and circulating video cameras emerged. (340)

While Quendler is indicating the relation between innovative development of new technologies and the foregrounding of heretofore unexplored narratives, the underlying message is that there has emerged in certain forms of filmmaking an ability and a subsequent desire to project individualized narratives that are drawn from a penchant for more personal stories of experience. This evolution in filmmaking toward a "personal essay" or diaristic format is cemented also by Pat Aufderheide, director of the Center for Social Media at American University, when she maintains that the mid-1980s made personal-essay documentaries "accessible beyond the reaches of film schools and art houses, and began to take place in the programming diet of television" (in Ellis and McLane 262). Aufderheide goes on to state,

> Personal essay documentaries were part of a trend in documentary work overall toward a more intimate approach, even in explicitly public affairs subject matter, with the goal of intervening in a shared understanding of meaning. In this documentary genre, the narrator takes clear ownership of the narration, at the same time that the narrator is a character. They are frankly, inevitably personal. (In Ellis and McLane 262)

What is perhaps most interesting about Aufderheide's statement here is the issue of ownership of the narration as it pertains to the narrator. This clearly echoes both the Latina Feminist Group and Beverley in placing control of the narration—the story and experience—as significantly "bearing witness to one's own becoming." In a genre like documentary filmmaking, this path to ownership may be problematized slightly in dissecting the relation between cameraperson or filmmaker and an object/subject who is carrying the film and its narrative but is not technically in control of the recording medium.

Visual Experience as Narrative Expression—How a Documentary Is a Text

The narrative strategies in *Which Way Home* are capable of being critiqued in the same manner that a written essay invites analysis. The concept of a personal-essay documentary to describe its rhetorical structure, purpose, tone, audience, and reception is not necessarily radical, yet it does give ample evidence that the film itself is not just a narrative—visual or otherwise—but also significantly in line with the testimonio narrative characteristics that are ultimately resistant to both the conventional narrative structure and to a larger understood historiography. This particular line of thought in regard to written testimonio narratives is transferrable to the more general descriptions by Jack Ellis and Betsy McLane in their *A New History of Documentary Film* where they discuss the purposes behind the creation of documentary film: "They [filmmakers] record social and cultural phenomena they consider significant in order to inform us about these people, events, places, institutions, and problems. In so doing documentary filmmakers intend to increase our understanding of, our interest in, and perhaps our sympathy for their subjects" (Ellis and McLane 2)

If this alone does not provide enough of a reason to see certain types of documentary as testimonio, Ellis and McLane go further to define the intended results that a documentary subject will elicit, drawing very specific connections with Beverley's extended characterization of testimonio that "aspires not only to interpret the world but also to change it" (Beverley xvi). In regard to this type of action, Ellis and McLane write of both the artistic and resistant space that a documentary film simultaneously occupies, leading to a unique stimulation among the audience or readership: "The audience response documentary filmmakers seek to achieve is generally twofold: an aesthetic experience of some sort, on the one hand; and an effect on attitudes, possibly leading to action, on the other" (Ellis and McLane 3). As with the written form of personal essay or testimonio, the focus given to rhetorical structure, purpose, and presentation creates a strong sense of the narrative as a compelling message with urgency and meaning for its individual subject(s) and for how the larger community receives and responds to the message.

The narrative of *Which Way Home* is set up by the cameraperson's involved experience with the protagonists. The moving images, scattered captions of description, and responses of the boys to probing questions are the means by which the story is conveyed to the audience. When looking back at the definitions of *testimonio* and testimonial writing, one of the more telling characteristics that Beverley illuminates when striving for a definition is that the stories are "told in the first person by a narrator who is a real protagonist or witness of the events he or she recounts, and whose unit of narration is usually a 'life' or a significant life experience" (31). Narration becomes a more complex structure in light of precisely how *Which Way Home* works. Technically speaking, the cameraperson who is embedded with the boys on their journey and controls the viewer's "gaze" by directing the camera according to his or her inclinations can be inferred as the narrator. The cameraperson also instigates the interview sessions with the boys by providing them questions to answer and ultimately concludes the presentation of the film in conjunction with director, film editors, postproduction teams, marketing strategists, and others. Thus it might be construed that the production of the film is technically in the first person of the director, cameraperson, editor, or some combination of collaborators who mandate a particular presentation. In some ways "first person" is accurate in that sense and may create a dubious depiction of Kevin and Fito as first-person subject-protagonists, instead highlighting their roles as objects of the film—certainly in control of their own fate but not particularly in control of telling their story.

One way to understand the complex relations in a different manner is to recognize the history of subject-driven testimonio from its early representations in, for example, oral history projects and large-scale survey initiatives intent on inviting previously marginalized voices into the larger narrative. The late nineteenth-century historian Hubert Howe Bancroft proposed to include *californios*,[5] among others, in his massive *History of California*.[6] However, Bancroft only intended to include their stories by backhandedly dispatching questioners to solicit responses from the californios to specific questions—leaving their subjectivity to a minimum. The objective of true testimonio in collecting oral history, on the other hand, is to purposefully give memories and experiences to the storytellers by conversing with them rather than directing them. A change in approach to the interview process can avert the type of oral history that John Beverley typically sees, and it instead approaches testimonio. Beverley outlines concerns with the collection of oral history—shedding light also on the similar potential of a documentary filmmaker to dominate the story over the subjects/protagonists: "In oral history it is the intentionality of the recorder—usually a social scientist—that is dominant, and the resulting text is in some sense 'data.' In testimonio, by contrast, it is the intentionality of the narrator [that is] paramount" (32). When the twentieth-century scholar Genaro M. Padilla looked back at the work of Bancroft to collect these stories of californios, he laid the groundwork for a different interpretation of the stories and answers to questions, to be seen not merely as "responsive," and therefore only in conjunction with the interviewer's itinerary, but rather as seminal works of testimonio in which both the nature and content of the narratives can be drawn as subject-driven experiences regardless of the impetus to speak. Padilla's *My History, Not Yours: The Formation of Mexican-American Autobiography* concentrates on the recovery process of Mexican Americans at the root of their experiences beginning in the nineteenth century.[7]

Padilla's assertion to seize control of one's own history, as evidenced by his book's title, can be applied to specific types of narrative, like written testimonios and documentary films, in the twentieth century. Padilla rightfully explores the aftermath of the 1848 Treaty of Guadalupe Hidalgo as the formation of a new voice in history and asserts that the tradition of Mexican American perspectives of their own unique history are not a novel twentieth-century invention. Padilla also notes that the narratives presented by Mexican Americans in the nineteenth century consistently had a distinctly "unofficial" quality:

> Whereas slave narratives were published and often widely distributed to promote the abolitionist cause, Mexican-American personal narratives—for example, the scores of personal narratives collected from Mexican Californians in the 1870s—were meant to function only as supplemental material for American historians and were, therefore, as we shall see, quite intentionally not published. (9)

This is the general treatment that much of testimonio narratives have received; there is the idea that even when recognized, they still serve as additional or "supplemental" perspectives to a strong and continuous narrative of history rather than effecting change within the whole composition of that history. It is crucial to note that this general reception is still alive and applied today among the testimonial narratives not only of Mexican Americans but also among all Latinos, including a group as specific as young immigrant children. By recognizing the urgency and the ability to reimagine and reconstruct acted-upon objects of oral history projects and of documentary films instead as acting subjects, there can be an extension of political implications made by unearthing the smaller, unknown stories of others presented *by* the filmmakers through the medium of documentary.

Part of reimagining perceived objects as subjects depends on the perception of the power structure within the interview process in a documentary film, regardless of whether that interview takes place in an after-the-fact setting, such as sitting in a chair in a studio being asked to remember the significance of an event, or as in *Which Way Home*, a component of recording the events as they occur. The interview is intended to act as a means of introducing another perspective into the larger narrative of the film, not unlike Padilla's incorporation of oral history as an active form of history that seeks to take control of the narrative rather than simply add to it. Jonathan Kahana writes about the way that the interview has been primarily used in documentary films:

> The power of the interview as a documentary technique has primarily to do with the temporal continuity between the event and its cinematic

representation embodied in the interview subject's voice. The synchronous recording of sound and sight in the documentary interview presents us, then, with another instance of the confrontation of the look and the gaze in cinema. To the viewer, this gaze takes the form of a question that can never be articulated: if I can hear, why do I need to see? (263)

In this sense, the interview can be shown to transform from merely asking the person being interviewed to provide the audience with some added information into a vehicle for the interviewed subject to assume the reins of the narrative by gaining first-person status. While the person recording, asking questions, and ultimately editing maintains the semblance of control, the gaze articulated in Kahana's description is strongly connected to the narrative of the interviewed subject.

In *Which Way Home* the style of interviews conducted is governed by the nature of the embedded-journalist process; they must take place along the route, both aboard the train and off, and must then always carry a more impulsive tone than a prepared one. In addition to this characterization, the strategy revealed at the onset and continued throughout is for the filmmaker-cameraperson to be diminished; this is further cemented by the absence of a controlling voice-over narration. There is almost a reluctance for the cameraperson to have her or his voice recorded as part of the filming and interviewing process; somehow doing so is seen as diminishing the intended purity of devotion to the actual protagonists. The first appearance and opening remarks of the two young protagonists are indicative of how the storytelling is being surrendered somewhat by the cameraperson and promoted to their subjects. Upon being introduced to Kevin and after seeing him playfully and successfully search the ground for an abandoned cigarette, we hear him speak his first words of testimonio:

> What I've always dreamed of was to be in the United States. Most of the children in Honduras, they grow up with that idea, "I'm going to the United States." The truth is my mother is really poor. The money she makes is barely enough to feed us. In my life I would like to help her and be able to buy her a house.[8]

Kevin speaks these words with a somber hope that he carries with him throughout the documentary, carefully showing a love for his mother and an ongoing penchant to dream big. There is also a conveyed sense of his having considered this prior to being asked about it; the idea of relating this information to somebody and giving somebody else the impressions of his particular plight and his harbored dreams has occurred to him before, and he participates by relaying these in his narrative.

In contrast, shortly after introducing Kevin, the documentary reveals his friend and traveling companion Fito, whose expressions are curt and delivered with a suppressed laughter. He requires the sparsely worded prodding that the cameraperson instigates to get him to develop his narrative further, but he does not readily react. After Kevin explains how they left together in a revelation that they should go "as wetbacks" (*de mojados*), he says they left without telling Fito's mother:

> Cameraperson: You didn't tell your mom?
> Fito: No. Because she was gone.
> Cameraperson: Where to?
> Fito: Partying. With her husband.
> Cameraperson: What about your dad?
> Fito: He died.
> Cameraperson: When?
> Fito: Years ago.

Fito's hesitancy to speak or to elaborate when pressed reveals two things of importance. First, it reveals a difference between Kevin and him that may simply be a personality trait but could also be related to Kevin having fostered a desire to express his experience that Fito has not engaged. Second and more significant to the construction of the narrative, Fito's reticence presents the intention of the filmmakers to draw out the words and stories from their subjects if necessary. Here, Fito's narrative willingness or ability is limited, but rather than deny him or ignore his testimony, the cameraperson continues to focus the camera on Fito and subscribes to the belief that limited prodding may be successful in creating a safe space for him to speak—the space that Kevin seems to welcome and embrace in his narrative moments. In referring back to Kahana's description of the power of the interview as a documentary technique, scenes like this one, in which Fito's few words, his refusal to look in the camera, and his nervous laughter and smirking face provide an attempted answer to Kahana's defining question developed by the constructed gaze, "If I can hear, why do I need to see?" Furthermore, the notion of "shared authority" as defined by Louise Spence and Vinicius Navarro emerges through the ongoing dialogue provided by the interview process as it develops. Spence and Navarro state that interviews "can help foster a genuine dialogue between documentary makers and their subjects. They create opportunities for spontaneous exchanges that can, in turn, help shape the documentary. . . . The documentary subjects become participants in the making of the film even if they do not have direct access to the filmmaking apparatus" (74). The boys' emerging relationship with the cameraperson and the filmmakers as a whole is paramount in depicting the shared authority between the filmmakers and these two boys as the subjects of this documentary and their words and experiences as testimonio.

Conclusion

In portraying documentary films like *Which Way Home* as a youthful expression of testimonio and using the guidelines pertaining to the more traditional written form of testimonio, there is an implied argument that the first-person account of experiences as a narrative matters, that it is monumentally substantial in the process of elaborating a confined sense of history, recent or long past. The process of writing or speaking as an individual about one's own perspective and experience is vital to the continued construction of historiography, especially to fully embrace history's organic, incomplete nature over its characterization as absolute, even official. The role that stories from all populations play in the notion of continued construction is important; more specifically, the role of nonfiction, documentary film as a way to utilize the first-person, witnessed account as a rhetorical strategy to deconstruct and reconstruct historical narrative has developed another option for the telling and retelling of historical perspective. Janet Walker writes about the contemporary penchant for using film to elaborate the understanding of the world and its people, "The will to collect and authorize oral testimony—including video testimony—as a significant historiographic tool has never been greater" (93). She continues, making the direct connection to the growth of a vaguely defined sense of seeing more perspectives represented in documentary form—specifically in referencing the interview and its subject as an evolutionary development in crafting the voice(s) of previously unheard populations: "If, in years past, documentary film scholars regarded the 'talking head' as evidence of a lack of expressive force on the part of film and film-maker, now, forty years after the birth of the direct cinema, film-makers are realizing the probative powers of testimony in the direct address documentary" (Walker 93). It becomes evident that, in Walker's view as well as in others,' the previous reading of talking heads in documentary films as a deviation from expression has been replaced by the more accurate and substantive view of that talking head as being vital and perhaps more directly instructive when allowed to express and emote rather than simply exist passively on the screen as data.

In light of that evolution, the necessity to recognize the act of testimonio as doing more than merely depicting stories but instead advancing them—drawing on their power—is tantamount. Once more returning to Beverley's careful distinctions in and allusions to the implicit power that should be revealed in the embrace of testimonio, he states in relation to the idea that representation is enough:

> The key issue in testimonio, it seemed to me, was not . . . "representation." If the point of testimonio were simply to represent the subaltern *as subaltern*, victims as victims, then . . . it would be little more than a kind of post-modernist *costumbrismo*, the Spanish term for local-color writing. To recall Marx's well-known distinction, testimonio aspires not only to interpret the world but also to change it. Nevertheless, how one interprets the world also has to do with how one seeks, and is able, to change it. (xvi)

With that analysis in mind, considering the conclusion of *Which Way Home* with summary knowledge of Kevin and Fito returning again to the train ride north and ultimately reaching the United States, the question of this documentary narrative's purpose is appropriate. Has there been any effect from presenting the story of these two subaltern immigrant youths? An article from the *New York Times* in June 2014 depicts several aspects of the developing situation at the U.S.-Mexican border of children immigrating alone. Julia Preston, the article's author, portrays the young travelers' vulnerability as well as the misinformation that surrounds their potential crossing and arrival in the United States. She goes on to chronicle current patterns: "More than 52,000 minors traveling without their parents have been caught crossing the southwest border illegally since October [2013], including 9,000 in May [2014] alone, a record. . . . [M]any, especially the youngest, are coming to reconnect with families, hoping to join parents or close relatives who live in this country, often without papers" (Preston). The message is clear, regardless of politics and social ideologies, that the increase of children emigrating from Mexico and Central

America to seek new lives in the United States is imminent, and their stories are only more recently being condensed and disseminated to the larger community. The potential for change, something with which Kevin seems to wrestle constantly in his wide-eyed optimism and naiveté, is both proposed and demanded in this documentary. Through Kevin's and Fito's words and experiences, the audience encounters their testimonios, their interpretations of what they have experienced; implicit in their testimonios is the impetus for change on both individual and communal levels for these representations of the young emigrants who live unstable lives.

Notes

1. Grupo Beta is a segment of the National Institute of Migration of Mexico designed to offer water, medical treatment, information, and protection to migrants traveling through Mexico regardless of their immigration status. The first group began in Tijuana in 1990, and now there are more than 20 Grupos Beta all throughout Mexico.

2. The concept of the subaltern comes from Italian theorist Antonio Gramsci and refers to those who have no power in the state or in the class system to which they are tied. Indian scholar Gayatri Spivak took the term and expanded it in Indian postcolonial studies to relate to all people who lack control of their own self-identity based solely on their status within the social system.

3. The Latina Feminist Group's book is not limited to one editor or author but is instead credited to the collective as a whole.

4. The Latina Feminist Group consists of Luz del Alba Acevedo, Norma Alarcón, Celia Alvarez, Ruth Behar, Rina Benmayor, Norma E. Cantú, Daisy Cocco De Filippis, Gloria Holguín Cuádraz, Liza Fiol-Matta, Yvette Gisele Flores-Ortiz, Inés Hernández-Avila, Aurora Levins Morales, Clara Lomas, Iris Ofelia López, Mirtha N. Quintanales, Eliana Rivero, Caridad Souza, and Patricia Zavella.

5. Californios were Spanish speaking people who came from Mexico or Spain to settle in California from the mid-eighteenth to the mid-nineteenth century.

6. Bancroft's work was published in seven volumes from 1884 to 1890.

7. Padilla focuses specifically on the Treaty of Guadalupe Hidalgo and 1848, "the year a vast part of northern Mexico was annexed by the United States in a war of conquest" (4), as the genesis of Mexican American narratives because a new identity and experience had been born.

8. All of the people in the documentary speak among themselves and to the camera operators in Spanish. Translations to English are provided in the subtitles and are used in the cited sections here.

Works Cited

Bancroft, Hubert Howe. *History of California*. (1884). Santa Barbara: W. Hebberd, 1963. Print.

Beverley, John. *Testimonio: On the Politics of Truth*. Minneapolis: U of Minnesota P, 2004. Print.

Chanan, Michael. "Rediscovering Documentary: Cultural Context and Intentionality." *The Social Documentary in Latin America*. Ed. Julianne Burton. Pittsburgh, PA: U of Pittsburgh P, 1990. 31–47. Print.

Ellis, Jack C., and Betsy A. McLane. *A New History of Documentary Film*. New York: Continuum, 2005. Print.

Gordon, Ian. "Map: These are the Places Central American Child Migrants are Fleeing." *Mother Jones*, June 2014. Web. 28 June 2014.

Gramsci, Antonio. *The Modern Prince, and Other Writings*. Trans. Louis Marks. New York: International, 1967. Print.

Hesford, Wendy S. "Documenting Violations: Rhetorical Witnessing and the Spectacle of Distant Suffering." *Biography: An Interdisciplinary Quarterly* 27.1 (2004): 104–144. Print.

Kahana, Jonathan. "'Other Languages': Testimony, Transference, and Translation in Documentary Film." *The Dreams of Interpretation: A Century Down the Royal Road*. Ed. Catherine Liu, John Mowitt, Thomas Pepper, and Jakki Spicer. Minneapolis: U of Minnesota P, 2007. 263–282. Print.

Kaplan, E. Ann. *Trauma Culture: The Politics of Terror and Loss in Media and Literature*. New Brunswick, NJ: Rutgers UP, 2005. Print.

Latina Feminist Group. *Telling to Live: Latina Feminist Testimonios*. Durham, NC: Duke UP, 2001. Print.

Padilla, Genaro M. *My History, Not Yours: The Formation of Mexican-American Autobiography*. Madison: U of Wisconsin P, 1993. Print.

Preston, Julia. "Snakes and Thorny Brush, and Children at the Border Alone." *New York Times*, 25 June 2014. Web. 25 June 2014.

Quendler, Christian. "A Series of Dated Traces: Diaries and Film." *Biography: An Interdisciplinary Quarterly* 36.2 (2013): 339–358. Print.

Spence, Louise, and Vinicius Navarro. *Crafting Truth: Documentary Form and Meaning*. Rutgers UP, 2011. Print.

Spivak, Gayatri. "Can the Subaltern Speak?" *Marxism and the Interpretation of Culture*. Ed. Cary Nelson and Lawrence Grossberg. Urbana: U of Illinois P, 1988. 271–313. Print.

Under the Same Moon/La Misma Luna. Dir. Patricia Riggen. Creando Films, 2007. Film.

Walker, Janet. "Testimony in the Umbra of Trauma: Film and Video Portraits of Survival." *Studies in Documentary Film*. 1.2 (2007): 91–104. Print.

Which Way Home. Dir. Rebecca Cammisa. HBO Documentary Films, 2009. Film.

❱ 9 ❰

Resistance in Motion

Small Cinemas by Cuban Women in the Diaspora

ZAIRA ZARZA

Since the foundation of ICAIC, the Cuban Film Institute, in 1959, the patriarchal dominance of the country's mainstream cinematographic institution has been a subject of critical debate on and off the island.[1] The underrepresentation of women in Cuban cinema, ruled by hegemonic masculinity, is still a formidable issue to overcome today.[2] According to Catherine Benamou, since the early 1990s,

> factors delaying the accession of women to the field of film production include the absence ... of opportunities for formal film study outside ICAIC in Cuba and the need for a costly technical infrastructure along with proximity to laboratory and distribution facilities, which have contributed to the concentration of production in centralized state institutions (with varying degrees of autonomy) located in the nation's capital. (63)

This situation has changed in recent years. The scope for women's inclusion in the panorama of Cuban cinema has opened as a result of a number of initiatives: the foundation of the International Film and Television School (Escuela Internacional de Cine y Televisión, EICTV) in 1986 and the School of Audiovisual Communication Media (Facultad de Arte de los Medios de Comunicación Audiovisual) of the Art Institute of Cuba (Instituto Superior de Arte de Cuba) in 1988 and its affiliated departments around the island as well as independent forms of filmmaking. However, many challenges remain, starting with the apparent need to fill the long-standing gap in Cuban film production by women. Yet, young Cuban female cineastes, perhaps even unconsciously, adhere to Marguerite Duras's idea that "the women who can get beyond the feeling of having to correct history will save a lot of time" (in Braidotti 137). I read Duras's expression here as a smart critique of how the very act of "correcting" as a form of punishment that generally implies some extent of resentment has been a drawback or a hindrance for many ideologies (and individuals) to move forward.

Documentary has been a recurrent genre for female film authors' engagement and resistance. It has also been the genre by which many independent filmmakers have found opportunities for experimentation. Documentaries tend to gather smaller crews and require more discrete budgets than fiction cinema. Furthermore, when they are done independently or as school projects, there is room for the filmmakers to engage in more personal, intimate types of filmmaking. This circumstance could create possibilities for a more feminist approach in both narratives and aesthetics as seen in the work of the women directors I discuss here.

In the Cuban case, most female filmmakers were able to finish their first documentary works while being trainees as assistant directors for male cineastes who by and large were making feature fiction films. For a young generation of women filmmakers in the diaspora, documentary is bringing new light to the question of mapping contemporary Cuban "accented cinemas."[3] The contradictory conditions of multiculturalism in their host societies, the gender perspectives connecting the notions of nationalism, and diaspora are some of the concerns of these cineastes in filmic processes through which they negotiate their identities and those of their films' characters. Different forms of domination and postcolonial practices, the memory of slavery, and ritual spaces of religiosity are also addressed and debated by these women. To criticize not only the hegemonic masculinity but the macho character of the nation-state as an institution, in the way these filmmakers do, is already a form of contestation. In their representations of the self through first-person cinemas, they are giving space to gendered experiences that are much larger than their own. Building on arguments by Levinas and Butler, Alisa Lebow states that "the self is always a relational matter, never conceivable in isolation. First-person film merely literalizes and makes apparent the fact that self-narration—not to mention autobiography—is never the sole property of the speaking self. It properly belongs to larger collectivities without which the maker would be unrecognizable to herself, and effectively would have no story to tell" (xii). As Lebow further asserts—and as I purposely relate to these Cuban cineastes—they are able to transform "the work from autobiographic (a study of one's own culture) to ethnoautobiographic (a culturally grounded study of oneself)" (151).

In the space of the diaspora women have been able to subvert the patriarchal predicament of Cuban cinema. I find such subversion in the works of emerging Cuban female diasporic cineastes and how they represent different kinds of connections to place according to contexts, to the particular experiences of the filmmakers as migrant subjects, and to the narratives of the films themselves. I consider diaspora an analytical tool to understand how certain types of social formations can challenge modernity's attempt to integrate differences through ideology, citizenship, and the nation-state (Bhabha; Brah; Gilroy). I am interested in understanding these diversities as they are "written" in the films. Rather than focus on one singular identity, I want to explore the contexts in which multiple identities are defined, subverted, and rearticulated, notably in the reproduction of misrepresentations and stereotypes. These women are dealing with a transnational set of economics and politics, especially in relation to their mobility, networks, references, and diverse possibilities of place-making. Their attachments to and detachments from home may be seen through the dynamics of their family relations, self-referenciality, and self-representation, but I am interested also in how they relate to the host societies across their gendered positionalities and their own displacements and reterritorializations. For these reasons I have chosen to analyze works by the documentary makers Heidi Hassan, Susana Barriga, and Daniellis Hernández, as they are helping to reshape belonging by mapping "variations on *cubanidad*" in locations other than the ones Cuban writer Víctor Fowler has finely interpreted. In his analysis, Fowler suggests some variants of "what is Cuban," mainly in the United States and more specifically in Miami. He sees the exile diaspora as a pedagogical project, by which he understands "an ordered and reasoned articulation of experiences to transmit a precise cultural heritage" (Fowler 110). While memory appears as an act of self-preservation of identity, Fowler argues that identity there, "more than a matter of culture, places itself on the terrain of the ideological with a strong class-based component" (110).

Preamble to Contemporary Films by Cuban Women in the Diaspora

In the foreword of the compilation *Cubana: Contemporary Fiction by Cuban Women*, the Cuban American anthropologist Ruth Behar was encouraged to answer the question "What is the nature of Cuban feminism?" She replies by paralleling her response to the verses of "Geography," a 1938 work by the Cuban poet Dulce María Loynaz: "Question: Define: Island. Answer: An Island is an absence of water surrounded by water: An absence of love surrounded by love" (in Behar vii). Behar's rejoinder: "Cuban feminism is a paradox: there are no feminists in Cuba and yet the island is surrounded by feminism." Why are there no feminists in Cuba? While struggling with the extent of this question, I realized that perhaps the problem lies in the affiliation with the fixed categorical realm of "feminism." The origins and outcomes of this dis(connection) are an inexhaustible source of curiosity and debate.

Although inclined to empower female subjects, the history of women's activism in Cuba—largely driven by the Cuban Women's Federation, founded and directed for almost 40 years by Vilma Espín—is not directly related to Feminism with a capital F as an ideology or movement of resistance. Feminist postulates and their emergence in capitalist societies were not an immediate frame of reference for the newly revolutionary Cubans of the 1960s. For many years, the political project of the 1959 Cuban Revolution became *la medida de todas las cosas*—the measure of all things. The ideals of feminism and its principles—not unlike racial, sexual, and religious diversities—defined forms of difference that were not welcomed by the egalitarian norms inspiring and regulating social change. It was assumed that the activist struggle for women's rights existed in societies where there were problems that the revolutionary process ostensibly eradicated on the island. In her prologue, Behar goes on to assert how Espín repeatedly stated that

> the federation is a "feminine" and not a "feminist" organization: an organization of women committed to a revolution that already speaks in their name. . . . With the state providing all women with free education, health care, birth control, access to abortion, nutritional support for pregnant mothers and young children, day care, the freedom to divorce, and the unequivocal defense of women's sexuality in its own right, who needs feminism? (ix–x)

This situation is also noticeable in Cuba's education system today. Very few classes in universities in the country at both graduate and undergraduate levels are devoted to gender studies or women's studies, let alone feminist studies. In addition, and maybe also as a consequence, very few Cuban women scholars or cultural producers who live and work on the island have the possibility to debate their positionality regarding feminism due to the overwhelming masculinism of public intellectual life that causes women's and feminists' voices to be drowned out. Still today, fear of the radicalization of feminism and insufficient understanding of its proposals have affected young Cuban women's affiliation with the term even when their ways of thinking and daily life practices are deeply associated with their own liberation and enfranchisement. Of course, this is a global issue not at all singularly associated with the Cuban reality.

Patriarchy reveals itself in Cuba not through income inequality or deficiency in the fairness of laws but in, for example, the normalized heterosexual street harassment and especially the "double shift" that Cuban women experience at home and at work, bearing most of the responsibility for domestic labor and care for children and the elderly. Their professional development has not reduced their leading role in the household. Women are also still a minority in decision-making positions even though Cuba proclaims a more balanced proportion between men and women in the workforce.[4] The vast majority of single parents are female, and although both fathers and mothers have access to parental leave, it is a benefit that fathers almost never use.[5]

Demographics have also been affected by gendered realities. The accelerated aging of the Cuban population is a result of a massive youth diaspora that started in the early 1990s and of the decreasing trend in birth rates. The decline in births has been attributed to the difficult economic conditions experienced in the country but also to the high levels of professionalization and empowerment of women in a place where the rights for free clinically assisted abortion, free contraceptive acquisition, and social assistance for family programming have existed for decades. Having autonomy over their bodies, Cuban women on the island are avoiding having children under harsh economic conditions and increasing professional responsibilities. Likewise, Cuban women living abroad are delaying motherhood as the processes of adjustment and settlement in the new societies take additional time and effort. Without a recognized system of either domestic or transnational adoption in Cuba, maybe this will be the moment when changes toward family sustainability should occur.

Given the status quo, then, what is the panorama of Cuba's film scene by women, and how has diaspora complicated a gendered approach? In their processes of identity construction and representation of "Cubanness," womanhood, and migration, the triad of filmmakers I study here has expanded beyond the national border to examine the intersections of sex and gender, racialization, and migration. These artists' journeys could even be read as nomadic routes. Heidi Hassan goes from Havana to Geneva and then to Madrid; Daniellis Hernández moves from Havana to Manchester, England, and then to Berlin. Susana Barriga travels from Santiago de Cuba to Havana, then to London, and finally settles in Spain. However, geographic movement is not enough to argue for the traveling nature of these women. Rosi Braidotti's notion of nomadic subjects is more attuned to their migrant practices. She states that "nomadic consciousness consists in not taking any kind of identity as permanent.... The nomad has a sharpened sense of territory, but no possessiveness about it" (Braidotti 64–65). More importantly, "the nomadic subject is not always in motion or fleeting—she also requires periods of rest or *stasis*.... Periods of recollection and temporary stability are necessary to produce the kind of syntheses and associations that allow for a sustainable notion of nomadic subjectivity" (Braidotti 65). These three filmmakers found periods of stasis while they were international film students in Europe.

The films I analyze are short feature documentaries made by young Cuban female cineaste graduates from the prominent EICTV in San Antonio de los Baños, Cuba, the first step for most filmmakers toward transnational cinema production in Cuba (Lord and Zarza 200). At the time Hassan was pursuing her master's degree at the Haute école d'arts et design (HEAD) in Geneva, Switzerland, Hernández and Barriga were producing documentary works while on exchange in England through an educational agreement between EICTV and the University of Salford in Manchester. An urban poem, Heidi Hassan's autobiographic *Orages d'été* (Summer storms, 2008) is an internal journey, a coming-of-age film about a woman at the edge of turning 30. And so, it deals with questions that the filmmaker is posing to herself as she starts to fall in love with a local musician. *Extravío* (*Lost*, 2008) by Daniellis Hernández is an ethnographic documentary in which the director addresses the problem of class difference within race as a new form of citizenship-making. She accomplishes this end by portraying different stories of first- and second-generation black Anglo-Caribbean and African migrants in Manchester. Susana Barriga's *The Illusion* (2008), on the other hand, registers the filmmaker's reunion with her father, a political refugee in the United Kingdom whom she hadn't seen in more than 20 years.

These women's first-person way of filmmaking engages in a cinema of affect, a process that involves the noncognitive, rooted in the psychological self. Therefore, disturbance, distress, disappointment, frustration, anxiety, and grief in addition to desire, anticipation, joy, and fear (that is, affect and emotion) take precedent over rational knowledge, and gestures are more relevant than consciousness. The narratives are those of observation and intuition centered, Benamou finds, "on 'intimacy' as a chosen space for women's communication and growth. . . . [T]his area of film practice tends to be defended as part of a larger struggle to decolonize the screen, taking its cue from the organized political efforts to improve the status of women, rather than as an oasis of personalized, politically noncommittal expression" (66). Even though their works could be considered unrelated to each other, they share, to say the least, a common "structure of feeling [that] corresponds to the dominant social character" with which they grew up.[6] They partake in a generational memory, a collective consciousness of a past marked by the Soviet Cuba of their childhood, the temporary bonanza of the 1980s, and an adolescence signaled by the beginning of the post–Cold War era. That is, they both experienced the scarcity of the Special Period after 1990, the dual currency, the industry of tourism, and the increasingly perceptible segregation between the haves and the have nots. Their lived culture is also one of broad transnational movement in the twenty-first century, when the pain of family separation and the fact of being young migrant women in Europe will be central.

Fragments of the Self: *Orages d'été*

A woman walks on a bridge overlooking the city. It is nighttime and she has been out. Very soon she removes her high heels and walks with bare feet on the concrete. It is breezy and chilly out, and the wind blows her hair and scarf. From the top of a small bridge she contemplates the river, the traffic, the street lights. Although peaceful, the urban space seems to reject her as she rests her head on the cold metallic structure of the bridge and massages her neck like it is sore from carrying a heavy burden. She is alone, and her name is Heidi Hassan.

So begins the fourth short film made by this Cuban diasporic artist during her years in Switzerland. While the initial difficulties of Hassan's integration to the new context begin to fade, she now discusses topics related to her individual experiences as a mature woman: the increasing transformations of her body, the intimidating possibility of motherhood, the memories of her childhood and adolescence in another land, and the evocation of past love stories. The filmmaker places herself in front of the lens for the first time to conduct the viewer through fragments of her first love relationship in the diaspora. In doing so, Hassan films dates, phone calls, trips, and intimate moments with her lover. And as she does so, her most vulnerable self will be on screen. With the use of a subjective camera style, she will be the spectator of her own reality, becoming both mind and body of the gaze.

Many of the film's scenes are related to Hassan's photographic series Retratos íntimos (Intimate portraits) and Autorretratos (Self-portraits), not yet exhibited but available online in the filmmaker's webpage.[7] About the conceptions of her work with still and moving images, she has said, "Initially for me there is a snapshot because still photography is what first came into my life. Then I became a cinematographer and then I got to filmmaking. When I took pictures I was left wanting more, but I think that photography gives value to what you want to say."[8] For a filmmaker who constantly questions her work, these photographic self-portraits have helped her stay active in cultural production and train her gaze when she is not making movies. It is a sort of method that allows her to exorcize emotions: "I use cinema as a therapy to have a dialogue with myself without feeling alone or lonely in the solitude of a project, in the unconsciousness of a creative process."[9]

Several years after watching Hassan's 2007 film *Tierra roja* for the first time in Havana and many months after reencountering and falling in love with it as an international student in the diaspora, I interviewed Heidi Hassan. Thus I learned that its plot had been the fictionalization of the story of her mother, who left Cuba when Heidi was a teenager and did not see her daughter for five years. The filmmaker was the child to whom the letters in the film were written. And the audiovisual piece—articulated around a continuing absence—was how she was able to make more sense of her lived experience and observe it from a distance. What seems to be anticipation in the film is nothing but Hassan's re-creation of her own memories: a flashback. In *Tierra roja*, the narrator—Hassan's evoked mother performed by Hassan's voice—speaks in future tense, as she is foretelling her and her daughter's future experience in the diaspora. In this form of autobiography, the goal was never to reproach the decisions of her mother but essentially to think them through now as a young adult in her work. For that matter, Hassan considers *Tierra roja* a truly egocentric film but has also realized it has a broader reach and effect than she could have ever imagined.[10]

Orages d'été reminds us that maybe instead of lamenting the diasporas, we should recognize the political potential of social change that the diasporic experience entails. Although it is almost imperceptible, she (Hassan, the filmmaker, the character) has an accent, dances salsa, and eats a fried egg over white rice, as is usual in Cuba. At some point she recalls with nostalgia her "childhood sea" and "that sun," but the poetics of this film are not those of the diasporic subject in an obvious manner, and certainly the film does not represent direct reaffirmations of nationality or ethnicity. Hassan does not hide her Cubanness, but it is also not obvious in the story. The home remains in the space of memory through evocative language and is perceived only at certain moments. Maybe in foreseeing her future moving from Geneva to Madrid, the film reveals Hassan's dreams about being a nomad who starts anew. She talks about how she might eventually meet new people, and share their petty problems, learn the names of the streets, decide on her favorite bakery, and maybe one fine day, resume the path (*Orages d'été*).

Most of Hassan's work belongs to a cinema of gestures and silence in which body politics are relevant. Still, only fragments, excerpts of the body, are always visible, as if the graphic representation would symbolically demonstrate the decentered and insecure nature of the diasporic subject. The Cuban film critic and researcher Dánae Diéguez has included one of the scenes in this movie among the most erotic moments in the history of Cuban cinema (figures 9.1, 9.2).[11] Diéguez describes the scene in this way: "She films him [her lover] with tenderness and curiosity, capturing the novel expressions of a face still almost

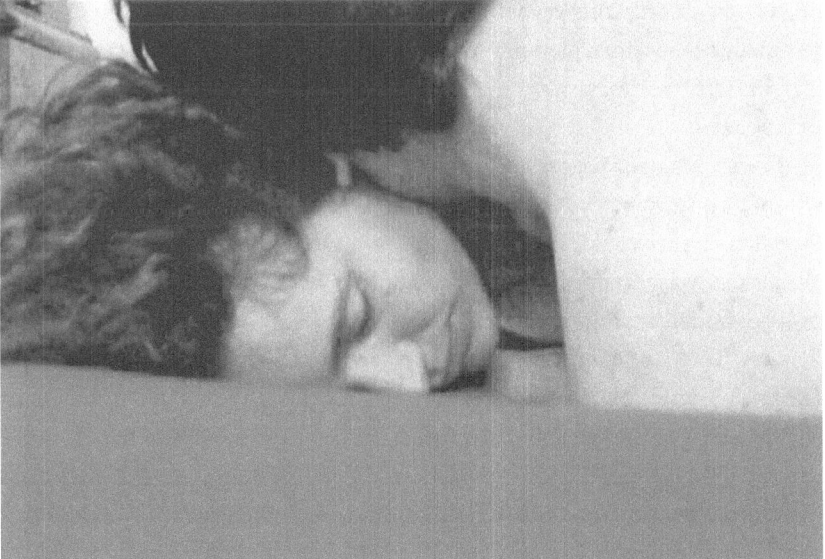

Figure 9.1. Lovers' intimate embrace (*Orages d'été*, 2008, Heidi Hassan).

Figure 9.2. Kaleidoscopic screen image of Heidi and Léonard (*Orages d'été*, 2008, Heidi Hassan).

unknown. Then the images become confused and all that remains is a play of lights, until the screen becomes a kaleidoscope."[12] The sequence of their sexual encounter is so personal that it engages a global language about the physicality of love, suggesting "the way vision itself can be tactile" (Marks xi). The lovers' self-made scene with a plethora of fragmented images of the body—arms, feet, legs, muscles, bones, veins, wrinkles, and beauty marks—proves the intimacy of the gaze.

As with Hassan's *Tierra roja*, in *Orages d'été* she again engages in the act of whispering for most of the tale and uses a voice-over that evokes her inner thoughts as she would be talking to herself. Once more, the artist is fictionalizing many aspects of her own life. She suggests a role play in the movie in order to understand the first steps of the relationship with her partner Léonard Plattner. The characters are all real, but many of their attitudes were changed. Differently from the film's depiction, "real-life" Hassan was the one who constantly asked him to stay and sleep over and always called him the day after their encounters looking for some kind of assurance from him. The male partner was the one who had a hard time committing at the beginning of their liaison. Even as an unconscious act, by inverting their relation in the film, Hassan participates in a thought-provoking gender-role switch wherein new dynamics of difference are revealed. This inversion works for her to intentionally disrupt the hegemonic positionalities prevailing in male-dominated societies. This way the filmmaker combines reality and fiction in a cathartic manner and prompts us to think about the endless power and outreach of one's imagination. Any woman in the world could be her, unsettled by those very same emotional challenges, as she constructed a filmic space for global female emancipation.

In and Out: The Borders of Race in *Extravío*

Daniellis Hernández has revealed herself as a noteworthy cultural producer of her generation by bringing to light racial issues in Cuba and abroad. As a documentary student at EICTV, she directed *Volver a El Fanguito* (Return to El Fanguito, 2006). The original on which she based her film is the 1990 classic *El Fanguito*, a documentary directed by black Cuban filmmaker Jorge Luis Sánchez that portrays the harsh living conditions and marginality of the inhabitants of the namesake neighborhood in the heart of Havana. Hernández also shot *Safari documental* in the Cuban province Isla de la Juventud about a pregnant Ethiopian woman. Afro-Cuban filmmaker Gloria Rolando discusses similar topics in her documentaries *My Footsteps in Baraguá* (1996) and *Cherished Island Memories: A History of Cubans and Cayman Islanders* (2007) about the presence of Caribbean diasporas in Cuba and their influence on Cuban cultural practices. Similarly, Hernández's second-year final exercise *Arriba de la tierra* (Above ground, 2006), centers on a black gravedigger in San Antonio de los Baños. During our interview in 2013, she indicated interest in developing a project related to Cuba's involvement in Angola's liberation war, following the steps of Rigoberto López, who was a film correspondent during the African conflict. Thus, her connection with the work of black Cuban filmmakers has been consistent and wide-ranging.

Once in the diaspora, Hernández continued to nurture her research topic. *Extravío* is a personal discovery in which the director contrasts her original expectations of people of African descent living in the United Kingdom with the actuality she encounters. Transgressing national boundaries in a process of cross-fertilization, this Cuban black woman, lost in the cold streets of Manchester, tries to find warmth and—as she states in the film—"the comfort of the known" in those with her same skin color, believing she might identify with them. But reality will change that search into further questions, and her quest will be more exhausting than she could have ever foreseen. In the film,

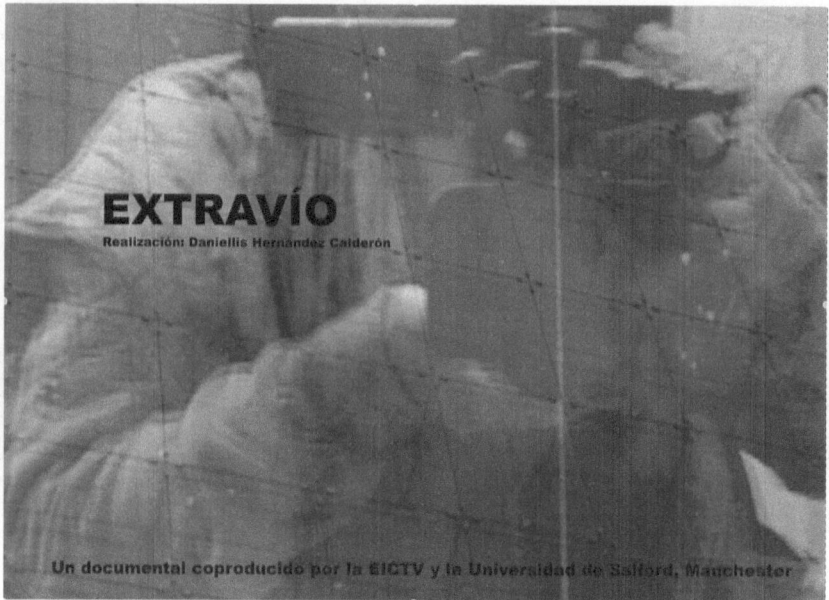

Figure 9.3. Promotional film poster (*Extravío*, 2008, Daniellis Hernández).

she narrates her accented cinema, as Heidi Hassan does in *Tierra roja* and *Orages d'été* and Susana Barriga in *The Illusion*.

In directing *Extravío*, Hernández, a nonreligious Afro-Cuban woman, portrays racial standpoints on religion and labor in a racialized urban setting. *Extravío* deals with the contradictory conditions of interculturation, such as the lack of freedom to film people, mistrust among the public and authorities in an era of surveillance and extended global sphere, and the constant process of negotiation with the subjects of her documentary (figure 9.3). In the initial scene, the monumental cathedral of Manchester is presented in a low-angle shot expressing the immensity of an overwhelming city with constant rain, cold climate, and tall buildings with glass windows. For her, time seems to go faster in this new scenery. The cineaste emphasizes the different pace with which black people live their lives in the North and the changes in rhythm and variety of responsibilities that the new habitat entails.

During the film, Hernández struggles to locate herself as a black Cuban woman—*extraviada*—lost in the new space where black people like herself are her only point of reference. Their transnational, transstate, and translocal relations become vital when measuring and analyzing the impact of the displacements, relocations, departures, and arrivals of information, human beings, and capital on contemporary Cuban cultural identities. With her film, I argue, Hernández engages in an act of media citizenship, as she uses the acquired information to deploy critical thinking about empire and condemn hegemonic structures of civil participation and implied violence (Flew; Rennie; Yu). Her first-person film is also a socially engaged practice. She criticizes the colorblind colonial discourse of the stories told at the People's History Museum, where blacks are erased from the institution's narrative on the "working people of Britain." Only images of submission and slavery are presented in the discourse, obliterating the recent history of blacks in England.

Throughout the film Hernández maintains a position that is both empathetic and distant. She identifies with the subject of her documentary as an autoethnographic study "concerned about the cultural connection between self and others representing the society" (Chang 207). However, her tone and approach are always from the perspective of a participant-observer in the conflated dyad of bearing witness and giving testimony. The academic background of the cineaste is noticeable in her work; she finished her bachelor's degree in sociology at the University of Havana in 2005. Therefore, perhaps her connection with the subject matter is less significant; she has a predisposition to register or document material from the scientific point of view of a researcher. That is why this is apparently the least personal work among the three women whose work I analyze.

Turning individual experience into necessary scholarship, Hernández portrays several social classes and genders among the black population in Manchester. The leader of worship, a young African woman who strives to find personal, professional, and spiritual satisfaction, introduces the idea of success, a concept similar to that of the American Dream. From that moment on, Hernández critically approaches the notion, indicating its falseness and how it is manipulated to import cheap labor from unequally developed locations in the world. She interviews recent immigrants and English natives: the supposedly successful Nigerian lawyer who has a house, a car, and a "good life"; a working-class immigrant striving for economic improvement; and inhabitants of marginal neighborhoods. She also visits Paul, perhaps the most interesting character of all, an Afro-Englishman who lives in Moss Side. He is awaiting a court case, and his teenage daughter is in prison. He shows Hernández pictures of his children and of himself during his youth when he wore long dreadlocks. Paul comments on the huge scar on his arm that is a consequence of a gunshot wound. Ironically and amid giggles, he says he lives as a good man now, as a Christian. Paul, who was born and raised in England, had a life that was far from the stereotype of success. Paul's story is a good example of how one can be in a place and not of it.

Avtar Brah notes that "discourses about the body have been crucial to the constitution of racisms" (3); the politics of hair in black culture is one of the most contested. So it is not casual that Hernández chose to film in an "ethnic hair" salon where a black woman comments on the need to ask her permission to film her hair, even if she cannot be identified on screen. For the woman who holds the camera and interviews people on the streets, the process of collecting information is constantly gendered. She is in a continual process of exchange with people she doesn't know and probably will never meet again. The guy in the hair salon asks the filmmaker whether she would take the male barber to Cuba with her; the lawyer mentions how he misses the obviously masculine "brotherliness" of African societies; the older man who approaches her in the park with unfriendly manners demands vigorously that, yet again, she turn off the camera.

The racial segregation of communities in the city and the overall white supremacy of England are also addressed. At one point Hernández is stopped by the police and prevented from filming in the streets of Moss Side. "We live in a state of mental slavery," says a middle-age African woman, referring to the threat that the mechanisms of state control find at seeing black people hanging out on the streets. "We come from a place where there is open land," she insists, while recognizing how they feel trapped as Africans living under Manchester laws. Suddenly, diegetic music starts playing from a car speaker. Gene Rondo's beats in "A Land Far Away" resonate, and a sense of belonging to Africa emerges then. Stereotypes and misconceptions are also described and contested. There is no balance in the foreign representation of Africa, as the media fail at showing "the true nature of Africans," according to an African man who refuses to accept the stereotypical colonialist image of his continent while resisting the notion of victimization.

Extravío may leave the viewer with mixed feelings. If on the one hand there is a sense of community among black people in the religious context and in the neighborhood collective way of life, on the other hand one can also appreciate what bell hooks states early in her book *Writing beyond Race*: "class difference disrupts notions of racial unity. And yet today, class differences coupled with racial integration have created a cultural context where the very meaning of blackness and its impact on our lives differs greatly among black people. There is no longer a common notion of shared black identity" (2). Hernández is well aware of that reality when she declares in *Extravío*,

> I am as lost as I was at the beginning. Every black face I see has a history I don't know. Who are they? Where do they come from? What do they believe in? Who do they love? What do they dream about? There are no certainties anymore. I find out that none of them is as close to me as I thought, but somehow they all are. It is not enough to look alike. It is not enough to have the same skin. Because in three months my skin is not the same, and in three years who knows how it will be?[13]

The filmmaker refers to the changes in her skin as a symbolic way of noticing the transformations of her personal and social life. The texture and tone of her identity, which she defines as her blackness, have been modified in the new diasporic condition as a symptom of her altered consciousness.

Contrasting Politics: *The Illusion*

The Illusion is a 2008 film by a young Cuban in diaspora, that represents one of the most radical forms of exilic experience. In our text "Intimate Spaces and Migrant Imaginaries," Susan Lord and I discuss various aspects of this film. Hopefully this new extension of the analysis will bring more light to such a relevant piece and to the study of diasporic cinemas in general. In this documentary we are reminded about political paranoia and the issue of family separation due to deep ideological differences when the 26-year-old filmmaker Susana Barriga visits her exiled father in London. A long-delayed reunion between the director and her father is filmed under odd conditions. This is the first time she has seen him since her childhood, and we become aware of the contrast between the kindness of her imagined father and the estrangement they experience during their actual encounter. Again, the filmmaker narrates and performs in the documentary. Thus, the enunciated first-person singular guides the aesthetic and discursive foundation of the film.

The male dominance of the father becomes evident when he blames his sister for putting their mother in a home for the elderly in Havana; images of the filmmaker's physically impaired *abuela* in the long hall of a seniors institution alternate with those of the London-based story. One can only ask rhetorically on what grounds he could judge his sister when he left 16 years earlier and never returned? Other family relations are discussed during the daughter's visit with her father. He finally has found someone he can ask about the rumors he heard about Maité, his younger daughter from a different mother than Susana's. And the question is followed by a cut to his entrance hall and a deep silence. "But you know that she died, right?" the filmmaker retorts.

The father's interventions in *The Illusion* could be read as a validation of the paranoia experienced by some members of the Cuban exile community. Viewers and even Barriga herself question her ethics in the documentary, as she mentions that she never told her father she was filming. She then becomes a spy or at least engages in a form of espionage, recording him without his consent. However, this occurs not on behalf of the political system he hates so much, but due to a daughter's intent to settle all matters with her father and what he represents in her memory and affect.

It could be argued that the film complies with the degraded image that the Cuban authorities gave to the post-1980 exiles, the alleged "lumpen" or right-wing *gusanos* who disagreed with the government. However, we are also challenged to believe there are strong reasons behind the father's actions. Through his comments we witness a family cycle of oppressive father figures. They represent the masculine nation-state and its political and social system as well as the forced, mandatory nature of the revolution even for those who never felt they were part of it and who experienced the impossibility of leaving because they were probably working-class, nonwhite Cubans like Barriga's father. Revelations about her father's past allow us to also recognize his need for affection. As a teenager in 1961, he was threatened by his strict father if he deserted the Literacy Campaign that he was forced to participate in as a *brigadista*, a volunteer teacher. Obviously, he did not feel connected to the project at the time. He was hurt by his father's fanaticism and pressured by the fear of failure, so he had to take the so-called step forward to prove his masculinity at age 14. The filmmaker's *abuelo* was blinded by the new revolution that defined severe borders between its supporters and detractors. Che Guevara's ideal of the New Man also settled at the time a notion of Cubanness that considered any love other than *amor por la patria* (love of the fatherland) unworthy. These multilayered intergenerational conflicts vis-à-vis Cuba's political leadership are registered in the story, and whether intentionally or not, the documentary criticizes both extremes and portrays the legacy and consequences for future generations.

The burden of the past weighs on the filmmaker's and her father's shoulders. He lives alone with a dog in London, isolated from the world, suspicious of everyone, and obsessed with the ghost of the Cuban regime, which manifests everywhere in his life, especially in his inability to communicate with his family. "When a family member leaves the country, you have to forget about their existence," he reminds his daughter. His false accusations of his daughter's collaboration with Cuban state security are a sign of the remaining hatred and distress with which some political refugees still live. He requires Susana's passport as proof of her identity, and he even blames her for wanting to go back to Cuba and not staying in London with him. The Argentinean columnist Quintín has written about *The Illusion* that "the film reveals something much deeper: a degree of violence of no return. Indeed, there might not be a more powerful testimony about the impossibility of reconciling the two sides in which Castroism divided Cuba."[14] The film can be interpreted as a dream of her childhood expectations. "How is this film similar to my dream?" Barriga asks as she recalls and reads through excerpts of the letters her father wrote to her years earlier.

The formal innovation is essentially geared by the camera shooting conditions: the recording device is hidden in her bag for most of the film—in the apartment and the street—and it is handheld by Barriga the rest of time in the London tube. The focus comes and goes, and sometimes the lens only finds a dim corner or a streetlight. Because the visuals are indistinct, largely shot with a camera hidden in a bag, sound plays a central role in this film. Different stages of surprise, suspicion, and denial are transmitted by the characters' voices and the movements of the camera, weaving, spinning, and shuddering. It is particularly the voice of the visually fragmented and blurry father that most clearly defines him when we notice the longing and waiting behind his question "Will I die here, or will I die in my country?" The difficulty or impossibility of return and his dream of homecoming "when there is democracy, when there is political amnesty, when that regime has disappeared absolutely," is a common remark in the global experiences of exile.

Although the film is more about the homeland and its implications in family ties than it is about the new context, the London experience for Susana Barriga is also connected to that city and the people who move in it. Even the London tube, where pedestrians rush pretty much disconnected from each other, seems distant and unsympathetic for the newcomer. We only perceive fragments of turning heads and of hands holding onto umbrellas, newspapers, and pipes. As in Hernández's *Extravío*, in *The Illusion* many pedestrians do no let Barriga film, and they question her right to use their images without their consent. Also, again there is fear of surveillance, but this time it takes an unexpected direction. A man in distress verbally and physically attacks Barriga, as the scene is recorded. She is genuinely scared and confused, and she asks the tube security to call the police.

The film contrasts the experience of the historical exile against the daughter's new diasporic subjectivity. For Barriga, the idea of her father was all in her imagination, a faux memory full of forgiveness and curiosity. Happiness was only possible before the encounter, when her father was an illusion that eventually turned into tangible reality. *The Illusion* became disillusion. Barriga states, "Yo misma pensé que había llegado a un lugar del presente. Pero sólo existíamos en el pasado. O al menos en un tiempo que yo había omitido para llegar hasta allí y luego irme, de regreso a la desmemoria" (I myself believed I had arrived at some place in the present, but we only existed in the past, or at least in a time that I had avoided in order to be able to get there and then return to nonremembrance). Of course, the documentary would have been different if the father responded to her visit in another way. As she reads from one of his letters she comments, "He needed some time." But that time turned into forever. Suddenly he was the distant man standing on a street corner and Susana, just a "woman who filmed him with a camera."

Conclusion

Explorations of the self in first-person documentary are more common so far among diasporic women than among their male counterparts. Distanced from the structures of media power and showing both vulnerability and courage, these stories are everything but spectacle. There is an underlying solemnity in them even if these types of documentaries could be, as Bill Nichols suggests, "characterized by a romantic individualism and a dramatic, fiction-like structure" (19). These films make us reflect on the negotiation of gendered and racialized spaces among the Cuban diasporic youth moving from a civil and political structure of late socialism to contexts of postindustrial capitalism. In that sense, their poetics could also be traced back to Afro-Cuban Sara Gómez's documentaries *Guanabacoa, crónica de mi familia* (Guanabacoa, chronicle of my family, 1966) and *Mi aporte* (My contribution, 1972), which the cineaste centers on untold race- and class-based stories of her family and herself. Her legacy among the younger generation of Cuban female filmmakers has been explored by a few authors,[15] but much remains to be analyzed in regard to the multiple elements of continuity and rupture between the different generations of Cuban filmmakers in the post-1959 era.

When asked about it, many Cuban female filmmakers in the diaspora say there is evidence of a feminine sensitivity at the center of their work because of the subject matter of their films and because the films were made by women. Although standing against cultural logics of normativity, many of them are still reluctant to identify as feminist. Why label the multiple forms of affiliation and understanding of community available for those who grew up in an environment where women's struggle for equal rights and empowerment was a social given without a name? Perhaps, for them, to embrace feminism means to engage in its mainstream, Western, white, liberal perspective, which would not be pertinent to their experience. Still, their shared meanings of womanhood are consistent in the complicated process of unlearning machismo and voicing their concerns; these presumptions are evident in their work.

A type of public intimacy is revealed as well through these cinematic journeys of the self that deal with racial discrimination, colonial power, and stereotyping; female subjectivity, embodiment, and nomadic selfhood; political paranoia; memory as illusion; and "the personal and family upheaval that results from the experience of migration and exile" ("Women at the Edge"). Hassan, Hernández, and Barriga were the camerapersons of their films, so they were mind and body—the two latter women even being on screen—but also the eyes and voices of these audiovisual pieces. In every case, their processes of migration were connected to institutional links. So, their film-school experiences abroad might have worked as a trampoline enabling a smoother readjustment and integration into their new surroundings. Their affective belonging is connected to a subjectivity that embraces the collective. Hailing diasporic subjectivity and family relations in a sort of visceral narrative, the films acquire a confessional tone that digs deep into these women's psychic landscapes. The three filmmakers analyzed here emerge, therefore, no longer in the dichotomy of creative subject/represented object but as represented subjects under construction, so much so that more than representing themselves, each of them will be "making" herself in the search of an "I" that is also an "us."

Many similar elements define the commonality of *Orages d'été*, *Extravío*, and *The Illusion*. The images are produced in situ with no use of archival material—a practice that is dear to the most traditional forms of documentary practice. They pursue an engagement with the city and the materiality of space since the filming subject in each work is exploring cityscapes and soundscapes of the new contexts still somewhat unfamiliar to them in their recent diasporic conditions. The three films, completed in the same year, are first-person texts told by the voice-over narration of the filmmakers themselves. They are, literally, the tellers of their own stories. References to the home as "imagined" in an important place of memory are present although tangential, while self-representation and affective engagement through bodily experiences are fundamental, given that each filmmaker physically performs a character. They cope with the responsibility of putting themselves in front of the camera. Sometimes it happens only through the voice and the subjective camera, as in *The Illusion* and most of *Extravío*. The vocal inflexions, tone, and pace also become part of their represented selves. They will all be living in a constant state of lack, sharing their individual anxieties in their self-reconstruction but also unaware of their privileges.

In Hamid Naficy's essay "Between Rocks and Hard Places: The Interstitial Mode of Production in Exilic Cinema," the author explores the masked, noncentralized, interstitial modes of film production of exilic, artisanal filmmakers. Emergent in opposition to hegemonic cinema, he argues that this mode of filmmaking will be driven by "the style's textual richness and narrative inventiveness, that is, its critical juxtaposition of audiovisual and narrative elements, discontinuity and fragmentation, multifocality and multilinguality, self-reflexivity and autobiographical inscription, historicity, epistolarity... and resistance to closure" (131). To a certain extent, *Orages d'été*, *Extravío*, and *The Illusion* share each and every one of these commonalities in a cohesive and affective manner. *Orages d'été* and *Extravío* also present clips from video shot by characters in the documentaries: Léonard films Heidi as she wakes up in the morning, and Paul films his neighbor's little girls to whom he acts as a father figure now that his kids have grown up and are estranged from him. This maneuver informs the collectivity of the filmmaking in a more plural, shared, and participatory audiovisual scape where several protagonists have not only the word but also the camera.

A show entitled "Women at the Edge of an Island/Mujeres al borde de una isla" opened in 2014 at the headquarters of the Aluna Art Foundation in Miami. It was the first art exhibition featuring only female diasporic artists from Cuba. Sixteen years after the publication of *Cubana: Contemporary Fiction by Cuban Women*, a collection of texts by Cuban and Cuban American poets and writers, the visual arts expanded in scope to include 23 women, the majority of whom were living in the United States and the rest in Spain and Colombia.

If all goes well, another 16 years will not go by before the next event involving all-female Cuban diasporic subjects takes place. When it does, I hope it has the creative field of film and media at its center and considers the Cuban diasporic experience of women in its truly diverse and multilocated dialogic dimensions.

Notes

1. Film critic and professor Dánae Diéguez has been an advocate for and historiographer of Cuban women's cinema in the postrevolutionary era. Writer Isabel Moya, director of the journal *Mujeres* (Women) and of the Cátedra de Género "Mirtha Aguirre" of the International Institute of Journalism José Martí, and the filmmaker and activist Marilyn Solaya have also done excellent work on the island. Ana M. López, Catherine Benamou, Susan Lord, and other scholars have written about Cuban cinema by women from different North American academic institutions, but the research field is still scant and dispersed, and a profound study on Cuban diasporic women filmmakers has yet to see light.

2. In the history of Cuban cinema only three Cuban women have directed long feature films on the island. Sara Gómez directed *De cierta manera* (*One Way or Another*) in 1974 but died at age 31 before bringing it to completion. In 2001 Carolina Nicola made *Así de simple* (Just like that), the first independent film conceived by a Cuban woman. In 2009, Rebeca Chávez followed with *Ciudad en rojo* (*City in Red*). Marilyn Solaya released *Vestido de novia* (*Wedding Dress*) in 2014 and Jessica Rodríguez presented *Espejuelos oscuros* (*Dark Glasses*) in 2015. The documentary *Deja que yo te cuente la historia* (Let me tell you the story, 2010) by EICTV graduate and Peruvian filmmaker Milagro Farfán is an interview-based film that complicates the outlook on the access of women film directors in Cuba.

3. According to the Iranian scholar Hamid Naficy, these forms of cinematic display are ways of translating personal experiences of postcolonial displacement into films. Not only are they created by cineastes who produce their audiovisual work in sites where they or their films' characters speak with an accent but also the works share commonalities in terms of their alternative modes of production, emergent styles and social impact.

4. The 2011 *Anuario estadístico de Cuba* presents data to that effect.

5. For more on the sociology of gender inequality, consult *Women's Work: Gender Inequality in Cuba and the Role of Women Building Cuba's Future*, from the Center for Democracy in the Americas.

6. The term was coined by Raymond Williams in the mid-1950s. "It suggests a common set of perceptions and values shared by a particular generation, and is most clearly articulated in particular and artistic forms" (Taylor). The concept has been also used by Jin Feng to analyze diasporic Chinese literature.

7. See Hassan's website, heidi-hassan.com.

8. Heidi Hassan, interview by Zaira Zarza, 10 May 2013, via Skype, Hassan in Madrid and Zarza in Kingston, Canada.

9. Hassan, interview, 10 May 2013.

10. Hassan, interview, 10 May 2013.

11. Diéguez and other film critics answered Juan Antonio García Borrero's call for comments in his post "Las cinco escenas más eróticas del cine cubano de todos los tiempos" on his blog *Cine cubano: La pupila insomne*.

12. Diéguez made this comment on García Borrero's blog post. All translations in this text are my own unless otherwise indicated.

13. "Estoy tan perdida como al principio. Cada rostro negro que veo tiene una historia que no conozco. ¿Quiénes son? ¿De dónde vienen? ¿En qué creen? ¿A quién aman? ¿Con qué sueñan? Ya no hay certezas. Me doy cuenta de que ninguno está tan cerca de mí como yo pensaba pero que, de algún modo, todos lo están. No basta con parecerse. No basta con tener la misma piel. Porque después de tres meses mi piel ya no es la misma y después de tres años, ¿quién sabe cómo será?"

14. "Pero la película revela algo mucho más profundo: un grado de violencia sin retorno. Efectivamente, no debe de haber otro testimonio más poderoso de la imposibilidad de reconciliar las dos partes en las que el castrismo dividió a Cuba."

15. A notable analysis of Gómez's legacy is Caridad Cumana and Susan Lord's "Deterritorialized Intimacies."

Works Cited

Anuario Estadístico de Cuba. Oficina Nacional de Estadística e Información. 2011. Web. 3 July 2014.

Behar, Ruth. Foreword. *Cubana: Contemporary Fiction by Cuban Women*. Ed. Mirta Yáñez, Dick Cluster, and Cindy Schuster. Boston: Beacon, 1998. vii–xix. Print.

Benamou, Catherine. "Cuban Cinema: On the Threshold of Gender." *Frontiers: A Journal of Women's Studies* 15.1 (1994): 51–75. Print.

Bhabha, Homi, ed. *Nation and Narration*. London: Routledge, 1990. Print.

Brah, Avtar. *Cartography of Diaspora: Contesting Identities*. London: Routledge, 1997. Print.

Braidotti, Rosi. *Nomadic Subjects: Embodiment and Sexual Difference in Contemporary Feminist Theory*. New York: Columbia UP, 2011. Print.

Chang, Heewon. "Autoethnography as Method: Raising Cultural Consciousness of Self and Others." *Studies in Educational Ethnography* 12 (2006): 207–221. Print.

Cumana, Caridad, and Susan Lord. "Deterritorialized Intimacies: The Documentary Legacy of Sara Gómez in Three Contemporary Women Filmmakers." *Hispanic and Lusophone Women Filmmakers: Theory, Practice, and Difference*. Ed. Parvati Nair and Julián Daniel Gutiérrez-Albilla. Manchester, England: Manchester UP, 2013. 96–110. Print.

Diéguez, Dánae. "¿Ellas miran diferente? Temas y representaciones de las realizadoras jóvenes de Cuba." *Cinémas d'Amérique Latine* (2012): 150–161. Print.

Extravío. Dir. Daniellis Hernández. 2008. EICTV. Film.

Feng, Jin. *Romancing the Internet: Producing and Consuming Chinese Web Romance*. Leiden, Netherlands: Brill, 2013. Print.

Flew, Terry. "Rethinking Public Service Media and Citizenship: Digital Strategies for News and Current Affairs at Australia's Special Broadcasting Service." *International Journal of Communication* 5 (2011): 215–232. Print.

Fowler, Víctor. "Variations on Cubanidad." *boundary* 2.29 (2002): 105–119. Print.

Gabriel, Teshome H. "The Intolerable Gift: Residues and Traces of a Journey." *Home, Exile, Homeland: Film, Media, and the Politics of Place*. Ed. Hamid Naficy. New York: Routledge, 1999. 75–83. Print.

García Borrero, Juan Antonio. "Las cinco escenas más eróticas del cine cubano de todos los tiempos." *Cine cubano: La pupila insomne*. 30 July 2012. Web. 3 July 2014.

Gilroy, Paul. *The Black Atlantic: Modernity and Double Consciousness*. London: Verso, 1993. Print.

González Mandri, Flora María. *Guarding Cultural Memory: Afro-Cuban Women in Literature and the Arts*. Charlottesville: U of Virginia P, 2006. Print.

Hassan, Heidi. Heidi-hassan.com. Web. 30 July 2014.

———. Interview by Zaira Zarza, on Skype. 10 May 2013.

Hernández-Truyol, Berta Esperanza. "Glocalizing Law and Culture: Towards a Cross Constitutive Paradigm" *Albany Law Review* 67 (2003): 617–628. Print.

hooks, bell. *Writing beyond Race: Living Theory and Practice*. New York: Routledge, 2013. Print.

The Illusion. Dir. Susana Barriga. EICTV. 2008. Film.

Lebow, Alisa, ed. *The Cinema of Me: The Self and Subjectivity in First Person Documentary*. London: Wallflower, 2012. Print.

———. *First Person Jewish*. Minneapolis: U of Minnesota P, 2008. Print.

Lord, Susan, and Zaira Zarza. "Intimate Spaces and Migrant Imaginaries: Sandra Gómez, Susana Barriga, and Heidi Hassan." *New Documentaries in Latin America*. Ed. Vinicius Navarro and Juan Carlos Rodríguez. New York: Palgrave Macmillan, 2014. 199–217. Print.

Marks, Laura. *The Skin of the Film: Intercultural Cinema, Embodiment, and the Senses*. Durham, NC: Duke UP, 2000. Print.

Naficy, Hamid. "Between Rocks and Hard Places: The Interstitial Mode of Production in Exilic Cinema." *Home, Exile, Homeland: Film, Media, and the Politics of Place*. Ed. Hamid Naficy. New York: Routledge, 1999, 125–147. Print.

Nichols, Bill. "The Voice of Documentary." *Film Quarterly* 36.3 (Spring 1983): 17–30. Print.

Orages d'été. Dir. Heidi Hassan, 2008. HEAD Genève. Film.

"Orages d'été." Review. artfilm.ch. N.d. Web. 14 Nov. 2013.

Quintín. "Ay, Cuba, si te dijera." *Otros Cines*, 14 Oct. 2008. Web. 3 July 2014.

Rennie, Elinor. "The Other Road to Media Citizenship." *Media International Australia, Incorporating Culture and Policy* 103 (May 2002): 7–13. Print.

Renov, Michael. *The Subject of Documentary*. Minneapolis: U of Minnesota P, 2004. Print.

Taylor, Jenny Bourne. "Structure of Feeling." *Dictionary of Cultural and Critical Theory*. Ed. Michael Payne. Oxford: Blackwell, 1997. Web. 2 July 2014.

Tierra roja. Dir. Heidi Hassan, 2007. HEAD Genève. Film.

Waugh, Thomas. *The Right to Play Oneself: Looking Back on Documentary Film*. Minneapolis: U of Minnesota P, 2011. Print.

"Women at the Edge of an Island/Mujeres al borde de una isla." Press release. Aluna Art Foundation. N.d. Web. 26 June 2014.

Women's Work: Gender Inequality in Cuba and the Role of Women Building Cuba's Future. Center for Democracy in the Americas, Washington, DC. 2013. Web. 27 July 2017.

Yu, Haiqing. "From Active Audience to Media Citizenship: The Case of Post-Mao China." *Social Semiotics* 16.2 (June 2006): 303–326. Print.

Yáñez, Mirta, Dick Cluster, and Cindy Schuster, eds. *Cubana: Contemporary Fiction by Cuban Women*. Boston: Beacon, 1998. Print.

Zurbano, Roberto. "For Blacks in Cuba, the Revolution Hasn't Begun." *New York Times*, 24 March 2013. Web. 3 July 2014.

10

Who Documents the Migrant?

Decolonial Aesthetics, Museo de América, and the Internet Documentary

JUAN G. RAMOS

The very form of the documentary lends itself to engagement with an audience through its emphasis on veracity and pathos. More often than not, however, the documentary form privileges a top-down approach to filmmaking in which the roles of filmmakers and objects of representation are clearly defined. In this chapter, instead, I am interested in discussing contemporary documentary forms that promote participatory and horizontal approaches to videomaking in which migrants engage in modalities of self-representation by employing Web 2.0 technologies. Throughout this chapter I explore the ways in which the Museo de América, in Madrid, devotes a section of its website to include new ways of conceptualizing how the stories and lives of migrants are visually documented.[1] As part of this effort, the traditional figure of the documentarian or documentary filmmaker has been altogether removed. Instead, the name of the museum often stands for the directorial figure while generating the Internet platform where migrants are able to narrate and document their own stories. In this way, the museum's webpage aptly named Migrar Es Cultura (To migrate is culture, MigrarEsCultura.es) hosts many of these videos. The museum's YouTube channel stores the same videos available on the museum's website but provides more visibility to a potentially wider audience.

Some of my interest in this collaborative and democratizing initiative is precisely the shift in how the documentary as visual text is now conceived. These short documentaries, for one, no longer need a director or documentarian. They also have a direct online platform for screening and are permanently visible, unlike many conventional documentaries that sometimes have restricted release, diminished availability for viewing, and limited circulation or dissemination. Internet documentaries readily embrace alternative modes of production and distribution through a variety of online platforms. In addition to this shift in production and distribution, it is important to note the museum's investment in emphasizing the role that migration plays to better understand the long-standing and complex relation between the Americas and Spain.

In emphasizing newer forms of Internet documentary filmmaking, I have selected examples of documentaries that appear on the Museo de América's Migrar Es Cultura webpage to examine in relation to theoretical discussions on the contours and redefinitions of the documentary form, given its changing and growing presence on the Web. Working with the critical perspective of decolonial aesthetics, I focus on how such Internet documentary examples open questions about contemporary definitions of documentaries, their aesthetic qualities and values, the shifting dynamics between producer and consumer, audience and screening venues, and documentary mainstream forms and new media sensibilities. While there have been a number of important studies on documentaries in Latin America, few if any have paid attention to the ways in which new media, particularly the Internet and visual platforms such as YouTube, might be utilized to create new types of documentaries in which the migrant has the ability to tell her or his own migratory story.

Notes on the Internet Documentary

In Julianne Burton's seminal 1990 study *The Social Documentary in Latin America*, the author presents a typology of five modes of documentary filmmaking. According to Burton, the use of an omniscient narrative voice that emphasizes objectivity is one the most salient characteristics of the expository mode; an example is Patricio Guzmán's *The Battle of Chile* (1975–1979). In contrast, in the observational mode the voice of the observed is prevalent and underscores the documentary's impartiality while paying close attention to personal stories; an early example W. L. Dickson's 1895 *Employees Leaving the Lumière Factory*. The documentarian's voice and intentions frame the presentation of information in the interactive mode, which often appears by way of interviews or monologues, as in Octavio Cortázar's *Hablando del punto cubano* (1972) and Michael Rubbo's *Sad Song of Yellow Skin* (1972). And in the reflexive mode there is often a self-awareness of the medium and genre employed in the creation of the documentary such as Dziga Vertov's *Man with a Movie Camera* (1929).

Lastly, Burton draws our attention to mixed modes that employ characteristics of the aforementioned documentary filmmaking strategies and how the term encompasses a variety of documentary subgenres, including biographical, poetic, and ethnographic; examples include Fernando Birri's *Tire Dié* (1960) and Fernando Solanas and Octavio Getino's *The Hour of the Furnaces* (1968) (Burton 4–5). I have highlighted these modes of documentary filmmaking, as suggested by Burton, to better situate the contours of traditional documentary films. Internet documentaries, however, are different in their approach to filming, technology used, and means of dissemination. Nonetheless, the Internet documentary employs some of documentary modes Burton highlights while also updating them to engage with shifting video and film sensibilities, formats, and technologies.

The "Internet documentary video," as I use the term here, refers to the variety of digital texts available online today; it encompasses full-length documentaries, short documentaries, video monologues and partial dialogues, poetic and experimental, biographical, autobiographical, historical, diasporic, archival, and transnational video recordings of nonfictional events. The key distinctions I make between conventional filmmaking and Web 2.0 documentary digital videomaking are that the figure of the documentarian or professional filmmaker is not essential for a documentary to be categorized as such and that we no longer need a physical screening space to view a documentary.[2] In the course of the past decade, file-sharing sites such as YouTube, Vimeo, or Dailymotion, have made it possible for almost any individual with access to technology and the Internet to create videos and upload them for the world to see. This is not to say, however, that every video available or uploadable ought to be categorized as a documentary.

Without falling into narrow definitions, essentialisms, or generalizations, the changing technologies and forms of documentaries, in fact, allow for a broader understanding of what documentaries have until recently been understood to signify. In the examples that I discuss, the migrants themselves have uploaded the videos that are available through the Museo de América's webpage to give personal accounts of their migratory journeys, which often take a transatlantic path from the Americas to Europe but also in other directions. For example, the Museo de América's portal also hosts videos that explore other migratory journeys in the Americas and from Africa to Europe. Given that the museum encourages anyone to upload videos without providing parameters, restrictions, or guidelines on their quality and length, it is not clear how and if the museum filters, categorizes, or curates what contributors upload. By not providing strict guidelines and by simplifying the upload process with three steps under the tab "crea tu historia" (create your story), the museum seeks to attract wide participation and contribution in the collective creation and exchange of videos that document personal migratory experiences. Migrar Es Cultura, the museum's webpage dedicated to this interactive interface, encourages Internet users and museum patrons to contribute to the growing and evolving repository of *historias mínimas*, by which I mean personal stories but also brief accounts that get to the core of the migrant's story with the due brevity characteristic of the Internet video format. The wealth of Internet documentaries available on Migrar Es Cultura ranges from personal accounts of the reasons that led to migration, how the migrant has adjusted to living in Spain, and aspects of food, cultural customs, and art forms that, if taken together, create a web of traveling cultures of the Americas.

In the specific case of Latin America, documentaries have a long-standing tradition that began to take shape in the late 1950s and 1960s with what is often called the New Latin American Cinema. Recently, the reinvention of the documentary genre has adjusted to the growing fascination with "instantaneity," which Michael Chanan has identified as the "*modus operandi* of the development and global spread of the Internet of the last twenty years" (147). The reach, circulation, and reception of documentary images create a cognitive geography that helps to understand not only pressing issues afflicting societies in Latin America, while it also provides a sense of how individual stories fit within broader political, cultural, and economic categories such as globalization and transnationalism. This is precisely the conundrum we face today: how might individual stories interact with globalizing forces such as the Internet? Chanan has convincingly argued that

> the computer screen and Internet connection obliterate distance more effectively than television—you just have to click another hyperlink, and without going anywhere, you're instantly somewhere else: not just a metaphor, but the virtual instantiation of globalization. None of this, however, provides a solution; what it does is create a parallel public sphere which repeats and multiplies the same disparities and contradictions. It is possible in the North to stream videos long and short from the South onto our desktops, yet major documentaries circulating in a growing number of small documentary festivals never reach our cinema

or television screens. In any case, globalization pulls in divergent directions. (153)

Chanan's observations hold true for a conventional conceptualization of documentary film as one that needs festivals and the stamp of approval of critics for recognition. Put differently, what Chanan is arguing here is that documentary filmmakers from Latin America, for instance, still need the approval of festivals from the global North to have a chance of exhibiting their work in a broader context. In contrast, the types of documentary to which I am referring do not necessitate a film festival, since the Internet or specific media-sharing websites are offering alternatives to the conventional notion of film festivals. More importantly, unlike conventional documentaries, which are created and edited to be screened at film festivals, the examples of Internet documentary videos available on the Museo's website are uploaded with the intention of reaching a broader audience that includes those visiting the Museo's website or its YouTube channel. Undoubtedly, the two screening venues—the Internet and the film festival—coexist. But with increasing limitations of circulation and distribution, as Chanan has described, the Web becomes a means through which documentaries can be at once exhibited, distributed, and stored for easy access and consumption.

Here it becomes important to bring an example from the Museo de América's webpage, *Viajes de ida y vuelta* (Roundtrip travels, 2012), as a way to highlight an Internet documentary video that was funded, created, and controlled by the museum. In the course of 13 minutes, a narrator-actor by the name of Daniel takes the viewers through a journey that explores the transatlantic connections between Spain and the Americas in what he calls a videoblog. The Museo funded the documentary, and the director's name only appears in the closing credits. In this videoblog, Daniel's narrative voice links the various approximations to migration as related to the ways that cultural customs, food, music, and people travel. The structure of this documentary is more or less conventional in that the actor takes us through locations in Madrid and Asturias to showcase examples of the embedded cultural connections that link Spanish émigrés to the Americas but also influences from the Americas in aspects of Spanish culture that are deemed quintessentially Spanish. Covering a span of seven days, Daniel shows how dishes like gazpacho, *tortilla de patatas*, and chocolate have their origins in the Americas. In music, the documentary shows how flamenco made it to the Americas and the end results of its return journey are *cantes de ida y vuelta* (songs of departure and return) that in turn give way to specific musical genres such as guajira, rumba, and colombiana. In other instances, the documentary aims to demonstrate how certain cultural products have a richer and deceptive history such as the Panama hat, which is actually made in Ecuador. Toward the end of the documentary, Daniel takes the viewers to the Museo de la Inmigración in Asturias, where historical artifacts, photographs, and documents serve as testament to the journeys of Spanish migrants to the Americas in the nineteenth and twentieth centuries and who returned to Spain after amassing considerable fortunes. The final sequence is an interview with Amalia Fernández, a woman born in Cuba but who has lived most of her life in Spain. Daniel asks Amalia if she has any recollections of Cuba, to which Amalia replies, "Todo. Yo creo que la gente que se sale de un lugar y se cambia, como yo, de continente, de tiempo, de espacio, de todo, la memoria se queda grabada a fuego" (Everything. I think that for people who leave a place, like me, and move to another continent, time, space, everything, memory becomes imprinted with fire) (*Viaje de ida y vuelta*).[3] In her mind it is the traditions of holidays, foods, customs, and memories that link her to her Cuban identity.

Given the brevity of this documentary and the variety of topics covered in a short time, *Viajes de ida y vuelta* intends to inform Spanish and Latin American audiences of points of contact among the various cultures while building a sense of acceptance and tolerance, and ultimately to underscore the values of interculturality and transatlantic exchanges. As an Internet documentary video that was funded by the Spanish Ministry of Culture and the Museo de América, the primary purpose of *Viajes de ida y vuelta* is to inform its audience and provide a different perspective on cultural aspects that are commonplace but often have a forgotten or multilayered history that makes discussion of the origin of a given food, song, dance, or customs an almost impossible task. The premise of the museum's participatory initiative is precisely to highlight how culture is in itself an already unstable, constantly shifting, and evolving concept, especially when linked to the complexities of migratory experience. This documentary serves to provide information in a short time, but it also invites viewers to rethink how culture must involve a reevaluation of historical premises as well as cultural and aesthetic values.

Keeping this example in mind, we might ask if it is possible to consider Internet documentary videos a mode of visual culture that is also part of a broadly construed art world. To begin addressing this idea, it is helpful to turn to T. J. Demos's work on how contemporary artists are redefining the documentary form to address global migrations. Demos's work is useful to question whether "'migration' remains both the capacious enough and the most accurate term to describe the multiple forms of movement and singular expressions of dislocation in contemporary experience" (3). In the case of the heterogeneity of Latin American migrations, it is important to remember the array of familial, personal, and economic reasons that lead migrants to travel "by choice"; according to Demos, it is "choice" that helps to distinguish migration from diaspora ("a geographical dispersal in the collective sense") and refugee ("the victim of persecution or forced expulsion") (3). Most of the videos found at the museum's site can be placed under the category of migration, though certain videos overlap with a diasporic sense of displacement, longing for home, and looking for a collective sense of identity and belonging.

While a museum traditionally holds artifacts that are considered valuable, unique, and prized for their inherent and assumed aesthetic value, might it be possible to consider these video uploads as a contemporary and democratic form of *arte povera*? In other words, and to return to the question of the film director as artist, can we begin to think of alternative modes of documentary video and filmmaking in which the figure of the documentarian as artist is demoted? These questions imply, of course, that anyone has the potential to be deemed an artist or, conversely, that only some have the capacity to produce documentaries that qualify as art. In Henry Jenkins's *Convergence Culture*, the author argues for a type of participatory culture that allows for new ways of producing and consuming media. In Jenkins's argument, however, he is thinking about Al Gore's cable news network initiative Current TV. Jenkins argues that "viewers were intended not simply to consume Current's programming, but also to participate in its production, selection and distribution" (240). Elsewhere in this discussion, Jenkins is cautious when arguing for this type of participatory culture, particularly in light of different web-based platforms such as ourmedia.org. While I would not go as far as arguing that what we see in the Museo de América is a fully developed form of participatory culture, since this would imply that producer-consumers have the autonomy to select and distribute their own work, the Museo's initiative is a step toward this direction at the very least in enabling migrants to produce how they want their personal stories to be told. In this sense, then, the opening of the documentary form to new possibilities allows for such questions to emerge in relation to new aesthetic dimensions while also engaging in questions linked to subjectivity.

On Decolonial Aesthetics and Subjectivity in Internet Documentaries

In its most basic and mundane function, the documentary ought to be primarily concerned with presenting information on social, political, and economic issues as they are. The end result has been thought to be that documentaries are meant to present information to raise viewers' critical consciousness or at least bring about awareness of specific issues. Needless to say, a number of studies and examples show how the documentary form has as much aesthetic value, artistic dexterity, and technical complexity as other film genres.[4] And yet, the documentary continues to be seen as a genre that documents and informs without necessarily entertaining and providing aesthetic pleasure.

These critical distinctions and aesthetic values have more to do with prevalent categorizations of film genres and understandings of aesthetic categories. Stemming from the work on coloniality of power (as introduced by Aníbal Quijano) and an array of decolonial positions (Walter Mignolo, Ramón Grosfoguel, Agustín Laó-Montes, María Lugones, and others), the critical endeavor of decolonial aesthetics provides alternative ways of understanding projects that do not quite conform to established parameters governing the arts. The concept of decolonial aesthetics has emerged in a variety of geographical coordinates from theorists working in Latin America, Asia, Europe, and the United States. Most notably, however, Walter Mignolo's recent work on decolonial thinking has focused on contesting and reframing Western aesthetics.[5] The particularities of each geopolitical space inevitably lead to distinct theoretical articulations, but the decolonial project moves toward a common goal of undoing, resisting, and challenging a hierarchical relation to Eurocentric aesthetics.

In Mignolo's articulation of decolonial aesthetics, he is most interested in contemporary forms of art that are linked to questions of race, gender, and identity in the context of globalization and what he terms "dewesternization of aesthetics," by which he means an undoing and decentering of Western aesthetics in favor of non–western European aesthetic models that have been traditionally silenced or neglected (30–34). A succinct and brief delineation of what decolonial aesthetics seeks to do is posited when Mignolo writes, "La estética, en el sentido moderno, es otra forma de control, menos visible, pero no menos eficaz: opera descalificando de las formas del *gusto* hábitos y emociones ajenas a la normativa olfativa, auditiva, táctil y gustativa" (In its modern sense, aesthetics is a less visible but equally effective form of control. It operates by undermining habits and emotions foreign to normative forms of sensing, pertaining to smells, hearing, touch, and taste) (44). Since the Enlightenment and particularly after the work of Alexander Baumgarten, Kant, and Hegel, aesthetics has become a field of philosophical inquiry with a certain scientific rigor seeking to demarcate the categories, values, and judgments governing taste and affective responses to specific works of art. Contemporary views on aesthetics have turned to a set of philosophical questions that necessitate a normative apparatus and language to categorize the inherent value, taste, and worth of art while also questioning the very foundations of Western aesthetic categories.[6] By doing so, these articulations of aesthetics have created a schism in which some works of art have long received attention and critical recognition due to an assumed value. In this sense, the traditional role of museums has served to advance specific aesthetic values since they have been the primary collectors and repositories of valuable art.

Moreover, the Museo's initiative redefines the conventional role of the museum to allow for direct contributions and participation from everyday people whose work becomes a visual and aural archive of personal stories of migration. Part of what I am claiming here is that the figure of the filmmaker or artist loses its place as the creator of visual works of art that encompass short documentary videos, reflections on culture, and simple interviews privileging the importance of an individual's story. A more nuanced understanding of what decolonial aesthetics can offer also leads us to rethink and reframe the position of the Internet documentary in contemporary articulations of film and aesthetic categories, especially in their engagement of a viewer's multiple senses.

The position of decolonial aesthetics, as I understand it, is to question the very foundations that determine and regulate artistic genres and what qualifies as art. Such a reframing of aesthetics allows for other ways of understanding the arts in terms that contest and resist Western and European categories and rubrics. In part, the project of decolonial aesthetics seeks to allow for a more expansive and inclusive participation of social actors or subaltern voices who have been traditionally categorized as second rate or popular artists. The videos hosted on the museum's website can be understood in terms of decolonial aesthetics by the way in which everyday individuals who are migrants are in a position to create videos and narrate their own lives. Especially when the migrant is able to have control over how she wants to tell her own story of migration, an undoing and redefinition of an aesthetic understanding of what counts as a documentary enables the migrant to record, self-document, and pass on to others elements of a migrant's own history through recourse to technologies capable of capturing and negotiating the interplay between orality and visuality. The role that Internet technologies have in relation to the transmission of orality and a rearticulation of visuality can be thought of as the migrants' participatory engagements with cyberorality and cybervisuality, which combined may lead to redefining sensorial and aesthetic engagement with Internet documentaries.

To illustrate some of the ways in which Migrar Es Cultura can engage with the potentialities that multimedia can offer, I now turn to a five-minute documentary called *Sonidos migrantes* (Migrant sounds, 2012). The structure of this brief documentary is one in which a narrator helps us make sense of how boleros, reggaeton, tango, son cubano, and other genres lend themselves to reinterpretations and adaptations to flamenco or rumba. It is precisely the mixture and travel of sounds, genres, instrumentations from Africa to the Caribbean and then to Andalusia or Catalonia that create an unforeseen network of musical semblances and familiar kinships. Other videos and images available on the Museo's website allow us to briefly reflect, for instance, on the role of Garifuna culture in Nicaragua, the importance of quinoa in Andean diets, or the role of photography to better understand the complexities of racial categories in understanding the Americas.[7]

This discussion of decolonial aesthetics' relation to Internet documentary videos leads to questioning the place of subjectivity in the creation of these new visual texts appearing online. We are reminded that with many documentaries, particularly those whose subject is the director, an individual, or a community, there are often multiple subjectivities at play. Alisa Lebow argues, "When a filmmaker makes a film with herself as a subject, she is already divided as both the subject matter of the film and the subject making the film" (4). In many of the documentary videos available through the Migrar Es Cultura webpage of the Museo de América, the authorial figure of the filmmaker is not immediately prevalent and takes on a secondary role in relation to the actual subject of the brief Internet documentary videos. Whether it is a community, an individual migrant, a musical style, or a broad array of cultural manifestations, the primary subject of the documentaries is the exploration of migratory processes that bring people, customs, and cultural products in contact and exchange with each other. Yet what many of the documentaries privilege is a first-person-singular account in which the perspective of the "I" is revealing and informative and creates an affective bond linking an individual's story to a broader collectivity of migrants of a certain national or regional identity. Some of what these videos seek to produce is precisely a transcendence of borders in favor of a borderless and almost utopian understanding of the benefits of migration and cultural exchange without problematizing the migratory experience.

One could go as far as speculating that the Museo's mission is to foster a welcoming and idealistic understanding between migrants (mainly Latin Americans) and nationals (Spaniards) by presenting instances in which migratory journeys have worked in both directions across the Atlantic. In other words, the videos seek to go beyond a formulaic and often redundant configuration of the migrant as either a victim or a vilified figure and instead position the migrant as one who seeks to insert herself into the social fabric of the host country by contributing to its culture and economy but also by adapting to the lifestyles of Spain. Precisely by enabling each migrant to tell her or his own story, the Museo creates a space to underscore the indeterminacy and multiplicity of the subject in the documentary videos. After all, in most of the documentaries available on the museum's website, the subject could be a person, a custom, a food, or a dance style. Behind every documentary is a recognizable human dimension that creates an affective link between migrant and host-country viewer by establishing a relation of cultural familiarity rather than dwelling on marked differences.

Continuing with this line of thinking, Lebow argues that we must also consider the relations between power and subjectivity: "If we then link the process of subjective representation to self-representation . . . , it quickly becomes clear that it entails a process of becoming the subject and object of the gaze, a somewhat autonomous position that is nonetheless constitutive of being able to reflect upon and represent the self" (4). This double perspective on subjectivity and self-representation is one that can be linked to Gloria Anzaldúa's conceptualization of the *mestiza* consciousness, *la conciencia de la mestiza*, in which "the *mestiza*'s dual or multiple personality is plagued by psychic restlessness" (100). In Anzaldúa's articulation of *mestiza* consciousness/*conciencia de la mestiza*, the double thinking, psychic fragmentation, and internal conflict jointly give rise to forms of artistic and quotidian expression that allow the subject-self to express her suffering and the embedded challenges and advantages of inhabiting two or more cultures.

In this respect, the migrant engages in a form of mestiza consciousness/*conciencia de la mestiza* when "she learns to transform the small 'I' into the total Self" (Anzaldúa 105). With this Anzaldúa is suggesting that a *mestiza* subject, unlike the Western subject, can only make sense of herself in relation to her community, ancestry, customs, language, even if they conflict with each other. It is in this process of self-assertion and self-understanding that the migrant is able to produce and share her story. The process of creating a video, even if it is not professional, enables the migrant to come to terms with her duality as both subject and object of her own documentary and storytelling. In other words, the migrants who contribute to the Migrar Es Cultura webpage not only participate in a process of self-understanding and self-representation but also engage in an active and intuitive redefinition of aesthetics by acknowledging the power of the word (orality) and of images (visuality). Anzaldúa notes, "An image is a bridge between evoked emotion and conscious knowledge; words are the cable that hold up the bridge. Images are more direct, more immediate than words, and closer to the unconscious" (91). While Anzaldúa is referring here to the images evoked through written language, we can extend her observation and theorization to the power that images and words have in the documentaries I discuss here. While there may be a certain level of narration, monologue, dialogue, or even accompanying written explanation, the images presented in a documentary can have profound effects on viewers and elicit new sets of relations among audiences, broadcasting technologies, and Internet documentaries.

Place and Format of Exhibition: Museum, YouTube

I want to briefly discuss how the place and format of exhibition, namely a museum and YouTube, change the terms of engagement with and understanding of documentaries. The primary exhibition space, or rather its platform, is the Museo de América's Migrar Es Cultura webpage, where a variety of documentaries, videos, art, photography, and other multimedia uploads are available. While a number of the documentaries are sponsored and created by the Museo itself, the novelty of the platform is also its emphasis on inviting people to upload their own images and have the ability to tell and share their stories. The videos do not have to be entirely about a migrant's journey from country of origin to host country. Instead, many of the videos move somewhat beyond this formula of the established documentary structure around migratory issues, especially as a way to illustrate that it is not only people who migrate, but also cultural forms and customs. More importantly, given the growing migration of Latin Americans to Spain, the Museo seeks to shift this unidirectional model of understanding migration by also looking at the histories behind Spanish migration to the Americas. In doing so, the Museo showcases the ways in which contemporary Spanish society cannot be understood without fully being aware of the mechanisms, exchanges, influences, and indebtedness to the long-standing and historically complex relations between the Americas and Spain. In addition to looking at the Americas, some video uploads allow for the self-representation of stories of African migrants to Italy and other parts of Europe. As such, then, the Museo's website is invested in exploring the unexpected migratory paths that can lead to a more nuanced understanding of how people, cultures, and customs move, evolve, and become recognizable and yet different through multilayered articulations of cultural migration.

In relation to the effects of Internet technologies as means of disseminating fragmented and brief images or personal accounts, Peter Hughes argues,

> The development of Web 2.0 is symptomatic of a significant change in media structures and cultures away from broadcast-based mass communication model (the model that has underpinned television and radio, large circulation of newspapers and mass market models of cinema exhibition and distribution) to a much more fragmented model of media in which audiences are more fluid and able to access a wider range of media forms at a time and place of their choosing: "a post-broadcast" model. (235)

In other words, Web 2.0 has shifted the relations between producer and consumer but also the means and format of information. If in the broadcast model narrative, coherence and longer forms were the preferred means of engaging with audiences, today given the wealth of competing information, videos, and images available on the Internet, the fragmented and almost minimalist mode of documenting and presenting individual stories has become more prevalent. Coincidently, however, while Web 2.0 has been noted to provide the possibility of individuals to connect with each other, it also emphasizes a growing sense of individuality and alienation.

As a way to make use of the new technological formats and modes of dissemination, Museo de América has also redefined its very role as a social and cultural institution. In terms of the relation between decolonial aesthetics and the museum, it becomes important to briefly reflect on the conventional role of museums as sites that hold and display artifacts, historical documents, and art. In their traditional role, before their presence on the Internet, museums were repositories of both foreign and local cultural artifacts, but the artifacts were only available to those who could visit the museum's physical space or have access to a printed catalogue. Today such museum holdings are increasingly available in digitized forms; thus museums acknowledge the need for information to become more widely available and accessible. The Museo de América has a variety of artifacts and documents that explore the longstanding and complex history between Spain and the Americas. In part, what I am arguing here, however, is that the Museo's turn to a participatory platform of exhibition, dissemination, and distribution of multimedia images, including the Internet documentary, has changed the very nature of how we conventionally understand and define the role of a museum. Put differently, now that an everyday person can share her story by posting a video or images, said individual as migrant is an active contributor and participant in building the virtual collection of the Museo.

The museum does not have a clear policy on the types of contributions it seeks or how the institution filters or curates Migrar Es Cultura. In fact, it appears as though the webpage is open to any contributions with minimal control on the museum's part. Its video that introduces the project opens with the premise "Porque entendemos que los museos están cambiando gracias a ti y tú eres el nuevo protagonista" (Because we understand that museums are changing thanks to you and that you are the new protagonist) ("Presentación Migrar es Cultura"). In this same video the museum announces that viewers and contributors will be able to watch videos on 10 channels, covering topics as diverse as food, music, art, literature, and memories (*vivencias*). Two converging messages appear at the end of the introductory video. The written words on the screen encourage migrants to upload videos, pictures, art, or memories linked to migration. Simultaneously, two of the museum's curators encourage migrants to consider the following: "Migrar es una web participativa, organizada en diferentes canales, para poder abarcar todos los aspectos de la cultura. Migrar es un espacio virtual de encuentro internacional donde puedes contar tu propia historia o continuar otros relatos similares" (Migrar is a participatory web space, organized under different channels, in order to cover all aspects of culture. Migrar is an international, virtual meeting space where you can narrate your own story or continue building upon similar narratives) ("Presentación Migrar es Cultura"). The museum's initiative is one that invites migrants to share at will their own memories of migration, but the framing of the project is one that is problematic in its search for a dual identification with migrants' countries of origin (in the Americas) and their new country (Spain). The underlying message is one that implicitly seeks contributions that affirm and share the museum's unproblematic views of cultural proximity and understanding. An interesting idea to momentarily entertain, though it is impossible to know, would be if the museum is open to accepting videos that do not present positive representations of migration and acceptance of migrants in Spain.

Despite having a seemingly implicit agenda of assimilation, the Museo's turn to new media, the Internet, and media-sharing sites and platforms shifts a common understanding of what a museum does and which cultural artifacts it decides to collect, catalogue, and exhibit as part of its holdings. The catalogue is now a searchable repository in which keywords, topics, and formats lead the viewer to explore its holdings, though there is a shared sense of ownership. Internet videos simultaneously belong to the museum, the migrant, and a potential global audience. Moreover, the mode of collection is not only the Museo's own website; the videos are available also on a YouTube channel linked to the Museo. By having this double visibility, it becomes potentially easier for audiences to search and find some of the Museo's videos. The Museo's turn to Web 2.0 technologies also engages with younger audiences, given that new modalities of creating, uploading, presenting, and consuming YouTube clips appeal to technologically inclined audiences. It can have a global reach, but the media also become embedded among the growing number of videos and clips uploaded every day. While the Museo seeks to democratize or at least create a horizontal structure of participatory cultural production, it becomes the reified and centralized virtual repository of these types of videos.

Keeping these observations in mind, I would like to turn to a video available through the Museo's website and its YouTube channel—*Las brujas migrantes* (The migrant witches, 2013). This Internet documentary focuses on the story of Alma Cruz from Guatemala, Jamileth Chavarría from Nicaragua, and Alicia Pacas from El Salvador and how they have become involved in social activism through the arts. At the beginning of the Internet documentary, Alma succinctly explains the circumstances of her journey to Spain when she discloses the following: "Estoy refugiada acá en España. Vengo de Guatemala y estoy acá por cuestiones de los asesinatos de mujeres en mi país" (I am a refugee here in Spain. I come from Guatemala and I am here because of the murders of women in my country) (*Las brujas migrantes*). Following Alma's story, Jamileth explains how she came to be in Spain: "Estoy aquí como migrante irregular y me he quedado para conocer también la experiencia de las mujeres europeas y porque tengo mucho interés en crecer" (I am here as an undocumented migrant and have stayed to also learn about the experience of European women and because I am interested in growing). The third self-identified witch, Alicia Pacas from El Salvador, explains that she is simply in Spain due to life's circumstances. Their video performance and theater group bear the same name as the documentary.

Jamileth Chavarría from Nicaragua explains in the documentary how they self-identify as witches and that they employ that term to bring together "un grupo de mujeres sin territorio y sin fronteras. Somos un grupo de autocrítica, feministas listas para enfrentar todas las formas de violencia que hay contra las mujeres de las muchas formas que lo sabemos hacer" (a group of women without territory or borders. We are a self-critical group, feminists ready to confront all forms of violence against women in the many ways we know how to do it) (*Las brujas migrantes*). The witches define themselves as women without borders, whether physical or cultural, who seek to place in dialogue a feminist consciousness with forms of violence afflicting migrants, particularly women migrants. In this six-minute documentary we see brief performances that question the embedded ideologies and global forces afflicting migrants on an experiential and quotidian level. Halfway through the video the women perform a chant with the following words: "Santo Eufemismo: quien inventó la frontera lo hizo para legalizar la discriminación, el racismo, la homofobia, el clasismo y todo lo que termina en sismo. Amen" (Saint Euphemism: whoever invented the border did it to legalize discrimination, racism, homophobia, classism, and all that ends in *ism*. Amen). Their chant appropriates and parodies a monastic song and denounces the injustices that migrants suffer. Such performances become an integral part of their Internet documentary, in which interviews, dialogues, and performances serve to document the struggles that Latin American women migrants face while seeking to change the perception that some Spaniards have of them as caretakers, maids, or factory workers.

It is unclear whether the museum curated *Las brujas migrantes* or if the three women in the documentary had absolute control over shooting, editing, and narrating their stories, as there are no closing credits except for a brief reference to Spain's Ministry of Culture and the Museo de América. While the primary emphasis of the museum's website is to give migrants a platform where they can upload their own stories, it is unclear whether migrants have unrestricted access to make use of the platform without always having to give credit to the museum. Nevertheless, as suggested in the brief discussion of *Las brujas migrantes*, the politicized, critical, feminist perspectives presented in the documentary are more valuable to renew and expand conversations in Spain about the role of migrants and their contributions to contemporary Spanish society. In having the ability to tell their own stories in their own words and by touching on thorny subjects, the three women in the video have made an important contribution by sharing their impressions of the factors that led to their transatlantic migratory journeys from Central America to Spain.

Moving from this discussion of the documentary, it becomes important to consider the wider implications of having access to such technology. The Museo's Migrar Es Cultura webpage is linked to a YouTube channel and thus allows anyone with access to technology to upload and share videos with the rest of the world. It should be stressed here that, unlike the Museo's website, a YouTube channel has the ability to track views. YouTube is also searchable and compatible with Google's search engine, since they are part of the same company. Moreover, portable electronics with Internet capabilities make YouTube videos readily available from anywhere there is access to the Web as opposed to the confinement of a screen's fixed physical location, the prevalent mode of viewership with traditional documentaries. The Museo's move to digital video format and engagement with Web 2.0 sensibilities of viewership—that is, shorter clips with boiled-down presentations of information—has empowered any migrant with access to video and computer technology to present and tell her story in a brief format. While the apparent loss of media specificity appears as a concern when delimiting the boundaries of traditional and Internet documentaries, one can, conversely, think about how viewers and contributors benefit from the multimediality of having the documentaries on YouTube and the museum's website (Snickars and Vonderau 14). The Internet documentary changes the understanding of what constitutes the documentary form, filming styles, and mechanisms of circulation, distribution, and storage. YouTube's motto, "Broadcast yourself," is one that resonates with the ways in which social media and other Internet platforms are connecting with contemporary users of the Web who seek to have immediate access to information, images, and videos as long as they are searchable. To this end, the museum's webpage and

YouTube channel serve as a dual repository; the museum provides visibility and institutional legitimacy to the videos. The migrants use the museum and its platforms to tell their stories, which would otherwise be untold aside from sharing such stories among trusted familial and intimate circles.

The Museo de América is not an isolated initiative, given that cultural institutions seek to have more visibility and meet the changes in technology and demands of visitors and audiences. A prime example is how the Library of Congress and other cultural centers also have YouTube channels. An interesting facet of the Internet documentary is its relation to open access. The traditional documentary is bound by copyright, unlike most Internet documentaries. These open-access videos allow sharing information in social media and thus have the potential for circulating among broader audiences, including migrant individuals and groups. The dilemma inherent in Internet documentary is twofold: Do such works benefit from becoming part of global corporate Internet companies such as YouTube and Vimeo? And should filmmakers continue relying on traditional formulas of documentary filmmaking, production, distribution, archive, and consumption? YouTube makes use of each user's data and information from searches to suggest videos and thus extend the network of visibility that Internet documentary videos can have. Due to rapidly evolving devices with Web capabilities, the documentary is no longer confined to the movie theater, film festival, or television screen. It can be watched from anywhere with Internet connectivity and has little monetary or time cost for the viewer. The growing emphasis and visibility of Internet documentaries is ultimately in tune with a market increasingly filled with images.

Conclusion

In discussing Internet documentaries as they relate to new modalities of representing and disseminating firsthand experiences of migration, I have traced some of the broader issues that ought to be considered when confronted with emerging technologies and growing availability of self-uploaded videos. The prevalent emphasis of Internet documentaries on brevity, fragmentation, and lack of conventional narrativity has begun to shift the very definition of a documentary. A brief exploration of the videos available on the Museo de América's website and its YouTube channel showcases newer forms of documentary that shy away from having directorial figures or even employing traditional film styles. Instead, the increasing emphasis on interviews, dialogues, and monologues gives primacy to the firsthand account and self-representation of the migrant as she wants to be seen. Unlike its place in the past, the creative control rests with the migrants who ultimately have the option of whether to submit their stories online and share them with the world with seemingly minimal intervention of the museum in the curatorial process.

The changes in documentary forms, styles, and engagement with shifting media sensibilities and technologies allow Latin American migrants to have more nuanced self-representation through the multiplicity of life stories succinctly presented in the short clips. Internet documentaries appear as a hybrid form that is at once a form of media communication and provides corrective information, that is, in correcting misrepresentations and stereotypes about migrants. Noteworthy, however, is how the detailed and graphic depictions of the process of migration take a secondary or background position in many of the documentaries I have discussed here. Instead, the migrants as inhabitants of Spain or the transformative impact of cultural objects from the Americas on Spanish culture are foregrounded on the videos available through the Migrar Es Cultura webpage. One could be critical by arguing that such representations emphasize the migrant's unproblematic assimilation. I argue instead that such self-representations build upon the idea that migrants are on an equal level or at least that they should be treated as equals to any citizens in the host countries. Ultimately, personal life stories or *historias mínimas* are essential to the Internet documentary because they show a different dimension of the occupations and professions migrants have but also introduce the plethora of circumstances that led them to leave their home countries and create new lives elsewhere. The migrants' ability to upload videos in which they can control how and for whom they are represented can be related to earlier discussions on decolonial aesthetics. After all, decolonial aesthetics seeks to challenge hierarchical and Eurocentric ways of understanding arts, including documentaries and the role of a museum, while also aiming to shift the modes of producing, consuming, and exhibiting artworks. In the examples of Internet documentaries I have presented, production is often in the hands of migrants themselves. With this in mind, it should be stressed here that for every personal story of migration or object represented in an Internet documentary video, a distinct and closely knit relationship to a migrant's life is introduced and ripples into a network of other migrants in search of new venues for self-representation.

Notes

Completion of this chapter has been made possible with the generous support of the Robert L. Ardizzone ('63) Fund for Junior Faculty Excellence at the College of the Holy Cross.

1. The term "migrant" is used here to refer to the heterogeneous experiences represented in the videos uploaded on the Museo de América webpage. The migrants are actors, journalists, maids, students; the reasons or the exact process of migration is not always made entirely clear. Because the migrants themselves upload these videos, the migrants as producers of their own videos are careful to choose what is revealed or omitted from their life stories and migratory journeys. Furthermore, the term "migrant" is used here instead of "immigrant" for three primary reasons. First, "migrant" encompasses and conveys the complexities of migratory journeys, in which the motivations for migrating are sometimes suggested and other times remain ambiguous. Second, the use of "migrant" mirrors what the Museo de América is doing through its Migrar Es Cultura page (MigrarEsCultura.es), where emigration, immigration, and migration are encapsulated under the category "Migration." Third, the term "migrant" is used here as a more humane and politically correct term to characterize a broad spectrum of migration stories.

2. For a discussion of authority in relation to documentary filmmaking and on the responsibility that documentarian and subject share, see Louise Spence and Vinicius Navarro's *Crafting Truth*, particularly chapter 3, which is devoted to an extended engagement with production and distribution mechanisms that grant authority to documentaries.

3. Unless otherwise noted, translations from Spanish into English are mine.

4. For recent studies on these questions, see Michael Chanan's "Going South: On Documentary as a Form of Cognitive Geography"; T. J. Demos's *The Migrant Image: The Art and Politics of Documentary during Global Crisis*; and *The Cinema of Me: The Self and Subjectivity in First Person Documentary*, edited by Alisa Lebow.

5. Other recent scholarship on this topic includes Juan G. Ramos and Tara Daly's edited volume *Decolonial Approaches in Latin American Literatures and Cultures*, particularly the chapters by Zairong Xiang and Javier Sanjinés, and Juan G. Ramos's *Sensing Decolonial Aesthetics in Latin American Arts*.

6. The work of Jacques Rancière has rekindled attention to aesthetics and politics within continental philosophy. Rancière's critical work moves away from discussions of aesthetics as either a discipline or a set of philosophical discourses and, instead, proposes the notion that works of art operate within a historical regime. For more detailed accounts of his concepts and reevaluation of aesthetics, see Rancière's *Aesthetics and Its Discontents* and *Aisthesis: Scenes from the Aesthetics Regime of Art*. In analytic philosophy, there is significant work done to move beyond traditional understandings. A useful work is Francis Halsall, Julia Jansen, and Tony O'Connor's edited volume *Rediscovering Aesthetics: Transdisciplinary Voices from Art History, Philosophy, and Art Practice*. In that

volume, for instance, Wolfgang Welsch's contribution helps us think about aesthetics' emphasis on the visual and the need to rethink how aesthetics engages the other senses as well. In relation to literary and cultural studies, Sianne Ngai's works *Ugly Feelings* and *Our Aesthetic Categories: Zany, Cute, Interesting* help us look at contemporary concepts and categories that might be useful in understanding articulations of what she calls the such zany, cute, interesting, or ugly feelings as animatedness, envy, and irritation. These positions on contemporary aesthetics stand simultaneously in dialogue and at odds with decolonial aesthetics, given that the latter seeks to move away from geopolitical articulations of aesthetics that maintain the centrality of Western aesthetics.

7. There are two illustrative videos on the role of quinoa in Bolivian and Andean diets, namely *La quínoa, un cereal milenario de origen andino* (Quinoa, an Andean thousand-year-old grain) and *La quínoa visita el Museo de América* (Quinoa comes to the Museo de América). Both videos are meant to bring about an awareness of the culinary diversity existing in various regions of the Americas. In other multimedia sections, the Museo allows contributors to upload videos and photography that can be accompanied with brief explanatory texts. Two examples of photography and questions of race can be found under the titles *Rostros andinos* (Andean faces) by Gabriel Barceló and *Entrevista con Dulce Pinzón* (Interview with Dulce Pinzón).

Works Cited

Anzaldúa, Gloria. *Borderlands: The New Mestiza—La Frontera*. 4th ed. San Francisco: Aunt Lute, 2007. Print.
Barceló, Gabriel. *Rostros andinos*. 2012. Web. Museo de América. 9 March 2016.
Las brujas migrantes. Museo de América. 2013. Web. 9 March 2016.
Burton, Julianne, ed. *The Social Documentary in Latin America*. Pittsburgh: U of Pittsburgh P, 1990. Print.
Chanan, Michael. "Going South: On Documentary as a Form of Cognitive Geography." *Cinema Journal* 50.1 (2010): 147–154. Print.
Demos, T. J. *The Migrant Image: The Art and Politics of Documentary during Global Crisis*. Durham, NC: Duke UP, 2013. Print.
Entrevista con Dulce Pinzón. Web. Museo de América. 2013. Web. 9 March 2016.
Halsall, Francis, Julia Jansen, and Tony O'Connor, eds. *Rediscovering Aesthetics: Transdisciplinary Voices from Art History, Philosophy, and Art Practice*. Stanford, CA: Stanford UP, 2008. Print.
Hughes, Peter. "Blogging Identity.com." *The Cinema of Me: The Self and Subjectivity in First Person Documentary*. Ed. Alisa Lebow. London: Wallflower, 2012. 235–249. Print.
Jenkins, Henry. *Convergence Culture: Where Old and New Media Collide*. New York: New York UP, 2006. Print.

Lebow, Alisa. Introduction. *The Cinema of Me: The Self and Subjectivity in First Person Documentary*. Ed. Alisa Lebow. London: Wallflower, 2012. 1–11. Print.

Mignolo, Walter D. "Rutas hacia la estética decolonial." *Estéticas y opción decolonial*. Ed. Walter Mignolo and Pedro Pablo Gómez. Bogotá: Universidad Distritral Francisco José de Caldas, 2012. 25–47. Print.

Ngai, Sianne. *Our Aesthetic Categories: Zany, Cute, Interesting*. Cambridge, MA: Harvard UP, 2012. Print.

———. *Ugly Feelings*. Cambridge, MA: Harvard UP, 2005. Print.

"Presentación Migrar es Cultura." Museo de América. 2012. Web. 9 March 2016.

La quínoa, un cereal milenario de origen andino. Web. Museo de América. 2014. 12 March 2016.

La quínoa visita el Museo de América. Museo de América. 2014. Web. 9 March 2016.

Ramos, Juan G. *Sensing Decolonial Aesthetics in Latin American Arts*. Gainesville: U of Florida P, 2018. Print.

Ramos, Juan G., and Tara Daly, eds. *Decolonial Approaches to Latin American Literatures and Cultures*. New York: Palgrave Macmillan, 2016. Print.

Rancière, Jacques. *Aesthetics and Its Discontents*. Trans. Steven Corcoran. Malden, MA: Polity. 2009. Print.

———. *Aisthesis: Scenes from the Aesthetic Regime of Art*. London: Verso, 2013. Print.

Sanjinés C., Javier. "Decolonizing Aesthetic Representation: The Presence of the European Savage in Bolivian Modernity." *Decolonial Approaches to Latin American Literatures and Cultures*. Ed. Juan G. Ramos and Tara Daly. New York: Palgrave Macmillan, 2016. 99-119. Print.

Snickars, Pelle, and Patrick Vonderau. Introduction. *The YouTube Reader*. Ed. Pelle Snickars and Patrick Vonderau. Stockholm: National Library of Sweden, 2009. 9–21. Print.

Spence, Louise, and Vinicius Navarro. *Crafting Truth: Documentary Form and Meaning*. New Brunswick, NJ: Rutgers UP, 2011. Print.

Viaje de ida y vuelta. Dir. Clara de la Flor. Museo de América. 2012. Web. 12 March 2016.

Welsch, Wolfgang. "Aesthetics Beyond Aesthetics." *Rediscovering Aesthetics: Transdisciplinary Voices from Art History, Philosophy, and Art Practice*. Ed. Francis Halsall, Julia Jansen, and Tony O'Connor. Stanford, CA: Stanford UP, 2009. 178–192. Print.

Xiang, Zairong. "The (De)coloniality of Conceptual Inequivalence: Reinterpreting Ometeotl through Nahua *Tlacuiloliztli*." *Decolonial Approaches to Latin American Literatures and Cultures*. Ed. Juan G. Ramos and Tara Daly. New York: Palgrave Macmillan, 2016. 39-55. Print.

CONVERSATIONS ON DOCUMENTARY FILM AND MIGRATION

11

Luis Argueta

Migrant Voices without Fear

INTERVIEW BY ESTEBAN E. LOUSTAUNAU

Boston, April 8, 2015

LUIS ARGUETA is a film director and producer whose work spans feature films, documentaries, shorts, commercials, and episodic TV. Born and raised in Guatemala, Argueta first came to the United States to study engineering at the University of Michigan. His college days in the Midwest were not only a time to learn about science and technology; he gradually developed an interest in film and labor migration issues. Argueta's first attempt at documentary film started when he and his college roommate grabbed a Super-8 film camera and went to Traverse City, Michigan, to interview cherry pickers. Although he never finished that film, the trip was the beginning of a successful film career that has included commercial television, feature films, and documentaries. Some of Argueta's early films include *The Cost of Cotton* (1978), a politically charged documentary that exposes the human cost of dumping U.S.-banned chemicals on cotton plantation workers in Guatemala. His 1994 film *El silencio de Neto* (*The Silence of Neto*) was the first Guatemalan film ever submitted to the Academy Awards competition; in 2015, Jayro Bustamante's *Ixcanul* became the second Guatemalan film to be submitted to the Oscars. After years of making TV commercials, in 2008 Argueta turned his attention to the issue of Guatemalan labor and migrant rights in the United States. That year he traveled to Postville, Iowa, in the aftermath of the largest single raid of a workplace by the

U.S. Immigration and Customs Enforcement (ICE). The raid that took place at Agriprocessors, Inc., the largest kosher slaughterhouse in the United States, resulted in nearly 400 arrests of immigrant workers, most of whom were undocumented and of Guatemalan origin. Since he first traveled to Iowa to learn about the mistreatment of Guatemalan migrant workers and their families, Argueta has produced three documentary films on this subject. Discussed in chapter 2 of this volume, the first documentary film in the series, *abUSed: The Postville Raid* (2010), focuses on the devastating effects of U.S. immigration enforcement policies on children, families, and communities. The film gathered wide acclaim and premiered on PBS in December 2012. The second film in the trilogy is *Abrazos* (2014), and the third film, *The U-Turn* (2017). At the 2015 premier of *Abrazos* in Guatemala City, the Guatemalan minister of foreign affairs awarded Argueta the Orden del Quetzal, the country's highest honor in the arts, humanities, and sciences. Our interview took place at the Park Plaza Hotel in Boston on the day Luis Argueta attended a screening of *Abrazos* at Emerson College.

How did you become interested in exploring migration through film?

Well, I've been saying that I first read an article on the front page of the *New York Times*, I think it was on July 11th of 2008, and it was written by Julia Preston, about Erik Camayd-Freixas, the interpreter who along with 25 other federally certified interpreters went to Waterloo, Iowa, to work on what they called a "continuity of operation exercise." The interpreters were called to Waterloo soon after 900 agents of ICE [Immigration and Customs Enforcement] executed a raid of Agriprocessors, Inc., the largest kosher slaughterhouse and meatpacking plant in the United States, located in the small town of Postville, Iowa. At the raid, 389 undocumented workers, mostly Guatemalan and Mexican, were arrested and processed for deportation soon after. Mr. Camayd-Freixas wrote a 14-page essay about his experience during the two weeks he was there. Every interpreter worked either in the arraignment of the detained immigrant workers the first week or the sentencing the second week. He stayed both weeks, and after that, he was so outraged by what he saw that he wrote the essay describing his experience, doing an incredibly thorough analysis of immigration policies and history. That essay really made me say I have to see this for myself because I couldn't believe that such a travesty of justice and of violations of human rights had taken place. So I went to Iowa. Originally, my intention was to be there only four days. I stayed two weeks. I intended to be there once and then go back to New York, but I stayed and went back 29 more times. So, usually that is my answer. Then, 29 months later, after 29 visits to Iowa and 17 trips to Guatemala, I finished *abUSed: The Postville Raid*. But then I realized that I have been interested in immigration and migration before I even realized it. When I was an undergraduate student at the University of Michigan and I began playing around with Super-8 films, I told my roommate, "Let's go to the fields in the upper part of the Lower Peninsula and do a documentary about cherry pickers." So we went to Traverse City, but we never did the film. Then in 1977, I read another article on the front page of the *New York Times* about the phenomenon of dumping in this case, dumping pesticides banned in the U.S. and Europe, into Third World countries. It was DDT that couldn't be used here but it was pushed, literary pushed, by a very strong advertising campaign as a solution to cotton pests. Alan Riding for the *New York Times* wrote an excellent exposé of how this overuse of pesticides was contaminating cattle, water, and people. So then I did a documentary called *The Cost of Cotton* [1978], which when I finished it, it was the reason why I didn't go back to Guatemala for many years because the film became a very highly politically charged documentary.

This was during the time of military dictatorship?

It was eleven years after the war had started, and there were guerrillas destroying spray planes because of the damage they were doing and as part of their insurgency campaign, but it was not yet in the levels of the war in that region in the 1980s. I was doing what you could say was an ecology-oriented documentary. It became politically charged, not allowing me to go back to Guatemala because I showed the migration of workers from the highlands to the coastal cotton plantations. I also used a couple of verses from one of Otto René Castillo's poems about cotton workers. He was, of course, a subversive poet by many right-wing accounts. The poem describes this phenomena of borrowing money, leaving the money with the family, and going to the coast to sell your labor very cheaply, living in horrible conditions and getting paid very little. Indeed, when I went to Postville I remembered *The Cost of Cotton*, which was 30 years old by then. I remembered it because there was a woman who I interviewed in Postville, and I said, "Well, you told me this horrible story of exploitation at the plant, of a trip that almost killed you, where you were almost raped, and where you had a lot to lose. Why did you put up with this?" And her answer was exactly the same answer that an older gentleman in the fields of cotton in Guatemala had given me 30 years before when I asked, "Why do you work for so little?" And he said the same thing that she said, "De algo a nada hay mucha diferencia" [From nothing to a little bit there is a big difference]. Suddenly it became clear to me that I had been interested in immigration. When I was at the University of Michigan I also worked two summers in the Human Services Department in Monroe, Michigan. My job was to intake immigrant workers that came with the seasons from Florida to northern Michigan, picking oranges in Florida and cherries in Michigan. There I saw that many of them had U.S. citizen children. I saw that while the parents may not have had access to any social services, the kids did, such as emergency systems or food stamps. This was a small way to help them to get started every year. There I also went to the camps, so I saw how migrant pickers worked and lived, but there was not really something that I focused a lot of energy on. You know, I did my job and then I went back to school in the fall. Then, after 2001, after 9/11, I had been doing commercials up to then, and that point I said, "No more." I wanted to save a tiny bit of my soul that was left. I told myself, from now on, I want to do something that I think is meaningful, at least to me. And I started visiting the Guatemalan consulate in New York. And I began visiting the mobile consulate where the office in New York will go to towns where there are a lot of migrants on Saturdays and Sundays, so that people wouldn't have to drive, wouldn't have to lose a lot of time from work. And the consul general there was a very good friend of mine, and she invited me to be involved. The first time I attended a mobile consulate was in Lynn, Massachusetts. There I began seeing large groups of Guatemalans coming for consulate services. At that time, I had just brought a video camera. When I did commercials, I always had a big crew, so I never touched the camera. We worked with 35-millimeter cameras, a soundman, an assistant of camera, a cameraman, and I directed, that was my job. But now that I had a small video camera I started holding it and experimenting with it when interviewing people. And I would do short interviews and then post them on YouTube. These are part of a small section that I called "Voices of Silence: Portraits of Immigrants." And I must have done about eight or ten of them. So, when I went to Postville, I thought, hey, I'll make a couple more interviews and add them to my collection. There was also another work that I did around ten years ago. It must have been in 2004 or 2005. I heard that there was going to be the first Spanish mass at St.

Patrick's Cathedral in New York, in honor of the Black Christ of Esquipulas, who is the patron saint of immigrants from Guatemala. Bishop [Rodolfo Quezada] Toruño was coming to say the mass. I wasn't there, but I hired a cameraman to go and do some filming during the mass. Then I bought the film that the church put out and edited a 15-minute documentary about that event, which became historical. Since then it has been a yearly celebration. Later I realized that it wasn't enough to have just those images. So I did interviews with different people who had been instrumental in planning the event. These included the Guatemalan consul, a couple of people who organized the mass, and a priest who had done work in Guatemala. This priest said something that really opened my eyes: "This event transcends its religious meaning. It is an event of identity and solidarity." It was a very moving experience to see St. Patrick's Cathedral packed with Guatemalan immigrants. So, when 2008 happened, the raid in Postville happened, I had been subconsciously getting ready for it.

How is a documentary like *abUSed* made? By this I mean how did you and your collaborators find a balance between managing the logistics and securing the financial investment required for making a film like this, and the high level of urgency that comes with telling a story about real, tragic events?

It wasn't easy, as you said. When I first learned about Postville, Iowa, I had to look it up in a map. Then I asked, where is the closest airport? The closest airport is two hours away, no matter where you look. So, I figured I had to fly to Rochester, Minnesota. That is the one airport that I thought was the most logical. I know there were flights to Cedar Rapids, but I didn't know where Cedar Rapids was, but I was familiar with Rochester because I knew about the Mayo Clinic. I then asked a friend of mine who had worked with me in many commercials and who's Guatemalan to see if she wanted to join me in Postville. "Where?" she asked. And I said, "Postville, a little town in Iowa where there was a huge raid and 389 workers were arrested, most of them were Guatemalan. Let's go to see what happened." And she did come. And I had a camera, and she had a camera. After four days I drove her back, as she had to get back to New York. You have to realize how far Postville was from New York. To get there we had to go fly to Chicago, change planes, go to Rochester, rent a car, drive down to Decorah, Iowa, first, because we had obtained three nights of free accommodations at the parish house in Postville, but the keys were at Luther College in Decorah. That was my first visit to Luther College. I didn't know what Luther College was before, and little did I know that it would become a second home. So, from the beginning I talked to people in Iowa and told them, "I'm doing this on my own dime. First, can you help me get some interviews? Second, can you find me a place to stay for free?" And they said yes to both. Later I found out that people were a little suspicious because there were a lot of press requests. And I quickly said I am not a reporter. I want to do a documentary. So I brought copies of *The Silence of Neto* and copies of the mass at St. Patrick's. Those were my introductory letters. And some people said, "Oh, it looks like this guy is for real." But again, there were the logistics of how do you manage to tell the story. I began by interviewing a couple of the women who had been given ankle bracelets and were left in town to care for their underaged kids without any means of doing this because they were not allowed to work. So they were living off the charity of strangers. Everyone whom I interviewed would mention somebody else. And I would write it down and say okay, how do I find this person? And it just became a big chain of people that I needed to interview not only to hear their own story but for me to understand what had happened. That took a lot of time. I did pay for my trip, and Vivian paid for her trip. What helped in this case was that after those two weeks I had enough footage to edit an eight-minute trailer, an extended trailer that had a beginning, a middle, and an end. And I began showing it around to anybody who showed some kind of interest and started to fund-raise for the documentary. The first grant we applied for was with the Iowa Historical Society, and they gave us $12,000. That was a good start, but of course, we didn't get the money for probably three months. The first few trips to Iowa I was paying for the trips with credit cards, but at least I didn't have to spend on hotels because I always found a place to stay. Once you are awarded your first grant you usually get more grants, and in this case that happened. With *abUSed*, you are talking about the urgency of telling current events. The way I managed it was by going around and doing an outreach tour with the eight-minute trailer, and I would speak about my experience, about what I was finding out, what I was doing. I was trying to make people aware of what only a few knew in Iowa, Chicago, or Minnesota but not in other places. A friend of mine recommended that I talk to the New York Immigration Coalition. They had actually sent a group of people to Postville to see what had happened, because they are an advocacy organization. And I asked them, Would you be my fiscal sponsors? And they said yes, and we signed a contract. That also opened doors to grants because nobody would give you money unless you have a fiscal sponsor, a nonprofit 501 organization. That brought in people in New York who were allies and that were interested in seeing how the film progressed. I went to Washington to the Migration Policy Institute, to Luther College, where some people there helped me, especially Pastor David Vásquez, he was terrific. He is Guatemalan, and he was a little suspicious of me at the beginning as well. Now we have become pretty much like brothers.

Speaking of Pastor David Vásquez, in the film he mentions that the raids reminded him of images of the disappeared from the time of the civil war in Guatemala.

Absolutely.

How did you react to this same footage?

Well, you know, this was so close to home. In Postville I was interviewing Mexican immigrants as well as Guatemalans, but the majority were Guatemalans. And people would tell me, "I remember my parents talking to me about the helicopters during the war in Guatemala and places being destroyed by soldiers that came in helicopters." So there was this image of helicopters and how this little town in Iowa had been attacked by helicopters. Even if those women that were working at the meatpacking plant were not adults at the time of the war in the 1980s, as some of them might not have been born yet, they had inherited memories. They had that, and I had lived through the 1960s and the 1970s in Guatemala, and I have personal experiences of friends who had been disappeared. When David said that, I said, "Absolutely." In addition, after the raid some people would say, "We have been trying to find my husband or my father and we don't know where he is. We called one jail and he is not there. We've called an 800 number that ICE has and we can't locate him." It was really hard. And later I would find men that were deported who said, "I have no money to call my wife." So, for five months, many had no contact with their families. It was extremely difficult to locate them. David Vázquez was absolutely right.

The spelling of the word "abused" in the film's title is perfect. How did the title come about?

In the opening credits of the film, the title appears "US" first, the "USed," and then "abUSed." It is totally deliberate. The film, of course, was not called *abUSed* in the beginning.

What was the original title of the film?

The original eight-minute film was titled *Postville, May 12th, 2008*. One of the things I really love is editing. I normally don't do the editing, but when I have to, I do. That eight-minute video I edited. Also, even before the eight-minute video, David Vásquez was invited, along with Sonia Parras, the attorney who defended many of the immigrants, to go to Washington. He was invited by Hilda Solis to attend a hearing. David called me and asked, "Luis, do you have something that we can show?" And I put together something like five minutes of testimonies by the women. That was the first public screening of anything that I had done. And people were very interested. I met another attorney, Leslye Orloff, with whom we are working on the third film now. Going back to the title. I hired an editor from Guatemala who was in Chile at the time to come and work with me on the film. He came for about three weeks, but he had a different idea about how the film should go. But he contributed with the title. His name is Rafael Valdeavellano, and he is a great filmmaker. Rafa and I played with all kinds of titles. And then he said, "Abused." And I said, "Absolutely!" And then I began to play with the design, and I thought it was just perfect, very provocative. Not only that, but in Spanish it is even better, "abUSAdos." Well, you know, it was provocative, and when we had the film's premier in Guatemala, sponsored by the Soros Foundation, we invited the U.S. ambassador, who said, "Before I decide to go, I want to see the film. Can you send a copy?" And we said no. So he didn't show up. Because, I mean, he was reacting to the title.

How did you build trust with the migrant workers and their families living in Postville?

That's a very good question. First of all, as I have said, I always thought, I am not a journalist. I am not a reporter. I am a filmmaker. This is what I did. I didn't show a whole film, but I would show the packages of my films. With the Guatemalans, I spoke Guatemalan Spanish, which helped. They didn't believe I was Guatemalan. And with the Anglos I spoke English. With them it was less of a problem earning their trust. With the Guatemalans, I would say, "I am interested in learning your story." Of course, they would not take me at my word. But early on, I realized I was going to have to spend time there. So, most journalists would come for a couple of hours and leave. And I was there for days and I wouldn't leave, and I would come back and see them at the church or see them in the streets. I would go where they were studying English, you know, go to the school. Yes, I would go in and out of the school. I had the keys! They were very good to me. So the kids would see me, and I became a familiar face. Early on that fall, a group of women got tired, and the attorneys said, "Your cases are very weak. You'll probably never get an adjustment of status. So we recommend you take voluntary departure. Instead of waiting to go to court to then be ordered to be deported, you can just go." And the church said, "We'll pay for your airfares." These were five families, four women and one man, and they all had kids. All had U.S.-born children. And I said, "Can I go? I'll pay my way." And they said sure. So, I accompanied these five families by land to Chicago. I flew to Postville, drove with them to Chicago, and then flew all together to Guatemala, and then went with them to the towns of El Rosario and Calderas. That was my first visit to their hometowns. During that trip, I also took letters and photos from other people who stayed in Iowa, to their relatives. And I would interview them on camera and asked them to send their regards. So I brought these video letters to Postville, and that helped to create trust because they thought this guy is crazy enough to go and send images of our families. This is something that has to be worked on. And I worked on this for 29 months. Along the way, I received a call from the Attorney General's Office in Iowa. And he said, "Luis, we understand you've been to Guatemala to several of the hometowns of these people, and there are four kids who were underage workers that were deported, and we are looking for them because we want them to consider coming back to testify at the child labor violations trail against the manager of the [meatpacking] plant." And I said, "I'll help you." And I found the four, found three more, and eventually brought seven kids to be material witnesses at the child labor violations trial against the general manager of the plant.

So you served as a go-between in this case.

Yes. I went, talked to them and their parents. We had conference calls on cell phones with the investigators and attorneys. I said [to the kids], "They want to offer you a trip back to Iowa without anything else. But they will pay your trip, some money to pay for food while you are there, but then you'll have to come back. At the most, you'll be there three months. This is your chance to tell your story in front of a court of law." And they said yes. And out of the seven, six received the U visa because they were victims of crimes. They collaborated with law enforcement, and it was determined that they had suffered considerable trauma and physical damage.

To my mind, no single subject in the film takes a dominant role. Instead, to me the people of Postville become the film's collective protagonist. How did you go about putting all the pieces and all the voices together in making this film?

It wasn't easy. Every interviewee would lead me to somebody else that I wanted to talk to. And it was not just immigrants. It was church people, school administrators, teachers, emergency medical teams, lawyers, and plain citizens that had come to volunteer their services. And it was the principal of the school. It was a lot of people! And I saw this town as a huge cast in a play, with the town itself and the plant's owners and managers. And then you had the attorney general and his investigators, and you had the Labor Department staff. Yes, it was a huge cast. I had over 500 hours of material. So, it was extremely difficult. We tried different structures. However, at one point I said to Ezequiel Sarudiansky, the editor of the film, "Zeeky, the way to go is this: let's take the eight-minute trailer and stretch it. Because I know that the beginning is the beginning and I know that the end is the end. We just need to insert pieces in the middle." And it worked. That was the way it worked. Then we developed themes and people, we used chronology. We determined that our time frame would be one year, from May 12th, 2008, to May 12th, 2009, the first anniversary of the raid, when there was a town march. Of course, we would do jumps at the end with updates of what was going on with the people. We developed some themes of abuse at the plant, the children, the parents, the deported families to Guatemala, the economic effects, and we had to develop each of those sections and find their appropriate place. But the beginning of the film is the beginning of the trailer, and the end of the film is the end of the trailer.

In the film, several migrant workers who were detained and taken away after the raid articulate a clear consciousness of the injustice they experienced. Did they already possess this consciousness by the time you arrived in Postville, or was it something that came about in the process following the raid?

In some of them, it was a process; in some of them I think it already existed. There was a man who was deported. He doesn't appear in the film, but he told me something that shows a consciousness of injustice derived from his biblical knowledge. He said, "When they would treat us so badly at the plant, I would think, 'You know, the Egyptians did it to them. They kicked them out of Egypt.'" He's talking about the Jews being victims, and now they were the victimizers. Another man, who is in the film, has a very elemental sense of justice when he says, "They accused me of stealing these documents. I did not steal them, I bought them!" So, what he didn't realize is that the documents were fake. But he had not stolen them. You know, to tell somebody that you stole something, it is a big insult. There is this dignified knowledge of injustice or an awareness of their dignity. However, in some it was a developed consciousness, especially among the women. And that is the subject of the third film in the trilogy, *The U-Turn*. That film talks about the group of women who gradually lost the fear of speaking out, telling the injustices and the crimes they had been victims of, and by doing so and collaborating with law enforcement, they were able to apply for a U visa. That was a gradual process. You know, take Pedrito, the little 12-year-old kid in *abUSed*, he had no idea what he wanted to be later in life. And this made him grow up very quickly. He said, "I want to be a lawyer." And he is on his way. He is now a sophomore at Luther College. There is a woman that appears in *The U-Turn* film that says, "They talked to us and they told us about our rights. We learned our rights and we decided to fight."

Speaking of mothers, in *abUSed* two of the mothers who were detained and eventually deported to Mexico and Guatemala, respectively, try to protect their families by denying having children when the ICE agents came to apprehend them. This shows their tremendous love and courage in the midst of fear and despair. In making the film, what impressed you the most about the migrant mothers?

The absolute dedication and conviction that no matter what they go through, it is because they have a very clear goal to have their kids have a better life than they did. And it is this love that they have for their kids and their families that is just remarkable.

A major theme in *abUSed* is the criminalization of undocumented migrants by U.S. Immigration and Custom Enforcement officials. In your films, how do you try to overcome this and other stereotypes about Latin American immigrants?

I am an immigrant, but I really didn't know anything about immigration prior to making the film. I got a permanent residency card through marriage and became a citizen 15 years later. I never thought that I would do it. I never saw any use for it. And then around 1999 or 2000, I saw how things were getting pretty tough, and a friend of mine said, "Luis, you should get your citizenship." And I did. I got it in July 2001. Little did I know that that fall things would really be getting very hard for people even with just permanent residency cards. So, this has been a great schooling for me. The main lesson I've learned is that each of these immigrants is an individual. That is the lesson that I try to keep in mind, and how they have touched my heart and changed my life is what I try to convey. Because I think that it is one person at a time that we need to change. [We need to] change the minds of people.

A very moving moment in *abUSed* is when a delegation from the congressional Subcommittee on Immigration led by Representative Luis Gutiérrez goes to Postville to hear the testimonies of migrant women and children, almost all of whom at some point worked for the meatpacking company Agriprocessors, Inc. What was it like for you and your crew to film this encounter on that particular day?

I think that was the moment when I said I have to stay here. I have to stay here and tell this story. That happened on the Saturday of the first trip. You know, I called the church after I read the article, left a message but didn't hear back from them for about a week. Of course, they were going crazy. But in New York I would say Why don't they call me back?! So, I called back and said I need to talk to somebody. So, they put me on the phone with somebody who was handling the press. And I said I want to come, and I want to come soon. And they said, "Well, you know. Maybe you want to come next week because there is going to be a big march on Saturday." And there was a big march. And I also learned when I got there that a congressional delegation would be there, and Julia Preston was there. A large Jewish delegation from Minnesota and Chicago also came. That moment, when the immigrants were telling their stories, it became so quiet that you could hear a pin drop. Everybody was absolutely quiet. But at one point, there was not a single dry eye in the house. It was absolutely impactful and moving. I said my God, I have to get to know the people who are telling these stories. I am very glad that I stayed and later went back.

In *abUSed* there is a scene that takes place in a barbershop in a small Guatemalan town where one migrant man now works after facing deportation from Postville. What's funny about this scene is that you are interviewing him while he is giving you a haircut. Is that right?

Yeah [*laughs*].

How do you see your role as filmmaker engaged in the very lives of the migrant subjects who appear in your films?

Rolando Calicio is his name, the barber of Postville. He would cut hair on Saturday because on Saturdays they didn't work at the kosher plant. He would say, "I make more money cutting hair on Saturdays than I do the other days." But of course, he couldn't cut hair every day because people were working. I see my [role as an engaged filmmaker] very naturally. I had never met Rolando until that day. I had spoken with him on the phone and said, "I want to talk to you." So I came and asked, "What is the easiest way to talk to you?" I wasn't going to say, "Stop cutting hair and talk to me." So, I said, "After you finish with [the clients] can you cut my hair?" He said yes. So, he cut my hair. I paid him for it. And while he was cutting my hair I said to my cameraman, "Roll!" We were very lucky because he was totally relaxed and said what he said. He was very candid. He actually wrote a song that I am considering using in *The U-Turn*.

Is he still in Guatemala?

He's still in Guatemala. He's still cutting hair, and his son is now cutting hair with him.

Nobel Peace Prize laureate Rigoberta Menchú appears in *abUSed* and addresses some of the social and political factors that have pushed many Guatemalans out of the country to seek a better life elsewhere. Has she seen *abUSed*, and what was her reaction after viewing the film?

She came to the premier of *abUSed* at the National Theater in Guatemala. I don't think [in *abUSed*] we have that image of a young boy and me that is going to be in *The U-Turn*, but she became very fond of Pedrito, the kid. She is a fan of the film and the story it tells. The story that I like to tell is how she got to be there. One day I said, "We have to go film this hand-painted sign that says 'Welcome to Postville.'" It was beautifully hand-painted. Unfortunately, it is not there any more. When we were filming it, I read it and said oh my God! Because it said, "Welcome to Postville. Boyhood Home of John R. Mott, Nobel Peace Prize 1946." And I didn't know who John R. Mott was until I later Googled it. But when I saw "Nobel Peace Prize 1946," I said, "Why didn't I think about it before? Rigoberta should be here!" So, I called a friend in Paris who I know had worked with her and said, "Vincent, can you get me a phone conversation with Rigoberta Menchú as soon as possible?" And he said yes. So we scheduled one for maybe three weeks in the future. In the meantime, I went to Pastor Vásquez, to Sister Mary, to the people in the town, the support group, and I said, "Listen. If Rigoberta Menchú were to agree to come and visit the immigrants who are here with the ankle bracelets, would you raise money to help pay for her trip?" And I said, "I also would ask her to come without charging her regular fee, which is quite high." And they said, "Yes, we would pay for her trip and her hotel." Three weeks from that day, I was in Guatemala. I got there the day before we were supposed to have the phone conference. And I called her assistant. No, Bea [Gallardo, the film's producer] called her assistant. And I said, "Ask her if I can come and have our conversation in person because I am here." And she said yes. So, I went to see her and interviewed her for the film, and then at the end I said, "Don't cut the camera because I want this to be recorded." And I said, "In the name of the Guatemalan immigrants in Postville, in the name of the Mexican immigrants in Postville, I would like to extend an invitation for you to visit them. They have agreed to pay for your travel, but no fee." She said, "Well. . . ." Then she turned to her husband and said, "Angel, bring me the calendar, please." And she looked at the calendar and said, "Well, we need to be in Mexico at the beginning of November, but maybe we can go a little later or a little before. What about around November 7th?" I said, "Perfect. That is my birthday!" So, we arranged a trip and she came. It was absolutely historical and very important for the women and for the support group. Some of the women did not know who she was. But they knew she was there. She was wearing a Guatemalan *traje*. She was very passionately interested in their stories. It was a great visit.

A common theme in many of your works, including the acclaimed feature film *The Silence of Neto* and documentaries such as *abUSed* and most recently *Abrazos*, is that of memory. How do you see the role of personal and public memory in your films?

Well, having grown up in a country where not only the society was repressive but where memory was not encouraged nor thinking either and where questioning was not encouraged, I was always convinced that I had nothing to say. And I had nothing to say because I couldn't remember anything. So, when Justo Chang and I began to write *The Silence of Neto*, which at first had a totally different name, it was *Guatemala, 1954*, we knew we wanted to tell a story around kids during the coup because that had marked my life and the life of many people in the country. My father was a judge and he lost his job, so it was a very personal story. You need to understand that I didn't learn the history of Guatemala in Guatemala. I learned it when I was at the University of Michigan. I lost my fear of speaking out in Michigan, in the U.S., and I also learned that I could express myself through film. All these things served to open the window to the past. And I began to remember and to associate the historical events with the personal story of my family and my life. So, it was a conscious decision to tell the story about something that people wanted to forget, because people didn't want to talk about it, and maybe they had forgotten about it. Certainly, kids today and the younger generations don't know about it. That is a period of history in Guatemala that is not taught. And in the U.S. it's the same thing. People don't know what happened in Central America in the 1950s. They don't know what happened in the '80s let alone in the '50s. So, I've made a conscious decision to speak about things that people wanted to forget or have forgotten. With *abUSed*, again, it was a conscious decision to talk about something that people really didn't want to talk about in this country. You know, I came [to the United States], literally, I ran away from Guatemala because I didn't want to be repressed and have found that I can say something about things that were uncomfortable or at least people didn't want to think about. And I became a citizen of the U.S. and I have a daughter here, I've made my home here, and as critical as I am of some of the policies and the history of foreign policy in the U.S., I am a citizen of this country because I think that people shouldn't have to fear to speak out. And the same way that I had felt that I was fed fear as a child, I realized that I would be fed fear as of 9/11, 2001. And I said, I didn't come here to be quiet or stay silent. I think it is extremely important to talk about the past, to bring back personal and collective memories, and reconstruct that base of identity. With the tour of *Abrazos*, I've realized that people with whom I am talking in colleges were in middle school or elementary school when Postville happened. They have no idea, not only about what happened in Central America in the '80s, but of what happened in Iowa six and a half years ago.

Something you do so well in your films is the inclusion of points of view and experiences of children. Why do you think it is important to look at past and present events from the perspective of children?

I think that it's a less adulterated point of view. It is less contaminated by pessimism, is more honest, and it's more fun. I really think that it is extremely important to keep the child inside in each of us alive because children don't have fear. At least that is what I have found out. I did grow up as a fearful child, but

I finally found a part that was not afraid. I think it is important to go to them because they are very honest and they teach me a lot.

abUSed is the first documentary film in a series that also includes your films Abrazos and The U-Turn. Can you describe these two most recent films and their connection to abUSed?

Abrazos had a historical connection, at the beginning at least, because while touring with *abUSed*, I came to Worthington, Minnesota, and after the screening, I met Lisa Kremer, who told me she knew Guatemala from her mission trips with her church but didn't know Guatemalans until she began working in Worthington. There she had met many immigrants who now were her friends. A few months later she told me that she had become a grandmother for the first time, that she loved spending time with her grandson, and that she realized that it would be unthinkable not to see her grandson when she wanted and that there were all these kids in Minnesota and Worthington who had never met their grandparents. She said, "What do you think if we take some of them to Guatemala?" I said, "It is a great idea. I'll help you as much as I can, and I would love to make a film out of it." So, that was the cause of the film. And it is a continuum in the sense that it is the stories of immigrant families from a slightly different angle. This is because very few of the Postville families that appear in the film had U.S.-born children. In this case, it was the total opposite. All of them had U.S. citizen children. The Postville families had been there for a relatively short period, five or six years at the most. There was a guy whom I met from Guatemala who had been detained at the raid, sent to jail for five months, and then deported. He had called his wife on Sunday the 11th of May to say, "I'm very happy because tomorrow is my first day of work." So he worked a couple of hours on Monday the 12th, and then the raid happened. In Worthington you have families who have been there 12, 16, 20 years, so they have made deep roots in Minnesota. There is a contrast, but there is also a good comparison. They are from different parts of the country. Postville families come from Chimaltenango and Sacatepequez, which are fairly close to Guatemala City, and the families from Minnesota come from San Marcos, which is far from the city, close to the Guatemala-Mexico border. Many of those immigrants had never been to the city. If they have a passport is because they got it at a mobile consulate. Those are the similarities and the differences. *The U-Turn* is very much tied to *abUSed*. *The U-Turn* was going to be the second film in what is now the trilogy. I really didn't think there was going to be a third film at the time. I thought it was going to be two films, and this was going to be the aftermath of the Postville raid and how the women lost the fear of speaking out, broke the silence, and collaborated with law enforcement, of how underage workers also lost the fear of speaking out and therefore told their stories and were able to normalize their immigration status and are now living in Postville with permits. Many of them have permanent residency, and some of them have traveled back to see their parents after eight or nine years of not seeing them. But then *Abrazos* happened, and that had an urgency and also had the support of Lisa [Kremer] and her husband. The kids were very much present and I, I was talking to my wife, telling her I'm going nuts because I'm trying to do two films at the same time. And she said, "Put *The U-Turn* away. The more time passes, the more changes in people's lives, and that won't hurt, that would be for the better." That was a very good advice. I did that and finished *Abrazos*. Now we have taken up the editing of *The U-Turn*. We did more filming in March, in Iowa, and we did another day of filming in Washington with an attorney. We are pretty much done. I think we might have one or two more interviews. I have an editor and an assistant editor working on the post-production of the film, and if we are able to raise enough money, I hope that we can finish it this year.

By now, you have presented *abUSed* and *Abrazos* across the United States and in many film festivals around the world. How have these films been received by different audiences?

Well, *abUSed* has been entered into 17 international film festivals, and I personally did about 160 presentations in colleges, faith-based communities, labor conferences, immigration conferences, one international conference in Guatemala, one international conference in Colombia. I also traveled to Helsinki with the film and to Gothenburg, in Sweden. One of the most common reactions that people have had is "I didn't know it's like that." This is a common demonstration of the ignorance of the situation of immigrants in the U.S. Law protectionists react with outrage about the violations of the Constitution and the comments that the lawyers and the judge make in the film. And there are some, you know, hard-core anti-immigrants who say, "Well, they broke the law and they deserved what they got." There's even people who don't accept that workers have rights independent of their immigration status. And you know, that is just simply denying the truth. So, I have to say that the film has been very well accepted in general. With *Abrazos* is a very emotional reaction, I think because the stories are about kids and about families, and people react to that first. They sort of forget about the immigration question. One of my purposes is to humanize the immigrants and to make them individuals, not numbers. As I said before, they have touched my heart and changed my life, and I think that we can try to continue to do that one person at a time.

Are you working with Ezequiel Sarudiansky as the editor again?

No, I am working with somebody else, but I did talk with Ezequiel last week, and I want him to be the supervising editor of the film. I think we can probably do that. He is now in Miami, so he is close. And his work is excellent. I also want to get some contemporary young people to work with the music with me. I used a lot of Americana music in *abUSed* and more Maya music in *Abrazos*. Here we have that song that the barber wrote, and I would like something else. I'm not sure what it is yet. Besides that, I have a fiction film that I have been developing with a friend of mine. It is an adaptation of a novel. It will be the story of Guatemala in the last quarter of the twentieth century seen from the point of view of a family. It is based on a book that was written by a Guatemalan writer. It will be very controversial because is about an intelligence army officer who at the end, he repents of what he did, burns his uniform and his medals. But again, it will be a family story with the background of Guatemala's history from the 1980s on. And then I have another story that I have been developing for a long time. I just signed an agreement with a writer friend of mine from California who is an excellent scriptwriter, and I think we have simplified the plot and we have gotten to the hard facts about illegal adoptions, a theme that, unfortunately, was very big in Guatemala until 2007.

One final question, in your view, what role can documentary film play in the struggle for immigrant rights and subsequently for comprehensive immigration reform in the U.S.?

Well, it's my hope that we can humanize immigrants, that people would realize that these are not numbers and that by reaching one person at a time we will change their minds and we will eventually change the laws. At the same time, this is my way to give some power to the immigrants because by them seeing their stories on the small or big screen they feel validated. In Worthington they said, "We feel important, we feel that people care about us." And they also lose the fear of speaking out. And that's crucial. They might one day become citizens if not through the grace of the U.S. Congress, then through their children's petition after they are 21. So, it might take a few years, but these are forces in the future. For people who do not know immigrants, I think it is very important to show that immigrants are not that different from them, from us and our ancestors and our own families. I think documentaries can educate and transform people. My film *abUSed* is distributed through New Day Films, which is the oldest co-op that distributes films for the educational market. We are able to reach quite a number of students and educators. It is by the help from people like you that we get the word out, and then people think about it. You know, I love that question "Do you ever think about the things you think about?" I think it is important that we educate the younger generations through thinking about the things that we think about, not just to act or react. There was a comment by Kent Ferris, the director of social action at the Diocese of Davenport [Iowa], who said, "Often we are just reacting to laws that are being passed or policies that are being created, but with this film we can get ahead and hopefully get into people's hearts so that things will be better for these families and for others." But we need all the allies we can get to get the word out.

12

Jenny Alexander

Breaking the Silence through Documentary Filmmaking

INTERVIEW BY ESTEBAN E. LOUSTAUNAU

Boston, March 23, 2016

Filmmaker, producer, and former community organizer Jenny Alexander has dedicated much of her professional life to advocating for the rights of immigrants in the United States, especially farmworkers, youth, and women. In particular, her work focuses on documenting personal stories of migrants who, after enduring violence and other forms of trauma and marginalization, find ways to transform themselves into vocal agents of change for their families and communities. Alexander's commitment to social justice and visual culture started when she was in college and studied abroad in Cochabamba, Bolivia. There, she completed a photography project on the Siglo XX mine, where the largest massacre of workers in Bolivian history had taken place in 1967. After college, Alexander spent 10 years as a union and community organizer. As a union organizer, she worked for the United Farm Workers and the Puerto Rican Workers Union (Sindicato Puertorriqueño de Trabajadores). At an immigrant workers organization in Boston, Alexander trained women immigrant workers in developing their public speaking skills. As part of this training, Alexander filmed the women so that later they could see themselves on camera. This not only helped the women realize their social empowerment as they listened to their own voices, it also enabled Alexander to come to understand filmmaking as a tool for social activism. After working with immigrant youth in East

Boston, Alexander completed a master's degree in film production at Boston University. She is a producer at Northern Light Productions, a documentary film production company in Boston. One of her documentaries is *Detained* (2007), which follows families affected by the 2007 U.S. Immigration and Customs Enforcement raid of more than 300 immigrant workers at a factory that produced vests for the U.S. military in New Bedford, Massachusetts. Another, discussed in chapter 3 of this volume, is *The Vigil* (2014), the story of Gina, Rosa, and other undocumented women who in 2010 became leaders of a peaceful vigil in the midst of a tough legislative battle over immigration in Arizona. We spoke in her office at Northern Light Productions.

Over the years, you have gained significant experience as a community organizer and filmmaker. How has your community activism influenced your work as a filmmaker?

I think that community activism actually has driven my work as a filmmaker in many ways. It all started when I was working with undocumented immigrant young people in East Boston and I did a documentary with them. This ended up being a collaborative project, which was used later as an organizing tool. I started following undocumented youth and students when the New Bedford raid occurred in 2007. Mario, one of the immigrant students I was working with, went to the church basement where families were going to try to find out what had happened to their loved ones who had been detained in the raid. I was already filming when I went to this church. However, I thought I was making a film about the students with whom I was working. But then I walked into this church basement, and I had never experienced anything like what I saw. There was such a feeling in the air of tragedy. People were coming together to try to support each other, and I knew at that moment that I had to document that. Every time we would interview a family, like when we interviewed a man named Lilo Mancia who had two small children, they would tell us similar stories of trauma. Lilo said, "My wife has been detained. I have two small kids." There was a woman named Sandra who had been detained, whose child was hiding under the table. There was another woman who was detained, Yamilet, who still had a breast-feeding baby. So we would interview people and then send the video clips to Senator Ted Kennedy, and we would ask, "Can you help get this person out of detention?" That actually helped the senator as he would then make the calls to immigration. We were able to get Yamilet out—she was the one that had the breast-feeding baby. At the same time ICE [Immigration and Customs Enforcement] was on the nightly news saying that no children had been left in unsafe predicaments and that everything was being done according to law, in the church basement you were seeing what that really meant. I knew that I wanted to document that because the reality of what was happening to people was so different from what was on the news. That is an example of how activism drives my filmmaking. This is how my film *Detained*, documenting the New Bedford raid, came about.

How was your film *Detained* received by the immigrant community and other audiences?

The film was used as an organizing tool. It was used in academic settings, it was used by Greater Boston Legal Services, and was screened at film festivals both within and outside of the United States. I think that one of the most powerful screenings we had was with the people who were in the film. Because most of the people had been traumatized by the raid experience, I had a friend who is a psychologist advise me, very intelligently, to make sure that the process for having the families view the film was one where you made sure that people were not going to be retraumatized. There was a therapist who had worked with the families during the whole process, and he came for the screening. We had the screening, but we also had a conversation facilitated by the therapist afterwards. It was very difficult for people to see the film, but at the same time they said, "It was important for us, because we want people to know our story." I think the power of film is that it can speak to different audiences very effectively. It can communicate the message of the human experience confirming what people went through acknowledging their experience, which is very important in terms of breaking the silence. In the case of the immigrant community, stories of injustice are too often silenced by the fear of deportation or the very shame and weight of the experience. For me this is a big theme: How can we use film to break silence? But this is also important in relation to the people who may not have been aware of what was really happening. There was a college administrator who couldn't believe the detainee's testimonies who said, "Did that really happen to people? Did they really put them in chains? Did they really do that?" Some people are always going to have faith in what the government does and says.

This reminds me of Luis Argueta's film *abUSed*, about a similar raid in Postville, Iowa, that happened in 2008. I think these films highlight very well your idea of breaking the silence.

Yes. Films like *abUSed* can provide a way for individuals, even an entire community, to share their experience and challenge the injustices they have experienced.

This film's ability to help break the silence is also a central theme in your latest documentary, *The Vigil* (2014). How did you first become aware of the vigil that a group of immigrant women created outside the Arizona state capitol building in 2010?

I have two answers to this question. First, because of the work I had been doing, I had a good friend who is a community organizer and who had moved to Arizona. She moved there to work with the immigrant community in Phoenix. She called me one day to say, "There is something amazing happening here on the capitol lawn! You have to come and film this." That was the last time she did that because I came to Phoenix and it quickly turned into a five-year project! So basically it was through my organizing relationships that I was aware of this. Second, I knew something had to be done about the Arizona Senate Bill 1070 and this idea that you would have to carry an ID with you at all times and that it could be considered a violation of the law to not have an ID with you. I come from a German Jewish background, so right off the bat I questioned what was going on there.

You mentioned that the process of making *The Vigil* took five years. How long did you stay in Phoenix, and how did you manage your time when making the film?

Well, the vigil began in April 2010. The purpose of the vigil was to keep it going on the capitol lawn as long as was needed to stop the law. The shooting of *The Vigil* occurred during April through early September of that year. It was the end of the summer when the vigil ended. In that period, I would say I went four or five times. I had a one-year-old daughter at that time, so it was quite something to do this. There were times when I brought her. Over that summer I probably spent altogether a month there. After that, there were probably four more shoots the following two years.

How did you begin to build trust with the migrant subjects in this film?

I would say that it was by going to the vigil. The vigil would be at the state capitol lawn by five in the morning. I would go to the vigil early, and I would just sit there. I didn't film right away, and then I started talking with people. I think it happened by showing up over time. The people would come up sometimes and ask who I was and how I was doing. I would just try to be very low-key and just be present, let people see me. Later, once I was able to start talking to people, I explained what I wanted to do, and then I started filming. But I also think by the second trip I took my daughter with me. I have a feeling that that helped too. They probably said, "Okay, she is a regular person." On the first trip there were some group events that I filmed, like the candlelight scene, but nothing personal. I really didn't start to film personal stories until the third trip I made to Phoenix.

Toward the end of the film, Gina, one of the central subjects in the film, describes her experience in the vigil as a transformation. This is after she realizes her power to speak. Can you tell me more about this process of transformation for people like Gina?

Gina represents, or reflects, what so many people go through, and she is very articulate about it. That is what I find so amazing about Gina. She speaks from soul to soul. When I first came to the vigil she didn't talk at all. I didn't think she could be a character in the film because she didn't talk. That was just how it was. Gina had only focused on work and on her son, on providing for her family. Basically, she would only move between work and home and was afraid of being stopped by the cops and getting deported, so she didn't speak up. She didn't do anything that she didn't absolutely need to do. Yet, inside of Gina was this strong and powerful person who has always been there, but her focus was on her family and building up a business. So when S.B. 1070 happened, it was a crisis moment. For Gina and the other women, that was the spark, which we talk about in organizing. There were many ingredients in that vigil. As a former labor and community organizer I could see that there were many nontraditional ingredients in the vigil. It was people coming together, but it was women's leadership. There were definitely men involved, but the heart of it and the persistence of it came from women every single day, all day, from morning until night. So one aspect of the vigil was the clear persistence by the women. The other was that the leadership was less about being the charismatic leader who is a very good speaker and who projects a persona. Instead, it was about listening. So, the women would sit there at the *vigilia* to listen to people come and share their *historias*, stories, share their *penas*, sorrows. And that is where the bonds were being made, in the listening. It wasn't about "Oh, that leader speaks so well, I will follow him," you know? And that was a huge difference. The women were there all the time, so they were present for people to come when they could, in their own time, and they would be there to listen. Rosa, another of the leaders of the vigil, is a great example of this. There was a man who said, "I used to come and speak with Rosa. I am a single dad and would tell her everything that I was going through, how difficult everything was, and she would listen to me. Through that process, I learned that I do have rights, that I am a human being, that I matter and am valuable." And that's big. That was a huge piece of the vigil. People were able to share their stories, and that is the key to breaking the silence. If you are able to share with others that thing that's holding you down and brings so much shame, you are able to break the silence. You realize that you can speak. And they created this environment with faith, for people to break the silence, to share their stories of shame. Because when you are the immigrant who is being told that you are the cause of everyone's problems, that you are one who steals, etcetera, it is shameful for people to go through this experience. So people don't talk. Gina wouldn't say anything about what she had gone through. She went through very difficult experiences that she never shared with others. So all of this was trapped inside. For Gina, breaking the silence happened through prayer. One day during a prayer session, Gina started to speak. And now she would tell you, "Since that moment, I have never stopped talking." The conditions were there. The women were sharing their stories. Their way of doing things was being honored because they had the Virgin of Guadalupe with them. The virgin was reinforcing that idea, so it was a huge transformation for Gina to find her voice. She became someone who was speaking out for herself. And in speaking for herself, Gina was representing others. The vigil evolved into a place where people actually came to listen and see how to respond to the daily threat of arrest, detention, deportation and anti-immigrant hostility. Being aware of how to respond to having their humanity questioned was a way of leading their community. Gina finding her voice is the root of the greatest social change that you can create. These are the seeds, *las semillas,* the key ingredients for social change.

How did the experience of making *The Vigil* have an impact on you?

My daughter was one year old at the time of filming *The Vigil*. First, I learned a lot from the women in the vigil about how to be a mom. They were very strong mothers in very difficult circumstances. As a woman, I learned a lot from them. Gina, for example, was running a business. She has her mother and two daughters in Mexico and her son here, all of whom depend on her, and on top of that, she became an activist. She was juggling many things in her life, and I was noticing her strength and determination, which gave me strength and inspiration.

The other piece had to do with my family history. You don't know when you are going into a new film project what you are going to learn and there is always something, something personal. But the thing is that you don't know until later because the work is so close to you. In my family, my grandparents and my dad, who was very young, escaped from Nazi Germany. When I was growing up I knew my grandparents and dad were refugees, but I didn't know many details of their story. Similar to what happens to immigrants in Arizona, the Jews in Germany went through a very shameful experience. I learned from my grandparents that you don't share the story loosely and that you have to be respectful of the story. It was when I was taking a class on immigration in college that I asked my grandparents to share their story with me.

My grandfather wrote me a letter, which included the story of an experience he had when the Nazis were in power and he was invited to visit a cousin in a distant part of the city. It was the day after Hitler had conducted a bloody purge within the Nazis. My grandfather was on the bus going to his cousin's when three SA guards got on the bus and surrounded him. Suddenly the SA guard grabbed his shirt and demanded to know why my grandfather had laughed at him. A fight ensued and my grandfather was taken to jail. While in the jail cell he realized that his cousin's invitation was still in his pocket because his cousin had moved to a new address. The invitation had contained criticism of the Nazis. My grandfather slowly tore pieces off the invitation in his pocket and ate them until the invitation was gone. He ended the letter with this story by writing, "My account is meant for you and the family. The less you circulate it, the better I will like it." I took this to heart, and so the story stayed in the letter. It was during the making of the film that the whole story was unlocked for me. I realized that in my own family there had been a kind of silence. I felt that out of respect that it wasn't my story to share with other people.

That story was written in a little letter. Maybe it was in my class paper, but that was it. This is why I find it so remarkable that the women in Arizona went through the process of breaking the silence by saying, "No, we have the right to be heard. We have the right to speak up. We have a voice." These were very difficult, traumatic experiences that had happened to them. And then they said, "Despite that, we are going to turn things around, and we are going to use it as a strength. In the presence of the Virgen de Guadalupe we are going to allow ourselves to share our stories of *pena* and *vergüenza*." *Vergüenza* is a difficult term for me to capture in translation, but it basically means shame. This made me realize that in my family we actually had had that too. Stories of experiencing the blow of oppression were still kept in the shadows.

When I was filming I saw a family seek the advice of one of the women at the vigil, María. The family asked María, "Should we stay or should we go? We don't know what is going to happen." She said, "You have to stay and fight." My own family had gone to a rabbi in Germany and asked him, "Should we stay or should we go?" Imagine if they had stayed! And suddenly I realized that the women were allowing themselves to take on the role of giving counsel in the midst of great upheaval and fear, with a spike in hate crimes and legislation intended to expel all undocumented people from Arizona. That is a huge leadership role. But they weren't practicing their leadership with a microphone. They were listening and inviting people to join their act of resistance. Watching the women create a space where people could share their stories and break the silence had a huge impact on me on a personal level. It allowed me to experience my family's story in a new way. It was after experiencing the vigil that I shared my grandfather's story in public for the first time at a screening of *The Vigil*.

Do you continue to stay in touch with Gina and Rosa? How has your relationship with them developed since making the film?

Yes, I've stayed in touch with Gina and Rosa. With Gina and Brian, her son, we became close through the filmmaking process, and to this day we continue our friendship. She has been on panels at several of the film screenings. She did a presentation in Seattle at the Social Justice Film Festival. That is something that I would like to continue to do. I plan to organize more screenings with Rosa, Gina, and Blanca so that they can speak in public because they are such powerful leaders. And again, I go back to the idea of your typical charismatic leader, but they are not like that. They are extremely articulate, extremely powerful in how they speak, but they lead more by example than by persuasion.

Music seems to play an important role in *The Vigil*. Some of the songs are sacred. Others are political. What connections do you see between reflective devotion and political action?

The connection between devotion and political action is definitely tied to liberation theology. That's what it was. I mean, Paulo Freire would have had a heyday with this vigil! The liturgical song "Pueblo libre" [Free people] that goes, "Pueblo libre que vas caminando por las aguas de la vida" [Free people walking along the waters of life] sends a message that is very much about liberation and faith. Song was a powerful thing that they were using along with their faith, and the songs really crystalized that. The song at the end of the film was written by the young singer Tomás Amaya. This song includes the youth's perspective about the vigil. Absolutely, music was a vehicle for social change and the political movement. I can't remember what song it was, but there was a song where the lyrics were masculine, "El hombre, ta-ra-rá" [The man, blah, blah, blah], right? But the women at the vigil changed the lyrics from "el hombre" to "el pueblo" [the people]. It was their way of trying to be more inclusive.

What impact do you think the Virgin of Guadalupe has in how women like Gina and Rosa come to redefine the notions of motherhood and of power for their lives?

I have a different perspective than how I think the women would answer this question. I actually would be curious to know how they would respond. My observation would be that La Virgen is about acceptance, about giving things time for acceptance because she has this unconditional love. As they would say, "La Virgen works in her own time, in her own way." So I think that maybe the challenge of being a mother is like accepting all of the aspects of how one is a mother and maybe not being judgmental with oneself. But my lens on it is political in the sense that I think La Virgen was very much influencing the women in terms of their roles as mothers and having a say in politics and having a say in how things are run. They took La Virgen and they put her on the state capitol lawn where legislators are making the decisions. It was like La Virgen opened a small space to help them say, "Aquí estamos. We are here and this is our message." So, for me La Virgen reaffirms the importance of the role of the mother but also that women and mothers have a voice that should be lifted, listened to, and should be heard. I think the women in the film used that to insert themselves into the political discourse and to provide a message that was not being heard at all. They also had a message against this very strong and hateful anti-immigration law and all the militia people that were there all around. The vigil is all about acceptance and love, which is very much the message of La Virgen. I think they positioned her in a very organic but powerful way.

The opening scene in the film shows Rosa about to set up the vigil. The Virgin of Guadalupe is shown as a companion to the women by riding in the passenger seat of Rosa's car wearing a seatbelt. How did you think of filming that scene?

Actually an editor suggested I film it. He said, "It is amazing how they are doing that." And then Rosa puts La Virgen on the bench to rest, her way of caring for her. Someone was always in charge of La Virgen. At the end of the night the women took turns taking care of her, putting her seatbelt on, taking her to the convent, bringing her back, *cuidándola bien* [taking good care of her]. The image we see in the film is Gina's Virgen. There were two statues, the travel statue and the statue set up every day at the capitol. The statue that was used the most was Gina's Virgin. It broke at the very end, and it was replaced by one belonging to the *abuelita* [the elder woman of the vigil]. *La abuelita* is *doña* María Nowaskowski, City Councilor Michael Nowaskowski's mother. She became a mother to all the women at the vigil, so she was very special. She died a little after the vigil was over. She was certainly very, very special. Then I think they had a smaller travel version of the statute, and that's the one they took to Washington, D.C. Every night around 11:30 p.m. they had to step off the capitol lawn. So there was this organization called Promise Arizona that was supporting the vigil. The women would go to Promise, which was located in a convent, and they would rotate sleeping next to La Virgen there.

Besides Gina and Rosa, can you tell me about other stories of resistance by women, men, and youth that appear in the film?

There was the single father with two kids who would speak with Rosa. The vigil completely transformed him. Also Brian, Gina's son, was very young at the time of filming, but I saw him later when his mom testified in Congress and he translated for her. As time has gone by, he is becoming more involved. I think at this age now is when I can ask him more about how the vigil changed him. I know it was very important for him to see his mom being very active. He was very proud of her, and he wrote about it in school. Another person who was transformed by her participation in the vigil and who appears in the film was a woman named Felipa. She has three kids, and her husband was deported during the process of the vigil. The vigil was very important for Felipa because she was going through a very difficult time, and she would come to the vigil, where she could get a little respite.

In the film, we see the presence of leading community activist Dolores Huerta, NPR host María Hinojosa, and the local Latino City Councilor Michael Nowaskowski. What did their presence mean to the vigil, and how did the local activists receive them?

Well, when you talk about local activists, there were many different groups in Phoenix. But when it comes to the women in the vigil, Nowaskowski was Abuelita's son, so he was considered part of the community. At that time, it was very important for him to come and be inspired by the vigil as well as acknowledge the vigil. He was involved in local politics, so he could take the message of the vigil to local decision makers. Dolores Huerta visited the vigil very early on. All the men and women who were at the vigil were very well received. It was very important to the men and women of the vigil to see these important people there. It would inspire and re-inspire them because the vigil was very hard. So to have someone from the outside say, "Wow, look at what you guys are doing!" was validating. But also, it was helping to get their message out to a much wider audience. Danny Glover came, and also Shakira came to the vigil. I think it was remarkable for people with a voice at a higher national and international level to have witnessed the vigil.

In the film we see some supporters of the vigil wishing the movement would take a more forceful stance against Maricopa County Sheriff Joe Arpaio and those who stood against the rights of immigrants in Arizona. How long was this debate, and how did Gina and Rosa manage to stay true to their peaceful beliefs?

That debate was going on the whole time, and it was happening also at the city level in Phoenix. You had different groups with many different thoughts on how to approach this. For example, the Puente Human Rights Movement is a group that held peaceful demonstrations but was much more confrontational and engaged in civil disobedience. They would block Arpaio's jail, among other things. That tension around strategy was going on within the vigil and among the wider immigrant and Mexican and Chicano community in Phoenix. That tension has been around a long time in social movements, of course.

There is a scene in the film where Gina says, "That's not our message" when two members challenge that the vigil should be more confrontational. There were definitely people who criticized the vigil as being ineffective, and there were disagreements within the vigil. However, despite all of that, the fact that the women were able to remain committed to the vigil is a testimony to their character as well as to their faith. Every day they were doing rosaries. So they had a ritual that was always grounding them.

Tell me a little about Doña Dora. Besides being a strong woman of faith, what was her role in the vigil?

She was similar to *la abuelita*. Doña Dorita and *la abuelita* were the two wise elders of the vigil. They were a rock for everyone, and they were both extremely spiritual. Doña Dora is from Bolivia, and she became the spiritual teacher for several of the women, especially for Gina. She will give spiritual lessons, like the heart lesson she gives Gina in the film.

In the film, the viewer assumes that several of the people who took the vigil to Washington, D.C., along with Gina and Rosa had no legal documentation to be in the U.S. Were they worried about being detained along the way and facing deportation?

That was always a risk they took, yes. Promise Arizona was the nonprofit organization that supported the vigil, and they helped plan the trip to Washington. If something were to go wrong on the trip, they would have helped. But there was always the risk of arrest or deportation in speaking out publicly.

Do you think the forces behind Sheriff Arpaio's strong anti-immigrant stance pertain only to border states like Arizona, or is this sentiment being felt across the country?

I think history has taught us that these flames can be whipped up. I wouldn't say that this could happen just at any time. The flames are always there, but I think that there have to be certain conditions that can make them catch on fire. I really believe that people's speech and people who choose to actually put an effort into this kind of rhetoric can be effective, unfortunately. That's why we have to be aware of this kind of demonizing and dehumanizing of people. Arizona is like the petri dish, but it is not isolated in any way. The fear of other, of new, of change, are human traits. And we see that throughout history. We have to be always aware that this fear is always there. I choose to always focus on stories like those of Gina, Rosa, and the men and women who were part of the vigil because they are the counterbalance to all of that. Many people targeted by SB 1070 were moving away. Many were hiding in their homes. The counterbalance to dehumanizing others is the people who are willing to take the risk to stand up and to speak out.

In many ways, *The Vigil* is about the strong bonds that women and children can establish in difficult circumstances. What connections did you see among the mothers and their children, many of whom are part of the DREAMers movement?

That to me was one of my favorite parts of the film because I could very clearly see how the principles, the faith, the beliefs, the actions, the role modeling of the mothers were like a gift that they were giving to their kids. In return, their kids were taking that and then adapting it to their experience and to their increasing familiarity with the American political system. Now we see the DREAMers often in the news, and they know the power of social media. They have been very successful in helping frame and reframe the story around immigrants and immigrant youth. Behind those kids are the parents with their values, the mothers who, like Gina, are willing to go and do a three-month vigil, like Rosa, who is dedicating her time to activism and to teaching her children to be brave. One of the most important moments in the film is when Rosa's daughter Dulce says, "My mom told me to never fear anything." And then later in the film when a man is interviewing her on local TV, she says, "We cannot let fear define our lives." To me, that crystalizes that mother-child relationship, when the mother is teaching this principle: "Mira, mija, you can't let this fear rule you." Dulce knows how to move in the system, she knows how to advocate, she's speaking flawlessly in English and Spanish, and now she is sharing that message. This is the message that is helping her figure out how to live in the world but also through which she is speaking about her community. This is very powerful. In any social movement we tend to focus on those who you see in front. And in the film you see the women who are shaping the most important part of the movement. To this day, Dulce continues to be involved with the DREAMers movement in Arizona. She is married and now has a son and works in real estate. She continues to be very successful.

How has *The Vigil* been received across different audiences?

To give you an example, a few months ago we did a screening at a university in upstate New York. The students who hosted the screening belonged to a Latino fraternity. The students on campus, many of whom were disconnected from the immigration issue, were really moved by the story of the film and actually started to speak about immigration issues. As a matter of fact, there was a little concern prior to showing the film on campus because someone had sent the equivalent of hate mail in relation to the screening. In many ways, I think it was important for them to still hold this event and have it be very successful and positive. The students who attended were able to relate the story to very different experiences and recent current events, such as the Arab Spring. One of the strengths of the film is that audiences can adapt it, in a sense, to what is important to them. That is what we have seen in many screenings. In religious communities we see the faith part being really motivating for them. Among younger audiences, we see how they connect the film to their parents' stories of migration and their social backgrounds. The PICO [Pacific Institute for Community Organization] Network is a national interfaith organization that used the film as part of their leadership development for their immigrant leaders. At one point Gina was in Washington, D.C., participating in a hunger strike for immigration reform. A man came up to her and said that he was in D.C. because he had seen her story and was inspired that if she could take action, he could as well. Those are the anecdotes that are the most inspiring coming from the screenings of *The Vigil*.

In representing the voices of immigrants through film, what messages do you wish to send to your audiences?

My first goal is to send their message, the message of the women and men of the *vigilia*. I understand that the filmmaker is like a filter and that we need to be aware of our voice as filmmakers. My intention is that people hear Gina and Rosa's message. I wish that, as much as possible, we are opening a space or a platform for their experience to be shared with a wider audience. With *Detained* it was people being able to share and tell their stories of what they had experienced, to be able to tell their truth because it is often mangled in mainstream media. I think this is changing a little now that there are more platforms for online and social media to influence mainstream media. I also think that the DREAMers movement has been exceptionally good at changing the narrative about immigrant youth and creating ways for people to tell their own stories.

What projects are you working on now?

I am working on organizing more screenings with *The Vigil* and finishing the film's study guide so that it can be used in schools and universities. Currently, I am working on a Northern Light project in San Juan, Puerto Rico, for the National Park Service. It is about the 500-year history of the fortifications and it is fascinating work. Also for Northern Light, I am working on two short videos and an audio program that will play on a Soviet Foxtrot submarine at the San Diego Maritime Museum. It tells the story of a little-known event that occurred on a Soviet submarine, the B-59, during the Cuban missile crisis.

# 13 k

Tin Dirdamal

Intimate Gaze of Significant Concerns

INTERVIEW BY LAUREN E. SHAW

Mérida, Mexico, March 11, 2016

Tin Dirdamal doesn't consider himself to be a filmmaker. But since he picked up a camera at the age of 22 in Orizaba, Mexico, to record a Central American migrant's story, he has made three films: *De nadie*, (2005), *Ríos de hombres* (2011), and *Muerte en Arizona* (2014). Born in Monterrey, Mexico, in 1982, he is the unique combination of his artistic mother and MIT-graduate father, both of whom hold a high regard for education. With a strong aptitude for math, Tin attended the Tecnológico de Monterrey as an industrial engineering student and nearly completed his degree there. However, he cut short his formal education in order to satisfy his curious nature in a different way. With no formal training in camera work or filmmaking he produced *De nadie*, his documentary on Central American migrants crossing Mexico. It has received prizes at Sundance, the Guadalajara Film Festival, and the Mexican Film Academy. *De nadie* is discussed in chapter 4 of this volume. *Ríos de hombres* deals with the water war in Cochabamba, Bolivia, in 2000 and tells this compelling story beyond what most filmmakers, academics, and journalists have attempted to portray and understand. *Muerte en Arizona* is a more lyrical and personal piece on his grieving process over an apparent lost love, though he characterizes this film as a futuristic documentary, choosing to emphasize the postapocalyptic narrative woven throughout. Though dealing in diverse subject matter, all three films share motifs and a personal vision of how human beings interact. Bringing his audiences to almost utter despair, Dirdamal does offer a glimpse of a possible and better option for humanity's seeming insistence on destruction and self-centeredness. This interview took place during the 17th International Conference on Hispanic Literature in Mérida, where Dirdamal was a participant in a panel organized by the book editors featuring his films.

You were one of the first to document Central American migrants crossing through Mexico on route to the U.S. What made you want to pick up a camera and film that experience?

I was volunteering on a project at that time that had to do with working with Central American immigrants in the Isthmus of Tehuantepec in Veracruz, where Mexico becomes narrow. There was an immigration checkpoint in the city of Orizaba where Central American migrants would get caught and put in Mexican immigration jails. The project had to do with visiting these jails and seeing what the immigrants needed.

How did you come to work on this project?

This all started by working with Jesuit priests in Monterrey, where I'm from. Monterrey is the industrial capital of Mexico. It's a very rich city. Back in the 1960s there were a lot of Jesuits there, and they taught at the biggest university there, el Tecnológico de Monterrey, a very prestigious but strict university. The Jesuits in the '60s didn't align with that vision. There was a student group that kidnapped and ended up killing the founder of the university, one of the wealthiest people from that city, who had studied at MIT and wanted to build his own version of MIT in Mexico. Influential members of society in Monterrey started blaming the Jesuits since they had helped develop student groups in general. So the Jesuits were expelled from the university and the whole city. In fact, the ultraconservative Catholic order the Legionaries of Christ, was founded in Monterrey. It along with the Opus Dei had strong influence in Monterrey when I was going to school. So the Jesuits began coming back little by little in the 1990s, and they established a cultural center. My mother mistakenly encouraged me to check out the cultural center and I did. That was the first time I heard these ideas that questioned life and even religion. So, actually for me to be going to this Jesuit cultural center was like going against everything I was taught. My whole education had been very conservative, and the Jesuits were very liberal. So the Jesuits put me in a project visiting the jails and seeing how immigrants were treated. And the reason I started doing the film was that one day one of the immigrants from Honduras needed a place to stay. So he stayed in our house in Orizaba. He had been cut really badly on his face by the Mara Salvatrucha. So, while staying with us he told us his story. And it was very moving to me. There was a camera in the house—I'd never used a camera before in my life—and I filmed him telling his story. After that I decided I would film other Central American migrants. My grandfather used to work in the cotton fields in California. I never knew him. He died before I was born. But he would never talk about how he was treated. So, in the whole Mexican imaginary, we all have a relative who either worked in the fields or went to work in the States and was poorly treated. So for me to see the same picture being repeated but with Mexicans mistreating Central Americans was very revealing. The story was about the human condition, not about Mexico versus the U.S. or Central America versus Mexico. So, I had a friend who had a camera, and I started making a film about it with no experience and with no concept for the film. I only had a camera. No sound equipment. So that's why all my shots are close, because my camera was my sound equipment. I knew that it was important to understand what these people were saying, so I wasn't interested in the composition of the image. The camera was just my microphone.

That's interesting, because something that stands out about your films is the intimacy you create on the screen. Part of that is the visual proximity of the subject, but also it seems as though you have created a closeness and trust with whomever you are filming. Can you talk about that?

Well, for me the film is always secondary. When I'm interacting with them it's in the same way I would if I didn't have a camera. I don't put on a persona for them. My job is to make that camera as invisible as possible. For example, I'll never take distance from you just to have a better shot. I'll just approach you and ask you things, and I won't repeat myself just to have a better line than what I'm filming. I think that not having studied film has actually helped me. I'm a very curious person, and I realize it's easier for me to get people to answer my questions if I'm holding a camera.

Can you tell me how Bishop Raúl Vera is connected to this project?

Well, when the Zapatista movement happened in the 1990s there was a very famous Catholic bishop in Chiapas who helped the movement. His name was Samuel Ruiz. The Catholic Church didn't approve of his actions. What the Church would do with these rebel bishops was to put a co-bishop with them. And this was Raúl Vera, a very conservative Franciscan that they put with Samuel Ruiz. But Vera changed and sided with Ruiz. So now the Zapatistas had two leftist bishops. The Church got really mad and tried to punish them by sending them to Saltillo, way up north. Vera has this clarity with no judgment, and he opened a shelter in the north. I needed some money to go shoot the immigrants, and I had met him and he said he could help me out. He's still there.

So, before volunteering in Orizaba, did you have a clearly formed idea about immigration policy?

No, not at all.

How did the filming of *De nadie* influence your way of thinking about immigration?

The way I obtain information about a problem is by just meeting with people until I end up with what I believe to be a semi-clear vision of the issue. But then as I keep questioning, I end up with nothing. It's like the more I find out about something, the more I see how difficult it is to have a firm grasp of an issue. And I think most people don't really have a real grasp on the immigrant issue. There's the human rights claim about how we should be free to move wherever. But that's not how we exist. As humans, we always separate ourselves, create borders, limits. That's inevitable. So when I try to talk about a solution, I find that something has been so wrong for so long that there's no clear way of fixing it. I would never dare to suggest a solution. I think it's out of our grasp. I think that we have difficulty seeing the impact of our actions. An example would be with the *Patronas* who help the immigrants by providing food for them. The priest in the town of La Patrona is not OK with their work. It's a Catholic community, and if these women go to church, he won't give them communion. When Raul Vera heard this, he went to La Patrona to give them communion. And there's something that priests can't interrupt in consecrating the host, but while he was giving communion you could hear the train coming. And he decided to interrupt what he was doing and he said, "Let's go and do what you do, help the immigrants." In essence he was sanctifying what the *Patronas* do, helping the immigrants. But what I really wanted to point out was something with the *Patronas* that shows how we don't realize how our actions will have an impact. Or if what we offer as a solution is really a solution. *Las Patronas* began to gain popularity because of the film. So you'd have universities that would watch the film, gather food, send it to the *Patronas* to the point where the president of Mexico invited them to come to Mexico City. But with all the new food coming so they could keep preparing it for the immigrants, the question became, where would the food be kept? In which woman's house? It became a power struggle and an issue of trust among the *Patronas*. It created such a division that when I last saw one of the women, she said she wished the film had never happened. There's something so wrong about our incapacity to see how our actions will evolve in time. We make assumptions, like the more food for these women, the better. But that was a false logic. The more, the better isn't necessarily what works. Coming from the outside and providing food affected the balance and the beauty of what these women did. In many ways I wish that I hadn't done that film.

Did you have any audience in mind when you were making *De nadie*?

No, just my parents. There was never any intention to be a documentary filmmaker.

Of all the people in *De nadie*, it seems that you became most involved with María, since you went to Honduras to connect with her family there. Do you know what happened to María?

No.

In an earlier interview I read that you feel now that *De nadie* is a naive film and that it has flaws. Can you tell me more?

When I made the film there was still this idea of good against evil. That's how I saw immigrants and the Mara, the police, immigration officials, etcetera. I think I was naive about it. It paints this simplistic picture of victim versus villain. There's another naivety that I do like and that I try to pursue, that the starting point be nothing, a void, so that it's a true exploration, letting the story become what it needs to become. I never wrote a script. That would inhibit the exploration. That naivety I like. That's why in my other film, *Rivers of Men*, the story I most like is the one of the military man because he's the supposed villain, but he isn't. There are no villains and victims in life. You only have these complex human beings dealing with their incapacities. We all have a villain and a victim inside of us.

Since *De nadie* was your first film, what did you learn about filmmaking in the process?

I still don't consider myself a filmmaker. I just gave an 18-month-long workshop in Campeche for people who'd never used a camera before, and maybe the first year and 3 months, there was no talk about how to use a camera or sound. To me that part is the least important. There are a lot of people who don't agree with that, with the lack of pursuit of form. The mass replication of an artistic expression in DVD is something that doesn't seem to hold a lot of beauty. Filmmaking is just my key to explore things. It's what I know how to do. If I could find a more accurate way, I'd abandon filmmaking in a heartbeat. I wish there were a more virtuous way. I'm sure there is, and I hope I can find it.

I'm not sure there is or who would make that judgment. So, moving onto *Ríos de hombres*, what made you film the water war of Cochabamba, why did you spend so much time there, and why did you identify so much with this struggle in the beginning?

I spent time there not because I identified with the struggle but more because I was confused about it. And the more I explored, the more confused I got. At a certain point, after two or three years, I thought about just abandoning the project. But the more confusing it felt, the more complex it got.

So, I understand it was booed at the Buenos Aires Film Festival. At what point did the audience start to boo?

At the end. That's one of my filmmaking milestones because you don't boo a boring film. I think it made the Argentines so angry because belief in social movements, for many of us, is the answer. Many South American countries rely on social movements, but I don't see a true break in logic with social movements. I don't think social movements are a space where one can really come up with a different logic. You would think that they are. It appears that way, but capitalism, neoliberalism is just a couple of degrees apart from social movements. No one has talked about the water war in its complexity. In Cochabamba, actually the majority of the water isn't public. It's private. Bolivian individuals have found a way to commercialize the water. Everyone is making their own well and being charged to do so. There's this whole commercialization of the water, which in its essence is the logic of the transnationals. There's no true rupture of the logic. It's a continuation of it. And I don't know of an indigenous community today that holds a different logic from the one of privatization. Maybe there is one that's cut off from the rest of the world. That's my same criticism with Evo Morales because sadly he just took the same logic in a reverse way—now we indigenous are going to oppress the rich and the white. When I got to Bolivia he was running for president and there was all this hope. But now you see it's just the same logic that he uses. That's why I think that social movements don't create a space to really break and find a new logic. I think in the end, we're so submerged in neoliberalism that we can't even understand the extent to which we are dependent on it.

I have this caricature in my head of San Luis Potosí, where the indigenous community considered the land sacred and a mine was going to be built there, pollute the water system, etcetera. So there were all these social movements manifesting against it. Yes, it's terrible to pollute the water. I understand the gravity and the violence of the mine. But the metal they were going to extract is needed for an important chip in cell phones. Yet everyone there who was demonstrating had a cell phone in his or her pocket. Maybe the solution is to go live in some isolated community in the Amazon, but no one is doing that.

Back to *Ríos de hombres*. I'm interested in the scene with the cattle being slaughtered. Is that your footage? Was that in Cochabamba? And did you film it with the idea of using it metaphorically?

What happened is that during the time I was making that film I became so confused that I just started filming like crazy. For a whole year I filmed different manifestations of water. With that idea I made a list of 100 ways in which we have contact with water, and one of them was at the slaughterhouse. That was such a headache because at that time I had like over 100 hours of material. Just to make sense of all that material was exhausting. It took 2 years to edit the film. In the end I had to work with an editor.

What did you know about the water war in Cochabamba before you went there?

I had just heard about it in conversations. There's something about me that I'm not ashamed of any longer. When I read, I don't absorb the meaning on the page. That's why I went into engineering, since I was always good in math and I didn't have to read anything. If I want to understand something I have to submerge myself in it entirely but not read about it. I don't read to learn about things.

Yet you quote Eduardo Galeano at the beginning of *De nadie*.

But I didn't read him. I heard the song written by the composer I worked with on the film. Before editing the film, I heard him play that song. That's why it's called *De nadie*, because of that song. Then I looked for Galeano for my second film, *Ríos de hombres*. I do have an understanding of Galeano's work, but through other people. I know of the profoundness and the poetry of his work.

Tell me about Galeano's appearance in *Ríos de hombres*, because you have him saying something on film that later you dispute.

That was a very painful thing to do. But it was speaking from my pain as well. It was hard for me because he and I became good friends. He watched *De nadie* and was so moved by it. I went to see him in Uruguay. But I know that if he saw the second film, he might not have wanted to ever talk with me again. It was painful to me not because of who he is and what he represents but because I considered him to be a good friend.

In *Ríos de hombres*, you narrate the transformation of how you think about the water war. Can you talk more about how you frame the event?

First there was no intention to have a first-person narrator, but it was the only way to make it work.

Is it your voice in *Ríos de hombres*?

Yes, but in *Muerte en Arizona* it's not my voice because I wanted to move away from that. I don't like that.

So, how did the film *También la lluvia* affect you since it came out one year prior to the release of *Ríos de hombres*?

Well, I'd been in Cochabamba for 6 years when they came to town. I was already working on the editing. But when I watched the film, it seemed that it was doing what it was trying to criticize—go to this place, extract what you want, and then leave. There's a violence in that. I thought it wasn't a very respectful act. Not to say that what I did isn't violent and disrespectful. I'm sure it is if you compare it to someone who goes there and stays for 50 years.

Why did you choose to use mostly English and a little Spanish in *Muerte en Arizona*?

I think English is more lyrical to me, even though I know people say that Spanish is more lyrical.

Did it have anything to do with the fact that that might have been the language you and your partner spoke in?

Yeah, that's the language we spoke in.

Did the people you filmed in *Muerte en Arizona* know they were being filmed?

No, and I didn't ask because we're so used to seeing human tragedy in images and we never question whether people in that tragic situation were asked if we could have access to their image. For example, we see images of people in war, at the worst moment of their lives, limbs blown off, etcetera. Yet we never question that. We're used to seeing that.

So you see the subjects in your film as equivalent to victims of war?

On the contrary. I think that raises the question Why not shoot the poetry of everyday life, then, the beauty in life? There's something personal about both, the tragic moment and the everyday. But we're not used to seeing that. We live in a public world—Google world, Google Maps, Twitter. You can find me on Facebook and Twitter, and nobody asked me for permission to use my image.

How in *Muerte en Arizona* did you film all those images from the apartment? Was it from different windows? Did you set the camera there, or were you always behind the camera?

I was always behind the camera, and yes, I moved from window to window.

So I'm interested in the title of *Muerte en Arizona*. Before viewing the film, I thought maybe it was about another border crossing. Can you talk about the title? I know that the fictional character dies in Arizona. Is there any more meaning in the title?

Well, most of my grieving for this woman happened in Arizona. I was living in Nogales at the time.

So, the grieving wasn't just in the apartment where you two had lived in Bolivia?

The grieving was never in the apartment. It was all in Arizona. But then she came back. And we moved to India and we had a kid there. And then we came back to Bolivia in the apartment where we'd been earlier. And for that year I started shooting *Muerte en Arizona*.

So, you were back together by then.

Yes, and we had a kid. So I had all these images of these people from the windows. And that's basically what I did for a whole year. But then I wanted to tell the story of this woman leaving me, so I just took the two things and made them into one. I was never in that apartment alone and grieving.

Isn't there a reference to migrants in *Muerte en Arizona*?

Yeah, a small reference, of my grandfather who was in the cotton fields. And there's a reference when I went walking in Arizona, finding a dry river and all the clothes left behind by migrants. Where I lived in Arizona, it was across from where you'd see lot of migrants. I always like to leave something in my films from another film. Even though these films don't connect to each other, they do to me. And after hearing your panel today I see how they connect even more. I do leave little hints or references in each film from a previous one.

So, I'd like to finish up by talking about the theme of transformation. *Ríos de hombres* traces your own transformation in how you frame and understand the Cochabamba water war, also, more obvious in *Muerte en Arizona* with the transformation through grieving. I guess you could say that in *De nadie* the migrants are hoping to transform their lives by migrating north for a better life. Also, in *Ríos de hombres* the army general underwent an amazing transformation that no one else mentions in their work about the water war. Is this an intentional theme for you?

The thing is, that if you have time on your side, you're always dealing with transformation. That's why Willie, the farmer in *Ríos de hombres*, transforms from a flower farmer into a welder, a tragic, poetic transformation. It's because of time, not necessarily me. If you're patient, things transform. Not so much in *De nadie* but in the other two films and the work I do now, that's what I'm looking for, transformation. People and their thoughts. Life and death. That's why I like working on projects over long periods of time.

So, in closing, can you tell me something about your next projects?

I'm working on *Ghosts of the Ship*, which portrays the strange and changing life of my children seen through the window of one month out of every year for the following 15 years of their lives. I'm also working on *Flesh*, a poetic portrayal of a delicate journey seen through the eyes of a man from the Yucatan Peninsula who believes [himself] to be 500 years of age and claims to be the keeper of the five elements of life since ancient Mayan times. It's a vexing story that strives to underscore our basic truths and questions our contemporary system of beliefs.

14

Heidi Hassan

Love and Identity in the Cuban Diaspora

INTERVIEW BY LAUREN E. SHAW

Madrid, May 2, 2015

Heidi Hassan began her artistic career as a photographer, graduating in 2002 with a degree in direction of photography from the Escuela Internacional de Cine y Televisión (EICTV, International School of Film and Television) in San Antonio de los Baños, Cuba. Later she emigrated from her native Cuba to Geneva, Switzerland, where she lived for eight years and received a degree in film direction from the Haute école d'art et de design (HEAD). She currently resides in Madrid, where she works as a cinematographer, photographer, and director. Hassan's films have been presented at prestigious film festivals such as the Journée Suisse at Cannes, Locarno Film Festival, and Havana Film Festival. Her 2014 feature-length documentary *Otra isla* has been screened at festivals and won awards in Cuba and off the island. The film centers around a family of dissidents sent to Spain in 2012. It poses many unbiased questions about the personal and political motives and expectations regarding migration from communist Cuba to Spain at a time when Spain was experiencing its own economic hardships and political transitions. In chapter 9 of this volume contributor Zaira Zarza discusses Hassan's *Orages d'été* (2008) and *Tierra roja* (2007), both of which also have been screened at notable film festivals and received awards. *Orages d'été* is a short autobiographical piece on falling in love with her partner, Léonard Plattner, and *Tierra roja* is a fictionalized account of Hassan's mother's migration to Switzerland. This interview took place in Hassan's home in Madrid and was translated from Spanish by Lauren Shaw.

I'm wondering if you have any feelings of indebtedness toward Cuba for having received your training there.

When I was living in Switzerland I tried to return to Cuba for a year. I was feeling, in a way, indebted to the Escuela de Cine there and felt like doing things in my country. But unfortunately I had an unpleasant experience that turned me off. I went with my partner, who is also a filmmaker, to make a documentary in the province of Guantanamo, in the eastern part of the country. It was about the legacy of the Taino in Cuba. We were interested in the topic since there's so little recognition of the Taino [indigenous] heritage in Cuba compared with the Spanish and African. We researched the project and got in contact with a very small community that lives in Yateras. EICTV, ICAIC [Cuban Institute of Cinematographic Art and Industry], AHS [Association of the Saiz Brothers], among other organizations supported the project by writing letters of recommendation. This community, despite being so isolated and difficult to access, became a site of interest in the '70s for American researchers and anthropologists. This created a tendency for the Cuban government to be paranoid about the visitors to the site, something entirely unjustified in our case. While we were filming, the people's leader showed up, surprised at our presence. We explained the project and showed him the official letters of support, after which everything seemed fine. But the next day the police arrived with an order to take us away. It was really unpleasant because they took us to the police station with the excuse that we didn't have any authorization, and they wouldn't let us finish filming. But for me the worst thing was when the police took me back to the little town to gather our things, no one would look at me or talk to me. Finally one of the women that had put us up in her house during our stay told me that I had betrayed them, that the police had told them that I wasn't Cuban, and that I was an American spy with the objective of hurting the government. I don't know how you can possibly respond to such craziness. She was so offended that she refused to hear any of my attempts to respond. I was overcome with a sense of powerlessness and shame in front of these people who had been so generous to us. That experience was a big blow because I realized that it wasn't possible for me to make films in my country, since my country felt the need to protect itself from me.

So now that you live in Spain, are you comfortable here with your work and the way of life here?

I think that my work would be very different if I had come directly to Spain from Cuba because the culture shock of being in Switzerland was much greater, and it made me develop in a different way and pay attention to other things. Switzerland was my first confrontation with emigration. In Spain perhaps the process of adapting would have been much simpler. Here in Spain I feel at home. But strangely, I have a much deeper connection with Switzerland because the things I experienced there taught me a lot. It was there that I had to reconstruct myself, and I think that in my cinematographic work one senses that my second home is in Switzerland.

Can you talk about your background, your education, and how you came to be an artist?

I suppose that in my case a lot has to do with being an only child. I was always a pretty solitary kid, and I remember entertaining myself even at a young age. I think that created the conditions that allowed for creativity, reflection, and introspection. When I was on vacation with my father, I spent hours in his workshop—he's an artist—inventing some kind of activity with the materials that he would be using. In that period for me it was heaven to be in the workshop. Later it became the library when I discovered the paintings of the vanguard artists of the twentieth century. Eventually it became the movie theater. As an adolescent I began to be interested in photography. In fact, with the first money that I earned I bought myself a camera, a very simple one, automatic, but with it I began to almost compulsively record my memories. It's something I continue to do even today, to the point that my memory has atrophied. I can only remember the moments that I have photographed. Later, then, my interest in photography brought me to film.

What directors, films do you most like?

I like lots of different kinds of film, and I admire many directors. Of course I have preferences, but they shift. I don't dare cite any for fear of leaving any out. I'm attracted to many different approaches, even the ones I don't particularly like. The time when I became interested in film coincided with filmmakers like Antonioni or Kieslowski, and I can't not mention that it was Terence Piard who made me discover the films of these two and many other directors, all of whom are European, and through them I discovered a sense of film that was completely different for me at that time. But I remember that it was a significant time in film that marked my decision to study cinematographic photography. I was watching *Joan of Arc* by Dreyer when I became conscious of the fact that there was a person behind the camera, and I understood the expressive capacity of the framing and lighting. I think that from then on the idea of going to film school to study photography started to haunt me. I was also interested in directing, but I felt a bit too young to have anything to really say.

Where did you study?

I studied direction of photography at the Escuela Internacional de San Antonio de los Baños in Cuba, and later I studied cinematographic direction at the École des beaux arts in Geneva, Switzerland. I complemented those studies with many workshops on different branches of film, photography, or painting.

Could you briefly explain the different roles involved with cinematographic direction versus direction of photography?

With cinematographic direction I'm involved in the entire process from start to finish. I'm responsible for everything, scriptwriting, financing, making the image, editing, and even distributing in some instances. As director of photography my job is to create the images that someone else has in mind and adjust them to the realities of filming.

So it seems that for you the relationship between photography and film is very close. Is that correct?

Yes, to me the two are very connected. Both are needed because they entail different ways of working. Film requires working with a team, and photography is a solitary job. I like the contrast between the two. Regrettably, of late I can spend only a little time on photography. I wish I could explore both artistic endeavors equally.

And your interest in exploring identity through film and the documentary?

I think that comes from my experience as an emigrant and my mother's as well. I believe that to leave your surroundings makes you see reality with some distance, and it requires you to ask new questions. You see with new eyes whatever you discover, but you also see anew what you left behind, and you notice things that you'd never even picked up on before. In general my work doesn't stem from a theme but rather from a feeling that I begin to investigate and develop. With my first pieces I never set out to engage with identity, but it became one of the principal themes because I had so many questions about it. For me film is a tool that I always have with me and that I use to explore things that interest me, while keeping a certain distance from myself.

How does *Otra isla* relate to the theme of identity?

I think it has a lot to do with that theme, with the way in which a group of people cling to their identity as their only means to survival.

Yes, but this film isn't as personal as your others. Or is it?

No, it's very different from the previous films. At the beginning I wanted to have a more personal approach. Then I realized that I was forcing a narrative onto the film, so I preferred to let myself be guided by the film, and the result is something very much mine but at the same time something I have trouble accepting that I could have birthed.

What was the point of view you wanted to present?

At the beginning I thought the film could be a metaphor of my relationship with my country, but I realized that the space I wanted to hold in the narration of the film was not needed. So I decided to change course, take myself out of the story, and let the situation speak for itself. I think that my point of view comes through anyway. The film might seem pretty neutral since I don't take sides or interact with the reality I'm filming. However, any filmmaker's point of view is present from the second they turn on the camera or even before that. In this case, I accompanied the Martín family during 6 months time but I only filmed 80 hours of that time. Of those 80 hours, only one hour made it into the film. What I left in and what I cut, of course, is one of the most obvious ways for my point of view to come across. Another example for this film is the decision I made about who would be the protagonist. It could have been the family as a whole, but I chose to make it the women. I could have made the film more political, but I decided to make its focus more human and social. I could have critiqued one of the groups represented in the film, but I chose to show them all as equally responsible. That's why the viewer doesn't quite know what to grab onto. Every film is the result of a series of decisions influenced by the filmmaker's principles and aesthetic preferences.

How much time did it take to complete the whole film, and what part of Madrid were you filming?

I met the Martín family when they had already spent two months living on the streets next to the Plaza Mayor in Madrid. I filmed them during six months, but the film took two years total for me to complete.

Were there others also living there with the Martín family?

At the beginning, no. The Martín family was in the plaza in front of the Ministry of Foreign Affairs, the ministry that had negotiated the agreement that brought them to Spain. Once they left the plaza, about 30 other people showed up, demonstrating and living there for almost two years.

How do you see a connection between film and immigration, in general?

I see the documentary as a tool for personal investigation. I feel that something changed in me ever since I left Cuba. Now I'm not sure about anything. I just have lots of questions. I think that the documentary helps me find paths that don't always bring me to answers but lead me closer. That's why I prefer to explore documentary or at least the hybrid form more than fiction film, because I think that it leads to a different kind of search.

And how has place influenced your documentaries?

As I said earlier, where you live shapes your experiences, which shapes your work. Some places make it easier to produce film. But in general it's pretty difficult to find support due to the many people making film today and the cuts in cultural spending that are happening everywhere. A lot of us are making films with our own funds, which is great but also makes it harder to be noticed. There are festivals that end up receiving 4,000 films, out of which only 30 are selected.

What festivals have you applied to?

Otra isla has been selected in Spain [IBAFF, International Film Festival of Murcia], in Cuba [Muestra de Jovenes Realizadores, Exhibition of Young Filmmakers], in the U.S. [Havana Film Festival of NY], and Puerto Rico LASA [Latin American Studies Association] Film Festival. Next it will be screened in Guadeloupe. But I've submitted it to around 90 festivals.

And *Tierra roja*?

It's been seen in many festivals despite the fact that it's a couple of years old now. At times I find out just by chance on the Internet that it's being screened in Los Angeles or in Mexico, for example, because many times the organizations that screen it don't notify me. I decided to send that short film only to La Muestra de Realizadores de la Habana because I thought it was important that it be seen in Cuba. But I myself didn't send it to any other festivals because it seemed to me to be such a personal film. Nevertheless, it's had a life of its own, completely unexpected. People seem to identify a lot with it. With that film I discovered that the deeper you go into yourself the more the film speaks to people.

What has been your greatest challenge in completing your projects?

My greatest challenge is to have confidence every day in what I'm working on. Because the relation with a project is very similar to a personal relationship. It passes through very different phases, from being head over heels in love, to having conflicts, to needing to take some distance. What is without a doubt is that there is a deep bond that connects me to my projects. When you work in isolation and it's so hard to find support to carry out projects, it's hard to not lose some motivation along the way. But that's a feeling that you have to learn to struggle with. The important thing is to always return to the essence, to the deep bond that connects you to the project, and there you rediscover your motivation.

When you made *Otra isla* were you thinking of a Cuban audience or a European audience?

It seemed important to me that *Otra isla* be seen in Cuba because I think that the film tackles some valid issues for our country that are made invisible by the official media. I think also that it reflects a situation with an impartial point of view and tries to show nuances that are usually hidden behind the usual extremist positions that normally accompany the theme of dissidence in Cuba.

Have you found other Cuban exiles who work in film and with whom you find support?

One of the reasons why I came to Spain is because an old friend who's also a filmmaker is living here, Patricia Pérez Fernández. She's a colleague from a long time ago, also a graduate of EICTV, and someone I worked with before.

We wanted to combine our efforts and work together again. We've been preparing for months now an autobiographic project that is expressed through audiovisual correspondences that we maintained since our emigration to Switzerland and Spain. We want to tell two different trajectories of emigration by two women near their 40s and who try to re-create themselves far from Cuba, interweaving perspectives on identity, professional life, and maternity.

And you have these letters?

Many, yes, but at any rate, they need to be rewritten, and some will be constructed along the way, since life and this project are in tandem.

So, the visual element, what will it be?

The film will alternate between staged scenes with scenes from daily life that have been filmed by us in the past. It will be a documentary with the presence of a very subjective camera.

Does it have anything to do with immigration, or is it mostly about the physical distance between people?

It's really about both things. The point of departure is the sense of longing for a friend and the necessity of making each other a participant in our lives, even through the distance. But it really is about immigration. It's the story of two filmmakers, women immigrants who try to re-create themselves in another country.

Returning to *Otra isla*, how was it received?

That depends on the country where it's screened, of course. It didn't pass censorship for the Havana Festival, but it did for the Muestra de Jóvenes Realizadores de Cine. I wasn't able to be at the screening there, but they told me it was well received, that people applauded a lot. I think that's so because it's a necessary film. It's a topic that gets no play in Cuba. A nice anecdote happened in New York when a Colombian woman who is completely supportive of the Cuban Revolution said to me, "Congratulations. This is the first time I've ever been able to even hear the subject of dissidence. For me dissidents have always just been some rejected group. But thanks to your documentary I was able to see them as humanity." I thought that I had achieved my objective with that comment. In Switzerland it was well attended, and when the film ended, everyone sat in silence. It was very strange and moving for me. In Murcia it went extremely well, since, of course, the film connects to Spain's reality in a different way and it speaks directly about the Spanish crisis. In Canada people were very curious, and there were a lot of postscreening questions and comments.

How do you see film giving a voice to the invisible people of the Latin American diaspora?

The new technologies facilitate the kind of filmmaking that doesn't depend directly on the film industry. Therefore, many themes that don't lend themselves to commercial film can be addressed with more freedom than ever imagined before and have access to audiences more than before.

Changing topics, can you talk a bit about feminism in Cuba?

I believe that it's a term that has been stigmatized. It's so often associated with a combatant attitude toward the male gender and to femininity itself, rather than what it really is, a search for equality of rights. Cuba is a country with a deep-rooted culture of machismo.

Do you feel the necessity to explore the theme of feminism or to express yourself through the theme of feminism?

I think that feminism is very present in my work, but I prefer to not use the label. I'm interested in speaking from the position of a woman and to emphasize the qualities that value the feminine and encourage authenticity.

Do you consider yourself more an investigator than a storyteller?

Yes, there are many people that I know who make films and have lots of ideas that they want to tell. For me it's certain themes that I want to delve into and just see what happens.

Do you begin with a theme as an intellectual pursuit or with something more visual?

I begin with a feeling.

Can you talk about the titles of your films?

I was about to call *Tierra roja* "Sopa de pollo" [Chicken soup]. I intended for it to reflect the yearning for our mothers' or grandmothers' cooking. Eventually I chose "Tierra roja" because it spoke better to the theme of the film. On the one hand, the color red is associated with communism, which could refer to Cuba indirectly. But on the other hand, that color suggests that the soil is not fertile, that it's dry and doesn't nourish or sustain life, which can make you think about emigration.

[I decided on] "Tormenta de verano" [*Orages d'été*] because this type of storm is very strong but fleeting, like the feelings I explore in the film. And *Otra isla* because the protagonists construct their house in the middle of the plaza, and visually it looked like an island. They left a real island and ended up on a symbolic one. I also have a short film titled *Miserere* that means "God, take pity on us." It's a story about a group of emigrants crossing the border. Another film is titled *Exilio*, and it's an experimental short, shot entirely with a subjective camera, where the main character seems to be looking at reality through a diving suit. My most recent work is titled *Los turistas*, and it's about the memories that inhabit an old hotel.

Do you feel part of a community of other Cubans or other Latin Americans here?

Now that I think of it, my best friends here are all Cubans, but I knew them already in Cuba. Other close people to me here come from everywhere. I couldn't point to one particular community. Also, what I like to do is pretty solitary so I don't usually participate in many social activities.

Are your plans to stay in Spain, go somewhere else, or return to Cuba?

I don't think that far ahead in the future. For me the future is extremely immediate. I never make plans, not even for summer. Right now I know that I feel good here. In reality, I'm so involved in my project currently that I could be just about anywhere in the world. But down the road, we'll see what happens. Life is very capricious. And despite everything regarding Cuba, I still think about working there.

And your last name, where is it from?

I chose my mother's maiden name as my artistic name. It seemed only fair to take her name, although I owe much to my father for my artistic vocation. But it was my mother who brought me up.

Thank you, Heidi. In closing I'd like to know if your mother has seen your films and if so, what she thinks. Your relationship to her seems deeply connected to the experience of emigration, hers and yours, so I wonder how she views your life and work navigating through the world as a filmmaker.

Well, it would be good to ask her if she were here. I've never directly spoken with her about this, so it's impossible for me to say. But what I do know is that she always has supported me and trusted me. And when she sees my films, she cries. And when we see them together we both cry.

15

María Cristina Carrillo Espinosa

Filming Common Experiences of Migration

INTERVIEW BY ESTEBAN E. LOUSTAUNAU

Madrid, June 5, 2015

Anthropologist and filmmaker María Cristina Carrillo Espinosa was born in Quito, Ecuador, and first migrated to Madrid in 2001. Her arrival in Spain coincided with a financial crisis in Ecuador that led to the dollarization of the national economy and a massive wave of migration to Europe and the United States. Between 2000 and 2004, near 1.5 million Ecuadorians left the country, many of them arriving in Spain and Italy. This migration phenomenon has become a central topic in Carrillo Espinosa's academic and artistic work, and it is the focus of her award-winning documentary *La Churona* (2010). After graduating with a degree in anthropology in 1995, she left Quito to study film at the prestigious Escuela Internacional de Cine y Televisión (EICTV, International Film and Television School) in San Antonio de los Baños, Cuba. Soon after returning to Quito, Carrillo Espinosa discovered documentary filmmaking as a way to bring together her passion for anthropology and her love for film. Prior to making *La Churona*, she directed two short fiction films, *Sabor a cebolla* (1997) and *Violetas* (1998), and collaborated in the production of *Un instante en la vida ajena* (2003). Discussed in chapter 7 of this volume, *La Churona* is the migration story of Ecuador's Virgin of El Cisne, represented in the film as a Virgin "without papers" looking for a place to live in Madrid. As such, the sculpted Virgin becomes an "object-metaphor" through which the film brings light to the invisible faces and unheard voices of the Ecuadorian diaspora arriving in Spain after the financial crisis of 2000. In this interview, Carrillo Espinosa discusses the ways in which *La Churona* became a bridge between her own migration experience and those of so many Ecuadorian migrants living in Spain. At the time of our interview Carrillo Espinosa had recently become a mother and was finishing her doctoral dissertation in anthropology at the Universidad Autónoma de Madrid. The interview took place at La CaixaForum in Madrid and was translated from Spanish by Esteban Loustaunau.

When and how did you discover an interest for documentary film?

Well, my interest in documentary film originates with my early studies in anthropology. A long time ago, after I finished college with a degree in anthropology, I felt a need for something else that would help fulfill my professional life. I remember going to the movies all the time, even when I was the only person watching in the movie theater. I've always had a passion for films. After finishing college, I didn't want to continue studying a master's degree in anthropology right away without first figuring out what I wanted to study exactly. After giving it some thought, I applied to graduate programs in visual anthropology and film school. I was very fortunate to be admitted into the Escuela de Cine de San Antonio de los Baños, in Cuba. I was very lucky to be admitted into such a competitive film school because back then I had not had any film training other than my interest in watching films. The year I applied, they only accepted one student from Ecuador, and I had the great privilege of being chosen to study in Cuba. But before starting film school, I had to decide whether I was ready to start from zero in a completely new field for me. I remember meeting someone who, although I didn't know at the time but who had studied at that film school, is now a good friend of mine. He told me, "If you love cinema, the best thing that could have happened to you is to be admitted into the Escuela de San Antonio." With that in mind, I made my decision and left for Cuba. But at that point in my life I still didn't know how to connect anthropology and film. After I finished film school in Cuba, I returned to Ecuador feeling a bit restless, asking myself what can I do with these two passions that I don't want to keep separate from each other? Suddenly, this is when I began to realize that documentary film could be a path where anthropology and film join each other. I started making a few short documentaries on cultural issues at the same time that I started studying migration flows at FLACSO [Facultad Latinoamericana de Ciencias Sociales]. Some time later is when I came to Spain to do an internship in a documentary film production company called Cero en Conducta. One of this company's most famous films is *Asaltar los cielos* [Storm the skies, 1999], about the life of Leon Trotsky's killer. I had seen that documentary in film school and loved it. So when I had the chance to apply to work in a film production company, I picked that one right away, trying my luck. I came to Spain to work with two directors, Javier Rioyo and José Luis López Linares. I was first hired as an intern without being directly involved in film production. They were working on a project that later became a documentary film that won a Goya. I believe the title of that documentary is *Los placeres y los días*. My first project with Javier and José Luis was viewing old footage of a film by a Catalan filmmaker from the 1940s and 1950s. We had many hours of never-seen-before footage, and that became my first task in the production company. I found it very interesting to view this old footage and learn from Javier and José Luis. But there was something else happening in Spain at that particular time. I happened to be living in Spain during the great Ecuadorian migration boom of 2000. This is when I told myself I must do a documentary about migration! This became a personal necessity for me, and it allowed me to put into practice some of the things I was learning at work. This is how the idea for a documentary on Ecuadorian migration to Spain came about. I first started filming a few scenes with various characters. I wasn't sure then what I wanted to do with the film. Even today, I still have old footage of when I would go to record soccer games, do interviews, attend meetings, take photos, etcetera. That's how I started working on documentary. This was sometime around the year 2002.

How did you become in touch with the Ecuadorian migrant community?

It was like a snowball effect. I had a Spanish friend who knew an Ecuadorian man who sold sunglasses in Puerta del Sol. They became acquainted with each other first. I find it funny that a Spaniard took me to meet a fellow Ecuadorian. Manolo was his name. That is how I met Manolo. He was very nice. Now I've lost track of him, but he was the first person I started to film and interview. He then introduced me to his friends, who then introduced me to other friends, etcetera. Soon after came the 2002 World Cup, and people would invite me to their homes to watch the soccer games. While we watched television I started making a few contacts. That's how it all started.

Now that I am writing my doctoral dissertation in anthropology, I find it fascinating to know that our own common migration experience puts us all on equal footing. This was very much unlike what happens in Ecuador, where people are split by clearly defined differences in ethnicity, class, or region. In Ecuador it is not easy to break these boundaries. But here in Spain it was just the opposite. To me as an anthropologist it was very interesting to see how we would have conversations not meant as strategies to bring us together but instead created absolutely real relationships based on common experiences. For example, we all shared the same experiences of standing in long lines at the consulate, our differences with Spaniards, especially when it came to language and tone. Speech marked a clear distance between them and us. This is quite strange because we all speak Spanish but it is not the same. These types of encounters, which I refer to as horizontal, became fascinating to me and would ease the fluidity of our relationships. This is how I started to make my first contacts with other Ecuadorian migrants. Then, of course, came the conflict at El Retiro. I started to go to El Retiro park at the same time that the conflict with Ecuadorian migrants started. This is what happened. In El Retiro there was an area where many Ecuadorians started gathering together. I am talking about families—men, women, and children. These gatherings were meant to build community. There were people selling traditional Ecuadorian food, playing music, cutting people's hair, drinking alcohol, and leaving the place a bit messy afterwards. Let me say that I witnessed the good and the bad. It was a great community-building site, but it was also a place that generated social problems, especially with local Spaniards.

Was this similar to what happens in Lisandra Rivera and Manolo Sarmiento's documentary *Problemas personales* [2002]?

Yes, it is exactly the same place. The problem began when people started calling the police. Just as the documentary shows, the police started to interfere, and Ecuadorians started to gain the reputation of being too loud, dirty, and unhygienic. The problem became so big that eventually the police displaced the Ecuadorian migrants from El Retiro. Later, Ecuadorians tried to revive the gatherings at the Parque del Oeste, but things were never the same again. Because of its central location in Madrid, El Retiro pulled more people together than any other location. That was what happened. Ecuadorian migrants occupied a central urban space for themselves, and this act eventually created problems with the local population.

Was this the moment of your arrival in Spain?

Yes, this was the context when I arrived. The situation was already complicated when I arrived. The migration curve was at the highest level in the period from 2000 to 2005. There were many, many Ecuadorians in Spain because there wasn't yet a visa requirement between these two countries. The visa requirement was imposed in 2003. Ecuadorian migration to Spain was at its highest point. Migration also had high political relevance. Spaniards began to realize just how many Ecuadorians were living in Spain. This was very significant, especially because at that time the average Spaniard had no idea of Ecuador's location in a map, and yet there were Ecuadorians everywhere. This is what it was like when I arrived.

How did you obtain funding to make a documentary about Ecuadorians living in Spain?

First of all, for my film *La Churona* I obtained financing through the Consejo de Cinematografía del Ecuador [Council of Cinematography of Ecuador]. From experience here in Spain, I can tell you that one can apply for funding to the Fondo Ibermedia [Ibermedia Fund] and grants from Fundación Carolina [Carolina Foundation]. Clearly, here in Spain film production is way more structured or industrialized than in Ecuador. In recent years, I've seen a few advancements in Ecuador toward film production. For example, I've started to see more international coproductions, better collaboration, better preproduction planning, better funding, and strong involvement by producers. Before, nothing of this nature ever happened in Ecuador, as things tended to be a bit more compartmentalized. Filmmakers in Ecuador had to be responsible for producing their own films. Nowdays, production companies are becoming more invested in helping you produce your film. But at the time of the making of *La Churona* I had to take care of every aspect of production, script writing, field research, executive production, financing, budget planning, etcetera. I had to be in charge of everything, and it gave me the chance to learn the system here in Spain. When I was working at Cero en Conducta I remember feeling jealous of the resources available to filmmakers and producers. When I first arrived here, back home we still didn't have the Consejo de Cinematografía del Ecuador. Therefore, there was really no comparison between making a documentary here in Spain and in Ecuador. Now, not much progress has been made. There is now the Fondo Ibermedia, and there is an increase on the level of professionalization in the sense of collaboration between countries.

For example, people from Ibermedia travel to Ecuador to lead workshops for emerging filmmakers. More and more people working in film participate with Ibermedia. When I was making *La Churona*, no one in Ecuador had anything to do with Ibermedia. This is why I was so impressed with Cero en Conducta, with the ease in which their documentaries would get funded, seeing how their films would actually be screened in movie theaters, perhaps not for too long, but they were being shown, and the financial backing to distribute their films in DVD format and to sell the television rights. It was definitely easier to obtain funding to make a film in Spain than in Ecuador. Another advantage of making films in Spain was the film distribution among countries. In Latin America this still continues to be an unmet need. Let me explain. In Latin America we still lack the international film distribution that you see here between Spain, France, Belgium, or Germany. This in Ecuador and other parts of Latin America is still missing. The biggest difference can be seen at the level of executive production of documentary films.

What does your own migration experience have in common with that of the subjects in your film?

A fundamental characteristic is our encounter with Spain. Despite the fact that we come from various regions and belong to different social classes in Ecuador, we share similar first impressions of Spain and its people. We shared many common understandings and misunderstandings in this other culture. Another shared characteristic is dodging administrative obstacles. You see, for a while I was also living here without legal papers. I think that shared experience was a key element in my close relation and contact with the subjects in my film. I also remember our connection to food. We would discuss our impressions of Spanish food and of how much we missed ceviche. We would spend time talking about food, about differences in the taste of beer. We were a bit nostalgic about our past lives in Ecuador. Even though I had already lived away from Ecuador during the time I was studying in Cuba, being in Spain made me miss Ecuador even more. Plus you have to keep in mind that communicating with family in Ecuador wasn't as easy as it is now. So, we would talk about our nostalgia for family, food, the mountains, music, pasillo, for example. When someone would play a pasillo at a party, I would say how much I missed not listening to Julio Jaramillo's song "El aguacate." All of these things can connect you with other Ecuadorians. You know you all share a common history. We would talk about politics, about the dollarization of our currency. Of course, each person would have their own particular opinion, but this wasn't intended to be an analysis of our country. The point was to share our common sensibilities about Ecuador, I think it is the common origin that brings people together. You know that there are real factors that divide you, but there are also plenty of characteristics that bring you together.

The other common experience that I was telling you about was the administrative one. This is very important to me because I experienced something I had never faced before in my life. When I lived in Ecuador and Cuba, I was always a student. Even when I first arrived in Spain to do an internship at Cero en Conducta, I came to this country as a student and never had any problems. But the problems came once I was left without papers. Soon after I arrived, things started getting a bit complicated for Ecuadorian immigrants. Too many Ecuadorians started arriving in Spain, and that forced the government to limit the flow of migration. In 2003 a visa requirement was imposed, and this started to slow down migration from Ecuador. At that time, I was working in the film industry, and it was very easy for someone from another country to apply for a work visa in this field. That is how the industry works here. For example, if a film production company needs to bring a cameraman from Mexico, there are proper channels to bring one.

By the time I was working in Cero en Conducta, many of my former film school classmates were here in Madrid. I'm talking about my inner circle of friends, all from different nationalities, and none of them had trouble obtaining a work visa. The first ones to arrive came to Spain just like I did, with a student visa to practice an internship. When their student visa expired they applied for a work visa. But just soon after I arrived, at some point in September of that year I was supposed to request my work visa, things started to change. Since I was planning on staying permanently in Spain, I did not apply for a work visa right away. This delay on my part complicated my immigration status. The producers at Cero en Conducta tried to help me, I hired lawyers to guide me in this process, but these attempts didn't move things any faster. I could stay in Spain without papers for one or two years, but the film production company could no longer offer me a job. Otherwise they would run the risk of losing their business. Suddenly, I was an immigrant without papers, without a job, but with the firm belief that I wanted to stay. At that point in time I wanted to stay. I loved living in Madrid, I had the support of my friends, I wanted to make a documentary, and I had lots of projects in mind. I can't remember exactly how long I was in that situation. I think it was about seven months.

This was an eye-opening experience for me, to live in a foreign country without papers. I had never experienced anything like it. It was tough. That experience enabled me to better understand the subjects in my film. I am not sure if this comes across, but for me it was a strong bonding experience. Being without papers brings about tremendous fear. Even though I do not fit the physical stereotype of most Ecuadorians, short and dark-skinned, walking by a Spanish police officer was very scary for me. Then the raids started happening. I was very afraid of being asked to show an ID because I didn't have one. Every time you go to a bank here they ask you for a legal ID. In those moments I remember thinking, oh, they are going to ask me for an ID and I won't know what to do! The feeling is something between fear and shame, anguish because you never know when your status is going to change. It is something that you feel through your body because it is embodied. One tries to become invisible. It is also mentally stressful because you don't know how to confront this fear. This sense of insecurity was awful for me. Not knowing when my status would change again was very difficult for me to handle. I wasn't able to apply for jobs. Even when I would think of applying for a job as a cashier, I knew they would ask me for documents. That was the toughest question. If I would say no, everything would be over. In this regard, Spain is not like the United States where one can find work without papers. Here things do not work that way. I couldn't find work, not even as a cashier. And I have two degrees! To apply for a job as a cashier was tough. It is hard to face that kind of fear and insecurity.

I remember talking with other Ecuadorians about our common experience. We would talk about our fear and feelings of uncertainty. Some of them would tell me how difficult it was for them to shop at a supermarket knowing that someone would ask for an ID when paying for groceries. Here is where nostalgia steps in. My friends would talk about the ease of life in Ecuador. Of course it may seem easier because there you are not under stress, living at the edge of legality, of the abyss.

When you were preparing the story of *La Churona*, did you have an ideal audience in mind?

I wanted Ecuadorians here and there and Spaniards here to see the film. Before making the film, I was very frustrated at the way Ecuadorian migrants were being represented in Ecuador and in Spain. After several months of living in

Spain without papers, I decided to return to Ecuador. I was never deported. My father became ill and he had to undergo surgery. That's when I decided to return home to Ecuador. This happened at the end of 2002, early 2003. Upon my return to Ecuador, I started working at FLACSO in the area of immigration. I did research with children of migrants. Years later as I was making *La Churona*, I wanted people from Ecuador to see it, and I also wanted people from Spain to see migration from the perspective of an Ecuadorian woman migrant. I was pretty disappointed with how Ecuadorian migrants were being represented, especially in Ecuador.

Earlier we talked about the film *Problemas personales*. I really like that documentary, but I also don't like that it is hypermasculine. It offers a hypermasculine gaze, but as a documentary it is very well made. Instead, I wanted women to speak in my documentary. Not only women but also yes, I wanted women's voices in my film. And I didn't want to tell a story of heroes and victims because most stories in the news media were very dramatic. Those stories showed families at the airport where everyone would be crying, showed abandoned children who ended up as drug addicts or as pregnant young girls. Most mainstream representations were an overdramatization of the problem, which of course is very traumatic, but because of its complexity it is also more than that. Since the beginning, I had a clear idea that I didn't want to portray migration from such a dramatic angle.

Here in Spain, I've always been bothered by that colonialist point of view that in many ways still remains. Most people in Spain think we've overcome that way of looking at Latin America, but it still remains here. That is the perspective of someone who lands in Latin America with a camera and quickly begins to photograph all the poverty. That is the image many in Spain still have, the Ecuadorian migrant who is escaping poverty and comes to find paradise in Europe. I wasn't interested in portraying that viewpoint in my film. Once I finished filming *La Churona*, director David Trueba made a comment that I cherish very much and that speaks of my intentionality as a filmmaker. He said, "I love the way everyone in the film speaks at the same level. Even the Virgin! I love your documentary because I had seen documentaries about religion that depict saints either from on high or from below, with much disdain or too much veneration. I also like that everyone who speaks is Ecuadorian. Here in Spain we are not used to listening to the voices of immigrants. Or maybe we have heard them speak but never at the same level of us Spaniards." I was so pleased when he said that to me because that is really what I wanted to show in my film. I wanted to represent migration from the perspective of an Ecuadorian woman.

How was the film received in Ecuador and in Spain?

This is a very good question. The film has been received differently in various places and contexts in which it has been viewed. Here in Spain I have not been able to show the film as widely as I would have hoped, but it has been received very favorably. Ecuadorian migrants here in Spain liked the film because it was a way of seeing themselves. They recognized familiar spaces, especially here in Madrid, and were able to say, "Hey look, Lavapiés! I was there!" That was the very first reaction I heard. They thought of the film as being nostalgic and fun. Even when I tried to avoid any sign of melodrama, the scene in the airport became very important for many migrants. They told me, "I've been there. I've arrived or said good-bye at [Madrid's] Barajas airport." I think this connection with the film is fundamental.

And in Ecuador, I've been surprised by some of the reactions to the film. Some people would say, "We were not aware of the extent of the Ecuadorian migration to Spain." They were also very impressed to learn how news about Ecuadorian migration would appear in newspapers like *El País* or on television and in the evening news. They were surprised by the media's recognition of Ecuadorians among the victims of a terrorist attack by ETA at the Barajas airport or by the reporting of the pro-immigration marches and the speeches by the representative of the Federación Nacional de Asociaciones Ecuatorianas en España [National Federation of Ecuadorian Associations in Spain]. This is what most caught their attention. They were used to hearing about migrants in Europe as only isolated or particular experiences. But the public displays like the takeover of public spaces like Plaza Mayor in Madrid were a real surprise for both Ecuadorians and Spaniards. The takeover of Plaza Mayor was tremendous for most Spaniards. Even my husband said, "How is it possible that such a large community of immigrants could have established itself in my neighborhood without me knowing anything about it?" The mass participation of Ecuadorian migrants at the San Lorenzo Church and Plaza Mayor was very impressive to everyone. Spaniards would say, "It's incredible that so many migrants could have taken over Plaza Mayor!"

The shot in the film with the plaza filled with people I had to get from *doña* Carmen [Barragán], the Ecuadorian migrant woman who first brought the image of the Virgin of El Cisne to Madrid, because at that time I had yet to start filming the documentary. But, of course, I said to myself, I need to show that event in the film. One can argue that the cinematic quality of that shot is not great, but it shows the magnitude of the mass demonstrations. Most people living in Madrid see the Plaza Mayor as the symbol of the city, of all things Spanish. So for them to see their plaza filled with thousands of people waving Ecuadorian flags and carrying on their shoulders an Ecuadorian Virgin was very shocking. What I loved the most about this scene is that it shows the immigrants' collective power, which was very important at the time. It became an occupied space to display the Ecuadorian nation. This is something I continue to study in my doctoral dissertation. This massive public event became a ritual, framed in space and time, to bring the Ecuadorian nation together. I am talking about a kind of nationalism that goes beyond any form of regionalism and classism that are so characteristic of the Ecuadorian diaspora. It was a space to reclaim *lo ecuatoriano*.

This is also meaningful because the Virgin of El Cisne is from the southern part of Ecuador. She is not like the Virgin of Guadalupe, who is a national symbol of unity in Mexico. But abroad, the Virgin of El Cisne does become that same type of unifying figure. In other words, outside of Ecuador regional differences do not matter, or do not matter as much any more. The other day I met a young woman and I asked her, "Tell me why, if the Virgin Mary is the same, you prefer the Virgin of El Cisne over the Virgin of Almudena? And her response reflected the obviousness of the question, "Well, it is not the same because I've known all my life the Virgencita de El Cisne." So, the regional Virgin from Loja has become a well-known unifying referent in the diaspora. In fact, I've interviewed many Ecuadorians who have told me that before migrating they were not strong devotees of the Virgin of El Cisne. In many cases, these people were nonbelievers but they saw her devotion as an opportunity to meet other Ecuadorians, to share life experiences, to remember, to be proud of who they were and where they were from. Unlike the time wasted waiting in the unemployment lines, these other gatherings are ways to claim something that belongs to them. It is something that gives people pride. This, I think, is very important.

As a sociologist, I was also surprised by an unexpected reaction to the film by the people in Loja. Maybe I had a false romantic expectation when I presented the film there, but the local people were not that impressed with seeing the Virgin of El Cisne's migration to Spain. I was a bit disillusioned, especially after all I had to go through to show the film in Loja, including putting some of my own money in the process. But the money did not matter to me as much as my ethical commitment to show the film in Loja. But the audience's reaction was completely unexpected. They said, "Yes, it is wonderful to see the documentary in a cinema, but for us, the original Virgin of El Cisne lives here with us." What surprised me the most, I guess, were the different expectations I had as a sociologist and documentarian and those of the people in Loja.

How can documentary film convey the voices of migrants in the diaspora?

In this film I was very interested in documenting transnational migration. I would ask myself how can I show this on film? I was very aware of this question as I was defining the structure of the film. The study of transnationalism has room for various fluid contexts where people come and go but also remain, for all the objects that are exchanged between migrants and nonmigrants. In the process of making the film I had to answer the question How can I transmit these messages through images? My attempt then was to show the link, the connection between those who migrate and those who remain. I was also interested in showing in every section of the film what's normally left untold and unseen. Let me explain. In Ecuador I wanted people to see "the footprints," as Tarkovski would say, the footprints, the traces of migrants in Spain. And in Spain, I wanted to raise awareness of life in Ecuador. For example, at the beginning of the film you see the historian telling the story of colonization, then you meet Jonathan, who talks about his mother who left Ecuador to seek employment in Spain. Then you see his grandparents showing photographs of their children. That's followed by a sequence with the town's mayor who talks about the community's connection with its migrants. Again you see the historian, then the priest who mentions the migrants and the idea of them bringing to Spain an image of the Virgin of El Cisne.

I had to cut a few scenes that included interviews with the staff of an international shipping company. This was nice because they told me about how many people in Ecuador would mail rosaries and scapulars to their relatives in Europe at this time of the year. However, in the end I had to cut out these scenes because the company did not allow me to show the scenes on film. From my interviews with the shipping staff I also learned about an increase of money flows and remittances from abroad to cover the cost of performances, rituals, and fireworks related to the annual festivities in celebration of the Virgin of El Cisne. These were some of the exchanges that I wanted to show in the film. Then when the film's storyline moves to Spain, I wanted to show the flow of the main object in the documentary. In fact, I wouldn't call the image of the Virgin of El Cisne an object. Instead, I would refer to her as an object-metaphor that represents not just the Virgin but all the people and objects that circulate in this migration cycle. Here we see objects that remind us of Ecuador. For example, in the first screening of the film, people who saw the festival of the Virgin of El Cisne taking place here in Ciudad Lineal would ask me, "Is this in Spain? It can't be! Where? In which park?" They experienced physical and cultural displacement when they saw the festival of the crazy cow, the fireworks, the image of the Virgin in the middle of the singers, etcetera. All of that reminds us of Ecuador.

That was one of my goals, and I believe that in documentary film image and sound are key elements, especially when projecting religious themes. As Jean Rouch says, the sensibilities that are found in ritual are impossible to describe with words. It is almost impossible. This is why it is important to show the devotion of the people for the Virgin of El Cisne in order to better understand what this Virgin means to migrants abroad. In the film you don't know what migrants are praying for, but their two major prayers are for their families' well-being and for papers, basically. From the research that I've read on migration and religious devotion, the question of geographical distance keeps coming up. When migration is not as long in terms of geographical distance, despair and longing for family is not as prevalent. Most Catholic migrants would pray to God and the Virgin asking for work, for example, for papers. But here in Spain, being so far away from Ecuador and when you add a prolonged time away from home, most prayers of intercession to the Virgin tend to be about family matters. This is another theme that brings you closer to the experiences and voices of migrants. My focus was to show the Virgin of El Cisne as another migrant herself. That was another conscious decision I made when thinking of the structure of the film.

In every interview I did with migrants, they always would talk about the moment they decided to leave Ecuador, of how their lives used to be prior to that, about their first impressions of coming to a new country, of their first encounters and clashes with Spaniards. And I wanted to show that same life story be about the Virgin. I wanted to represent the Virgin as another migrant. A sacred object, yes, but a migrant one. This is why in the film I present her origin, her story of migration, how she travels by plane, and once in Spain, I wanted to show the places where she is first welcomed and where she is not. When you see her story you realize that many factors related to her migration are out of reach, just like it is for migrants themselves. I remember the advice from a colleague in a film workshop while I was making *La Churona*. You see, as I was working on the film many Ecuadorian migrants started leaving Spain after they couldn't work legally here any more. I became frustrated with this new change because I felt I could no longer justify my argument in the story. Many Ecuadorians left, including Manolo, whom I mentioned earlier. This is why I was a bit frustrated until my colleague told me, "The fact that many are leaving Spain makes me think of the value of your documentary. Because if migrants do not move any more, are not adrift, you can't sense what continues to force them to be vulnerable." I kept this advice with me all along. It is important to remember that these sensibilities can be transmitted through cinema.

How did you decide on the stylistics and animation techniques that you employ in the film?

To me, *La Churona* is like a phrase I once heard that says "To speak about the mail tell me about the letter. Don't tell me about the mail." That's what I tried to do in the film. Having studied migration, being a migrant myself, I found Ecuadorian migration to Spain to be a bit complex and diverse. There were too many ways of looking at it, and at one point I felt overwhelmed. My background working with children of migrants helped me to focus on what was happening to young Ecuadorians living in Spain. I was interested in exploring many topics, such as racism, patterns of communication, etcetera. I knew I had to focus my attention on something very specific. I said to myself I want to address the link between migrants and their families and communities at the transnational level. That became, let's say, my overall theme. From there, I started looking for specific cases. With this in mind, the diversity of technical resources I use in the film share a common purpose of telling the story better. Once I had the story in my mind, I made use of all the tools and resources at my disposal to tell it well. Because I arrived in Spain in the middle of the Ecuadorian migration crisis, I had to look for material in various places. I reviewed material from television newscasts and newspaper coverage to show the relevance of migration in mainstream society not only in Ecuador but also in Spain. We often forget that transnationalism also has an effect in the places of new arrival. This is why clips from the newspaper *El País* had to be included in the film. Once I learned that television crews had been covering the story of the Virgin of El Cisne in Madrid, I knew I had to find that footage somewhere.

The shots from Plaza Mayor are essential to show the large presence of Ecuadorians and their activism in Madrid.

I am aware that some viewers prefer the use of animation while others do not. I applied animation because I wanted to reconstruct the original myth of the Virgin of El Cisne. I first thought of other techniques to re-create the myth, but all of them failed. In the end, I went with animation for this part of the film. I was pretty happy with the end result because it opens up space for my own subjectivity. I did the same thing in a few of the interviews in the film where you can hear my voice asking the questions. I wasn't interested in taking the main role in the film as first-person narrator, but I am happy to be present in the film at least subtly through my own voice. As I said, this is why I also relied on the use of animation.

When writing the part of the myth of the Virgin in the screenplay, I first thought of including a discussion between various people, a schoolteacher, a historian, a priest, and a few local people from the town of El Cisne. In my mind, it was going to be great to show the differences of opinion among these people. However, when I filmed this scene, one of the people manipulated the conversation. The owner of the restaurant where we filmed the scene kept interrupting his daughter and others who wanted to speak. Everyone stopped talking, plus the sound was not very good in that location. Another idea I had was to include a radio announcer from Loja to tell the story of the myth. I really liked the way he would tell the story, making all the sound effects of the wind and the rain, the flooding, for the radio. But I ran into copyright problems. The radio station wanted to charge more than the cost of making the entire film! Then I considered telling the myth story as a comic strip, but the quality on film wasn't very good. This is when I decided to go with animation. My animation designer came up with a few options. We considered the line drawings of Guaman Poma and we liked them. They are not exactly the same drawings, but they follow the same rudimental aesthetic. Basically, this was the thought process that led to the use of animation in the film.

What were your greatest challenges in telling a story of Ecuadorian migration in Spain?

More than facing challenges in terms of migration issues, the greatest challenge has been at the religious level here in Spain. That was one of the issues when making the film that I really did not expect would have been a problem. But here in Spain, religion is very much tied to right-wing politics, to the most conservative sectors of society. Even in terms of film distribution, works that discuss religious issues do not do so well. To have the film shown on Spanish public television is basically impossible. Someone turns on the TV and watches a couple of minutes of religious programming and immediately switches the channel. They don't like it. What's interesting is that they enjoy watching programming that deals with, let's say, Salvador Allende. That's what they want to watch. To talk about religion is horrific and tedious to them. I still remember a film workshop I took with David Trueba. He read my screenplay, gave me a few tips, and even watched the first montage of the film. I had the privilege of getting his feedback. He told me, "I really like it, but you are going to have a very hard time distributing this film in Spain." Then my husband, Adolfo, saw the film and said to me, "Let's see how we are going to do this because in this country we are very antireligious, and it is going to be complicated." This is why in every screening I would stress the fact that this was a film about migration. When I was trying out the film among friends and with small audiences prior to making the final cut, the most common complaint among all Spaniards was the religious overtones in the film. My former boss Javier Rioyo commented, "Thank you for showing the pageant contestants because I was pretty fed up of seeing so many priests and Virgins!" It is true.

In Cuba they also told me to cut the whole religious part that takes place in Ecuador. I edited lots of it, but it got to the point when I said I can't cut this! I can't cut out the section in Ecuador! I had trouble even at the 2010 International Film Festival in Havana, where I eventually won the Postproduction Award. In this festival one meets with the jury before they make their final decisions. The members of the jury told me, "Cut out the part about Ecuador and the award is yours." But I had to tell them, "I can't cut out Ecuador because later in the film when the Ecuadorian migrants speak about Loja and El Cisne the viewer would not understand what they would be talking about. One has to be patient when watching the film." This is what Patricio Guzmán means when he describes documentary film's "otro tiempo," another time, things happen in another rhythm. You must change gears. It is not like when you are watching a Hollywood film. This is what my film editor would say to me, "If you keep in mind that *La Churona* is a documentary the section in Ecuador fits well. But if you don't realize that, the part about Ecuador seems a bit long." But I needed to keep that section in the film. The documentary required that section. I think that was my greatest challenge, not so much the questions about migration but the viewers' reactions against religion.

My other challenge came from the priests, more so with one of them because the older priest died while I was still making the film. More than anything else, I had to deal with the priests' perceptions. For example, the younger of the two priests in the film insinuated his dislike for appearing to be competing against doña Carmen for the control of the Virgin. This is because he considered that it was the priests, more so the Church, who had the final word with regards to the Virgin. After all, his impression was that the Virgin belonged to them. The priests were opposed to how in the film I place doña Carmen's perspective at their level and opposite to theirs. His vision was very paternalistic, even when speaking to me. He wanted to control the camera shots, wanted to preview each scene. At some point he offered to find funding to finish the film so that he could take full control. In making the film, my interactions with religious and public figures in Spain carried a mixture of discrimination and political correctness. They still saw me as just another Ecuadorian immigrant. Their attitudes toward me were both politically correct and condescending, two things at once.

How did you earn the trust of the various social actors that appear in your film?

With lots of patience! [*Laughs.*] For example, it took over a year for doña Carmen to agree to an interview with me. Another struggle was earning the trust of Jonathan and his family whom we see in the airport scene. At first, doña Carmen seemed to agree to be on film because she was seeking media attention. She wanted to have a voice. But later she became reluctant to speak with me, as she didn't know how her words would be interpreted by other Ecuadorians. At that point she was worried about protecting her image as a community leader. You have to keep in mind that as a leader she was politically ambitious. She actually ran to be an assembly representative. She was very much interested in protecting her public image. The priests had a different attitude about this. Their strategy was to remain away from the media as long as doña Carmen appeared in it. They were against giving any interviews. Their excuse was that they wanted to avoid any conflict with doña Carmen. To earn the trust of various people in the film, I had to do a lot of fieldwork. Whenever possible, I tried to be reciprocal and help people without being manipulative. Doing a film like this sometimes seemed like an exchange of demands because I wanted to film and investigate. For example, to earn doña Carmen's trust, I assisted her with some administrative work related to the Asociación Virgen de El Cisne [Virgin of El Cisne Association]. I transcribed letters for her, that sort of thing. With the priests, they would ask me to photograph some of the masses.

On the one hand, doña Carmen avoided doing an interview with me until one day she agreed to do it. However, the day we tried to do the interview I ran into some major technical problems. She asked to be interviewed in her home, but on the day of the interview she had people working on home repairs. The environment was very noisy, and then suddenly the power went out. This was a very challenging interview. In fact, I wanted to redo it one more time. Doña Carmen agreed to do the interview one more time, but she never committed to any given day. On the other hand, the priests agreed to an interview about a year after my initial contact with them. They were the ones who requested an interview. I must say that although they wanted to be interviewed, their one demand was that I could not ask questions about the conflict with doña Carmen. These negotiations took much time and patience, but they ended up being crucial for the film.

What happened to the original sculpture of the Virgin that doña Carmen brought with her from Ecuador?

That figure ended up in doña Carmen's home. In fact, when I started the documentary the priests had not yet gone to Ecuador to bring their own sculpture. It was one of those things that you can't anticipate at the beginning, but then in the end you notice how reality can surprise you. I found it very interesting that there were two migrant images of the Virgin in Spain. When that happened, I asked myself what am I going to do with two images of the same Virgin? I was focused only on the image that at that point was in doña Carmen's bar in Madrid. I thought the story in the film would develop in a different way. I expected that in the end the priests were going to finally welcome doña Carmen's image into their church. But only in the end of the film did I realize the meaning of the two Virgins and of the symbolism behind the priests being the ones going to Ecuador! Doña Carmen also thought that the Virgin would eventually return to the church.

When the priests brought theirs from Ecuador, doña Carmen immediately started looking for a new church. This is not mentioned in much detail in the film because she didn't tell me this, and I couldn't find a way to fit it in the story. If I had to do the film all over again, I would try to incorporate this to the main storyline. But it was beautiful for the film that doña Carmen decided to go searching for a place for her Virgin and in all these churches they would tell her that her figure wasn't welcome because she lacked papers. To me that was fantastic! In the interview I tried many times to have doña Carmen explain that, but she didn't say it. When she first told me about it, I thought it was amazing. I also learned that the priests from the church in Lavapiés were the ones who wrote to the bishop asking him to deny the Virgin to be admitted into any church in Madrid. They are the ones plotting to shut down any entryway for the Virgin. This is why in the film we see that the Virgin is first welcomed in the Our Lady of Reparation Church, but later, after a phone call from the bishop, the Virgin is taken out of the church. Seeing that there was not a single sacred place for the Virgin, doña Carmen has to bring the image to her home. What happened, clearly, is that she had less and less space to move around in the city.

Doña Carmen is a very complex woman, as you can see in the film. She is a fighter, as in the moment when she comes up with the idea of organizing an Ecuadorian fair. At another moment in the film, doña Carmen takes the Virgin out of the church without asking anyone. Here in Spain, I learned that if you want to take a sacred sculpture out of a church for a procession, you need both authorization form the church and a city permit. Whenever doña Carmen would take out the Virgin for a procession in Ciudad Lineal, she would say, "What can they do to me? Arrest me? So be it." But each time she had fewer and fewer places to move around. It's been a while since doña Carmen decided to move back to Ecuador. However, I've been told that the sculpture remains in Madrid, moving from home to home. But I don't know where it is.

Another theme in the film is the passing of time. After watching the film and considering our current economic crisis, you realize how many things have changed. For example, there are fewer Ecuadorian migrants in Spain, the Virgin of El Cisne Association does not exist any more, and not as many people attend Catholic mass as they once did. I continue to attend the November mass in honor of the Virgin of El Cisne. Now the church is only half full, whereas before there wasn't enough room for all the people. In Lavapiés, people continue to do the annual procession, but it is much smaller than it once was. Before, the procession was massive, a bit shocking for the neighbors in that part of Madrid. The documentary shows Ecuadorian migration at its peak, with the families and work demand. Now one doesn't even think about that. Now you go to a job interview, and everyone around you is considering whether to stay, go back, or move on. Many families have left Spain and moved elsewhere. For instance, nowadays there are many more Ecuadorians in London. We are living a totally different moment today. Of course, the collapse of the mortgage bubble keeps coming again and again in the interviews I've been collecting lately.

Tell me about the collapse of the mortgage bubble.

The 2008 financial crisis hit people in Spain pretty hard, especially immigrants and within the immigrant enclaves, the Ecuadorian community. Why? This happened because of the sheer number of Ecuadorians living in Spain and because a few years later they had started buying homes and property in Spain. By the mid- to late 2000s, many Ecuadorians were already established in Spain and had steady jobs. Also you have to keep in mind that back then banks would give you the moon and the stars. Another factor was that most bank loans required people to have a cosigner. Of course, their cosigner was usually another Ecuadorian. When things started to go bad, the collapse caused a chain-link effect. When the mortgage bubble burst, many Ecuadorians suffered a tremendous financial fall. Many of them had to go back to Ecuador, walking away from their homes here. Some others are deeply in debt.

The problem was two-sided. It was terrible that the banks gave out so many loans, and the Ecuadorian migrants were also at fault for agreeing to purchase homes at very high prices. I am talking about homes that would go for two hundred, three hundred thousand euros. These were incredibly overvalued homes, but the banks were inflating the cost. Keep in mind that in order to make these expensive homes affordable, banks would offer mortgage loans with adjustable rates for sixty-year periods. The crisis happened when the flexible interest rates started going up. The starting interest rates were very deceiving. Homeowners started paying five hundred or eight hundred euros a month and then later a thousand, a thousand five hundred. Imagine what it is like in Spain to pay a thousand five hundred euro mortgage? The mortgage crisis brought tremendous stress to the Ecuadorian community here.

What are your next short-term and long-term projects?

I can't help it, my next film project will most likely have an Ecuadorian theme. Earlier I thought about making a film related to either the mortgage crisis or about the experience of second-generation Ecuadorians in Spain. I find the mortgage crisis theme fascinating because of the role the Ecuadorian government tried to play in it. When it comes to migration affairs, the Ecuadorian state sees itself as a transnational entity, concerned with the mortgage problem

Ecuadorian migrants faced here in Spain. This was particularly true at the vice-presidency level. The government of Ecuador opened a support office here in Spain which many people have found very useful. This office has given people basic advice on how to negotiate with banks and other lending institutions.

That came about from the work done by the Plataforma. I am not sure how many people are aware of the Plataforma de Afectados de Hipoteca [PAH, Platform of Mortgage Victims], a citizen social platform that offers, first of all, advice on how to save one's home and second, organizes groups of people to prevent home evictions. Interestingly, the Ecuadorian government has joined forces with PAH to give advice among the Ecuadorian community. For example, the Ecuadorian government and PAH together presented an official demand to the European community on behalf of an Ecuadorian who had been evicted. Today, the case is still being discussed. At first, I wanted to do a film about this particular case, which to me is quite symbolic. But I am also interested in studying the *generación uno y medio* [generation one and a half]. These are children and youth who arrive to a new country either with their parents or after their parents as part of a family reunification process.

Lately, I have been conducting interviews with young Ecuadorians, 20-somethings mostly, and I've been fascinated by the connections they maintain or generate anew with Ecuador. Their connections are totally different from that of their parents,' but they are still meaningful. Even though their memory about Ecuador refers to their early childhood—many of the youth I've interviewed left Ecuador when they were five or six years of age—they still consider returning to live in Ecuador at some point later in life. Their relationships continue to remain with other Ecuadorians, or they may branch out to other Latin Americans living in Spain. This is something that I thought would have changed or not have lasted after several years of living in Spain. Instead, many Ecuadorians continue to date and marry other Ecuadorians. The photos of them with their friends show mostly young Ecuadorians, with a few [other] Latin Americans here and there. They may have a Colombian friend, but for the most part they remain segregated. For now, I cannot see myself thinking of making a documentary that is not about the Ecuadorian migrant experience.

Appendix

The films analyzed in this volume are listed here by chapter, with information on where to find them.

CHAPTER 1

Harvest of Empire (dir. Peter Getzels and Eduardo López, 2012) is available at HarvestofEmpireMovie.com, and Amazon.

CHAPTER 2

abUSed: The Postville Raid (dir. Luis Argueta, 2010) is available at abUSedthePostvilleRaid.com, New Day Films (NewDay.com), and Kanopy.com.

Sin país (dir. Theo Rigby, 2010) is available at Vimeo.com, NewDay.com, and Kanopy.com.

CHAPTER 3

The Vigil (dir. Jenny Alexander, 2014) is available by contacting the filmmaker directly at activevistamedia@gmail.com.

CHAPTER 4

De nadie (dir. Tin Dirdamal, 2005) is available at Netflix, Amazon, and YouTube.com/watch?v=uX4X1YhW-sY or by contacting the filmmaker directly at tin.dirdamal@gmail.com.

Los invisibles (dir. Marc Silver and Gael García Bernal, 2010) is available at YouTube.com/user/invisiblesfilms.

CHAPTER 5

Del otro lado del cristal (dir. Mercedes Arce, Guillermo Centeno, Marina Ochoa, and Manuel Pérez, 1995) is available at CubaCollectibles.com/cuba-documentales.html.

The Lost Apple (dir. Cliff Solway, 1962) is available at the Pedro Pan Exodus YouTube channel, YouTube.com/watch?v=WK0JKF-FtS4.

Operation Peter Pan: Flying Back to Cuba (dir. Estela Bravo, 2010) is available by contacting the filmmaker at estelabravo.com/contact.html.

CHAPTER 6

Abuelos (dir. Carla Valencia Dávila, 2010) is available by contacting the filmmaker at carlavalenciad@gmail.com.

CHAPTER 7

La Churona (dir. María Cristina Carrillo Espinosa, 2010) is available by contacting the filmmaker directly at lachurona@gmail.com.

CHAPTER 8

Which Way Home (dir. Rebecca Camissa, 2009) is available at WhichWayHome.net, Netflix, and Amazon.

CHAPTER 9

Extravío (dir. Daniellis Hernández, 2008) is available by contacting the filmmaker directly at daniellisht@gmail.com.

The Illusion (dir. Susana Barriga, 2008) is available by contacting the filmmaker directly at excenter.av@gmail.com.

Orages d'été (dir. Heidi Hassan, 2008) is available at Vimeo.

Tierra roja (dir. Heidi Hassan, 2007) is available at Vimeo.

CHAPTER 10

Videos from the Museo de América series *Migrar es Cultura* are available at MigrarEsCultura.es.

Contributors

Ramón J. Guerra is associate professor of English at the University of Nebraska-Omaha. His research focuses on the placement of Chicano and Latino literature within the larger named American literature, particularly in the late twentieth and early twenty-first centuries. He specifically examines the significances of nonfiction witness accounts, oral histories, and memoirs, all under the category of *testimonio*, as a means to expand historiography through literature. He has published work on testimonios of Latinos from the time of the Mexican Revolution to the present day. He also teaches about the American Dream mythology in literature and about Latino cultural representations.

Lizardo Herrera is associate professor of Spanish at Whittier College. He earned a PhD at the University of Pittsburgh and a master's degree in cultural studies at Universidad Andina Simón Bolívar in Quito. He has published numerous articles in journals such as *Revista Iberoamericana*, *Chasqui*, *Revista de Literatura Latinoamericana*, *Cultural Studies Review*, and *Procesos: Revista de Historia Andina*, among others. In 2009 he was awarded the Cultural Studies Fellowship at the University of Pittsburgh. He was an associated writer at Plan V (planv.com.ec), an online news site, and writes for *La línea de fuego* (lalineadefuego.com), an online journal in Quito.

Jared List is assistant professor of Spanish at Doane University in Crete, Nebraska. He obtained his PhD in Latin American literatures and cultures at Ohio State University in 2013. His research and publications focus on representations of life and death in Central American documentaries, including a published essay on Marcela Zamora Chamorro's documentary film *El cuarto de los huesos* (*The Room of Bones*). His interests include (de)coloniality, subaltern studies, memory studies, and oral history.

Esteban E. Loustaunau is professor of Spanish at Assumption University in Worcester, Massachusetts. His main areas of teaching and scholarship are contemporary Latin American literature, film, and music as they intersect with issues related to migration, youth cultures, subalternity, decoloniality, and Internet studies. His work has been published in several edited volumes and refereed journals including *CR: The New Centennial Review*, *Revista Iberoamericana*, and *Revista de Literatura Mexicana*

Contemporánea. His current research project examines the possibilities and limitations of literary journalism, music, and documentary film to represent acts of defiance and recognition by people who have had to confront social, political, and economic expulsions in the forms of dispossession, displacement, and violence in Central America's Northern Triangle, Mexico, and the U.S.-Mexican border. Combining teaching and civic engagement, he has developed various workshops and cultural programs to empower Mexican immigrant families in the Midwest and Central American unaccompanied refugee minors in New England.

Manuel F. Medina is professor of Spanish at the University of Louisville. His main areas of research and teaching include Latin American and U.S. Latino film, narrative, cultural studies, and technology in education. He has published extensively and delivered papers at domestic and international conferences on Latin American narrative and film within the context of border and cultural studies. He has authored a book on the representation of history in the Mexican novel of the late twentieth century, *Archivo y discurso en la nueva novela histórica mexicana*. He is completing a book project on the study of space in Ecuadorian film. He is president of the Asociación de Ecuatorianistas. At Louisville he has organized an annual Latin American film festival since 1995.

Ada Ortúzar-Young is professor emerita at Drew University in Madison, New Jersey. She has held professional offices at the local and national levels. She was elected to the Executive Council of the American Association of Teachers of Spanish and Portuguese. She regularly teaches courses in contemporary Hispanic literatures and film centering on gender issues, diasporas, migrations, and globalization. She is a frequent presenter at national and international conferences. Her publications have focused on diasporic subjects such as the representation of Caribbean women in recent Spanish film and on literary works depicting migration to the United States.

Thomas Piñeros Shields is lecturer in the Department of Sociology at the University of Massachusetts at Lowell. Prior to joining the faculty at UML he worked for a decade as a full-time research associate at the Heller School for Social Policy and Management at Brandeis University, where he conducted multisite, mixed-methods evaluations of community-based organization initiatives to promote civic engagement. He has developed community-based and participatory research projects with youth in Waltham, Massachusetts, and with undocumented immigrant young adults. Prior to working at Brandeis University he worked in youth development and community development fields, participating in the East St. Louis Action Research Project with the University of Illinois. His dissertation in sociology and social policy at Brandeis was an ethnography of the student immigrant movement that explains how the DREAMers emerged as new political actors.

Juan G. Ramos is associate professor of Spanish at the College of the Holy Cross in Worcester, Massachusetts, where he teaches courses on Latin American poetry as well as literature and language courses at all levels. He is the author of *Sensing Decolonial Aesthetics in Latin American Arts* (University of Florida Press, 2018), which focuses on the concept of decolonial aesthetics in relation to the development of antipoetry, third cinema, and the "new song" movement during the 1960s and early 1970s in Latin America. He is coeditor, with Tara Daly, of *Decolonial Approaches to Latin American Literatures and Cultures* (Palgrave Macmillan, 2016). He has published on the connection between poetry and film and the historical *crónica* during *modernismo*. He also researches and presents on aesthetic and postcolonial approaches to poetry and film.

Lauren E. Shaw is professor emerita of Spanish and Hispanic studies and coordinator of foreign languages at Elmira College in New York. There she taught courses on Spanish language, literature, film, and social issues of the Hispanic world. She continues to teach courses in the Spanish and Hispanic Studies Department at Hobart and William Smith Colleges. Along with her concerns around immigration, her research focuses on the Cuban *trova* as testimony of the social-political changes on the island. Her edited collection of essays titled *Song and Social Change in Latin America* was published in 2013 by Lexington Books. She received her PhD in Hispanic and Luso-Brazilian literatures from the Graduate Center at the City University of New York.

Zaira Zarza is a Killam Memorial Postdoctoral Fellow at the University of Alberta. She continues to teach courses in the Spanish and Hispanic Studies Department at Hobart and William Smith Colleges. She worked in the Department of Social Research of the Cuban Film Institute. Her book *Caminos del cine brasileño contemporáneo* was published by Ediciones ICAIC in 2010, and she coedited the special issue "Havana" for the Canadian journal *Public* of winter 2016. She is the founder and coordinator of the project Roots and Routes: Cuban Cinemas of the Diaspora in the 21st Century, a platform for the promotion and study of film and media works by young Cuban artists who live off the island. Her current research focuses on creative industries in transitional Cuba. She obtained her PhD in cultural studies at Queen's University and holds a master's degree in art history from the University of Havana.

Index

Page numbers in *italics* refer to illustrations.

Abandonment, 96, 102
Abrazos (2014), 11, 242, 254–58
Abuelos (2010), 8–9; awards for, 137; cinematographic technique in, 144–48; identity search in, 140; immigration in context of, 136–37; junked cars image in, 143; letters presented in, 149–50; photography utilized in, 139–48; violence presented in, 151–52
abUSed: The Postville Raid (2010), 7, 11, 59–62, 63n1, 242–57; audience reach of, 259; exploitation, dispensability and, 41–50; film festival entries of, 257–58; injustice challenged by, 263; as performance of memory, 40
Activism: belonging recognized through practices and, 5; documentary, art and, 6; for immigration reform, 89; as social movement, 69; *The Vigil* (2014) representing political, 77. *See also* Community activism; Grassroots activism
ADAC. *See* DREAM Act Coalition
Adams, Randall, 6
Adichie, Chimamanda Ngozi, 4
Adoption, as illegal, 258
Affect, concepts related to, 28–30
Affective turn, 28–29
The Affect Theory Reader (Seigworth and Gregg), 28–29
Agamben, Giorgio, 41
Agriprocessors Inc., 47, 50, 242, 252
Ahmed, Sara, 25–26
ALA. *See* American Library Association
Alexander, Jenny, 6, 7, 11, 67, 71, 81, 110n5, 260–74

Allegory, 161–63, 165
Allende, mi abuelo Allende (Beyond My Grandfather Allende), 14n2
Allende, Salvador, 138, 141, 145–46, 312
AlterCine Foundation, 3
Alterglobalization social movement, 76–77, 84n3
Aluna Art Foundation, 212
Amaya, Tomás, 268
Amazon, 3
La americana (2011), 110n5
American Dream, 51, 205; as illusive, 10; mythos of, 177; portrait of, 176
American Library Association (ALA), 31–32
Amnesty, 209
Amnesty International, 94, 110n9
Animation, 310–11
Anzaldúa, Gloria, 227–28
Arce, Mercedes, 120
Arellano, Elvira, 88–89, 108, 109n1, 109n2
Arendt, Hannah, 41, 56
Argan, Giulio Carlo, 171n15
Argueta, Luis, 6, 7, 11, 40–50, 241–59, 263
Arizona Senate Bill 1070 (2010), 80; as unconstitutional, 83–84; vigil to resist, 68–70, 72–73, 75–78, 81, 84, 263–71
Arpaio, Joseph, 68, 77–79, 270–72
Art Institute of Cuba (Instituto Superior de Arte de Cuba), 193
Aruca, Francisco, 130
Attenborough, Richard, 128
Audio and visual effects, 4; innovation through, 209; nature used for, 139–41, 148–52; visibility created through, 95–96
Audiovisual correspondence, 293
Aufderheide, Pat, 183
Avila, Ernestine, 89–90

Baker, James, 129–30, 132
Bancroft, Hubert Howe, 185, 191n6
Bare life, 41
Barnard, Sheila Curran, 6
Baroque ethos, 158–59, 166
Baroque replica, neobaroque nationality and, 160–65
Barragán, Carmen, 166, 306–7, 313–15
Barrie, James M., 120
Barriga, Susana, 10, 195, 198, 207–10, 211
The Battle of Chile (1975–1979), 143, 218
Bautis, Marta, 110n5
Bay of Pigs (1961), 125, 132–33
the Beast, 9, 94, 100, 104, 106, 175; children on, 177; as main migrant transportation mode, 110n6; as *Which Way Home* primary narrative, 176
Behar, Ruth, 195–96
Behavior, dialogical nature of, 60
Belonging: activism and practices used to recognize, 5; community and, 54, 295; to nation, 26
Belsham, Bruce, 30
Benamou, Catherine, 193, 199, 213n1
Benjamin, Walter, 52, 161
Bennet, Mark W., 45
Berlin Wall, 1
La Bestia. *See* the Beast
Beverley, John, 9, 181–82, 183, 185
Beyond My Grandfather Allende (*Allende, mi abuelo Allende*), 14n2
Bienvenido a tu familia (*Welcome to your family*) (2009), 136
Birthplace, citizenship, race and, 47
Birth rates, in Cuba, 197
Black identity, 10, 206–7
Bollaín, Icíar, 156
Border crossing: companionship and, in *Which Way Home*, 179–80, 188; dangers of, 175; undocumented migrants jailed for, 276–77
Border Patrol, violence by, 179
Bourgeois, Roy, 26
Bracero program, 42

Bradford, Anita Casavantes, 132
Brah, Avtar, 206
Braidotti, Rosi, 198
Bravo, Estela, 120–21, 131–32
Brewer, Janet, 67, 70, 73
Bruckner, Nicholas, 110n5
Las brujas migrantes (*The migrant witches*) (2013), 231–33
Bruzzi, Stella, 4, 91
Buchanan, Patrick, 36n10
Bureau of Prisons, 44
Burlington Coat Factory, 79–80
Burton, Julianne, 91, 218–19
Bustamante, Jorge, 110n8
Bustillo de Oro, Juan, 165

Cabrera, Mariana, 27
Cafferty, Jack, 21–22, 26
Calicio, Rolando, 253
Californios, 185, 191n5
Camayd-Freixas, Erik, 44–45, 242
Cammisa, Rebecca, 9, 175
Canler, Ed, 128–29, 133
Capitalismo gore, 102
Caravan of Mothers of Disappeared Migrants (Caravana de Madres de Migrantes Desaparecidos), 111n12
Cárdenas, Maritza, 5
Carillo Espinosa, María Cristina, 9, 12–13, 136, 155, 163, 171n6; documentary film interest of, 298; Ecuadorian migrant community relationship with, 299–300; future projects of, 316–17; migrant children researched by, 305; personal migration experience of, 302–4; religious challenges faced by, 311–13; Spain arrival of, 301; on Virgin of El Cisne sculpture, 314–15
Carter, Jimmy, 27
Casa de las Américas, 133
Casa del Migrante (Home of the Migrant), 100
Castillo, Laura, 46, 63
Castillo, Otto René, 243
Castro, Fidel, 125, 130

Castroism, 209
Catholicism: indigenous people conversion to, 156–57; rituality of, 158, 167
Cautious complicity, 105
Censorship, 34
Centeno, Guillermo, 120
Central Intelligence Agency (CIA), 130–31
Cero en Conducta, 301–2, 303
Cerrando el círculo (Operation Peter Pan: Flying back to Cuba) (2011). *See* Operation Peter Pan: Flying Back to Cuba
Chanan, Michael, 1, 3, 32, 220–21
Chang, Justo, 254
Chavarría, Jamileth, 231–32
Chavez, Leo, 22
Cherished Island Memories: A History of Cubans and Cayman Islanders (2007), 203
Children: on the Beast, 177; Carillo Espinosa research on migrant, 305; emotional burden of, 153; family reunification for, 256–57; Flores, as seen by, 107; ICE proclaiming safety of, 262; importance of perspectives of, 255–56; increase in immigration of, 190–91; love for, 99–100; memory of, 108; mothers modeling courage for, 84; optimism of, 177–78, 191; parents spied on by, 131–32; quality of life sought for, 166–67; relocations places for, 120; as sent away, 120; stories from, 49; undocumented migrant mothers fear for, 96, 124; vulnerability of, 190; women transformed by, 99; worry and fear for, 90. *See also* Pedro Pan children
The Children Who Cheated the Nazis (2000), 128
Chovel, Elly, 127, 128, 134
La Churona. *See* Virgin of El Cisne
La Churona (The Migrant Virgin) (2010), 9, 12–13, 136, 156, 163, 297; discontent expressed in, 165; exclusion refused in, 170; film techniques utilized in, 310–11; funding for, 301–2; intended audience for, 304–5; as migration experience bridge, 298, 309–10; pilgrim songs in, 155, 159; reception of, 306–8; three day pilgrimage presented in, 164; time as theme in, 315–16
CIA. *See* Central Intelligence Agency
Cinema Novo, 14
Cinematographic direction, 289
Citizenship, 1, 47, 63, 195
Civil disobedience, 82
Climate change, 1
Codigofagia, 158–60, 165, 167, 170
Cold War, 124
Collective memory, 59, 62
Collective mobilization, 72
Colonialism, 93, 156, 170n2
Coloniality of power, 224
Coming to Our Senses (Reber), 29
Committees for the Defense of the Revolution, 131
Common Core educational standard, 32
Communism, 125, 144, 295
Community, 5; belonging and, 54, 295; of Hassan, 295; need for, 97
Community activism, filmmakers and, 261–62
Co-move, 108, 113n27
Companionship, 179–80, 188
Conciencia de la mestiza (mestiza consciousness), 227–28
Conde, Yvonne M., 120, 127
Conquergood, Dwight, 64n9
Conquistadores, 156–57, 161–62, 169, 170n2
Convergence Culture (Jenkins), 223
Cortázar, Octavio, 218
La cosecha (The Harvest) (2011), 110n5
The Cost of Cotton (1978), 241, 243
Costumbrismo, 10, 190
Council of Trent, 157
Counter-Reformation, 157, 170n4
Coutin, Susan Bibler, 55–56
Crafting Truth (Navarro and Spence), 236n2
Creole elites, 162–63
Crime-suppression sweep, 80
Crowdfunding platforms, 3–4
Cruz, Alma, 231–32
Cuando los hijos se van (When the kids leave) (1941), 165, 167

Cuarón, Jonás, 94
Cuba, 120–22; birth rates in, 197; education in, 196–97; filmmakers as women from, 213n2; Hassan feeling indebted to, 287; intergenerational conflicts in, 208; patriarchy in, 197
Cubana: Contemporary Fiction by Cuban Women (Behar), 195–96, 212
Cuban feminism, 196–97, 294
Cuban Film Institute, 193
Cubanidad, 195
Cuban missile crisis, 120, 129
Cuban Refugee Center, 123
Cuban Revolution, 10, 124, 131, 196
Cuban Women's Federation, 196
Cultural *champús*, 164, 166, 169, 171n10
The Cultural Politics of Emotion (Ahmed), 25–26
Cultural preservation, 2
Cyberorality, 226
Cybervisuality, 226

Dailymotion, 219
Dávila, Remo, 138–41, 147–52
Dean, Caroline, 158
De cierta manera (One Way or Another) (1974), 213n2
Decolonial aesthetics, 224–28, 236n6
Decolonial consciousness, 91–93
De Genova, Nicholas, 41, 46–47
Dehumanization, 43, 272; from deportation, 62–63; documentary film eliminating, 258; documentary role in, 50; exposing of, 93
de la Peña, Pedro, 163
de las Casas, Bartolomé, 156
Deleuze, Gilles, 171n9, 171n15
Del otro lado del cristal (1995), 8, 120, 123–26
Democracy Now!, 24
Democratization, 217–18
Demos, T. J., 223
De nadie (2005), 8, 12, 90–91, 110n5, 278–79; awards for, 102, 112n23; documenting by obeying in, 100–108; learning experience from, 280; making of, 276–77; poverty statistics in, 112n20; transformation shown in, 284

Department of Homeland Security (U.S.), 37n11, 109n2
Department of Justice (U.S.), 44–45
Depersonalization, 43
Deportability, 46–49, 109n2
Deportable life, 40–50, 62
Deportation, 2, 11, 180, 250–51; dehumanization from, 62–63; family separation from, 53; fear of, 47–49, 271; process of, 54; of removable aliens, 37n11; trauma associated with, 40–41
The Deportation Regime: Sovereignty, Space, and the Freedom of Movement (Peutz and De Genova), 46–47
de Robles, Diego, 155, 160–62
Desierto (2015), 94
Desolation, 97
Detained (2007), 11, 261–62
Development, Relief, and Education for Alien Minors Act (DREAM), 81. *See also* DREAM Act Coalition; DREAMers
Dhuway (Griffiths), 30
Diarios de motocicleta (The Motorcycle Diaries) (2004), 29
Diaristic filmmaking, 182–83
Diaspora, 195–201, 207, 297–98, 307; subjectivity and, 211–12; voice and, in documentary film, 308–10
Díaz, Junot, 24, 26
Dictatorship, in Argentina, 78
Didion, Joan, 120
Diéguez, Dánae, 201–2, 213n1, 214n11
Digitization: of museum artifacts, 230; sense of ownership from, 231
Dignity, 106, 251
Dirdamal, Tin, 3, 8, 12, 90–93, 110n5, 275–85; background of, 102; Flores relationship with, 103–5, 107–8; proximity practice of, 102–3; role respected by, 105–6; subjects met by, 100
Dispensability, exploitation and, in *abUSed: The Postville Raid*, 41–50
Displacement, 11, 90; fear of, 47; history, memory and, 50–59; trauma from, 57
Disposable life, 41

Documentary film: access to viewing, 3; approval needed for, 221; art, activism and, 6; audience impact of, 2; Carillo Espinosa interest in, 298; definition of, 4, 130; dehumanization eliminated through, 258; dehumanization in, 50; dialogue created by release of, 131; exclusion overcome through, 39; female engagement and resistance through, 194; humanity reclaimed in, 95; identity explored through, 289–90; immigrant rights role of, 258–59; Latin America proliferation of, 3; location influencing, 291; memory separation from, 62; as performance of memory, 59–62; personal-essay concept of, 183; persuasive power of, 7, 80–81; power of interview in, 186–87; reality captured by, 91; resistant space in, 184; sensibilities transmitted through, 310; subgenres of, 219; testimonio traits in, 182; as transformative, 63; as vehicle for expression, 58; veracity and pathos in, 217; voice and diaspora in, 308–10. *See also* Internet documentary filmmaking

Documentary Now, 3

Documentary Storytelling: Creative Nonfiction on Screen (Bernard), 6

Dollarization, 9, 159

Doss, Erika, 29

DREAM act. *See* Development, Relief, and Education for Alien Minors Act

DREAM Act Coalition (ADAC), 81

DREAMers, 68, 81–83, 272

Drowning, 176–77

Duras, Marguerite, 194

Echeverría, Bolívar, 158, 170

Economic globalization, neoliberal, 84n4

Ecuador, 9, 136–37; Carillo Espinosa relationship with migrant community of, 299–300; Cuenca region in, 138, 140, 147; diaspora in, 307; dollarization in, 9, 159; exceptionalism in, 164; family separation in, 167; financial crisis in, 297; geography of transatlantic, 168–70; identity failure of, 167; media recognition of, 306; memory of, 168, 309; migration phenomenon in, 297, 299, 310; protests in, 306–7; segregation in, 317; shamans in, 148; social differences in, 300; stereotypes of people from, 304; Virgin of El Cisne as patroness of, 162

Education: in Cuba, 196–97; of filmmakers, 211; of Hassan, 286–87. *See also* Common Core educational standard

84 Lumber, 2, 33–35

Eisenhower, Dwight D., 129

Eisenstein, Sergei, 95–96

Ellis, Jack, 183–84

Emilia (2007), 137

Enlightenment, 225

EpiCentroAmerica, 5

Eroticism, 201–2, 214n11

Escaleras, Máximo, 166

Escuela Internacional de Cine y Televisión (International Film and Television School) (EICTV), 193, 198, 286, 297–98

Espada, Martín, 26

Espín, Vilma, 196

Espionage, 208

Esteva, Gustavo, 113n27

Euskadi Ta Askatasuna (ETA), 159

Even the Rain (También la lluvia) (2010), 156, 162, 282

Exceptionalism, in Ecuador, 164

Exclusion: documentary film used to overcome, 39; feeling of, in Spain, 165, 169; humiliation and, 169

Exhibition, places and format of, 218–35

Exile, 11; adaptation to, 153; global experience of, 209; reasons for, 137; support for victims of, 292–93

Exploitation, 170n2; dispensability and, in *abUSed: The Postville Raid*, 41–50; suffering from, 97

Expressionless, 53, 59

Expulsion: types of, 14n3; of women, 109n4

Extravío (2008), 10, 198, 203–7, 211–12

False narratives, 4, 19–22

La Familia Unida, 109

Family separation, 88–89, 126; from deportation, 53; due to ideological differences, 207; in Ecuador, 167; as immigration motivation, 178–79; tragedy of, 261; trauma from, 128–29
Feeling soma, 29
Felman, Shoshana, 52–53
Feminism, 10; engaging in, 211; expression through, 294. *See also* Cuban feminism
Fernández, Amalia, 222
Fernández, Manolo, 136
Ferris, Kent, 259
Fertility, 20
Figueroa, Rubén, 109n1
The Figure of the Migrant (Nail), 4–5
Film festivals, 3, 137, 221, 257, 262, 286, 291–92
Filmmakers: admiration for, 288–89; assumptions made by, 129; as black, Cuban, 203; challenge for, 292; community activism and, 261–62; as Cuban women, 213n2; defined roles of, 217; education of, 211; physical transformations used by, 207; point of view shifting in, 290; resistance represented by, 97; resources for, 301; role respected by, 105–6; solidarity between subject and, 91–92; subject relationship with, 103–9, 189, 253, 267; trust building by, 248–49, 264, 313–14; unknown stories presented by, 186; violence towards, 210; visibility promotion role of, 108–9; women proximity with, 98–99; words drawn out of subjects by, 188
First-person filmmaking, 9, 12, 176, 181–89, 194, 205, 207; cinema of affect engaged by, 198–99; exploration of self in, 210
Fishbowl (*pecera*), 123–25
Flesh, 12, 285
Flores, María, 106; Dirdamal relationship with, 103–5, 107–8; rape of, 107; as seen by children, 107
FMLN. *See* Frente Farabundo Martí de Liberación Nacional
Fondo Ibermedia, 302–3
Ford Foundation, 3

Foreign policies, U.S.: consequences of, 28; reform for, 23; uninhabitable conditions created by, 22
Foster, David William, 14n1
Fowler, Victor, 195
Frente Farabundo Martí de Liberación Nacional (FMLN), 27
Frontier (1996), 30
Fuentes, Ileana, 125
Fundación Virgen del Cisne (Virgin of El Cisne Foundation), 166

Galeano, Eduardo, 100, 282
Gálvez, Alyshia, 72
García Bernal, Gael, 3, 8, 90, 110n5; interviewee relationship with, 93–100; listening role of, 108
García Borrero, Juan Antonio, 214n11
Genasci, Sharon, 110n5
Generational divide, 29
Getzels, Peter, 7, 36n1
Ghosts of the Ship, 12, 285
Globalization, 175, 221
Golash-Boza, Tanya Maria, 109n2
Golden Eye (L'Oeil d'or), 3
Gómez, Sara, 10, 210–11, 213n2
González, Juan, 36n1; demographic changes statement by, 33; *Harvest of Empire: A History of Latinos in America* by, 7, 20; as *Harvest of Empire* film narrator, 19, 23–24, 25
Goodman, Amy, 24
Goodman, Melvin, 26
Gordon, Rogelio, 136
Gore, Al, 223
Goulding, Jim, 128
GPS monitoring devices, 45
Gramsci, Antonio, 191n2
Grandfathers. See *Abuelos*
Grassroots activism, 2–3
Grassroots Journalists Network (Periodistas de a Pie), 101
Grau, "Mongo," 132–33
Grau, Polita, 129, 132–33
Grau San Martín, Ramón, 132–33

Gregg, Melissa, 28–29
Grey Gardens, 3
Griffiths, Lew, 30
Grupo Beta, 191n1
Gruzinski, Serge, 157
Guanabacoa, crónica de mi familia (Guanabacoa, chronicle of my family) (1996), 210
Guardad, María, 27
Guerra, Ramón J., 9–10
Guevara, Che, 29, 36n7, 208
Guissani, Bruno, 33
Gusanos, 208
Guterres, António, 33
Guthrie, Woody, 42, 49–50
Gutiérrez, Luis, 47–48, 252
Guzmán, Patricio, 218

Hablando del punto cubano (1972), 218
Hacker, Melissa, 128
Hainer-Violand, Julia, 32
Harris, Mark Jonathan, 128
The Harvest (La cosecha) (2011), 110n5
Harvest of Empire: A History of Latinos in America (González, J.), 7, 35; comparison between book and film, 19–23; countries discussed in, 23; as required university text, 30
Harvest of Empire: The Untold Story of Latinos in America (2012), 6–7, 35; audio and visual elements in, 21–22; awards for, 31–32; bias against, 31, 36n8; capitalism presented in, 29; comparison between book and film, 19–23; directors of, 36n1; distribution patterns of, 30; experiences represented in, 28; González, J., as narrator of, 23–24, 25; opening of, 31–32, 36n9; pain as shaping, 26; task of appealing to, 33
Hassan, Heidi, 10, 12, 195, 198, 211–12; community of, 295; on Cuban feminism, 294; education and career of, 286–89; feeling indebted to Cuba, 287; filmmaking influences for, 291; film titles of, 294–95; future projects of, 293; greatest challenges for, 292; identity explored by, 289–90; intimacy images of, 201, 202; name origin of, 295; personal relationship to films, 290; photographic series by, 200; relationship with mother, 296; Spanish lifestyle of, 288
Here and There (Vengo volviendo) (2015), 136, 171n12
Heritage, 20, 71
Hernández, Daniellis, 10, 195, 198, 203–7, 211
Herrera, Lizardo, 9
Hinojosa, Maria, 73, 270
Hirsch, Marianne, 126, 134
La Historia de Nuestras Vidas: The Story of Our Lives, 61, 63n1
Historias mínimas (personal stories), 220, 235
Historias paralelas (Home Is Struggle) (1991), 110n5
Historiography, 181, 183, 189
History: displacement, memory and, 50–59; of immigration in U.S., 52; story divergence with, 22–23
History of California (Bancroft), 185
History of the Eagles, 3
Hoffman, Martin, 42
Holocaust, 41, 127–28, 134
Home: creation of, 137; as imagined, 212; as memory space, 201; need for, 97
Home Is Struggle (Historias paralelas) (1991), 110n5
Homelessness, in *Which Way Home*, 176
Home of the Migrant (Casa del Migrante), 100
Hondagneu-Sotelo, Pierrete, 89–90
Huerta, Dolores, 270
Hughes, Peter, 229
Hurricane Mitch, 104, 112n24

ICAIC. *See* Instituto Cubano de Arte e Industria Cinematográficos
ICE. *See* Immigration and Customs Enforcement, U.S.
IDA. *See* International Documentary Association
IFC. *See* Independent Film Channel
The Illusion (2008), 10, 198, 207–10, 211–12

Imagen de la Virgen María (Sánchez, M.), 163
Immigrant rights, protests for, 68, 109n1
Immigration: *Abuelos* context of, 136–37; benefits of, 227; Carillo Espinosa personal experience of, 302–4; of children, increase in, 190–91; *La Churona* bridging experience of, 298; documentary film connection to, 291; documentary film on, 136; dual experience of motherhood and, 88–89; family separation as motivation for, 178–79; from Latin America to North, 1; memory, identity and, 8; memory of, 230–31; as recreation opportunity, 293; severe experience of, 100–101; socioeconomic conditions forcing, 101, 105; unidirectional model of, 229; U.S. history of, 52
Immigration and Customs Enforcement, U.S. (ICE), 44, 242, 247, 251, 261, 262
Immigration policies, U.S., 39–40; contradictions to, 50; justice absent in, 51–52; protesting of, 61
Immigration reform, 1, 109n1, 258–59; activists for, as targeted, 89; symbols of, 88
Impossible subjects, 40. *See also* Deportable life
Impossible Subjects: Illegal Aliens and the Making of Modern America (Ngai), 39–40
Inca elites, 158–59
Independent Film Channel (IFC), 3
IndieGoGo, 3–4
Indigenous people, religion conversion of, 156–57
Information Agency, U.S., 120
Un instante en la vida ajena (2003), 297
Instituto Cubano de Arte e Industria Cinematográficos (ICAIC), 120, 193
Instituto Superior de Arte de Cuba (Art Institute of Cuba), 193
Interculturation, 204
International Documentary Association (IDA), 2
International Film and Television School (Escuela Internacional de Cine y Televisión) (EICTV), 193, 198, 286, 297–98

Internet documentary filmmaking, 218–34
Intimacy: filming of, 199–200; Hassan images of, 201, 202; proximity related to, 102–3, 277; as public, 211
Into the Arms of Strangers: Stories of the Kindertransport (2001), 128
Introduction to Documentary (Nichols), 51, 64n8
Invisibility. *See* Visibility
Los invisibles (2010), 8, 90–91, 108, 110n5; availability of, 110n9; critical distance performance and, 93–100; as expedited, 94; main subjects in, 111n17; undocumented migrant mothers in, 98
Iowa Historical Society, 246
Iowa Workforce Development (IWD), 48
Irigoyen, Rosa, 124–25
IWD. *See* Iowa Workforce Development

Jail, undocumented migrants sent to, 276
Jaramillo, Antonio, 163–65
Jelin, Elizabeth, 58–59
Jenkins, Henry, 223
Jesuits, 157, 163, 276–77
Jiménez, Diego, 164–65
The Juridical Unconscious: Trials and Traumas in the Twentieth Century (Felman), 52

Kahana, Jonathan, 186–88
Kanopy, 3
Kickstarter, 3–4
Kidnapping, 100, 104, 112n20
Kindertransport, 127–28
Kremer, Lisa, 256–57

Labor opportunities, lack of, 92
Lafaye, Jacques, 156–57, 161, 162
LASA. *See* Latin American Studies Association
Latina Feminist Group, 183, 191n3, 191n4
Latin American Documentary Filmmaking (Foster), 14n1
Latin American Studies Association (LASA), 13

The Latino Threat (Chavez, L.), 20
Latino threat narrative, 20, 22; countering of, 28; replacing of, 26
Leading by obeying (mandar obedeciendo), 105
Leal, Eusebio, 130
Lebow, Alisa, 227
Levinas, Emmanuel, 95
Lily, Aunt, 142, 143, 144, 146, 150–51
List, Jared, 7
Literacy campaign (1961), 124, 208
Longing, sense of, 293
López, Alex, 129
López, Ana M., 143, 171n13, 213n1
López, Eduardo, 7, 19–20, 26, 30–31, 36n1
López, Rigoberto, 203
López de Solís, Luis, 163
López Linares, José Luis, 299
López-Marroquín, Isaías, 48, 63
Lord, Susan, 207, 213n1
The Lost Apple (1962), 8, 126, 133; central theme of, 123; Pedro Pan children in, 120–23
Loustaunau, Esteban, 8, 11–12
Loynaz, Dulce María, 196
Luna, Diego, 3

M-13. *See* Mara Salvatrucha
MacArthur Foundation, 3
Las Madres de la Plaza de Mayo, 78
Maeckelbergh, Marianne, 76–77
Maid in America (2005), 110n5
Maldonado-Torres, Nelson, 92–93
Mandar obedeciendo (leading by obeying), 105
Man with a Movie Camera (1929), 218
Mara Salvatrucha (M-13), 112n26, 277
María en tierra de nadie (2010), 110n5
Maricopa County, 68, 79
Martínez, Emeteria, 111n12
Masculinity, 193–94, 206, 208, 305
Mazariegos, Juan Carlos, 63
McLane, Betsy, 183–84
Media citizenship, 205

Medina, Manuel F., 8–9
Mejía López, Luis Enrique, 26
Mejía-Pérez, Dulce, 53, 55, 63
Mejía-Pérez, Elida, 50–59, 63
Mejía-Pérez, Gilbert, 50, 54, 57–58, 63
Mejía-Pérez, Helen, 53, 55, 57–58, 63
Mejía-Pérez, Sam, 50–59, 63
Memorabilia, of Pedro Pan children, 126
Memory: of children, 108; definition of, 60; displacement, history and, 50–59; documentary film as performance of, 59–62; documentary separation from, 62; of Ecuador, 168, 309; as generational, 199; home as space for, 201; identity, migration and, 8; of immigration, 230–31; of Pedro Pan children, 125–26; perceptions enhanced by, 146; physical remnants of, 134; production of, 59; role of personal and public, 254–55; for self-preservation of identity, 195; through storytelling, 62; triggers for, 124. *See also* Collective memory
Menchú, Rigoberta, 24, 26, 253–54
Mestiza consciousness (*conciencia de la mestiza*), 227–28
Metaphorical resignification, 6
Mexican Railway Transportation (Transportación Ferroviaria Mexicana), 101
Miami (Didion), 120
Miami Catholic Welfare Bureau, 120–21, 129
Mi aporte (My contribution) (1972), 210
Mieleş, Fernando, 136
Mignolo, Walter, 41, 92–93, 224–25
Migrant consciousness, 103–6
The Migrant Virgin. See *La Churona*
The migrant witches (Las brujas migrantes) (2013), 231–33
Migrar Es Cultura web portal, 10–11, 217–35, 236n1
Migration Policy Institute, 247
Militarism, of police, 80
Military aid, 27–28
Ministry of Culture (Spain), 232
Mirar (viewing), 92

Mobility: as derivative and lacking, 5; social conditions of, 4–5. *See also* Collective mobilization
Modernity, 92, 165, 171n13, 195
Montalbán, Ricardo, 120, 122
de Montesinos, Antonio, 156
Morales, Evo, 281
Morris, Errol, 6
Morrison, Toni, 108
Mother, idealization of, 165–68
Motherhood, 8; courage modeled by, for children, 84; critical consciousness of, 89–90; delaying of, 197; DREAMers and, 81–83; dual experience of immigration and, 88–89; of immigrants, as defiant, 91; as intimidating, 199; negotiating new notions of, 89–90; Virgin of Guadalupe connected to, 82, 268–69. *See also* Transnational motherhood
Mothers, undocumented migrant, 8; critical agency of, 89; danger exposure of, 108; deportation of, 251; fear of, for children, 96, 124; in *Los invisibles*, 98; unique experience of, 109n4
The Motorcycle Diaries (Diarios de motocicleta) (2004), 29
Mott, John R., 253
Moya, Isabel, 213n1
Muerte in Arizona (2014), 12, 275, 283–84
Multiplicity, of subject, 227
Museo de América, 10–11, 217–35, 236n1
Muslim-majority countries, travel ban for, 2
My contribution (Mi aporte) (1972), 210
My Footsteps in Baraguá (1996), 203
My History, Not Yours: The Formation of Mexican-American Autobiography (Padilla), 185–86
My Knees Were Jumping: Remembering the Kindertransports (1996), 128

Nacify, Hamid, 212, 213n3
"*Los nadies*" (The nobodies) (Galeano), 100
NAFTA. *See* North American Free Trade Agreement
Nail, Thomas, 4–5, 14n3, 109n2

Nanook of the North, 3
National Cattle Congress (U.S.), 44, 46, 61
National identification cards, 56, 80, 263
National Institute of Migration of Mexico, 191n1
Nationalism, 137, 307
Natural disasters, 92, 104. *See also* Hurricane Mitch
Naturalization Law of 1795, 52
Navarro, Vinicius, 2, 188–89, 236n1
NeMLA. *See* Northeast Modern Language Association
Neobaroque nationality, baroque replica and, 160–65
Netflix, 3
New Documentaries in Latin America (Navarro and Rodríguez, J. C.), 2
New Documentary (Bruzzi), 91
A New History of Documentary Film (Ellis and McLane), 183–84
New Latin American Cinema, 220–23
New Man, 208
Newman, Alberto, 144, 147
Ngai, Mae M., 39–40
Nichols, Bill, 33, 51, 64n8, 122, 124–25, 210
"The nobodies" ("*Los nadies*") (Galeano), 100
Nonverbal communication, 91
North American Free Trade Agreement (NAFTA), 6, 28
Northeast Modern Language Association (NeMLA), 13
Northern Light Productions, 261
Nostalgia, 147, 201
Nowaskowski, María, 269
Nowaskowski, Michael, 76, 269, 270
Nuremberg trials, 52

Obama, Barack, 110n6
Objectivity, 4, 91, 124, 149, 218
Object-metaphor, 297, 309
Ochoa, Marina, 120
L'Oeil d'or (Golden Eye), 3
O'Farrill, Albertina, 132–33
One Way or Another (De cierta manera) (1974), 213n2

One-way ticket (Pasaje de ida) (2003), 136
Operation Babylift, 128
Operation Pedro Pan, 8, 120–34
Operation Pedro Pan Group, Inc., 127
Operation Peter Pan: Flying back to Cuba (2011), 8, 120–28; dialogue created by release of, 131–32; key voices in, 129–30
Oppenheimer, Deborah, 128
Orages d'eté (2008), 10, 199–203, 211–12, 286, 295
Orality, 228
Ordoñez, Gilda, 47, 49, 63
The Origins of Totalitarianism (Arendt), 56
Orloff, Leslye, 248
Ortuño, Diego, 136
Ortúzar-Young, Ada, 8
Otra isla (2014), 12, 286, 290–94

Pacas, Alicia, 232
Pacific Institute for Community Organization (PICO), 273
Padilla, Genaro M., 185–86, 191n7
Paéz Hernandez, Gabriel, 136, 171n12
Page, Joanna, 4
País, 53–54
Paranoia, 207–8, 287
Parental authority (*patria potestad*), 124, 131
Parras-Konrad, Sonia, 44–45, 48, 248
Pasaje de ida (One-way ticket) (2003), 136
Patria potestad (parental authority), 124, 131
Patriarchy, in Cuba, 197
Las patronas, 278–79
Pecera (fishbowl), 123–25
Pedro Pan children: becoming prominent figures, 128; first arrival of, 130; in *The Lost Apple*, 120–23; memorabilia of, 126; memory of, 125–26; understanding of, 133; voices of, 126–28
Pedro Pan of California Responds to Estela Bravo's Documentary, 131
Pérez, Manuel, 120
Pérez Fernández, Patricia, 12, 292–93
Performances: *abUSed: The Postville Raid* as memory, 40; as bearing witness, 61; as gendered, 78; *Los invisibles* and critical distance, 93–100; of memory, 59–62; photography capturing, 142; prefiguration and contentious, 75–77
Periodistas de a Pie (Grassroots Journalists Network), 101
Personal portraiture, 25
Personal problems (Problemas personales) (2002), 136, 300, 305
Personal stories (*historias mínimas*), 220, 235
Peutz, Nathalie, 46–47
Photography, 2, 288; *Abuelos* utilizing, 139–48; direction of, 289; tragedy emphasized by, 144–45, 153
Piard, Terence, 288
PICO. *See* Pacific Institute for Community Organization
"Piedra y camino," 152
Piñeros Shields, Thomas, 7–8
Pinochet, Augusto, 142, 145–46
Plane crash, 41–42, 62–63
Plan Frontera Sur, 112n22
Platform of Mortgage Victims (Plataforma de Afectados de Hipoteca) (PAH), 317
Plattner, Léonard, 202, 212
El pliegue (Deleuze), 171n9
Podalsky, Laura, 36n6
Police, militarization of, 80
Political crisis, 1–2
The Politics of Documentary (Chanan), 1, 32
Polytheism, 156
Portable electronics, 233
Postville, Iowa, 42–50, 61, 63, 241–60
Poverty: as deep, 24; *De nadie* statistics on, 112n20; visibility, violence and, 102
Powers, Penny, 129, 132
Prado, Anayansi, 110n5
Prakash, Madhu, 113n27
Prefiguration, contentious performance and, 75–77
Preston, Julia, 190, 252
Problemas personales (Personal problems) (2002), 136, 300, 305
Professionalization, 197, 301
Prometeo deportado (Prometheus deported) (2011), 136

Promise Arizona, 269, 271
Protests, 2; in Ecuador, 306–7; for immigrant rights, 68, 109n1
Proximity: Dirdamal practice of, 102–3; between filmmakers and women, 98–99; intimacy related to, 102–3, 277
Pueblo, 54
Puerto Rican Workers Union (Sindicato Puertorriqueño de Trabjadores), 260

Quendler, Christian, 182–83
Quinoa, 226, 237n7
Quiñones, Alfredo, 28

Race: citizenship, birthplace and, 47; locating of, 204–5; segregation of, 206
Raids, 6; as botched, 51; Burlington Coat Factory, 79–80; increase in, 109n2; Postville, Iowa, 42–50, 61, 63, 241–60
Railway system, Mexico, 101–2, 110n11, 112n19
Ramírez, Gilberto, 63
Ramos, Juan G., 10–11
Rancière, Jacques, 236n6
Rape, 107
Read, Sue, 128
Reagan, Ronald, 27
Reber, Dierdra, 29–30, 34
Reception theory, 28
Reconquest (*reconquista*), 20
Removable aliens, 35, 37n11
Repertoires of contention, 7, 68, 69–70, 77–81
Return to El Fanguito (Volver a El Fanguito) (2006), 203
Rigby, Theo, 7, 40, 51
Riggen, Patricia, 179
Ríos de hombres (2011), 12, 275, 280–82
Rioyo, Javier, 299, 312
Ritualized practices, 55
Rivera, Lisandra, 136, 300
Rockefeller Media Artists Fellowship, 3
Rodas León, Isabel, 136, 171n12
Rodríguez, Juan Carlos, 2
Rolando, Gloria, 203
Romero, Anthony, 26

Romero, U. Roberto, 110n5
Rouch, Jean, 309
Roundtrip travels (Viajes de ida y vuelta) (2012), 221–22
Rubbo, Michael, 218
Ruiz, Samuel, 278
Rutherford, Anne, 29–30

Sabor a cebolla (1997), 297
Sad Song of Yellow Skin (1972), 218
Said, Edward, 137
Salles, Walter, 29
Salvadoran migrant artists, 5
Sánchez, Jorge Luis, 203
Sánchez, Miguel, 163
Sánchez Soler, Martha, 109n1
Santiago, Fabiola, 26
Sarmiento, Manolo, 300
Sarudiansky, Ezequiel, 250, 258
Schechner, Richard, 60
Seeger, Pete, 42
Seigworth, Gregory J., 28–29
Self-assertion, 228
Self-improvement model, 72
Self-privilege, 93
Self-representation, 212, 234–35, 236n1
Semantic duplicity, 53–54
"Señora Santana," 122–23
Shamans, 148
Shame (*vergüenza*), 267
Shared authority, 188–89, 236n2
Shaw, Lauren, 2, 6–7, 12
Siglo XX mine, 260
Silence, breaking of, 11, 48, 123, 257, 262–67, 272
The Silence of Neto (El silencio de Neto) (1994), 241, 246, 254
Silver, Marc, 90, 94, 110n5
Sindicato Puertorriqueño de Trabajadores (Puerto Rican Workers Union), 260
Sin país (2010), 7, 40, 50–62
Smith, Wayne, 132
The Social Documentary in Latin America (Burton), 218

Social empowerment, 6
Social status: expulsion from, 4–5; sacrifice for, 166; shift in, 5
Solalinde, Alejandro, 94, 112n22
Solaya, Marilyn, 213
Solidarity, 6, 245; as ethnic, 73; between filmmaker and subject, 91–92
Sommer, Doris, 103
Sonidos migrantes (2012), 226
Sosa, Candi, 129, 133
Space: as cinematographic, 147; creating of safe, 99; home as memory, 201; as listening, 77; materiality of, 211–12; as resistant in documentary film, 184; subjects creating, for control, 104; transforming from public to sacred, 73–75
Spain, 155–56, 167–68, 288; Carillo Espinosa arriving in, 301; challenges with religion, 311; colonialist view point in, 305; complexity between Americas and, 218, 221, 229–31; exclusion felt in, 165, 169; Hassan lifestyle in, 288; immigration from Latin America to, 12, 136, 159, 164, 220, 228–29, 231–32; lifestyle in, 227; mortgage bubble collapse in, 316; social diversity in, 300; visa requirements for, 303
Spanish Conquest, 16th century, 20, 71, 156–57, 170n3
Spanish language, promotion of, 23
Spanish Ministry of Culture, 222
Spence, Louise, 188–89, 236n1
Spivak, Gayatri, 191n2
Starvation, 160
Stasis, 198
State of Emergency: The Third World Invasion and Conquest of America (Buchanan), 36n10
State Repression and the Labors of Memory (Jelin), 58–59
Stereotypes, 195; descriptions of, 206; of Ecuadorians, 304; of Latinos, 19–20; overcoming of, 251–52
Subjectivity, 211–12, 224–28
Support Our Law Enforcement and Safe Neighborhoods Act. *See* Arizona Senate Bill 1070
Susskind, David, 120

También la lluvia (Even the Rain) (2010), 156, 162, 282
Tambutti Allende, Marcia, 14n2
Taylor, Diana, 61, 62, 78
Technology, 2–3; access to, 233; family brought together by, 146. *See also* Web 2.0 technologies
Television, 31–32, 36n2, 183, 312
Tepeyac Hill, 71–72, 74
Testimonio: On the Politics of Truth (Beverley), 182
Testimonios, 9–10, 176; as bearing witness, 181; documentary film traits of, 182; drawing on power of, 190; history of subject-driven, 185; impetus for change in, 191; as supplemental, 186; as visualized, 180–83; will to collect, 189
Textocentrism, 62
The Thin Blue Line, 3, 6
Thompson-Márquez, Wendy, 30–31, 36n1
Tierra roja (2007), 10, 200, 202, 286–87, 292, 294–95
Tilly, Charles, 7, 68, 69
Totalitarianism, 56
Tourism industry, 199
The Tower of Snow, 123
Transnational film production, 156
Transnationalism, 308, 310–11
Transnational motherhood, 89–90
Transportación Ferroviaria Mexicana (Mexican Railway Transportation), 101
Transvestism, 162, 166, 171n8
Trauma: advice for dealing with, 262; from deportation, 40–41; from displacement, 57; enduring of forms of, 250; from family separation, 128–29; sites of, 123
Travel ban, for Muslim-majority countries, 2
Treaty of Guadalupe Hidalgo (1848), 186, 191n7
Troubled Harvest (1990), 110n5

Trueba, David, 305, 312
Trujillo, Rafael, 24
Trump, Donald, 1–2, 35, 37n11

UFW. *See* United Farm Workers
Under the Same Moon (2007), 179
Unemployment, 97
United Farm Workers (UFW), 73, 260
Urban island, 99
U.S.-Mexican War (1846-1848), 29
The U-Turn (2017), 11, 242, 251, 253, 256–57

Valarezo, Galo Ramón, 171n6
Valasco, Dorothy, 110n5
Valdeavellano, Rafael, 248
Valdez, Jaime, 101
Valdivieso, Teresa Mora, 160
Valencia, Sayak, 102
Valencia Dávila, Carla, 8–9; aunt Lily of, 142, 143, 144, 146, 150–51; awards for, 137; family research of, 136–41, 147–48; recording utilized by, 145–46; role importance of, 138–39, 149
Valencia Hinojosa, Juan, 138–39, 142–47
van Alphen, Ernst, 59
Vásquez, David, 247–48, 254
Vega-López, Pedro Arturo, 43–44
Velez, Yamil, 35
Vengo volviendo (Here and There) (2015), 136, 171n12
Vera, Raúl, 102, 278–79
Vergüenza (shame), 267
Vertov, Dziga, 218
Viajes de ida y vuelta (Roundtrip travels) (2012), 221–22
Videoblogs, 221
Video recording, 10
Vietnam War, 128
Viewing (*mirar*), 92
Vigil, resisting Arizona Senate Bill 1070, 68–78, 81, 84, 263–71
The Vigil (2014), 7, 11, 110n5, 261; audience reception of, 273; bonding capacity presented in, 272; making of, 263–67; message desired from, 273–74; music importance in, 268; political activism represented in, 77; prefiguration in, 76; resistance stories in, 269–70; themes emerging from, 68–69; violence portrayed in, 78; Virgin of Guadalupe represented in, 70–75; women resistance in, 67–81, 84
Vimeo, 3, 219, 234
Violence, 90; by Border Patrol, 179; faith-based movements against, 84n4; towards filmmakers, 210; images of, 27; persuasion over, 157; poverty, visibility and, 102; *The Vigil* portraying, 78. *See also* Rape
Violetas (1998), 297
Virginia Foundation for the Humanities, 32
Virgin of El Cisne, 9, 313–15; appearance of, 160; Carillo Espinosa on statue of, 314–15; celebrations of, 158, 164, 166, 170n5, 308; children of, 167; Ecuador journey of image of, 155; as Ecuador patroness, 162; functions of, 160; myth of, 311; as object-metaphor, 297–98, 309; original sculpture of, 314–16; peace brought by, 159; presidential sash worn by, 170; regional influence of, 307; replicas of, 163; three day pilgrimage for, 160, 162; transvestism of, 162, 166, 171n8
Virgin of El Cisne Foundation (Fundación Virgen del Cisne), 166
Virgin of Guadalupe, 7–8, 67; as companion to women, 269; devotion to, as political resistance, 68–73; as inspiration, 265, 267; motherhood connected to, 82, 268–69; physical transportation of, 73; space created by, 74–75. *See also* Virgin of El Cisne
Visa waivers, 130–31
Visibility, 294; audio and visual elements creating, 95–96; challenge to, 93; distorting of, 92; filmmakers role in promoting, 108–9; through Internet documentary films, 233–34; journalism promoting, 111n18; poverty, violence and, 102
Voice: diaspora and, in documentary film, 308–10; filming techniques conveying, 122; of Pedro Pan children, 126–27; realizing power of, 264; self-representation through, 212

Voluntary departure, 249
Volver a El Fanguito (Return to El Fanguito) (2006), 203

Waldman, Diane, 90
Walker, Janet, 90, 189–90
Walsh, Bryan O., 121, 129–34
Water: as symbol, 139–41, 148–51; war on, 280–82, 284
Web 2.0 technologies, 217, 219, 229
Welcome to Your Family (Bienvenido a tu familia) (2009), 136
What Makes a Film Tick? Cinematic Affect, Materiality, and Mimetic Innervation (Rutherford), 29–30
When the Kids Leave (Cuando los hijos se van) (1941), 165, 167
Which Way Home (2009), 9–10, 175, 190; backdrops in, 178; the Beast as primary narrative for, 176; cameraperson involvement in, 184–85; companionship and border crossing in, 179–80, 188; homelessness articulated in, 176; narrative strategies in, 183; protagonists in, 177, 187–88
White, Robert, 36n3
Who is Dayani Cristal? (2013), 94
Wilhem, Silvia, 128
Williams, Raymond, 213n6

Women: bonding of, 265, 272; children transforming, 99; as Cuban filmmakers, 213n2; emotional challenges of, 203; engagement and resistance of, through documentary film, 194; expulsion of, 109n4; filmmakers proximity with, 98–99; gender identities of, 166; hearing voices of, 90, 108; important figures influencing, 254; inclusion of artists as, 212–13; professionalization of, 197; as protagonists, 290; public speaking skills for, 260; recognition demanded by, 105; resistance of, in *The Vigil*, 67–81, 84; sensitivity of, 211; underrepresentation of, 193; Virgin of Guadalupe as activism focal point of, 67, 70; Virgin of Guadalupe as companion for, 269. *See also* Feminism; Motherhood
World War II, 127–28

YouTube, 3, 110n9, 219, 228–35, 244
Yupanqui, Atahualpa, 152

Zamboni, Mariana, 27
Zamora, Marcela, 110n5
Zapatistas, 105, 278
Zarza, Zaira, 10, 12, 286
Zedillo, Ernesto, 101

REFRAMING MEDIA, TECHNOLOGY, AND CULTURE IN LATIN/O AMERICA

Edited by Héctor Fernández L'Hoeste and Juan Carlos Rodríguez

Reframing Media, Technology, and Culture in Latin/o America explores how Latin American and Latino audiovisual (film, television, digital), musical (radio, recordings, live performances, dancing), and graphic (comics, photography, advertising) cultural practices reframe and reconfigure social, economic, and political discourses at a local, national, and global level. In addition, it looks at how information networks reshape public and private policies, and the enactment of new identities in civil society. The series also covers how different technologies have allowed and continue to allow for the construction of new ethnic spaces. It not only contemplates the interaction between new and old technologies but also how the development of brand-new technologies redefines cultural production.

Telling Migrant Stories: Latin American Diaspora in Documentary Film, edited by Esteban E. Loustaunau and Lauren E. Shaw (2018; paperback edition, 2021)

Mestizo Modernity: Race, Technology, and the Body in Postrevolutionary Mexico, by David S. Dalton (2018; first paperback edition, 2021)

The Insubordination of Photography: Documentary Practices under Chile's Dictatorship, by Ángeles Donoso Macaya (2020)

Digital Humanities in Latin America, edited by Héctor Fernández L'Hoeste and Juan Carlos Rodríguez (2020)

Pablo Escobar and Colombian Narcoculture, by Aldona Bialowas Pobutsky (2020)

The New Brazilian Mediascape: Television Production in the Digital Streaming Age, by Eli Lee Carter (2020)

Univision, Telemundo, and the Rise of Spanish-Language Television in the United States, by Craig Allen (2020)

Cuba's Digital Revolution: Citizen Innovation and State Policy, edited by Ted A. Henken and Sara Garcia Santamaria (2021)

Afro-Latinx Digital Connections, edited by Eduard Arriaga and Andrés Villar (2021)

The Lost Cinema of Mexico: From Lucha Libre to Cine Familiar and Other Churros, edited by Olivia Cosentino and Brian Price (2022)

Neo-Authoritarian Masculinity in Brazilian Crime Film, by Jeremy Lehnen (2022)

www.ingramcontent.com/pod-product-compliance
Lightning Source LLC
Chambersburg PA
CBHW031755220426
43662CB00007B/411